D0857159

HOUDINI!!!

Also by Kenneth Silverman

Edgar A. Poe

The Life and Times of Cotton Mather

A Cultural History of the American Revolution

Timothy Dwight

HOUDINI!!!

THE CAREER OF EHRICH WEISS

American Self-Liberator, Europe's Eclipsing Sensation,
World's Handcuff King & Prison Breaker–
Nothing on Earth Can Hold HOUDINI a Prisoner!!!

KENNETH SILVERMAN

NEW HANOVER COUNTY
PUBLIC LIBRARY
201 CHESTNUT STREET
WILMINGTON, N.C. 28401

HarperCollins*Publishers*

Greek papyrus quoted from Hans Dieter Betz, ed., *The Greek Magical Papyri in Translation Including the Demotic Spells* (1986), with permission of the University of Chicago Press.

HOUDINI!!! THE CAREER OF EHRICH WEISS. Copyright © 1996 by Kenneth Silverman. All rights reserved. Printed in the United States of America. No part of this book may be used or reproduced in any manner whatsoever without written permission except in the case of brief quotations embodied in critical articles and reviews. For information address Harper-Collins Publishers, Inc., 10 East 53rd Street, New York, NY 10022.

HarperCollins books may be purchased for educational, business, or sales promotional use. For information please write: Special Markets Department, HarperCollins Publishers, Inc., 10 East 53rd Street, New York, NY 10022.

FIRST EDITION

Designed by Laura Lindgren

Library of Congress Cataloging-in-Publication Data

Silverman, Kenneth.
    Houdini!!! : the career of Ehrich Weiss : American self-liberator, Europe's eclipsing sensation, world's handcuff king & prison breaker / Kenneth Silverman. — 1st ed.
       p. cm.
    Includes bibliographical references and index.
    ISBN 0-06-016978-8
    1. Houdini, Harry, 1874–1926. 2. Magicians—United States—Biography. I. Title.
GV1545.H8S55   1996
794.8' 092—dc20
[B]   96-7163

96 97 98 99 00 ❖/RRD 10 9 8 7 6 5 4 3 2 1

For Brenda Wineapple and Michael Dellaira

And in memory of
Peter Shaw (1936–1995)

For release from bonds: Say, "Hear me, O Christ, in torments; help, in necessities, O merciful in violent hours, able to do much in the world, who created compulsion and punishment and torture." Say it 12 times by day, hissing thrice eight times. Say the whole name of Helios beginning from ACHEBYKRŌM.

"Let every bond be loosed, every force fail, let all iron be broken, every rope or every strap, let every knot, every chain be opened, and let no one compel me, for I am"—say the Name.

—GREEK MAGICAL PAPYRUS, FOURTH CENTURY A.D.

CONTENTS

METAMORPHOSES

HANDCUFF KING

THE UPSIDE DOWN

A MAGICIAN AMONG THE SPIRITS

PALIGENESIA

APPENDIX AND SOURCE GUIDE

METAMORPHOSES

First, hee must be one of an impudent and audacious spirit,
so that hee may set a good face upon the matter.
—*Hocus Pocus Junior*, 1634

He runs face forward. He is a pursuer.
He seeks a seeker who in his turn seeks
Another still, lost far into the distance.
Any who seek him seek in him the seeker.
His life is a pursuit of a pursuit forever.
—ROBERT FROST, "ESCAPIST—NEVER"

What is your favorite motto?
"Do others or they will do you."
—HOUDINI, ANSWER TO A QUESTIONNAIRE, 1909

ONE

1874—1898

MAYER SAMUEL WEISS AND HIS SON, EHRICH WEISS

A STUDIO PHOTO taken in America shows the Reverend Doctor Mayer Samuel Weiss wearing a *barrett*—the four-cornered miter of German Reform Judaism. He is bald or balding except for a salt-and-pepper mane, nearly shoulder-length. Through his dark mustache and gray whiskers his mouth makes an unsmiling stripe, so that with his small spectacles he seems intent and solemn, perhaps severe. Whatever he thought about his life in the United States he took with him to the grave. No record of his impressions survives, if he kept any. But to judge from the known circumstances, he found little in the New World but disappointment and failure.

When he departed Europe, Weiss (originally Weisz) was no longer young. A rabbi with several years' education at German universities and some training in law, he emigrated from Budapest in 1876, when he was forty-seven. He temporarily left behind his family: his second wife, Cecilia Steiner, a small, stocky woman twelve years younger than he; their four sons, ranging in age from infancy to six years; and a fourteen-year-old son from his first marriage. After two years in America he located a rabbinical post in the Midwest, where Cecilia and the children joined him. They embarked from Hamburg, among 322 steerage passengers of the single-screw steamer *Frisia*. After a fifteen-day voyage they reached New York

City on July 3, 1878, in ninety-five-degree heat. By September the family had reunited and settled in Appleton, Wisconsin.

Mayer Samuel could scarcely have found himself or his family a nicer situation. Set amid farms, meadows, and woods, Appleton was a classic American small town—a progressive, expanding place of nearly seven thousand, surrounded by flourishing towns like itself. Appleton supported three newspapers, two fire companies, several hotels and banks, and retail stores galore. Humming mills powered by the Fox River converted grain from the nearby fields into flour, and forests of white pine into paper. The general prosperity gave rise to roomy houses shaded by giant elms, public parks for picnicking, and opportunities to see plays, concerts, or the cannonball catchers of P. T. Barnum's "Greatest Show on Earth." The presence of Lawrence College distinguished Appleton from similar semi-rural towns and lent to its air of well-being a dignity of purpose: "it would be difficult to find in the very center of civilization," the local *Crescent* boasted, "a more intelligent or genial community than this."

Mayer Samuel's new home also offered a promising professional life, or seemed to. Tolerant Appleton supported Episcopal, Methodist, Baptist, and Catholic congregations that amicably contributed to building one another's churches. A Jewish congregation had been organized in 1866, but lacked a settled rabbi until Mayer Samuel's arrival. He presided over some fifteen Jewish families, more than seventy-five worshipers. They had no synagogue but planned to build one. Meanwhile they gathered on Friday and Saturday evenings in a hall donated by the local Odd Fellows on the town's main street, College Avenue. On the High Holy Days, Jews from nearby towns and as far away as Green Bay came to the hall, as did many non-Jewish Appletonians, curious to learn about unleavened bread.

In his cassocklike black *talar* and white neckbands, Rabbi Weiss cut an exotic figure on College Avenue. The *Crescent* called his appearance "venerable" and remarked that it commanded "the most profound respect." Townspeople may not have known that he wrote essays and poems (and apparently published some), but they recognized his erudition. He was praised for his eloquence, quiet humor, and ability to speak Hebrew, Hungarian, and German. The *Volksfreund*, the local German-language newspaper, called him *gebildeter*—"very cultured."

Despite the picnicking parks and the respect for his age and learning, Mayer Samuel lasted barely four years in Appleton. His congregation, synagogue still unbuilt, let him go. They may have considered him not so much "venerable" as simply too old. Even on his arrival the *Volksfreund* described him as *schon bejahrter*, "already advanced in years." Or, becoming Americanized themselves, they may have found him too Old World. According to one longtime Appleton resident, they wanted an English-speaking rabbi while he, a native of Hungary under Hapsburg rule, spoke and conducted services in German. For whatever reason, they offered his post to a rabbi from Westphalia. To weigh on the family's already oppressive situation, during their four-year stay Cecilia had given birth to a son and a daughter. At the age of fifty-three, Mayer Samuel found himself adrift in the United States with a wife, seven children, and no job.

A failure in idyllic Appleton, he fared worse in booming Milwaukee. Although the "Deutsch Athens" contained some five hundred Jewish families, a population that increased as pogroms drove thousands more from Russia, it supported just two synagogues, with only about 125 members. Even so, many Jewish businesses stayed open on the Sabbath, leaving the pews empty. "The greatest majority of men of Jewish descent in this city," a visiting journalist observed in 1880, "are almost unacquainted with the principles which make our religion the light of mankind." The notorious ignorance and indifference created little demand for rabbis.

Mayer Samuel became a Milwaukee rabbi without a congregation. He found none even when a third synagogue went up in 1886, and a fourth in 1887. To maintain his family, he seems to have conducted some services outside the city's organized religious life. In 1883, for example, he borrowed a shofar and Torah just before the Rosh Hashanah holidays, apparently to use in services. He also reportedly opened a "private school" on Winnebago Street. Whatever his efforts, they did not spare his family from having to beg. As the Weisses moved from one address to another, Cecilia was forced to appeal to the local Hebrew Relief Society for a half ton of coal against the winter, and a few dollars for provisions.

Mayer Samuel watched the decay of the city's Jewish life touch his own children. His son from his first marriage, Herman (originally Armin), married a woman named Dollie Patterson, a churchgoing Congregationalist. Herman not only married outside the faith but also loitered there. He and his new bride gave his half-brother Ehrich a book of children's stories entitled *Our Boy's Chatterbox*—as a present for Christmas. But Mayer Samuel saw worse than assimilation overtake Herman. The young man developed tuberculosis and was sent to New York in hopes that a change might improve his health. He died in Brooklyn during the Christmas season of 1885, at the age of twenty-two.

Ehrich's development also gave Mayer Samuel plenty to think about. Born Erik Weisz in Budapest on March 24, 1874, he was the middle son among Mayer and Cecilia Weiss's five boys. To ease the family's need he shined shoes, sold newspapers, and ran errands. But he also gave signs of becoming the archetypal Cantor's Son of the Yiddish stage, seduced from the tragic spirituality of Judaism by the bright lights of modern secularism. He brought with him to Milwaukee his excitement over a trapeze artist he had seen in Appleton, and tried to imitate. At around age nine, he made his debut as a contortionist and trapeze artist, in what seems to have been a five-cent juvenile circus assembled by a friend. He wore red woolen stockings and called himself "Ehrich, The Prince of the Air."

When Ehrich was about twelve he ran away from home, perhaps twice. Intending to stay away a year, he hopped a train for Texas, but entered the wrong freight car and arrived in Kansas City, Missouri—no routine escapade in a traditionally closeknit Jewish family, much less a rabbinical one. On either the same or another flight, he headed for Delavan, Wisconsin, about fifty miles from Milwaukee. Working as a shoeshine boy, he was discovered in the local business district by a middle-aged couple, the Flitcrofts. They gave him a bath and a bed, mended his clothing, and then took him in for the summer, believing him to be homeless.

Humbled in Milwaukee, his family feeling the strain, Mayer Samuel tried New York City. As with his emigration from Europe, the move meant a separation, but this time he had company. He and Ehrich came on first, sometime in 1887, and lived for several months in a boardinghouse on East Seventy-ninth Street, run by a Mrs. Loeffler. Cecilia and the others joined them the following year, in time to see the Great Blizzard topple telegraph poles and pile up thirty-foot snowdrifts. New York drew the largest part of the ongoing exodus of Eastern Europe's Jews, some two hundred thousand arriving there in the 1880s. Mayer Samuel chose to settle not in the Lower East Side, the Jewish cosmopolis, but in an ethnically mixed immigrant neighborhood, largely Irish, Italian, and German. The family found a second-floor flat at 227 East Seventy-fifth Street—a four-story tenement on a street of lookalike tenements, a few doors down from a firehouse and a public school, bounded by the rumbling Second and Third Avenue elevated railroad lines.

The move to New York improved Mayer Samuel's situation little if any. He had business cards printed up introducing himself as MINISTER OF THE CONGREG. ADATH JESHURUN. That the congregation went unlisted in city directories of the period, however, indicates that it was a small group with no synagogue. Otherwise he sought work as a rabbinic jack-of-all-trades: "all religious Services a Specialty," his business card put it, "Marriages and Funerals, also practical MOHEL." Yet circumcisions and burials failed to provide his family with even the necessities. For aid he called on Bernard Drachman, rabbi of a neighborhood congregation, Zichron Ephraim. Drachman offered to give or lend him money or commend him to possible benefactors. Mayer Samuel declined, but offered for sale part of his large library of Hebrew books, from which Drachman bought a set of the *Codes of Maimonides* at the asking price. Driven to join other Jewish immigrants who found jobs in the ready-made clothing industry, Mayer Samuel reportedly worked at a Broadway neckwear-cutting firm. If he did, the experience brought humiliation along with income: his son Ehrich, now a teenager, worked there too.

Ehrich took other odd-jobs. He scurried as a uniformed messenger boy for the Mutual District Messenger Company and the American District Telegraph Company, large firms with offices throughout the city. He also worked in a tool-and-die shop, and perhaps a printing establishment. The jobs cannot have left much time for schooling, although he became a pupil in the Talmud Torah of Zichron Ephraim, according to Rabbi Drachman, and was apparently bar mitzvahed by him.

What play and amusement Ehrich found centered on sports. Milwaukee's "Prince of the Air" was New York's avid swimmer and boxer. Had illness not kept him from competing, he believed, he could have won the 115-pound title at the Amateur Athletic Union; he had already beaten the boy who was eventually crowned. Passionate about athletics, he pasted in a scrapbook colored lithographs of Paddy Fitzgerald and other current bicycle champions. But most of all he liked to run. Living only five blocks from the hills and meadows of Central Park, he allegedly did ten miles a day there to train himself for long-distance events. In September 1890 he won a prize in a mile race sponsored by the Amateur Athletic Union. When the officials realized that he was under the age limit, they revoked the prize but soon gave it back to him.

A photograph of Ehrich around age seventeen shows him in running shoes, shorts, and the tank-top shirt of the Pastime Athletic Club, to which he belonged. Poised to race, he appears determined—a gaunt-faced, handsome boy with close-cropped dark hair, powerful neck, and muscular calves, slightly bowlegged. A half-dozen medals spangle his tanktop. Some represent actual contests won, some are merely self-glorifying fakes. It is the picture of a scrapper who feels he can never do enough, who wants all the medals there are and more—the picture of a title-taker.

Mayer Weiss's sixteen dismal years in America ended with his death at sixty-three, on October 5, 1892. The family having made still another move, to a flat at 305 East Sixty-ninth Street, he developed cancer of the tongue. He died after surgery at Presbyterian Hospital, of the epithelioma and what the death certificate calls "shock following operation." According to Ehrich, on his deathbed his father asked him to promise that Cecilia would suffer no want. He would later speak of his father affectionately and with admiration for his learning. But he disclosed nothing of what he had borne as the son of a parent who could not clothe him: "such hardships and hunger became our lot," he would remark, "that the less said on the subject the better."

Mayer Samuel left two adult offspring: twenty-two-year-old Nathan (Nátán) and twenty-year-old William (Gottfried Vilmos); and three minors besides eighteen-year-old Ehrich: Theodore (Ferencz Deszo), sixteen; Leopold, thirteen; and Carrie Gladys, ten. Ehrich long recalled his mother's weeping at the time of Mayer Samuel's death. But her words, as he recorded them in his faulty German, sound less full of grief than of accusation: *"Weiss, Weiss, du hast mich verlassen mit deiner Keinder!!! Was hast du gethan?"*

Weiss, Weiss, you've left me with your children!!! What have you done?

THE HOUDINIS; METAMORPHOSIS

Visitors to the 1893 World's Columbian Exposition in Chicago could sample Aunt Jemima pancake mix, ogle belly-dancing-great Little Egypt, rotate in George Ferris's 264-foot bicycle-wheel-in-the-sky, and hear Paderewski play Chopin. In the sideshow on the mile-long midway, they might also see nineteen-year-old Ehrich Weiss performing as Harry Houdini—one-half of a magic act called "The Brothers Houdini."

The transformation was not sudden, although its history is obscure. Ehrich's interest in magic may have been wakened when he bought or received a dollar box of tricks as a child in Milwaukee; he may have given his first public show at the Pastime Athletic Club in New York, when sixteen; the same year he may have returned to Milwaukee and performed professionally during Christmas week, for twenty dollars. How he became "Harry Houdini" is clearer. Probably in 1891 he teamed up with a slender, mustachioed youth named Jacob Hyman, a friend from the neckwear-cutting firm. They called their act the Brothers Houdini. Which partner devised the stage name is unknown; it alluded to the French conjurer Jean Eugène Robert-Houdin (1805–1871), esteemed as the founder of modern magic. The -i ending had a long tradition among magicians, many having used it to invoke the famous eighteenth-century Tuscan conjurer Pinetti (1750–1800 or 1805). Ehrich's nickname, "Ehrie," modulated into Harry. Harry Houdini.

The personnel of the Brothers Houdini proved changeable too. Euphoniously describing themselves as "The Modern Monarchs of Mystery," Harry and Jacob Hyman played not only the Columbian midway but also dime museums and small theaters in upstate New York and the Midwest, billed with burnt-cork artistes, Bohemian glassblowers, and "Oklahoma Bill, the scout, and his prairie wife." But Jacob dissolved the partnership in early 1894 and took off on his own as "HOUDINI Oriental Conjuror and Mysterious Juggler." For a while his brother Joe appeared with Harry as "The Brothers Houdini." With three Houdinis afoot, behold a fourth: Joe dropped out, and his place was filled by Harry's real-life brother Theodore. Theo shared Harry's interest in magic, and his ruggedness. Rightly nicknamed "Dash"—an Americanizing of his Hungarian middle name, Deszo—he was two years younger than Harry but heftier, a "harum-scarum, hell-raisin' boy," Joe Hyman said, who could "fight like a wildcat."

This latest "Brothers Houdini" act, as Dash recalled it, opened with the sudden appearance of a flower in an empty lapel-buttonhole. ("Harry's buttonhole, of course," Dash said, his older brother being "very decidedly the boss.") The act included some card tricks and the production of a handkerchief from a candle flame, but featured and ended with the trunk effect called Metamorphosis. Harry and Dash got some good notices but achieved no great success. After deducting living and traveling expenses, each kept only about two dollars a week for pocket money and sent what earnings remained to their mother.

"The Brothers Houdini" broke up permanently in the summer of 1894, when Harry married. His bride was a diminutive eighteen-year-old brunette from Brooklyn, Wilhelmina Beatrice Rahner, called Bess. Many

conflicting accounts of their meeting survive. The most likely version, cor-
roborated by Joe Hyman, came from Dash. He said that he met Bess first
himself, when she was performing in "The Floral Sisters," a song-and-
dance act, and introduced her to Harry. After a quick courtship (three
weeks, according to Bess), the couple married on June 22 and honey-
mooned in Coney Island—"cheap," Bess said, "but glorious." Like his
deceased half-brother, Harry wed outside the faith; Bess came from a
family of immigrant German Catholics. Cecilia seems to have accepted the
match without complaint, but the also-widowed Mrs. Rahner, again
according to Bess, at first objected to Harry because he was Jewish.

The meager earnings of the Brothers Houdini could not support three
performers. Bess took Dash's place, thereby breaking up the act, which
became "The Houdinis." Husband and wife complemented each other's
appearance as magician and assistant. Harry no longer looked gaunt, as he
had in adolescence, but strong and compact, despite his baggy evening
clothes. He was short, only five-five or five-six, yet seemed larger beside
Bess, who was barely five feet tall and weighed only about ninety pounds.
Her elfin qualities were heightened by her big dreamy eyes and soft voice,
and exaggerated onstage by the costumes she wore: tights and bloomers, or
a Little Lord Fauntleroy outfit of black knickerbockers, white shirt with
flowing lace collar, and jaunty velvet jacket. Harry kiddingly referred to her
as "my large wife."

"The Houdinis" started out where the Brothers Houdini left off, in one
of the ubiquitous dime museums. After appearing in Richmond and
Hampton, Virginia, at the end of 1894, they were booked for two weeks in
January 1895 into Huber's Palace Museum on East Fourteenth Street, close
to the Union Square entertainment district. They were billed as "The Houdi-
nese"—one of many garblings of the name. (Thanks to other misspellings
and typos, Harry also appeared as "Houdin," "Hunyadi," "Hondini,"
"Robert Houdini," "Harry Houdine," and "Professor Houdinis.") In the
hierarchy of the theatrical world, dime museums ranked just above beer gardens. They offered chambers of horror, waxworks, and live human oddities
who exhibited themselves on high wooden platforms in the 'curio hall.' Most
museums set up in unrented stores in busy neighborhoods, marching out
their attractions over and over throughout the day and into the evening.
Harry later recalled that he did nine to fourteen brief shows daily, introduced
by the words: "Your attention towards this end of the hall! Here you will find

a clever young man; he will mystify you if he can. . . . Houdini, look at him."

At Huber's the Houdinis shared the bill with performing monkeys and a sprinting contest for fat ladies. Harry apparently tried to increase his take by 'graft,'—namely, hawking a twenty-five-cent pitchbook entitled *Mysterious HARRY HOUDINI: TRICKS Requiring no practice or special apparatus*. His first publication, it revealed such elementary secrets as "How to Pull a Tape Through your Neck" and explained, less practically, how to hurl battle-axes at but not into an assistant standing before a board, setting the handles on fire for a finale. He may have made some money. In the diary he began keeping, in a small red notebook issued by the *Detroit Free Press*, he entered: "Graft Big."

However undignified, the dime museum grind was valuable practice. But Harry and Bess disliked the work and the atmosphere. For a while she refused to appear at Huber's, leaving him to perform alone. For his part, he later said, he "kept very quiet, and tried to make a living." He did enjoy knowing the freaks. They were the museum stars, capable of drawing large crowds and matching salaries. Harry worked with and befriended Count Orloff, the atrophied "Human Window Pane" ("You Can See His Heart Beat! You Can See His Blood Circulate!"), who gave him a picture and autograph—"To my friend Hondinis [*sic*]." He also got to know Unthan, the armless wonder who could play the violin with his toes, and Thardo, a beautiful woman who submitted herself to repeated rattlesnake bites, after demonstrating the lethal powers of the venom by injecting it into a rabbit that died in agony. He corresponded, kept in touch, and developed longterm friendships with them. Having journeyed from the *Codes of Maimonides* to the curio hall, a sort of two-headed man himself, he felt a kinship with human anomalies—"being classed a 'freak' " too, he said.

The Houdinis' engagement at Huber's went unnoticed in the press. So did their next booking, with trick riders who maneuvered their bicycle down a ladder at Tony Pastor's Fourteenth Street Theater, close to Huber's. Pastor, known for his waxed mustache, many rings, and shiny opera hat, was becoming a power in the entertainment business. But after a week Harry and Bess inspired no warmer endorsement from him than: "The Houdinis act as performed here I found satisfactory and interesting." Until early fall they worked mostly in a circus playing Apollo, Driftwood, Renovo, and other Pennsylvania hamlets, alongside Scoffield the juggler and gun-drill artists. By Harry's account Bess doubled as a singing clown while he also did the Punch-and-Judy show. He carved some of the figures from cedar blocks with a jackknife, using his own face as a model. He doubled as a freak too—Projea, the Wild Man of Mexico. His eye stayed closed for three weeks after being hit by raw meat thrown into his den.

What small impression the Houdinis made came from an effect Harry had used since starting out: Metamorphosis. The apparatus consisted of a so-called substitution trunk and a cabinet to enclose it. The subtrunk resembled a steamer or costume trunk save for a row of airholes near the bottom; it was large enough to comfortably hold a person. The cabinet stood about seven feet high and ten to twelve feet wide. Topped by a wide valance and open in front, rather like a proscenium, it could be closed by drawing a dark curtain across it.

In the basic effect Harry, tied in a sack and locked in the trunk, changed places with Bess outside, who was then found inside the same locked trunk, inside the sack. As fully described in a magazine article:

> . . . to the audience and to the close inspection of the volunteers upon the stage, the time-worn trunk was shown, and its four sides, bottom and cover well sounded to prove the absence of trickery. Next there were given for examination a black flannel bag, seven feet in length, a yard or so of heavy tape and some sealing wax.
>
> Houdini's next request was that his committee securely encase him in the previously examined sack, tightly bind its mouth together with heavy tape already in their hands, and secure the knots with sealing wax.

With Harry bagged inside, the trunk was padlocked, trussed with heavy knotted ropes, and wheeled into the cabinet. As the curtain was drawn across, he could be heard knocking and shouting inside the trunk—proof he was still there. Then:

> Mrs. Houdini, standing at the open curtain, makes the following brief announcement. "Now then, I shall clap my hands three times, and at the third and last time I ask you to watch CLOSELY for—the—EFFECT." At this, she rapidly closes the curtain and vanishes from sight, yet instantaneously the curtain is reopened—this time by Houdini, himself.

The trunk was rapidly unroped and unlocked. Bess, now inside it, was assisted to a standing position, "though imprisoned in the identical sack and bonds which just a moment or two before secured her husband."

The impact of Metamorphosis depends on speed, which demands agility and smooth teamwork. To stun and baffle as it can, the exchange must occur in a blink. One instant the assistant is standing beside the locked trunk, the magician bagged inside; suddenly beside the trunk stands the magician, his assistant bagged inside. Bess's tiny physique was ideal for scrambling in and out, and she and Harry made the subtrunk seem a minor miracle. "Just think over this," he announced in his earliest advertising for "The Houdinis." "The time consumed in making the change is THREE SECONDS!" Several newspapers, too, commented that they switched places in "an incalculably short space of time," with "lightning-like rapidity," as "quickly as one can fire a self-cocking pistol." The suddenness, one paper said, left spectators "almost too astonished to applaud."

Harry rang many changes on Metamorphosis to keep it fresh. Sometimes he led up to the substitution by first having his hands tied behind his back with rope or black braid and borrowing a coat from a member of the audience. He would step into the cabinet, emerge after a moment wearing the coat, his hands still tied behind him, and then perform Metamorphosis: "the trunk trick in connection with the braid trick," he called it. Other times he wore the borrowed coat inside the sack, and it reappeared on Bess when she turned up there in his stead. Or he might bring an audience member with him into the cabinet, sometimes a confederate, sometimes not. Although his own hands remained tied, the helper emerged with broad daubs of burnt cork on his face: "allowing a man in the cabinet," he called this one, "and making a dummy of him."

Harry saw the potential of Metamorphosis and trumpeted the Houdinis' handling of it. "Our act is the supreme cabinet mystery in the World," he proclaimed on an 1895 advertising card. "[It] has been featured at . . . the Oxford London and has created a sensation in Europe, Australia, and America." Far from wowing audiences at the famous London music hall and on two other continents, of course, it was worming an extra few cents' admission from circusgoers in American podunks, in the 'concert' after the main show. But it was getting attention. "Who would cavil on a matter of a dime or even more," asked the newspaper of Pottsville, Pennsylvania, "to see the great illusive trick of the Houdini Box mystery?"

THE AMERICAN GAIETY GIRLS; THE MARCO COMPANY; THE CALIFORNIA CONCERT COMPANY; THE WELSH BROTHERS CIRCUS

Encouraged, and having passed his twenty-first birthday, Harry ventured on what he called "my first enterprise." In September 1895 he bought a half interest in the American Gaiety Girls, a financially-shaky traveling burlesque show. The move is surprising, given his prim morals. On tour, he and Bess met up with an acquaintance, Kate Gregors, who had become a prostitute: "invited us up house," he huffed, "but *We* declined!!!" Something of mixed pride and embarrassment lingers in his later description of the Gaiety Girls as "the finest, cleanest, and largest show of its kind on the road that season. . . . Of course I mean burlesque shows." Clean and fine maybe, but the company drew a men-only audience, and the costumes pitched flesh and form. "Many portions of the dialogue and much of the stage business is vulgar," a Massachusetts reviewer commented, "and some of it positively indecent in tenor and allusion."

In five or so months as the Gaiety Girls' part proprietor and manager, Harry played through eastern Pennsylvania and upper New York State, and into New England. The touring provided plenty of headaches. He no sooner took over than he found the baggage delayed in Reading, Pennsylvania, forcing the troupe to perform in street clothes. Some of his thespians turned out to be tipplers too. He and Bess presented Metamorphosis—they were billed as "European illusionists"—but also doubled in the farcical musical skits that opened and closed the show. In "The Bloomer Club," a satire on the period's New Woman, he acted as one of the club's "fun-makers," in the getup of a rahrah college student. Between this curtain-raiser and the closing burletta, "Rob-Hip-Hur-Roy," came a colorfully costumed Amazon march and some novelty acts, notably 140-pound May Morgan. She wagered to wrestle for a purse any woman at the same weight or man at 122—Greco-Roman, catch-as-catch-can, or collar-and-elbow style. The company also sometimes gave away a turkey.

Harry tried his own methods of filling the house. In Manchester, New Hampshire, during the second week of November 1895, he announced that before being locked in the subtrunk he would allow his hands to be secured not with rope or braid but with handcuffs borrowed from the audience. This come-on may have marked his first public performance of a handcuff escape. It occurred to him to expand the stunt to advertise the Gaiety Girls' arrival in town. When the company moved to Gloucester, Massachusetts, he exhibited his skill at the local police station. At his invitation officers clapped him into old-fashioned as well as modern cuffs, but none held him.

Four days later Harry repeated the feat with some novel wrinkles at a newspaper office and a police station, before the company's first evening performance in Woonsocket, Rhode Island. Under the headline HAND-CUFFS DON'T COUNT, a local reporter described how Harry allowed himself to be braceleted by six different pairs of handcuffs at once, including a set of double-locking cuffs, which required a different key to unlock each hand. He ducked into a "private room" and returned dangling opened cuffs—once in forty-eight seconds, another time in eighteen. His exhibitions reaped prominent, and free, publicity. The Woonsocket paper announced that he would try similar tests at the Gaiety Girls' evening performance. Having hit on a surefire promotion, he repeated the police station displays as the company moved to Worcester and then Holyoke, Massachusetts. The local press reported that he unlocked the cuffs with "as much ease as if they were strings wound around his wrist."

The up reviews perhaps came in places too small to count much, or averse to burlesque, for they did not help. Despite giveaway gobblers and some good-size houses, the Gaiety Girls folded, owing twenty dollars for railroad fares and unable to meet its payroll. Wrestling May Morgan, wife of the company's business manager, was charged with having fraudulently collected money for costumes she never delivered. Her husband was arrested, though protesting that he was a financial ruin, "not having a 'sou markee.'"

Harry and Bess may have been out of the Gaiety Girls by that time, but its collapse still left them with debts. In the spring of 1896 they joined the Marco Company, a magic show playing the Canadian provinces. No less a gamble than the Gaiety Girls, it was the dreamchild of a professional church organist from Connecticut, Edward J. Dooley. An amateur magician as well, he aspired to head up a full-rigged magic show on the scale of the leading nineteenth-century illusionists, and featured large stage effects with names like "Mystery of Mahomet" and "The Cremation of Floribel." He billed Bess as his daughter, "Mlle. Marco," and Harry as his son-in-law and successor.

Harry often stole headlines from his fellow performers. In a demonstration at the Halifax, Nova Scotia, police station, he had a card selected, then asked that a messenger be sent to Mademoiselle Marco at her hotel, with the question, "What card was thought of?" Bess named it correctly—a routine bit of mindreading but dramatically fancied-up enough to make the newspapers. In the St. John, New Brunswick, police station, Harry invited the chief to fetter him in leather cuffs, recently adopted by insane asylums to keep inmates from harming themselves. This "maniac cuff and belt" consisted of hard leather mittens that prevented digital movement, attached to a leather belt cinching the waist. The device was difficult to escape. Harry had to grip and turn the key with his teeth, and work the belt down toward his feet until it reached the floor, when he could step free. He was out, the St. John's newspaper said, "after a few minutes' work."

But the Houdinis had boarded another sinking ship. Having failed to sell tickets, Marco disbanded his company in Halifax. Bess and Harry bought or were given some of his apparatus, and by July were adrift again in Maritime Canada, advertising a program of MAGIC MIRTH AND MYSTERY—a corny tag used by countless magicians before them (and after). From the summer of 1896 through the fall of 1897 the Houdinis wandered the Northeast and Midwest in pursuit of work. A record of their activities survives only in a handful of unidentified clippings, undated programs, unexplained contracts, laconic diary entries, and later misrecollections, revealing little more than that they offered a changeable mélange of subtrunk, handcuffs, and conventional magic, playing an occasional one-week stand in variety shows and dinky dime museums.

While knocking around, the Houdinis tried to find a successful formula, some strong selling-point or arrangement of effects that would establish them in show business. They often overhauled and renamed or even scrapped their act. For a while they put together their own version of Marco's show, including his "Mysteries of Mahomet," a levitation illusion in which Bess, a reviewer wrote, "actually floats in space without any visible means of support." Taking over Bess's maiden name, the Houdinis for a while appeared as "The Rahners, America's Greatest Comedy Act." In a variant, Harry played one summer garden as "Harry Raynohr, Sleight of Hand," Bess as "Beatrice Raynohr, The Melodious Little Songster." For other stints Harry worked as "Cardo," doing card magic exclusively. Probably during this period, he became also "Professor Murat," a hypnotist. He learned the rudiments from an ex-newspaperman, Billy Diamond, who once earned his living as a "horse"—a professional mesmeric subject. Diamond taught him 'geek effects' too, he later claimed, like "sewing buttons on my bare chest, running needles through any part of my anatomy, without any preparation of the body, such as cocaine, morphine, etc., and not feeling the pain."

The shifts and turns, so far as the sparse evidence indicates, brought mostly more restlessness. Harry and Bess offered to work for Harry Kellar, the leading American illusionist, but he said he had all the assistants he needed. They considered teaming up with a smalltime magician stage-named Abd-el-kadir to play resorts, or forming a troupe to play Europe with Alexander Weyer, a dime museum strongman who could pound nails through two-inch planks with his hands. They probably felt pinched— Harry shot craps in Chicago, losing sixty dollars—but kept up a prosperous front. Booked by chance in Appleton, Harry returned for the first time in fifteen years to the scene of his childhood and of his father's first defeat in America. He went from one end to the other of the changed town, scarcely recognizing the Fox River around the paper plant but meeting people who remembered him and his parents. Interviewed by the local press as "Mr. Weiss, the magician," he let out that Appleton's native son had performed in England and "studied and practiced for a considerable time in London."

The need to flaunt more fake medals was relieved by occasional real successes. During an exhibition at the Grand Rapids police station, Harry was cuffed, in the words of a local paper, "until the blood stopped circulating and the veins stood out in knots on his arms." To ensure the irons against tampering, the sheriff pasted postage stamps over the keyhole and pencil-marked the paper for identification. Harry removed the cuffs and gave them back with the marked seals unbroken. Although an effective touch, the stamps—easily lifted off and restuck—presented no extra obstacle to unlocking the cuffs. But in the wake of the impressive escape, "The Houdinis'" follow-up presentations of Metamorphosis at the opera house sold tickets and brought cheering reviews as "the finest [illusion] ever seen on a local stage." "*Created a Sensation*," Harry wrote in his diary, "Act Wonderful."

Near the end of 1897 Harry and Bess found three or four months' steady work with the California Concert Company, a midwestern medicine show then playing Cherokee, Weir City, and similar outposts in Kansas. Like dime museums, medicine shows existed on the far side of show business, and often of the law as well. Given mostly on outdoor stages or in tents, they brought smalltown working people a taste of theater, alternating entertainment with hustles for nostrums like Kickapoo Indian Sagwa. The California Concert Company was headed by an oldtime pitchman, "Dr." Thomas Hill. It featured Swiss bellringers, a German dialect comedian, and an all-purpose dancing/acting/cornet-playing team called the Keatons, with whom the Houdinis became close friends. (Joe Keaton later wrote to Harry that his undersize eleven-year-old son, Buster, would grow up to be not much larger than "little *Bessie*," but was "excruciatingly funny.") Harry and Bess made twenty-five dollars a week, plus board and traveling expenses, as the "Great Wizard" and the "little vocalist." When the company moved through the adjacent Indian Territory (soon to be Oklahoma), he sold medicine in the streets. The milieu made for some choice experiences. He took a spectator inside the Metamorphosis cabinet, presumably to blacken his face in the variation called allowing-a-man-in-the-cabinet-and-making-a-dummy-of-him. This prospective dummy pulled a gun—"jokingly," Harry noted in his diary; he turned out to be a former member of the Jesse James gang.

Harry again experimented with a new kind of act. Many medicine shows of the period exploited the rage for Spiritualism that had overtaken the United States, and much of England and Europe, for half a century. The California Concert Company having fallen on hard times, Harry offered to fill seats by presenting a fully-lit séance, on a program with the perennial *Ten Nights in a Bar Room*. "Only Time a Seance in Public Ever Given By Houdini," the show advertised, "except in large cities, and then at advanced prices." He promised to manifest spirit hands and faces, make musical instruments fly through space playing sweetly, and transmit messages from the departed. While his performances fell far short of the promises, they paid off. Day after day he recorded the take: "Played to about 700.00 [seven hundred dollars, in Galena, Kansas] on 8 shows"; "Broke the record at Garnett for paid admissions. Spiritualism cause of it—Bad effect—1034 Paid Admission to see spiritualism."

For Harry the lively sales did not justify the "Bad effect." A straight-shooter, he felt guilty hoaxing his audiences, particularly in one case when he purported to convey a spirit message from a black man who had been murdered. The conflict eased in the spring of 1898, when the California Concert Company went the way of the Gaiety Girls and the Marco Company. Its demise left Harry and Bess to join a traveling repertory group to act for a while in melodramas. The lure of big paid admissions apparently proved too great, however, and they returned to the séance business. Now "The Great Mystifier" and "The Celebrated Psycrometic Clairvoyant [*sic*]," they worked local union halls and such places, levitating tables and answering sealed questions about past, present, and future. Whatever the guilt, it had its rewards—"lived like a king," Harry noted in his diary. He also produced his first known publication in a magic journal. The June 1898 issue of *Mahatma* ran his "Silent Second Sight" effect, explaining the talking and silent codes by which he could communicate to Bess whatever someone wrote on a slate or pad: "I have even trained my right ear to move up and down to thus give my assistant the tip."

But like their other ventures, the foray into Spiritualism brought Harry and Bess full circle back to the dime museums. This time they descended into the Eden Musee of St. Joseph, Missouri: "Received all our money," Harry noted there. "No one else did."

Turning twenty-four in the spring of 1898, and barely surviving, Harry sought a niche in still another branch of show business. He and Bess accepted a six-month return engagement with the Welsh Brothers Circus, for which they had worked briefly in Pennsylvania three years earlier. In this Golden Age of American circuses, Welsh Brothers mounted probably the best and largest ten-cent show in the country: leaping greyhounds, wirewalkers, Arabian jugglers, contortionists, clowns, an orchestra, and much more under a waterproof big top that could seat two thousand people. Headquartered in Lancaster, Pennsylvania, Welsh Brothers promised a "Grand Holiday for the Toiling Millions."

It was no holiday for the performers. In the Houdinis' earlier tour with the show, Bess had had to double as a singing clown, Harry as a wild man. Now they signed on to do Metamorphosis, Bess to give in addition her "serio-comic specialty and work in side-show if necessary," and Harry, with the other male performers, to "go in daily street parades, if required." On the other hand, Welsh Brothers paid the cast promptly and fed them, Harry said, "extra well." Better still, reviewers in Kutztown, Shenandoah, and similar towns singled out "The Houdinis" for praise. By late summer the circus was using Metamorphosis to close the show.

Reviving his early days as Ehrich, Prince of the Air, Harry began seriously training himself as an acrobat. He had kept in shape during the Houdinis' years on the road, in part by speedy bike riding (gleeful to have "run away," he noted, "from all bike cops"). To build up his wind, he now added a mile-or-more run every day, on at least one occasion playing baseball as well, which left him sore for a week. Working out with the Bard Brothers, an acrobatic troupe, he learned how to get around on the horizontal bar and was soon swinging on it publicly, in clown costume ("went big and funny"). He kept at it and advanced quickly. Aided by a guy wire, he learned to somersault coming off the bar, and by early summer was daily practicing strenuous back and double somersaults. By the fall, he had bought his own acrobat's tights and slippers, and could chalk up no small athletic achievement: "1st double out in front of audience."

But along with opportunities, notice, and a modest living came blue funks and hassles. "Rottenest bus[iness] of season," Harry recorded in Norristown, Pennsylvania. "Fearfully Hot. I slept on side walk of Main Street." "Rain hard," he noted in Paw Paw, "No dinner." Usually friendly with the freaks, he got into a mean scrape with Bill the Dog Boy. He "worsted" Bill, but began carrying a gun for protection against him. By the time the traveling circus shut down, in October, he had had enough: "Last two weeks seemed like eternity." Before leaving he obtained a written endorsement from the Welsh brothers. They recommended Metamorphosis as "the strongest drawing card of its class in America," and praised the Houdinis personally as "a lady and gentlemen [*sic*] in all that this term implies."

THE SCHOOL OF MAGIC

Bess and Harry returned to New York to recoup, apparently staying with his mother. Harry mailed flyers for the 1898–99 season notifying managers that the Houdinis had refurbished their act with elegant new costumes and new stage settings, "handsome, gorgeous and bewildering with bright hued plush embellishments and variegated colored electrical effects." In the new season they would offer THE FINEST FINISHED MYSTERY IN THE WORLD, a program that would "reflect credit on any house we may be booked at."

This was an SOS—not a promise of things to come but a plea for work. By the end of 1898 things had become "so bad," Harry wrote later, "that I contemplated quitting the show business, and retire to private life, meaning to work by day at one of my trades . . . and open a school of magic." He came close to doing that. From the address of his mother's Sixty-ninth Street flat he sent out a sixteen-page catalog for "Harry Houdini's School of Magic." Its mishmash of items for sale included egg bags, card swords, and other apparatus; lessons in Punch and Judy; and cheap how-to books, such as the ten-cent *Dogs and How to Keep and Train Them* and the twenty-five-cent opus, *Guide of Flirtation with Fan, Eyes, Parasol and Gloves.* In desperation it would seem, Harry also marketed his hand-cuff come-on: "You defy the police authorities and sheriffs to place hand-cuffs or leg shackles on you, and can easily escape. Price on application." He even offered to teach Metamorphosis—the price, on application, to include "right of exhibiting same; drawings, complete instructions, expla-nations, introductory speech and all secrets of box, sack, coat, braid and quick method of working." In effect, he put on the block the centerpieces of "The Houdinis'" whole act.

Brought low enough as an entertainer to consider bowing out, Harry left late in December for the Midwest to complete his prior contracts. He began at Middleton's in Chicago, still another dime museum. Here the "Wizard of Shackles" shared the platform with a brace of nine-pound infants, "Tiniest Triplets Ever Born." While in town he received a letter from Albini (Abraham Laski [1860–1913]), an immigrant Polish-Jewish magi-cian temporarily turned booking agent ("Nothing But the Elite of the Pro-fession . . . Theatrical Experience from Russia to California"). In some earlier correspondence Harry had bristled at Albini's offer to serve as his press agent, loftily replying that his reputation was such "as to render the insertions of the press un-necessary." Albini now haughtied him back: "I am surprised that a man of such reputation . . . to work in a Dime Museum." With the dank reminder that Harry did not have to "sit on a platform" with mismade creatures, he urged him to call: "We will try to raise the name of Houdini to where it ought to be, and not in a Museum."

As the roving, protean Harry Raynohr, Cardo, Professor Murat, Projea, and Wizard of Shackles, Ehrich Weiss had been actor, acrobat, bur-lesque impresario, wild man, spirit-worker, puppeteer, merchandiser, illu-sionist, hypnotist, and fun-maker of the Bloomer Club. Rather like the scholarly Dr. M. S. Weiss—"all religious Services a Specialty, Marriages and Funerals, also practical MOHEL"—he had been many things, but not a winner.

TWO

1899

MARTIN BECK

UNEXPECTEDLY, in the early spring of 1899, after a half-dozen years idling in museums and smalltown bigtops, Harry's career skyrocketed. In fourteen dizzying months he became a star of American entertainment.

The reversal began at a St. Paul, Minnesota, beer hall, the Palm-garden—one of the earlier contracts Harry meant to fulfill as he considered retiring. A party of sightseeing theater managers dropped in. One of them, Martin Beck, challenged him to escape some handcuffs—"perhaps more in a joke than sincerity," Harry thought. Beck brought a few pairs the next day and sent them onstage; Harry escaped. On March 14, Beck telegraphed him from Chicago: "You can open Omaha March twenty sixth sixty dollars, will see act probably make you proposition for all next season." Harry carefully preserved the message, and at some time wrote across the bottom of it: "This wire changed my whole Life's journey."

Martin Beck brought Harry not only the highest weekly salary he had ever earned, but also the perfect vehicle for his ambitions, temperament, and gifts. By the first decade of the new century, with perhaps two thousand theaters in the United States and Canada devoted to it, vaudeville was coast to coast the most popular form of entertainment in North America. Big-time vaudeville, which Beck personified, was no scramble of fourteen platform shows a day and one-night stands in Pottsville. Acts played a pre-arranged circuit of larger cities in generally handsome theaters, appearing twice a day and staying a week or more in the same place before moving on to the next appointed job on the circuit. Steady work in relatively comfortable conditions, before a national audience, at a high salary.

Not only the comforts, but also the atmosphere and the demands of top-line vaudeville particularly suited Harry. Unlike burlesque and medicine shows, it cultivated a middle-class wholesomeness meant to bring families into the theater—an ideal that would become unprofitable to maintain against the nation's loosening moral standards, but congenial to Harry. ("INFERIORITY," he printed in one of his diaries, motto-like, "IS THE MOTHER OF PROFANITY.") The typical vaudeville program of eight to ten acts thrived on novelty, and not just novelty but singularity. In a comedy singing duo, she must be very tall and he very short; in a family of acrobats, one must be hardly out of diapers. This, and the ten- to thirty-minute time limit of the vaudeville turn, led many magicians to abandon the varieties of conjuring (and bulky apparatus) that characterized the two-and-a-half-hour, 'full-evening' magic shows of the nineteenth century. Instead they specialized in one kind of magic distinctive to themselves—coins, cards, cigarettes, or, for Harry, escapes.

And Martin Beck, his new mentor, was a vaudeville tycoon. A stoutish, jowly figure in pince-nez, he had come to the United States at sixteen, among a small troupe of German actors. By now he oversaw a monopolistic chain of theaters that extended from Chicago to the Pacific Coast. His Orpheum circuit, in the West, virtually divided the management of American big time with the partners B. F. Keith and Edward F. Albee, whose circuit dominated vaudeville in the East. By the 1920s Keith's and Orpheum owned all the major vaudeville houses in the country. A no-nonsense businessman, intelligent and well-traveled, Beck tried to lend his circuit a touch of class, defying the many who sneered at vaudeville as a mass opiate. He insisted that his acts stay at the best hotels, booked Sarah Bernhardt (at seven thousand dollars a week), and built vaudeville its shrine, the Palace Theatre in New York.

The contract Harry signed with Beck, on April 27, came like a rebirth, even a better birth. It placed him, before the end of the year, at leading vaudeville houses in Kansas City, Chicago, Pittsburgh, Cincinnati, and St. Louis, and took him for the first time farther west to Denver, San Francisco, and Los Angeles. The Orpheum circuit cooperated with Keith's eastern circuit, so at the New Year Beck booked him into major Keith houses in Boston and Providence. Accustomed to $25 weekly, when paid at all, Harry found his initial, decent $60 escalating every few weeks—to $125, $150, $175, $250. Beck took a hefty cut: 15 percent of all dates Harry played in Orpheum theaters for up to $150, and 20 percent when he earned more, an additional 5 or 10 percent occasionally going to intermediate agents. On the other hand, Beck earned his money, and in Harry's interest. "I have laid out the plan for you very carefully," he told him. "My aim especially is at present to make a name for you." As he did.

NEEDLE SWALLOWING; THE STRAITJACKET ESCAPE; THE JAIL ESCAPE

Harry met these large opportunities with a crowd-pleasing creative burst, some of it from out of nowhere. While retaining Metamorphosis, he introduced major new effects into "The Houdinis'" old repertoire. The first to attract notice—Needle Swallowing—came in one of his earliest appearances under Beck's management, at the Kansas City Orpheum on April 10, 1899.

In a typical performance, Harry invited a committee onstage to watch him closely as he placed a number of sewing needles in his mouth. Sometimes with humorous patter about "taking iron for the blood," he began chewing them, loudly. "You can hear the steel crush and snap under his iron teeth," a reporter said. A light was held close to his face and he opened his mouth to show the committee that the needles had disappeared, apparently swallowed. The reporter continued:

> He is then given a long piece of white linen thread, peculiarly knotted by some one of the committee for future identification; one end of this he places in his mouth and begins swallowing. This operation is continued until only the smallest particle of an end is visible in his throat. Then with open mouth and in the glare of a bright light, he catches the end of the thread and slowly draws forth, not only the same knotted thread, but on this thread are strung the identical number and kind of needles given him by his judges.

Although such performances made review headlines—"Houdini in His Weirdest Trick of Chewing Needles"—the effect was almost a century old, and despite the seeming pain and danger it can be done by quite young or amateur magicians, even using razor blades instead of needles.

What set apart Harry's performance of Needle Swallowing was his boldness in presenting it on large stages, where the slender thread and needles are hard to see. The trick is meant for the close quarters of a small room or nightclub; in fact he carried it in his pocket as part of what he called his "hanky-panky stuff," ready to perform anytime, anywhere. To make the basically small effect convincing in a vaudeville theater took unusual showmanship. He built it up by bringing onstage the committee to examine his mouth, and perhaps by increasing the usual number of needles. One newspaper gave the number he swallowed as a dozen, another as about twenty. Although Harry himself later said that he used, depending on the size of the theater, from 50 to 150 needles, and ten to thirty yards of thread, a surviving packet of his later needles, set up for performance, contains only about twenty-five.

Under Beck's management Harry also made news with his card magic. In Cincinnati he vanished twenty-five cards at his fingertips one by one— according to the city's *Enquirer*—then made them one by one reappear there, using the so-called back palm, a moderately difficult sleight introduced in the late 1890s. At a publicity demonstration in Denver he instantly produced from a pack any card called for by a spectator, and performed the classic card-stabbing effect: a selected card was returned to the deck, which was then spread out haphazardly on the table, face down. Blindfolded, Harry clasped a penknife, moved it above the scattering, and, casually it seemed, speared one of the facedown cards, which turned out to be the one selected. He later said that during this period he kept a pack of cards in his hands all day long—not unusual for a serious card manipulator—continually mixing, shuffling, and manipulating them. "I practice seven or eight hours a day as conscientiously as a Paderewski at the piano," the *Denver Times* quoted him saying. "But my handcuff tricks are best."

Harry was right. Having started out as a magician, making a flower appear in his buttonhole, he learned on the Orpheum circuit that his greatest appeal lay in escapes. A week after signing with Beck, he tried slipping some cuffs onstage without pulling the cabinet closed around him: "1st time I took off cuffs with curtain open," he wrote in his diary, "was the hit of act." Among many other innovations he also emphasized escapes from unusual cuffs. In Boston he got out of thumb cuffs, a small, highly effective stocklike shackle, used to pin the thumbs together. In Omaha he undid cuffs fitted with time locks. In Providence he attempted leg-irons made locally during the Civil War, fitted with so powerful a spring that putting them on and closing them, by means of a screw key, took six minutes (Harry escaped in two).

In satisfying the big-time, Harry reached not only to the exotic but also to big-time excess. He brought new excitement to his police-station promotions by allowing himself to be festooned in as many as a dozen handcuffs and leg shackles. In San Francisco four hundred officials and patrolmen from all over the county came to see him fastened with four varieties of handcuffs (three containing double springs) and two pairs of leg-irons, another set of handcuffs being used to lock the hand and leg shackles together. "This brought him to a crouching posture," the *Chronicle* reported, "and made him to all appearances helpless to use a key even if he had one." He escaped in seven minutes, producing the manacles interlocked in a long chain. His ankles, wrists, arms, and legs beringed with cuffs of all sorts, he made a grotesque human package. To a Los Angeles reporter he was "trussed like a turkey at a Thanksgiving shoot." A Buffalo newspaper said the haltering put him "in danger of tearing up the floor with his nose." The danger was real, the tightly ratcheted irons often bruising and bloodying his skin and making his wrists swell.

A sensational new handcuff test arose out of Harry's confrontation, in San Francisco, with a bearded young English magician who called himself Professor Benzon. On July 9 Benzon published in the *Examiner* a long article, with photographs, entitled "Expose of Houdini's Trunk and Handcuff Trick"; it was reprinted next day in the *Los Angeles Record*. Benzon charged (correctly) that others before "The Houdinis" had performed Metamorphosis, and gave a presumed exposé of Harry's handcuff escapes. Only a few models of handcuffs were manufactured, he explained, and all cuffs of the same manufacturer could be opened with the same key. Harry's simple secret consisted of his having "conveniently about him all keys known to the handcuff trade."

Martin Beck urged Harry to ignore would-be exposers: "The more he writes and tries to expose you, the more he is advertising you." Savvy advice, but on its part it ignored Harry's style of redress, which was not Turn-the-other-cheek but Do-the-guy-in-fast. On an early road trip he was effecting the exchange in Metamorphosis when a committee member brought up from the audience stood on a chair and peeped over the top of the cabinet. Harry bounded out "white with rage," by newspaper report, and before the "paralyzed" audience denounced the man "in a by no means gentle manner." In Benzon's case he shot back first through an article in the *Call* on July 11. He laughed off Benzon's explanations as "absurdly simple" and plagiarized from a ten-cent book on magic, both of which were true.

That all handcuffs of the same model made by the same manufacturer could be opened by the same key was no secret. Harry himself wrote that twenty-five keys could unlock all the handcuffs made in the United States, and some of the companion leg-irons as well. But although only a few kinds of cuffs may be in active police use in one country at one time, there exist in the world hundreds of varieties of cuffs. Some are named for their inventors, such as Tower cuffs, others for their shape or method of construction, such as Plug 8s. Ranging from five-inch thumb cuffs to giant Oregon boots, they differ in weight, complexity, and design, and use different locks. Even if one possesses the scores of keys required to open them all, the problem is to recognize, on taking the cuff in hand, which key is needed. Harry's surviving apparatus includes large, numbered burlap pouches, rather like snap purses with overlong bags. He *may* have used them as a filing system for classifying keys and picks to various kinds of handcuffs. Even if he did, however, the rest of what he had to do remains a question. How did he get to the keys? Where did he hide them for use?

Benzon's pseudo-explanation hinted at none of this, but Harry took sensational advantage of it anyway. To demonstrate that he did not need keys at all, he offered to perform a handcuff escape nude. He did so at the San Francisco police station on the night of July 13. Stripped before a dozen detectives, he was examined by a police surgeon and two assistants, who after searching from his hair to between his toes certified that it would be impossible for him to conceal a key, wire, or anything else. As an extra precaution his mouth was tightly taped shut. The detectives then fettered his wrists and ankles with ten pairs of their own handcuffs, using another pair to fasten the wrist and ankle shackles together. Carried buck naked into a closet off the detectives' room, he emerged five minutes later, naked still but with the cuffs removed and strung ponderously together.

The nude test could not be presented at theaters, but Harry kept the press and public aware of him by adding it to his police-station exhibitions.

A New York newspaper reported in December that as he started to strip in the station, a sergeant protested, "That don't go. . . . You've got to keep your clothes on." At least once, at a Philadelphia police station, he also did his Needle Swallowing effect "in charming and total dishabille," as a reporter put it, to show he had nothing to hide. Proud of his muscular physique, he had many publicity pictures taken of himself laden with cuffs, adamically clad in no more than a jockstrap-size loincloth.

During the same Benzon-inspired demonstration for the San Francisco police, Harry introduced another spectacular escape. He asked the superintendent of the local "Insane Ward" to strap, lock, and lace him into a straitjacket. Such restraints are put on the reverse way from an ordinary coat—solid side in front, open side to the back—the arms going into long baglike sleeves, closed at the ends and sewed to heavy straps. The open back is firmly buckled together. Then the arms are crossed and wrapped around the chest in a self-embrace, their end straps tightly drawn around the back and buckled too. (A crotch strap is often used as well, extending from the front of the jacket to the back between the legs, to prevent the jacket from being moved up and down.) Harry freed himself in San Francisco and repeated the feat in Los Angeles three days later, walking into the city receiving hospital and, according to the *Call*, asking to see "the best strait-jacket you have in the place." He got the attendant to put it on him securely, then asked to be taken to a room where he could be alone. After about ten minutes the attendant heard "violent knocking" and opened the door, to find Harry freed, the straitjacket draped over his arm. "It was a hard one," he reportedly said, "but I did it."

By his later account Harry conceived the escape while touring the Canadian provinces with the Marco Company. In St. John, he had met a doctor in charge of an insane asylum, who invited him to visit. Straitjackets and similar 'mechanical restraints' had largely been given up in England; many medical authorities and reformers condemned their continued use in North America as archaic and cruel. Through the small bars of a cell door, Harry saw a "maniac" struggling on the canvas-padded floor, "rolling about and straining each and every muscle," he said, "in a vain attempt to get his hands over his head and striving in every conceivable manner to free himself from his canvas restraint." Next morning Harry got permission to try to escape from a jacket. He practiced for a week afterward, perhaps even performing the feat publicly at a provincial theater.

With its note of sadism and overtone of social controversy, the Strait-jacket Escape became a mainstay of "The Houdinis"—which was becoming more and more just Houdini. Harry blazoned his new escapes on business cards:

POSITIVELY

The only Conjurer in the World that Escapes out of all Handcuffs, Leg Shackles, Insane Belts and Strait-Jackets, after being STRIPPED STARK NAKED, mouth sealed up, and thoroughly searched from head to foot, proving he carries no KEYS, SPRINGS, WIRES or other concealed accessories. . . .

under Management of Martin Beck, Chicago

At least as concerns straitjackets, this was frank. Harry neither used nor needed "concealed accessories." The escape can leave skin abrasions and charleyhorses but, as is true also of handcuff escapes, it can be easy or near impossible. The difficulty depends on the size and cut of the jacket, the number and position of the belts and buckles, the presence or absence of a crotch strap, and the tightness of the buckling or lacing done by the stage volunteers. The material counts too, most jackets being made of heavy canvas, some of canvas and leather, and the most difficult of leather entirely. "The more inflexible the material," Harry noted, "the more diffi-cult and longer the time necessary for making your release." One "mur-derous" escape a few years later took him over an hour: "The pain, torture, agony, and misery of the struggle," he said, "will forever live in my mind."

On a creative high, Harry outdid himself again at Chicago's central police station by escaping, on April 5, 1900, from a jail cell. After being searched for hidden picks and keys by the jailkeep and four detectives, he was led into a cell with two locks. One was an ordinary cell lock with a key-hole. The keyhole, however, was covered by a hinged iron tongue that extended to the outer frame of the cell, where it notched over a staple that was then padlocked, out of the prisoner's reach. Harry had to open the remote padlock, swing the hinge back to expose the keyhole, then open the door lock. Once the detectives and jailer left the cell, it took him three min-utes to get out.

Harry repeated this eyepopper five days later in Kansas City, Missouri.

This time he was undressed and searched by several detectives, who also taped his mouth. They locked four pairs of police handcuffs on his wrists and shackled his ankles, crossing the shackle chains over the short handcuff chains, which forced him to waddle into the cell crouching. The lock here was innovative, "recently purchased under a guarantee of absolute safety," the *Star* reported, and requiring two keys to open. "These locks cannot be sawed or picked, the guarantee is, and it is backed up by signed testimonials from experts in the penitentiaries." A sheet was thrown over the cell to conceal Harry's activities. In just under seven minutes, he threw open the door and stepped out—to shouts from the spectators—holding in his hands the four pairs of handcuffs, the shackles, and the new, guaranteed lock.

SUCCESS

By the time of his first Jail Cell Escape, after a year under Martin Beck's management, Harry had attained a weekly salary of four hundred dollars. The amount was ninety dollars less than the entire annual budget, in 1905, of the entire family of an American factory laborer. Playing top vaudeville houses in sizable cities, Harry was often featured on the bill and sometimes held over a second week. Leading newspapers in one city reported his feats in another, in terms from super to superduper: "one of the biggest hits in the history of the Orpheum"; "the greatest juggler and mystifier ever seen in the city"; "the English vocabulary promises to be exhausted in the efforts of people to describe their astonishment." Merchants draped their wares in his sudden renown, such as the Omaha butcher who ran an ad showing shackles flying off Harry, above a price list for pork loin and round steak: "HOUDINI can get away from these handcuffs, but you can't get away from these facts. . . . The Best Meats, The Lowest Prices, at the Central Market."

American newspaper readers wanted to know not only what Harry did onstage, but also how he did it and who he was. He dodged questions about his methods with a stock reply: "Please excuse me from answering. . . . If I were to do so, my bread and butter would be gone." Perhaps because of the snobbish appeal of foreign performers—or perhaps to explain away his grammatical blunders and uneducated speech—he portrayed himself as a Hungarian or Austrian who had arrived in America only within the last several years. Interviewers often referred to him as "a magician from Buda-Pest" or "an Austrian and has been in the United States about 10 years." (In Boston he was billed as "The Weird, Mystifying and Inexplicable Hungarian Magician.") "I expect to go back to Hungary some day," the *Buffalo Express* quoted him as saying; "speaks good English," the paper added, "learned it no one knows where." Perhaps forever to bury Ehrich Weiss and Projea, the Wild Man of Mexico, he said nothing of his family's coal-less sweatshop years in Wisconsin and New York, and of his own freak-show days he gave out only a distorted and blandly abstract account: "Coming to this country, he was virtually driven from pillar to post," a Denver paper related, "until finally he got a start in Omaha, was sent to the coast by the Orpheum people and created a sensation in police circles."

Reporters offered impressions of Harry's appearance. They stressed his smallness—"somewhat undersized"—and angular, vivid features: "He is smooth-shaven with a keen, sharp-chinned, sharp-cheekboned face, bright blue eyes and thick, curly, black hair." Some sensed how much his complexly expressive smile was the outlet of his charismatic stage presence. It communicated to audiences at once warm amiability, pleasure in performing, and, more subtly, imperious self-assurance. Several reporters tried to capture the charming effect, describing him as "happy-looking," "pleasant-faced," "good-natured at all times," "the young Hungarian magician, with the pleasant smile and easy confidence."

Harry's well-exercised physique, now much displayed, became a news story unto itself. Under the heading MARVELOUSLY DEVELOPED FOREARM OF MAGICIAN HOUDINI the *St. Louis Post-Dispatch* published parallel photographs of the thickveined forearms of Harry and of the Prussian strongman-wrestler Eugene Sandow, heralded as the most perfectly developed man in the world. The newspaper observed that despite Harry's much slighter frame, his overall muscular development "almost, if not quite" equaled Sandow's, and his arm muscles bulged "proportionately larger." It gave Harry's measurements as wrist, seven and a quarter inches; forearm, eleven and a quarter inches; fist doubled, eleven and a half inches. Since the girth of the average man's forearm exceeded that of his wrist by only about two inches, it could readily be seen that Harry's muscular development was "prodigious," his forearm "a pillar of steel." (Other measurements proved, the writer added, that he could not possibly escape from handcuffs by sliding them over his hands, as many believed he did.)

The press measured Harry against the strongmen of magic, too. The Orpheum-Keith circuit at times presented more than one magician on the same program, Harry appearing over the year with the rising star Howard

Thurston (1869–1936) and the renowned Chinese magician Ching Ling Foo (Qua Chee-ling [1854–1922?]). Foo introduced to Western magic such standard effects as the Torn and Restored Paper, and the Foo Can—a small pitcher that pours forth a seemingly endless supply of water, though repeatedly shown to be empty. At Keith's flagship theater in Boston, he enjoyed the longest engagement ever recorded by a magician on the Keith circuit, begetting so many imitators that, Martin Beck wrote, "The country is pested with Ching Ling Foo acts." Yet when Harry joined the bill, for the week of January 8–13, 1900, the press described him as a "formidable rival" to Foo, and "more talked about." Harry stuck the notice in his thickening scrapbook, exclaiming in the margin, "and Ching Ling Foo on Same Programme."

With newspaper readers eager for anecdotes and human-interest items about him, Harry no sooner established a reputation than he began acquiring a legend. The *Boston Herald* covered his meeting early in 1900 with Capt. Charles Bean, inventor of several ingenious police restraints including the Bean Giant handcuffs. Most handcuffs connect the wrists by a flexible chain, affording them play. But Bean Giants were tooled from flat sheets of steel that, pillory-like, prevented the wrists from moving toward or away from each other. To thwart further any lockpicking attempt, Bean Giant keyholes were made small and set beyond reach of the prisoner's fingers. Bean had offered a five-hundred-dollar reward to anyone who could escape from the cuffs, even using a key. As the press reported their meeting, Harry said: "I have spread your fame for making handcuffs all over the United States. I take my hat off to your Yankee ingenuity." Then he slipped a pair of Bean Giants—hands fettered behind his back! Bean reportedly gulped, "Well! Well! I couldn't believe it unless it took place before my eyes. I have probably fastened 10,000 prisoners in my time with those handcuffs, and have met with all sorts of experiences, but—you beat me."

If the *Herald* account has rather much the glow of Famous Mantles Handed Down in History, it pales beside other encounters with Harry retailed in the press. In Joplin, Missouri, a white man in a brown derby hat reportedly broke into his dressing room and stole Bess's thousand-dollar diamond brooch, "given her by the Czar of Russia." Denver police reportedly cut the eyes out of several station-house portraits and pasted gauze over the holes to spy out his method of undoing an Oregon Boot. The story-of-stories, in the timeworn mold of the Trickster Tricked, concerned the perverse defeat of Harry's skills by everyday objects: While calling from a phone booth, he was locked in by a practical-joking traveling salesman, and unable to escape (HOUDINI LOCKED IN); he missed a train after failing to unbuckle the straps on his luggage, to get out his tickets (HOUDINI KNOCKED OUT?).

The publicity also gained Harry spoilers and critics, magnified his (very few) failures, and exposed his limitations. He required that handcuffs secured on him must be in working order, and looked out for those that had been "crabbed," as he called it, for example by jamming the locks with BBs. Just the same, a policeman in Evanston, Illinois, manacled him with fixed cuffs, earning a rare "SOAB" in Harry's clean diary. One of several pairs of cuffs in a Kansas City performance simply froze on his wrist, making an embarrassing headline in next day's *Star:* HOUDINI COULDN'T GET IT OFF. Here or there reviewers faulted his grammar, complained that his escapes did not show up well onstage, zonked his "very bad palming," deplored his self-praise. "Houdini wastes a lot of valuable time in telling the audience how good he is," one commented; "He would be even more interesting," another wrote, "if he said less about being the 'greatest ever.'"

In fact, Harry was beginning to manifest a godlike ego, which while provoking criticism also insulated him from it. Although pained by his lack of formal education, he would not stand by to hear it called a fault: "While I have not studied grammer [*sic*] as thoroughly as I should have done, I never the less studied Locks, and that is a good excue [*sic*] for me." Knowing how locks worked was more than a good excuse for his imperfections. It was a badge of his singularity, of being, as he wanted to be, like no one else, ever: "the Handcuff act can not be done searched and naked after my style by *any one on Earth,*" he wrote at this time, "no one else can do it or *explain* how I do it." In godlike terms indeed, he advertised the act as ONE OF THE GREATEST MAGICAL FEATS SINCE BIBLICAL TIMES.

Despite the few stabs at his card-palming or grammar, Harry felt cheered by his growing celebrity, especially given the failures of the past— his own and his father's. A turning point came on May 1, 1899, when the *Chicago Journal* published a drawing of him shedding cuffs and leg-irons at police headquarters. He cut it out to keep and wrote next to it: "first time my Picture ever appeared in a newspaper." As Bess recalled the day, he burst into their hotel room with the paper, shouting, "Bess we're made! I'm famous!"

AT ODDS WITH BECK

Martin Beck contributed much to Harry's success. Having promised to "boom you to the top notch," he kept him booked, publicized him everywhere, and craftily guided his progress. Determined to get Harry noticed in New York, for instance—which had not yet happened—he passed up the chance to introduce him there in summer, "the dull season," proposing instead that he spend the time playing Saratoga, Newport, or some other ritzy resort, "to boost you up before fashionable audiences." He wrote to Harry often and encouragingly, passing along tips: hold out for suitable salaries; buy an album for notices ("your clippings is what gets you the engagements"). Careful not to trigger Harry's quick temper, he listened patiently to his penny-pinching gripes about railroad fares, massaged his hurt feelings when critics carped: "since the 'knockers' have been at work . . . I just set my mind on it that I will work three times as hard to make a star out of you." Harry's brother Dash estimated how much Beck's pushing, coddling, and expertise accomplished. "Although many persons claim to have made Houdini," he wrote later, "all credit should go to astute Martin Beck."

Yet as Harry ended his first Orpheum tour, in December 1899, he felt restive under Beck's management. With his tireless hard work and despotic independence—and dozens of dazzling reviews behind him—he balked at laboring under someone else's direction. He also begrudged Beck his 20 percent cut, and told him so. Beck knew his own worth too, however, and remembered well enough Harry's situation at the time they met: "no managers would believe that your act was fit for vaudeville," he reminded him, "they all considered it a museum act." This was not the right thing to tell Harry, nor was Beck's reply to his continued grumbling about the cut: "whatever I get, you are not losing anything by it, as I certainly ask managers a price which they would never have given to you." In an I'll-show-you spirit Harry sometimes sent Beck less than the contractual commission, forcing him to write for the rest, then wire.

By February Harry had become dissatisfied with his salary and bookings as well. He complained that a friend described him as "the cheapest headliner in the business," and told Beck to demand more money for him. Beck had had enough. "I do not want instructions from you," he snapped. "I am fully capable to know what to do. It is of no use for you to get the swelled head, as we are cutting heads off every day." Unscared, Harry also questioned dates in Buffalo, Toronto, and Cleveland that Beck had arranged for him earlier in the year, at only $150. But Beck knew how to bellyache too. "I do not like to be questioned by you," he wrote back. "At the time I made the contract . . . nobody knew that you are on earth, and it was only through my prestige and influence that you received these dates, which you seem to have forgotten so very soon." For good measure he observed that Harry had identified him, in an ad, as his "manager and backer." "Permit me to say that the word 'backer' I will never stand for. I am not handling a prize-fighter"—about which he was not exactly correct.

Despite their bickering, Beck had large plans for Harry, and was arranging for him to become known in Britain and continental Europe. Harry's intended tour abroad had been announced in the fall of 1899, but preoccupation with the Boer War, which was depressing British show business, delayed his departure until the end of the following spring—the first spring of the twentieth century. Planning ahead, Beck also booked Harry again on the Keith circuit for mid-August, when he would return to New York.

During his big year on the circuits Harry had added several advertising slogans to his long list, including "The Celebrated Police Baffler." But he began using one tag more often than others, and then exclusively. The new generation of vaudeville magicians often titled themselves king of some specialty—"King of Cards," "King of Billiard Balls," "Paper Tearing King." Having arrived in the United States twenty-two years earlier, as four-year-old Ehrich Weiss, Harry sailed from it at the end of May as HARRY HOUDINI, THE KING OF HANDCUFFS. SS *Kensington*, bound for Southampton.

HISTORICAL NOTE

THE MATRIX OF PERFORMANCE

BY THE TURN of the century Houdini had introduced the basic handcuff, jail, and straitjacket escapes that have preserved his fame. But his career as an escape artist, and as Houdini, was just beginning. In order to follow his early rise in American vaudeville undistracted, little has been hinted about the historical and social origins of what he performed. This matrix of influences, sketched below, bears on his biography at no one point but at every point. In retrospect it shows that Houdini began his career by combining several popular practices of his culture to startlingly original effect. In anticipation it suggests how much his later career was the mirror image of his earlier. And it involves persons and events that stirred his imagination all along.

On the genesis of Houdini's passion for locks, handcuffs, and other security devices, the press printed dozens of conflicting accounts. Reporters often misquoted or misrepresented what he said and did, often stretching the facts to make news. And magicians are in the deception business: in more than a few, the disposition to mislead operates onstage and off, a trait aggravated in Houdini's case by an unusually bad memory for dates and places, a family habit of fabulation, and a can't-get-enough hunger for publicity.

Every time Houdini answered a reporter's questions about his early interest in locks, he gave or was reported to give a different story. "[M]y

ancestors were locksmiths," one went, "and I followed the calling of a professional locksmith for some years." His mother, in another tale, baked
such great pies that he could not keep his hands off them: "No matter
where she hid the pies," he said, "I always managed to discover the hiding-
place. And so she tried locking them up. But I opened the locks without any
difficulty. That is how I began my career." For other storytelling occasions
the pies became a horse that stepped on his hand when he was nine,
sending him to the hospital. Bored there, he looked around for something to
do: "I saw a pair of double racket [*sic*] handcuffs which the superintendent
brought in to put on a crazy man," this tale went. "The click of the lock
amused me. . . . I got them down, put them on and then sat down and figured out how I could get out." And so on.

By contrast with this whatever-you-want about his discovery of locks,
on the question of how he mastered them Houdini said nothing. A noted
locksmith who knew him, Charles Courtney, wrote that he was not expert
"mechanically," but nevertheless had "a remarkable knowledge of locks
and locking devices." Over his lifetime Houdini collected hundreds of locks,
and must have pulled hundreds apart to see how they worked. What he saw
he remembered. In some unpublished manuscript notes he set down what
he called "one of my great challenge secrets which I am now giving to
Mankind." The secret was his "photographic eyes." Seeing a lock or handcuff he would get a "vision of the key," he said, "just like photographed in
my mind, which was of much importance to me in preparing for the
opening of the lock." He could retain the vision for weeks, and even late in
life could recall almost the exact sizes of the various "keys etc." of jail cells
he had opened. Concerning the deepest secrets of his lock magic he said
and wrote no more than this little.

On the other hand, the foundations of Houdini's *escape act* can be
traced fully. They lay in the history of Spiritualism, the worldwide religious
movement that lasted from the late 1840s to about the Second World War
(and survives weakly today), its popularity now waning now resurging.
Like other supernaturalist revivals in the West, it was the counterspinning
twin of science. Much as the witchcraft epidemics of the seventeenth century gave the lie to Newton's mathematical universe, Spiritualism reaf-
firmed the reality of spirit in the face of modern scientific materialism,
allaying anxiety throughout Christendom about the immortality of the soul
and the fate of the self after death.

Spiritualism sprang into being in rural Hydesville, New York, on March 31, 1848. For several nights rappings and other mysterious noises had disturbed the humble home of a farmer named John Fox, his wife, and their daughters Katie and Margaret, aged twelve and fifteen. On the night of the thirty-first, one of the girls induced the raps to sound as many times as she snapped her fingers, suggesting the presence of some intelligent agency. In the following days the girls became able to elicit the raps by merely asking, and began using them to signal responses to questions they posed (Was the agency an injured spirit? One rap for yes, two for no). Within a year or so the phenomena turned rambunctious. Visitors to the Fox home told of being slapped by invisible hands, feeling the floor vibrate, hearing the sound of sawing, seeing window shades roll up, drawers fly open. Similar manifestations began appearing throughout upstate New York, and within two or three years throughout the state and region. For tens of thousands of people the Fox Cottage in the village of Hydesville soon became no less sacred than the birthplace of Jesus in Bethlehem.

Not everyone was swept away. Emerson, for one, condemned the movement as a caricature of religion, a "gospel that comes by taps in the wall, and thumps in the table-drawer," a "Rat-revelation." But by the time of the Civil War a militant national religious revival was underway, assembled in leagues, associations, and churches. One of its leaders, Mrs. Emma Hardinge, estimated that the United States then contained no fewer than eleven million adherents to Spiritualism. "It is in the cabin of the miner, in the heart of the Rocky Mountains," she enthused, "and consoles the toiling emigrant in his nightly camp on the desert waste or the wild prairie." Spreading from Hydesville to the West Indies, South America, China, Turkey, and throughout Europe and Britain, Spiritualism won disciples not only by demonstrating God's immanence in the world but also by linking up with women's rights, temperance, organized labor, and other reforms, offering itself as a revolutionary movement that could rebuild society.

Enter Houdini and his escape act. As the Spiritualist ranks swelled, demonstrations came to be given not only at home but also by professional mediums on the concert stage. One reason for the movement's wildfire success, in fact, was that its eerie manifestations, whether in a sitting room or a public hall, could be enthralling theater. And magicians quickly understood that the floating objects, jingling bells, and unfurling curtains opened up for them a rich new vocabulary.

Many magicians reproduced Spiritualist phenomena in their shows. Touring the United States in 1860, the Scotsman John Henry Anderson, "the Wizard of the North" (1814–74), had spirits rap out the results of the Lincoln-Douglas presidential race. In the 1870s the popular English magician-pianist Robert Heller (William Henry Palmer [ca. 1830–78]) tipped tables, rocked chairs, and made words appear on his bare arm, written in blood. Other conjurers advertised a "Wonderful Spiritual Seance" or a program of "Spiritualism illustrated" (forerunners of the "Grand, Brilliant, Bewildering and Startling Spiritualistic Seance" Houdini guiltily gave with the California Concert Company). Spiritualist effects became so established a part of the magician's repertoire that Robert-Houdin, in his *Les Secrets de la Prestidigitation et de la Magie* (1868), included among the six "branches" of conjuring "*The Medium Business*—Spiritualism, or pretended evocation of spirits, table-turning, -rapping, -talking, and -writing, mysterious cabinets &c."

In a shift decisive for Houdini's career, Spiritualist mediums, and afterward their magician counterparts, became the first 'escape artists.' That happened as the mediums' more and more spectacular results—up to full materialization of departed spirits—brought on widespread accusations of fraud. In the 1870s mediums countered by offering to produce their phenomena under test conditions. These included confinement in cabinets or cages, prior searches when nude (perhaps the model for Houdini's nude jail escapes), and subjection to various restraints. During some 1875 test séances in London, for instance, two mediums were tied around the waist and ankles by leather straps fastened with combination locks, then hitched by further locks to marble pillars. A "materializing test medium" named George Everett similarly advertised a "HANDCUFF TEST!!," offering a five-hundred-dollar reward for "the four pair of Handcuffs to hold him."

By the time Houdini started out, in the mid-1890s, he encountered a public familiar with mediumistic handcuff tests, if not by experience at least through the press. As an 1897 article in *Scientific American* described them for its readers:

> The handcuff test is a great favorite of the "medium." In this test the performer uses any pair of handcuffs furnished by the audience, and by them put on him. Yet, in a very few moments after he takes his place in the cabinet, his coat is thrown out, but on exami-

nation the handcuffs are found to be on his wrists just as they were placed by the audience. As a final test, the performer comes out of the cabinet holding the handcuffs in his hand, removed from the wrist but locked.

Houdini himself had met a Spiritualist escape artist in 1892, while playing a Milwaukee dime museum. A Bavarian medium, Dr. Josef Gregorowitsch, gave him a private demonstration, using Houdini's own tape, bandages, nails, and needle and thread: "I tied Dr. Gregorowitsch's wrists together, sewed the knots, put the surgeon's plaster over everything," Houdini recounted later. Inside the cabinet he tied the medium's feet to a chair and his neck to a board. "I did not think he could move—in fact, I was positive he couldn't." Yet from behind the curtain a cup, saucer, and spoon began rapping out answers to questions.

Gregorowitsch told Houdini he had learned his methods not from another medium but from a magician. In fact, Spiritualist mediums no sooner began having themselves bound and handcuffed than magicians followed. They presented their feats not as tests, however, but as outright entertainment, often exposing fraud by showing how precisely the same, apparently supernatural effects could be produced by natural means. One near model for Houdini was the magician S. S. Baldwin, "the White Mahatma" (1848–1924). During the 1870s he had himself handcuffed before stepping into the spirit cabinet—from which bells nevertheless rang—and allowed his legs to be cuffed, then emerged from the cabinet with the shackles undone. By the mid-1890s—when Houdini befriended him—Baldwin was offering a thousand dollars to anyone who could produce a pair of handcuffs that would hold him three minutes.

Houdini credited Baldwin with having given him the idea for an act made up mostly of handcuff escapes. But he credited the escape itself to Ira and William Davenport (1839–1911, 1841–77), a superlative pair of medium-magicians who ambiguously merged Spiritualism and conjuring. According to Dash, Houdini was "a great worshipper of the Davenport Brothers in his youth." The Davenports stood only about five feet six inches tall. Their twin heavy drooping mustaches and twin narrow pointed goatees gave them the look of desperadoes. From 1855, at the dawning of Spiritualism, they produced Spiritualist-type manifestations although tied with copper wire (twisted on with forceps), locked in police handcuffs, or secured by an iron plate with thumb- and finger holes, their digits fastened in place by twine, the knots sealed with wax.

In the Davenports' most famous feat, three knee-high trestles were set out on center stage, deliberately isolated from the wings and back wall to eliminate the possibility of confederates. Raised from the floor on the trestles—eliminating the possible use of stage traps—was a large mahogany cabinet or armoire, seven feet long and six feet high. With its three doors, it looked like three closets hitched together. Inside the cabinet were wooden seats at each end, joined by a shelf along the back. A committee brought up from the audience was asked to encircle the cabinet, thereby cutting it off even more from any possible aid. Then a tambourine, guitar, violin, recorder, and handbells were placed on the shelf inside or hung on the back wall. The brothers seated themselves at either end, and were bound to their seats with sash cord passed through holes in the benches and heavily knotted, immobilizing them. The doors were no sooner closed than suddenly and all together the tambourine banged, the guitar strummed, the bell rang, all the other instruments joining in. Amid the musical crash the doors were thrown open, revealing all the instruments hanging in place, neat and orderly, the ornery-looking brothers still lashed to their seats.

The "never-to-be-forgotten Davenport Brothers," as Houdini called them, neither claimed nor denied supernatural gifts. Spiritualists and anti-Spiritualists argued over the nature of their abilities. Many magicians tried to imitate them, although the secret of the so-called Davenport Rope Tie was known to very few. As Houdini admiringly understood, their career demonstrated that the Spiritualist-magic-escape performance could be a ticket to world fame. The Davenports appeared before Napoleon III, Czar Alexander II, and Queen Victoria, as well as the kings of Italy, Belgium, the Netherlands, and Prussia. Storms of applause and pages of newsprint greeted their performances—as did fights, mob threats, and lawsuits. Sensationally able to "stir up two continents," Houdini wrote later, the "Davenports stand forth in [the] nineteenth century history of magic as its most dramatic figures."

Indirectly the Davenports probably also inspired Metamorphosis. The English magician J. N. Maskelyne (1839–1917) presented a version of the effect in England as early as 1865, to prove that he could outdo the Davenports' manifestations. He curled up inside a smallish wooden box that was locked and corded, then covered with canvas and laced—and escaped.

Many versions of the effect followed. In a show that included a conjuring version of a séance, the French magician Cazeneuve (1839–1913) presented the Double Indian Mail, setting a locked, roped trunk inside another trunk, which he similarly locked and roped and moved into a cabinet. His assistant entered the cabinet and a little more than three minutes later was found in a tied sack within the nested trunks, their locks and ropes still intact. Something of this quasi-Spiritualist ancestry of Metamorphosis survives in Houdini's calling his cloth cabinet a "ghost house."

Had Houdini kept his escapes within the setting of Spiritualism, he might have lost his identity in the crowd of other mediumlike magicians of the time. But except for his early flirtation with séance-magic, he reoriented his escapes, breaking their connection with Spiritualism. Again and again he emphasized to reporters that he worked by natural means: "Whenever any of these alleged spiritual mediums tell you that they have supernatural aid in freeing themselves from handcuffs and ropen bonds," he told one, "you may safely set them down as frauds. The handcuff trick is merely a matter of sleight-of-hand."

Casting escapes in a surprising new light, Houdini moved them from the world of Spiritualism to the contemporaneous religion of Strenuosity. He had of course cultivated the brawn and limberness indispensable to his escapes through years of running, swimming, ballplaying, boxing, and circus acrobatics. But he was not alone. The word "conditioning" came into general use around 1890, as not only Houdini but also millions of other Americans (and Europeans) began devoting themselves to rugged exercise. Cramped by urban life or deskbound at sedentary jobs, they complained that the price of modern civilization was dyspepsia, tameness, and enfeeblement, and joined in a crusade for physical vigor. It gave birth to many now-familiar revitalizers—rowing machines, 'physical education,' professional trainers, and corn flakes, also producing ten million bicycles a year (in the United States in 1890) and Houdini's Sandowesque forearms. Sandow himself circulated beefcake pictures of his anatomy, and exhibited it in "plastic poses" on the stage. Houdini gave his escapes the atmosphere of this Gospel of Health, and the feel of a sporting event. "If it had not been for my athletic boyhood," he was later reported saying, "I would never have been Houdini."

The physicality of Houdini's escapes, emphasized by his semi-nude display of muscle, set him apart from mediumlike competitors. He lengthened the distance, though, and cast his escapes in a still stranger light, by so often exhibiting them at jails and police stations, and publicizing their relation to crime and punishment. For all his rabbinic austerity, the ex-runaway was fascinated by criminals, and in this too was not alone.

Houdini's struggles with Bean Giants and newfangled cell locks gratified a widespread interest in the technology of professional criminals and crimestoppers, a new caste that had come into being with the emergence of the great American cities. Works of the period such as Inspector Thomas Byrnes's *Professional Criminals of America* (1886) and George Walling's *Recollections of a New York Chief of Police* (1887)—rogues' galleries of key-fitters and till-tappers—included illustrations of such nifty tools of the trade as the "Burglar's lead-filled mallet," "sectional jimmy," and "Key nippers." The pictures look like nothing so much as the surviving sets of miniature implements Houdini used. Books by professional burglars were popular too, such as the safecracker Langdon W. Moore's *Own Story of his Eventful Life* (1893), which related his devoted study of Lillie and Yale bank locks and explained how he "solved the problem of lockpicking by putting pressure on the bolt."

Houdini publicly allied himself with such representations of the professional thief not simply as a threat to society but as a person of remarkable skill. He told a reporter in Buffalo that his education in locks came from "persistently meeting criminals in New York upon their release from prison and learning from them what they knew." "I carry a lot of burglar tools in my baggage," he acknowledged. His freedom to use them, it is worth adding, often hung on having the favor of the police, whose manacles and jails were after all not meant to be broken. A friend shrewdly commented that he "had to have either opposition or assistance from the Police in order to make a success when he was doing his handcuff act." Because their word counted with the public, moreover, he prominently printed testimonials from the police in his advertising.

For these reasons Houdini cultivated lawmen and stayed abreast of their affairs. He bought tickets for the Policemen's Ball, kept a folder labeled "Police Cuttings," and owned a *Directory of Police and Prisons*, which named the chief of police in every sizable town in the country, and the wardens of state and federal prisons. "It has been my good fortune," he wrote later, "to meet personally and converse with the chiefs of police and the most famous detectives in all the great cities of the world." By the end of his career he owned a New York City Police Department pass, authorizing him to cross "all police lines."

Houdini's unique performances, then, grew out of an unlikely fusion of the worlds of Spiritualism, conjuring, physical culture, and professional crime, combining features of the séance, the magic act, the muscle show, and the burglary.

HANDCUFF KING

... all dependance on the security of common Locks, even of those which are constructed upon the best principle of any in general use, is fallacious.

—JOSEPH BRAMAH, *A Dissertation on the Construction of Locks* (SECOND EDITION, 1815)

The most difficult task before the novice must be to identify the particular type of lock he is trying to pick. Is the lock a WAFER or PIN-TUMBLER? Or, in the case of a raw beginner, is the lock a LEVER or PIN-TUMBLER? There is no simple answer. The ability to identify the particular types comes only with practice and study. Open as many old locks as you can and study the principles, LOOKING ALL THE TIME FOR WEAK POINTS which are built into the design. Believe me, ALL locks have weak points.

—DAVID DE-VAL, *Lock Picking* (1987)

The path of a handcuff king is not all roses.

—HOUDINI, INTERVIEW WITH *San Francisco Examiner*, JULY 28, 1899

THREE

1900—1905

THE ALHAMBRA DEBUT

Houdini's continental tour began with some jolts. Days before leaving New York he received a cable from an international agent, Richard Pitrot, who worked in cooperation with Martin Beck. Pitrot was to have accompanied Houdini overseas. Instead the agent wired him that on reaching England he would find contracts waiting for dates in London, Paris, and Berlin. But there were no contracts. Pitrot turned out to be, Houdini said, a "*Dam [sic] Liar.*" What he found was that after his year-long winning streak in the United States, he had come abroad to be out of work.

This time there was no thought of opening a magic school. Houdini settled with Bess into a theatrical boardinghouse favored by American acts, at 10 Keppel Street in London, and gave a private showing of his skills at Scotland Yard. In later years he often bragged about this demonstration at the famed CID; the detectives had no fear of his escaping, he said, and so used easy locks. But the press did not cover the event, and it earned him no bookings. Those came through a man named C. Dundas Slater, manager of the Alhambra theater. While crossing the Atlantic, Houdini had appeared in a shipboard show for the Seamen's Fund, and often did card tricks in the smoking room. A fellow passenger gave him a letter of introduction to

Slater, who had brought to the Alhambra such specialty acts as the Georgia Magnet, the much-imitated weight-resister who could not be pushed or lifted off her feet. Slater arranged for Houdini to give a private performance at the Alhambra on Wednesday, June 27; if he impressed, a booking would follow. London newspapers described the program as a "press rehearsal." Houdini called it, resentfully, a "trial." (It was conceivably merely a publicity stunt.)

Located in Leicester Square, the Alhambra was only one of five hundred variety theaters in and near London, but one of the top. Notable for its Moorish decor, recalling the Alhambra in Granada, it had seats for eighteen hundred people, and promenades around the stalls and tiers that brought the capacity to four thousand. It was the scene of many royal visits. Although he performed in the afternoon that June 27, Houdini appeared in full dress, wearing a black frock coat, white dickey, and white bowtie around a stiff, chin-high collar. The audience consisted of representatives of the London press and of Scotland Yard, evidently not more than twenty. Houdini gave them printed testimonials from American police chiefs, and did his basic vaudeville act, now polished by long experience: a few card manipulations, the subtrunk with Bess, and some escapes using new and old shackles brought by the pressmen. Pushing back his coat sleeves, he rolled up his shirtsleeves to allow himself to be trussed and retrussed. He worked not inside his cloth cabinet but behind a simple three-sided screen, his body hidden but his face visible and toward the spectators.

Predictably Houdini astonished. Londoners soon read about "a marvelous gentleman, who frees himself in marvelously quick fashion of fetters, manacles, and all sorts of frightful things." Houdini was booked into the Alhambra for two weeks at the beginning of July, then held over until the last week in August, and after a first trip to the Continent was reengaged for the Christmas season—"making it the record," he pointed out, "for quick return engagements." He or Slater hired a dozen men to parade outside the theater in sandwich boards announcing "ALHAMBRA/HOUDINI."

At the Alhambra Houdini found himself in a more lavish theatrical setting than any he had known. As distinct from American vaudeville, English variety theater had roots in a boisterous past of local tavern entertainment, where patrons sat at tables to drink, guffaw, and sing along. In the last quarter of the nineteenth century, these earlier music halls had given way to respectable showplaces with ornate architecture and uniformed ushers. The largest offered star-studded programs that included not only variety acts but also plays, operas, ballets, and even circuses adapted to the stage. Houdini shared the stage with the celebrated Australian dervish Saharet (whom he and Bess befriended); "Animatograph" films of the Boer War, followed by a patriotic military display, "Soldiers of the Queen"; and "The Gay City," a sumptuous musicale featuring clog dancing by costumed Dutch peasants and a floral ballet by the Alhambra corps.

Although billed as "King of Handcuffs and the World's Greatest Mystifier," Houdini took no risks in his first appearances abroad. He presented his well-oiled cards-handcuffs-subtrunk routine. But each element got rave notices. His cards were "uniquely clever"; his escapes, from a crouching position behind a small curtained enclosure, "eclipsed anything yet produced in this line, either by mediums or magicians"; his Metamorphosis topped all others: "Since the days of the Davenport Brothers we have had many bewildering box tricks. . . . It is, however, no exaggeration to say that the latest seen in this country is far and away the most skillful." A reviewer for *The Showman* called Houdini flat-out "Probably the most mysterious and wonderful entertainer the world has ever seen."

In the wake of the hurrahs came another, smaller jolt. When Houdini set out from London to work the provinces, he found managers unwilling to book him. They considered an escape act too exotic for their family theaters, which had hung on to the older working-class tradition of popular songs and local jokes. Houdini had in effect to undergo a second audition. The head of one of the provincial circuits, Frank McNaughton, gave him a week in Bradford, textile capital of Yorkshire, at sixty pounds. The tryout did such good business that he engaged Houdini for his entire circuit at one hundred pounds, after which provincial managers fought one another for the privilege of hiring him.

Houdini toured without benefit of Martin Beck's guidance. Awaiting news from Houdini about his success at the Alhambra, Beck had been uncertain what to do about the Keith bookings he had arranged for Houdini's return in August. Houdini meanwhile was full of offers from Europe, and resented Beck's and Pitrot's mishandling of his overseas debut. "I had to give all kinds of trial shows," he complained to Beck, "and if you had followed your original intention of sending a man over with me, it would have been 100 percent better for all concerned." As Houdini lingered abroad, doing well, Beck postponed the Keith dates for three months, then six, then for as long as necessary. Assuming that Houdini would eventually return to America under his management, he proposed having a play written around his act that could be mounted in legitimate theaters in the United States. But even from abroad he ruffled Houdini by treating him as a fledgling, for instance when Houdini balked at paying Pitrot a commission. "It does not pay in this World for either an artist or manager who wants to stay in the business to break his word," Beck lectured him from Chicago. "I assure you it is my experience that it is necessary in order to gain full success to do the right thing."

Houdini had his own ideas about what paid and how to get ahead. In July 1901 he wrote to Beck asking to be let out of his contract: "I would like to know how much you want to call all things off, and return me my signiture [sic]." He calculated that he owed Beck in foreign commissions about $425, but was willing to offer more to terminate, "as I am more than satisfied to pay you for your trouble that you had with me in America." Five hundred dollars was settled on as the price of Houdini's release, payable within six weeks—which as usual he dragged out, to three or four months. He stayed friendly with Beck but over the years erased his help from public view. "In magical history generally the manager had a great deal to do with a performers rise to fame," he wrote later. "Am not complaining, but have had to be my own manager."

Houdini may have planned the break with Beck well in advance. At the least it seems likely that he accepted the Keith bookings and agreed to return in August only as insurance, in case he flopped overseas. When he swore out his passport application before sailing for England, he stated that he intended to return to the United States within two years. But he spent most of the next four and a half years in Britain, Europe, and Russia, making himself an international star.

THE PACKING CASE ESCAPE; THE HODGSON ESCAPE; THE MIRROR CUFFS

Houdini shuttled back and forth between Britain and the Continent. He kept to a more-or-less fixed route of cities and theaters, through repeated tours of performance. In each circuit of Britain, for instance, he regularly played most cities of one hundred thousand or more, moving south from his base in London to the Channel resorts around Brighton and Portsmouth; west by the Great Western Railway to Bath and Bristol; north through

Birmingham and along flat, hay-colored fields to the sootstained row-houses of Huddersfield, Bradford, Hull, Leeds, and other coal and wool towns; farther north to Glasgow and Edinburgh, and then back to London through Manchester, Liverpool, and Cardiff.

To depict this five-year span of Houdini's career chronologically would mean following him through repeated Channel crossings, to towns visited and revisited, in theaters played, replayed, and played again. It would highlight the cyclical sameness of his tours. But viewing the same years country by country and otherwise ignoring his schedule throws into relief the challenges each country presented and the spectacular ways he met them.

"Most of my success in Europe," Houdini wrote, "was due to the fact that I lost no time in stirring up local interest in every town I played. The first thing was to break out of jail." Having introduced the Nude Cell Escape only two months before leaving the United States, he used it to trumpet his arrival in a string of English provincial towns—Halifax, Bradford, Newcastle, Birkenhead, Leicester (where he foiled the military prison in which Oliver Cromwell had locked his captives). The exploit became "town talk at once," he said, "with the result that the man in the box-office had to work overtime counting his receipts."

It became national news when, in Sheffield, Houdini escaped the murderer's cell that had held Charles Peace—"the greatest criminal that London ever had," he noted in his diary. "Never saw such crowds." Hanged in 1879, Peace had worked respectably enough as a picture framer, sent his children to Sunday school, and collected birds. But because of his violent nocturnal burglaries, which had terrified London, he never managed to stay out of jail long. (He tried: once while in custody he jumped, manacled, from the window of a train going fifty miles an hour.) With Houdini inside Peace's cell, on the second tier, Sheffield police triple-locked the door; they placed Houdini's clothes in another cell, also triple-locked. To bar his escape further they fastened the iron gate leading to the cell block with a seven-lever lock. Yet five minutes later Houdini stood before the very surprised chief constable, clothed. "This feat has been discribed [sic] in almost every newspaper," he reported to his diary, pleased with himself. "Makes me one of the most noted foreign performers in England. Every illustrated paper has my portrait."

Perhaps because he was a foreigner, however, Houdini found the English police less willing to cooperate than the American, especially in large cities. London police denied him permission to take on the Old Jewry or any other London prison; the police chief of Birmingham turned him down too, wary of being used for publicity: "He would not stand for it," Houdini griped in his diary. "Said Houdini would not get any advertisement out of him. Good boy." Elsewhere he appeased the constabulary by promising to perform at their charities, not knocking the security of their jails—"I tell them just what they wish, that they are great, etc."—and maybe, as one diary entry suggests, paying them off: "Superintendent Moy again to hand. Very touching man. Touched me for five Quidlest." Sometimes he simply worked around them, as happened in Wigan. Having breezed out of the county jail there in just two minutes, yet being forbidden to advertise his escape, he got a stooge to help him boom it from the stage. "Was not allowed to publish fact," he recorded, "but had boy planted in gallery to ask me if I had broken out. Good gag."

Houdini's jail escapes could not be shown onstage, but during his English tour he presented a facsimile for theater audiences. Something between an escape and an illusion, it involved a large barrel in which he was tunned. With him handcuffed inside, the barrel was padlocked and rolled into a compartment painted to represent a prison cell. Its door was locked with a key turned three times, and a curtain was thrown over the whole. Then the shocker. The curtain was removed, the cell door opened, the barrel rolled from the compartment and unlocked. Out climbed not Houdini but Bess— who had been on the stage until moments before.

Effective as the mock-jail-cell transposition sounds, Houdini seems to have used it only a few times. But he had stored up plans for other escapes and wanted, he wrote a friend, "to experiment with all of my former ideas and inventions, that I was unable to attempt in America"—"and do you know," he added, "all the ideas are great." The greatest of them was what he called the "nailed up in the box gag." A few years later he gave a hokey-sounding account of its origins, which he traced to a bitter winter in St. Louis early in his career. Lacking money to buy firewood, he rummaged up a discarded packing case. "I knew I would make myself too conspicuous by carrying so large a case through the streets, and further knew that no police officer would permit me to break it apart in so crowded a thoroughfare, so I conceived a method of taking it noiselessly apart."

In one way, the Packing Case Escape improved on Metamorphosis. The subtrunk was a piece of magic apparatus, a bought prop; the packing case was just a packing case. It brought with it free advertising, too, and good public relations. As a challenge to Houdini, the crate for each perfor-mance was locally built by some department store, warehouse, cabinetry firm, or other town business that used large wooden boxes. Eager to pub-licize and profit from their connection to his feat, local merchants adver-tised it on their own, making him seem a welcome, exciting community friend.

Houdini introduced the escape in the summer of 1902 in Germany; a standout performance, however, came on September 22, 1904, in Glasgow—a city he liked for its bustle and flourishing music halls. The announcement that he would be encased and nailed up in full view of the audience drew such a rush to the Zoo-Hippodrome theater—so named for adjoining a zoo—as to block streetcar traffic: "You might have walked on the heads of the surging, struggling, swaying mass of people," the *Evening Citizen* observed. Although the management doubled ticket prices for the event, thousands attended. The luckier part of the overflow had seats temporarily set on stage; many who were not let in waited around the Zoo-Hipp merely to learn whether Houdini managed to get out.

According to the Glasgow press, representatives of the firm that built the packing case had visited the theater during the day, and protested the center-stage trapdoor. They proposed erecting a platform over it, on which the case could be elevated off the floor. When Houdini made his entrance, just before 10:00 P.M., a team of eight carpenters threw off their coats, dragged stout beams onto the stage, and began hammering the platform together. The whacking all but drowned out the pit orchestra. Supported on struts, the platform stood three or four feet high, giving the audience a clear view of the floor beneath. As Houdini stood by, the crate was hoisted onto it—a squarish wooden box made of solid planks about three-quar-ters of an inch thick. After an inspection committee confirmed its solidity, he crouched inside, the house cheering. The carpenters nailed shut the top planks as a lid, then bound the case on every side with thick rope of the kind used for mooring ferry boats. An extra-large cloth cabinet was moved around the platform and case, its red plush curtains drawn.

The audience remained quiet as the orchestra played popular tunes, softly enough so that any loud noises inside the cabinet could be heard. After fifteen minutes, during the closing bars of "Rule, Britannia," Houdini pulled aside the curtain and stepped from the platform to the stage—

minus his dress coat and shoes, his shirtfront accordion-wrinkled, but free. On the platform sat the packing case, still roped and nailed.

When Houdini left the theater that evening he walked into a living hero-fantasy. "Mob waited for me," he wrote proudly in his diary, "took me shoulder high, carried me home and upstairs. Had to make a speech from the window."

Houdini performed this amazing escape often. Without revealing his method, it can be said that it involved no stage traps, but depended in part on leaving one side of the box weak. Bess or another assistant had to steer the preliminary stage business so that fewer nails were driven into this exit side. In unpublished notes headed "PACKING BOX ESCAPE," Houdini explained that:

> a capable manager is absolutely necessary, he is useful in more ways than one. He mingles among the committee as one of them and (unostentatiously) directs, assists and steers the committee from placing too many nails in the part of the box that the per-former intends to direct his attention to when imprisoned.

A subtlety here is that, once the performer has entered the case, the lid can be clinched with hundreds of nails, since it plays no part in the escape. But because the lid represents the natural means of egress, the final nailing blitz leaves the impression that the whole box has been stitched closed till doomsday: "the lid should receive a liberal supply of nails," Houdini remarked, "as the audience's attention is drawn to same as the most invul-nerable part."

Two more of Houdini's escapes in England got him mobbed, one for its brutality, the other its complexity. The near-killer occurred in Blackburn, population 120,000, a major cotton-producing center topped by spinning-blocks and mill chimneys. On October 24, 1902, Houdini played the Palace Theatre there, a pennanted hodgepodge of classical, Moorish, Dutch, and other architectural styles. Throughout his circuit of the provinces, he posted a standing offer of twenty-five pounds to anyone who could cuff him so that he could not escape. Just before ten-thirty that evening, the bet was taken up by a handsome, clean-shaven young man named William Hodgson. Hodgson brought with him onstage six pairs of heavy irons with clanking chains and padlocks. The anchorings, one journalist observed, "would have put the instruments of torture on board the Spanish Armada to shame in point of weight and formidable appearance."

Houdini always carefully stipulated that he would free himself from any "regulation" cuffs that were in working order. He saw that some of the locks had been tampered with, the keyholes battered, so he objected that Hodgson's restraints did not meet the terms of his standing offer. Hodgson countered that Houdini had challenged audience members to bring their own irons. Something in the situation goaded Houdini into taking a big chance. He said he would go on if given time to deal with the unforeseen difficulty. "This announcement was greeted with great cheering," the local *Argus* reported, "and the work of pinioning proceeded."

Houdini had less to fear from Hodgson's irons than from Hodgson. The son of an Anglican priest, Hodgson had taken up bodybuilding and judo to fortify his slight physique. He succeeded to the point of writing muscle articles for *Sandow's Magazine* and opening "W. H. Hodgson's School of Physical Culture." Among his scholars were the Blackburn police, whom he conditioned. His biographer called him "easily one of the most powerful men, pound for pound, in all England." He was also one of the more eccentrically fastidious. After opening letters he would wash his hands to kill germs sent by mail; when his youngest brother left for Canada and asked a word of advice, he counseled him never to sit on a public toilet seat.

With his understanding of muscle interaction, Hodgson knew what pulled what, and he torsion-tied Houdini in chains. He fixed one set of irons on Houdini's upper arms, passing the chain behind his back and pulling it tight to pin his elbows to his sides. He fixed another pair the same way, padlocking the two sets together behind Houdini's back. With Houdini's arms yanked hard behind him, Hodgson then cuffed Houdini's wrists, counterwrenching the arms forward. "The pulling and tugging at this stage was so severe," the *Argus* reported, "that Houdini protested that it was no part of the challenge that his arms should be broken." After latching a second pair of cuffs on Houdini's wrists, Hodgson got him to kneel down. He looped the chain of a pair of heavy leg-irons through the chains binding Houdini's arms together, bowstringing his arms to his ankles behind his back, hogtie-style. Houdini seemed to one observer not just helpless but suffering, "in great agony . . . his contracted and pinched arms and hands turning blue-black." Drawn, crosstrussed, and torqued, he was placed in the ghost house.

After fifteen minutes the cabinet curtain was opened. It revealed the snaffled Handcuff King lying on his side, so exhausted-looking that he seemed to have fainted. He asked to be set upright, which Hodgson did. The curtain was closed again. Now or earlier, several others had come onstage, including Houdini's brother Dash—watched carefully by Hodgson—and a physician named Bradley. When the cabinet was reopened, after another twenty minutes, Houdini asked to speak with Bradley. He explained that his hands had gone numb, and requested that they be freed awhile to restore circulation. Hodgson reportedly squawked, "This is a contest, not a love match, if you are beaten, give in." At this, the *Argus* said, "Great shouting and excited calling followed, which was renewed when Bradley, after examining Houdini, said his arms were blue, and it was cruelty to keep him chained up as he was any longer." Hodgson still refused, however, although he allowed Houdini a drink of water. Appealing to the growingly impatient audience for more time, Houdini reentered the cabinet and reappeared fifteen minutes later, to loud cheering, with his hands, at least, liberated.

It was shortly after midnight when, after an hour and forty minutes, Houdini staggered from the ghost house for the last time. Panting, "half-dead" as he recalled it, he threw the last of the shackles on the stage. According to one reporter, "the vast audience stood up and cheered and cheered to give vent to their overwrought feelings." After escaping from cuffs Houdini often soothed his mangled hands with lotion; while working in Bradford he had even ruptured a small vein in his left arm. But this time his arms were swollen and discolored with welts where the irons had nipped them, bleeding where he had had to tear flesh to get free, looking, a reporter said, "as though some tiger had clawed him." The physician speculated that a few more minutes of compression might have left the arms paralyzed.

Houdini's shredding did not impress the physically cultured Hodgson. Interviewed a day or two later by the *Blackburn Star*, he denied that he had locked Houdini in crabbed cuffs or roughed him up, much less nearly paralyzed him: "absolute nonsense," he said. He maintained that he had passed his fingers around the inner ring of each cuff to be sure it did not squeeze Houdini, and knowing something of anatomy, he had been careful not to compress his brachial artery. He griped about the suspicious presence onstage of Bess and Dash, and exhibited a pair of handcuffs he had locked on Houdini. One iron link had been cut through and others showed deep file marks. The slicing suggested that Houdini had gotten hold of some tools, and used them. The *Star* backed up Hodgson, remarking that four other irons he had put on Houdini had not been returned to him.

Houdini was not likely to sit still for charges that he had cut his way out, with help from others—the less so as they were probably true. Although he had left Blackburn by the time the interview appeared, he returned just to show up Hodgson's "miserable falsehoods" and defy taunts from his supporters that he "dared not come back." Speaking from the footlights of the same Palace Theatre, he accused Hodgson himself of having cut the handcuff links after the event, in order to discredit him.

Houdini's cyclical tours returned him to Blackburn, but never eagerly. It remained a "wretched" place to him, its gallery the worst of "all the hoodlum towns I ever worked." Hodgsonites did not fancy him either, or forget him. The mutual contempt boiled over during a reengagement in December 1903. When a challenger refused to let him examine the cuffs he had brought on stage, Houdini grabbed them and disdainfully cuffed himself. "Well," he wrote afterward in his diary, "you ought to have heard the booing that was my share to obtain." When he entered the cabinet he found that the inside of the lock had been fooled with, giving him a tough ten minutes' work to get out. And when he did, the audience reaction stunned him: "Instead of applause," he recorded in disbelief, "once again I was booed." Burned up, he snapped the cuffs on some rods near the footlights, leaving his challenger to spend twenty minutes opening them, and getting razzed again.

The going-over in Blackburn stayed with Houdini, and he privately referred to it as "that terrible Hodgson night." But part of his power as an entertainer came from presenting himself as undefeatable, and for a long while he publicly proclaimed the ordeal his "greatest conquest."

Houdini's most baffling escape from a single pair of handcuffs came during his run at the London Hippodrome in March 1904. For this engagement, signs mounted across the whole length of doubledecker streetcars carried a large picture of him around the city, with the legend HOUDINI HIPPODROME KING OF HANDCUFFS FAMOUS JAILBREAKER. As a prelude to his opening, he accepted (or arranged) a challenge from journalists of the *London Weekly Dispatch*. Employing an armory of British police shackles, household locks, and unusual historical cuffs, it surpassed the Hodgson Escape, not in tortuosity but in weight.

Stripped to his stockings, trousers, and a collarless shirt, Houdini submitted first to Bastille irons loaned by John Tussaud, owner of the London waxworks. Accounts of the event vary; apparently a gigantic set of the manacles was loaded on his ankles, arms, and waist, and fastened by triple-locking padlocks, each weighing two and a half pounds. His ankles were also secured by three-inch-wide steel bands that had once hobbled the legendary English criminal Jack Shepard, hanged in 1724 at the age of twenty-two. By means of a chain, the Shepard anklets were then padlocked to armlets; to work on the anklets, Houdini would have to slip the armlets first. Police who attended the event also braceleted him with the cuffs used on Charles Peace, several pairs of British cuffs then in use, more ankle and arm restraints, and an assortment of large and small locks. Finally a chain was wrapped around his legs, cinched by a combination lock that opened upon setting the correct three-letter word.

Altogether this hardware store reportedly weighed more than 131 pounds, not much less than Houdini himself. He estimated that he could escape, concealed by a screen, in half an hour. After eleven minutes of silence broken only by rattling chains and Houdini's heavy breathing, the audience of journalists and police saw an armlet fly over the top of the screen, then heard a crash. After another three or four minutes the Jack Shepard anklets were placed outside the screen by an arm bare of any cuffs or chains. After twenty-seven minutes Houdini himself emerged, shackle-less, and spoke the word that sprang the combination lock.

This wonder ushered in Houdini's uniquely intense escape during a Hippodrome matinee on Thursday, March 17. Five days earlier a representative of the *London Daily Illustrated Mirror* had stepped onstage and challenged him to overcome a single pair of cuffs made in Birmingham—the center of British handcuff manufacture—by the blacksmith Nathaniel Hart. The smith claimed to have spent five years tooling the restraint, a week on the key alone. "It cannot be picked," he said, adding that he could not pick the lock himself. Before an excited audience, Houdini agreed to try.

Four days of nonstop publicity followed. Crowds gathered before framed portraits of Houdini posted in the Hippodrome's windows. Newspapers printed drawings of the "terrible" cuffs and discussed their difficulty in awed absolutes: "They are locks within locks and there is not a similar pair in the world." With England experiencing trade problems, cartoonists romped. The *Chronicle* depicted John Bull constrained in the

Mirror Cuffs, labeled "Chinese Labor," with the tag, "Beaten John Bull. He can't get out of that." "London in an uproar," Houdini delightedly noted in his diary. "Press full of 'match,' Mirror, and Houdini."

Home to many famous performers, the Hippodrome was the newest and best. Opened in 1900 at a cost of a quarter of a million pounds, it sported carved marble columns, velvet pile carpeting, and a nautical-style grand salon walled with fumed oak. A novel ventilating apparatus kept the inside air sweet. Convertible to circus, water spectacle, or music hall performance, the theater was equipped with an arena and an eight-foot-deep hundred-thousand-gallon water tank, lit from below by portlights. The fifty-foot stage could be raised or lowered on hydraulic rams.

For Houdini's Mirror Cuff Escape, by existing accounts, some four thousand spectators and more than a hundred invited journalists crammed the Hippodrome from stalls to gallery. When Houdini appeared in the arena, following a full variety program of six turns, he "received an ovation worthy of a monarch," a London paper said, "one of the finest ovations mortal man has ever received." Dressed in his habitual black frock coat and high white collar, he began with matter-of-fact solemnity: "I am ready to be manacled by the *Mirror* representative if he be present." The journalist, Frank Parker, stepped into the arena, shook hands with Houdini, then called up a large committee from the audience to see that the cuffing was fair. Houdini summoned his own entourage to look after his interests. Perhaps as many as a hundred in all, the two groups of overseers made a long chorus line in front of the stage.

The cuffs were clicked on Houdini's wrists. The key was inserted and turned six times, laboriously, to secure the bolt. Then Houdini said: "I am now locked up in a handcuff that has taken a British mechanic five years to make. I do not know whether I am going to get out of it or not, but I can assure you I am going to do my best." Wildly applauded, and with Bess standing by in her black knickerbocker outfit, he entered his red-curtained cabinet. The Hippodrome orchestra began playing. It was then three-fifteen.

What confronted Houdini inside the ghost house looked formidable, looked forget-about-it. These were inflexible handcuffs, without a chain or swivel, the wrist holes coupled to cylinders that housed the intricate locks. The locks were of a type invented in the eighteenth century by Joseph Bramah. They were the first high-security mechanisms, used for guarding state secrets. The key was a metal tube with slots cut in the end. When the key tube entered the lock it pushed a number of slides, each to a different depth. The key could be turned only when all the slides were depressed the correct distance, which required endway pressure and many delicate rotations. Bramah had offered a two-hundred-guinea prize to anyone patient, knowing, and lightfingered enough to pick the device. His money stood unclaimed for sixty years, until reaped in 1851 by the famed lock-picker Alfred Hobbs, an employee of a Boston lock manufacturer.

To open the Bramah lock, however, took Hobbs forty-four hours. And the Bramah lock and key to the Mirror Cuffs were even mazier than the originals. In his five-year labor, the Birmingham blacksmith fashioned a one-of-a-kind device consisting of *two nested* Bramah locks. Opening it required a key with a double tube: an inner barrel with six slots, recessed into and protruding from a wider barrel with seven slots. The Mirror Cuff lock was probably more complicated than the most complicated safe locks of the period.

As Houdini worked inside the cabinet, there was nothing for the audience to see but its curtains now and again rippling. After twenty-two minutes, he stuck his head out, prompting a volley of cheers and shouts of "He is free!" But he only wanted to get a better look at the lock in strong light. As he disappeared again inside, the orchestra struck up a waltz.

Houdini did not reappear for another thirteen minutes. Perspiring this time, his stiff collar broken, he explained that he needed to stretch his aching knees but was determined to continue. "The 'house' went frantic with delight at their favourite's resolve," the *Mirror* noted. Memories of the Hodgson Escape may have stirred, for Parker—or by one account, Bess— gave Houdini a glass of water and consulted with the manager of the Hippodrome, who directed an attendant to bring a large cushion. "The *Mirror* has no desire to submit Mr. Houdini to a torture test," Parker announced, "and if Mr. Houdini will permit me I shall have great pleasure in offering him the use of this cushion." Houdini pulled the knee rest back into the cabinet. The band played on.

Twenty minutes later Houdini stepped out once more from the cabinet, still handcuffed. "Almost a moan broke over the vast assemblage as this was noticed," the *Mirror* reported. "He looked in pitiable plight from his exertions and much exhausted." Bess was reportedly so "overcome" that she had to leave the theater. Houdini asked to have the handcuffs removed a moment, so he could take off his frock coat. Wary this time—especially since Houdini had never seen the cuffs being unlocked—the *Mirror* representative considered a moment, then said he could not open the cuffs unless Houdini admitted defeat.

The refusal pricked Houdini to a moment of high spontaneous drama. Maneuvering until he got hold of a penknife from his vest pocket, he opened the blade with his teeth. Then, flipping his coat inside out over his head, he slashed at the cloth until the coat hung from his arms in pieces. The audience, the *Mirror* said, "yelled themselves frantic." A committeeman helped him out of what strips remained of the coat, to contending cries of "Why don't you give it up?," "Don't let him do it," "Go on Houdini." It was recorded that he had toiled for one hour.

Ten minutes later the orchestra was completing a march when Houdini bounded from the cabinet with a shout, holding the shiny Mirror Cuffs in his hands. "The scene of enthusiasm which followed is indescribable," one reporter wrote. "Cheer after cheer burst from the delighted spectators." Amid the roaring and hat waving the orchestra struck up "See the Conquering Hero." Houdini left the arena a few moments, by several accounts "hysterical and weeping." But the applause continuing he returned, self-possessed, and made a short speech, confessing that he once or twice had thought of giving up.

Next day, London and provincial newspapers headlined Houdini's victory: HOUDINI'S TRIUMPH; STRUGGLE WITH HANDCUFFS; HANDCUFF KING. Elated by captivating "great, big, conservative London," he was able to fatten his scrapbook with no fewer than seventy-five separate newspaper stories about his feat. Reported back in the United States too, it brought him many more telegrams and letters of congratulation than he could answer. He acknowledged his wellwishers in a large ad, consisting of the words LETTER OF THANKS repeated in a column, like a roll call. For the rest of his engagement the Hippodrome management gave him the program spot usually reserved for the big production number, and plastered stands outside the theater with his name. "Talk about being billed big," he wrote back to the States, "you ought to see London, and look about. Nothing on the walls but Houdini."

The *Mirror* affair stayed news for weeks, helped by Houdini's offer of one hundred guineas to anyone else who could get out of the cuffs. He had a close call when a longhaired, abstracted-looking young man named Beaumont turned up on stage, with hands so small that he could slip them in and out of the closed rings. Resourceful as ever, Houdini simply locked the cuffs and handed them to Beaumont to open. When the outwitted youth began addressing the house on fairness, the orchestra was ordered to play over him and the stage was cleared fast to make way for the plunging elephants.

The excitement may have worn Houdini down. By the end of his Hippodrome run—on a bill with Sandow striking "plastic poses"—he caught a heavy cold, could hardly speak, and was laid up in bed for twelve days. For the first time he had to cancel a date, in Newcastle, because of illness. The press attributed his breakdown to overwork. In another sour fillip, on his last night at the Hippodrome the stagehands slighted him. "Although I tipped the men £5 ($25)," he grumbled in his diary, "none of them remained to help me pack up. Bravo!!"

How did Houdini escape the Mirror Cuffs? Hart, the Birmingham blacksmith, contended that he had a malformed hand, whose bones he could contort at will. But some magicians think Houdini and Hart schemed the event from the beginning, perhaps in cahoots with the *Mirror*, and that Houdini's drawing out of the test to more than an hour was only showmanship. In his time and later, Houdini was often charged with spending more time in his cabinet than he needed, letting the audience grow tense and chew their nails while, inside, he read a newspaper or twiddled his thumbs—a charge he firmly rejected. A modern lock expert, Bill Liles, is even more skeptical. Like British police cuffs of the period, he points out, the Mirror Cuffs were nonadjustable. Just as bobbies often had to carry several different-size cuffs, the creator of the Mirror Cuffs needed to know Houdini's wrist size in order to forge cuffs that fit him. This and other evidence led Liles to believe that Houdini designed the cuffs himself. Many magicians assume Houdini must have had a key to open the Bramah locks. The Amazing Randi, the outstanding American escape artist since Houdini's time, put it bluntly: "I can *assure* you that the *Mirror* handcuffs were not opened with anything but the key."

But how did Houdini get the key? His friend Will Goldston, a British magician, asserted that Bess smuggled it to him when she gave him a drink of water. This seems unlikely considering the size of the key, not to mention that it could be more easily passed to Houdini in the knee cushion or that, being clothed, he could have concealed it on himself. But it may be worth adding that the bringing onstage of a glass of water for Houdini to drink does figure in several of his most phenomenal escapes, including the Hodgson torturing.

IMITATORS, RIVALS, MANAGERS

Houdini's conquests inspired scores of imitators. "In England we have 55 Kings of Handcuffs," he complained. "[I]f you throw a stone in the air it will fall down and hit some one who has a handcuff key in his pocket and a 'Handcuff King' idea in his head." Magicians hotly argue the ethics of their profession: imitation or pilfering of tricks and sleights invented by others, without giving credit, is constantly denounced but commonly practiced. For himself Houdini never concealed the long history of his escapes in Spiritualist magic. And at least for now, he claimed no more than to have been the first escape artist to challenge the police, the first to do the act or escape jail cells naked, and the first to use police testimonials in his advertising. Nor did he object when others performed handcuff escapes: "we must all make a living."

On the other hand Houdini demanded entire credit for inventing Houdini. And others not only aped his act but also copied his publicity, his evening dress, his picture poses, his handcuffs, even his name. He stuck their reviews and pictures in the back of his scrapbooks, where, clad in his style of frock coat and his A-to-Z array of prison jewelry, they make a weird gallery of Houdini clones and mutants—all, he complained, "using names as near to mine as possible . . . Hourdene, Whodini, Cutini, Stillini, etc." Early during his stay abroad he took large ads in London newspapers, as well as in U.S. magic journals and theatrical papers, threatening to prosecute anyone who ripped him off:

> STOP THIEF! I, Harry Houdini, do hereby give notice that I have fully patented my handcuff act or show, according to the laws of Great Britain, and I will positively prosecute any and all managers playing infringements or colorable imitations. Letters patent No. 14327, granted August 10, 1900.

This was just a bluff, actually, for patenting his handcuff act would have meant publishing its secrets in detail. (The British patent office listed his application as "Abandoned.") When not railing at the Houdini-ettes he sometimes grandly shrugged them off: "all England is full of Handcuff

Kings," he wrote a friend, "but through this all, there is but one Houdini, and that is the Houdini from the city called New York."

The most successful of Houdini's imitators was in a sense his own creation—his brother Dash, formerly his partner in "the Brothers Houdini." Only a few months after his first successes abroad, he cabled Dash: COME OVER, THE APPLES ARE RIPE. "By the time I [arrived]," Dash recalled, "he had my act framed—settings, handcuffs, a substitution trunk, a girl assistant—even bookings in opposition to his own. He had even picked out the name by which I was to be known." Dash would use the name for the rest of his life: *Hardeen*. He was somewhat taller and beefier than his younger brother, with thick wrists and heavy forearms. But his chest expansion— important for gaining slack in straitjacket escapes—was by his own measurement at least an inch less than Houdini's seven and a half. Following Houdini's summons he remained in Great Britain and Europe successfully for seven years, virtually duplicating his brother's handcuff act, once before the Swedish royal family in Stockholm. He begot his own imitators as well, Houdini's-brother-ettes. They provoked Houdini into placing a large ad, notifying the public that "I HAVE ONLY ONE BROTHER AND HE IS THEO. HARDEEN." One imitator of them both even melded their names, performing as "Hardini."

Hardeen near worshiped his older brother and stayed contentedly in his shadow, "very proud," he wrote, "of the confidence he showed in me by electing me to be Houdini's leading rival." On his side Houdini felt an easy sense of superiority to Dash and equally real love for him, nurtured by a childhood of shared poverty and dislocation. He enjoyed passing a day with him in London, or bumping into him on a train when their routes crossed. Just the same his brother *was* another Handcuff King. Houdini pasted clippings about him at the back of his scrapbook—beside those of his other imitators—and needed to know that Hardeen did not outclass him. He asked a friend about Hardeen's reception in Europe. "It seems to be the prevailing impression," the friend let him know, "that while he does the Handcuffs etc etc apparently as good as Houdini *He does not make it go* with the audience—or in other words—he is not the *showman* Houdini is." That was the right answer to give Houdini, and happened to be true. Leslie Guest, a magician who saw Hardeen perform some time later, said the act gave him "the creeps. First, Houdini's curtain. Then Houdini's set, and Houdini's props. . . . It only remained for Houdini to walk out." But when

Hardeen walked out, Guest said, The Uncanny departed: "Instead, a man who looks something like him, and has some of his mannerisms. The spell is broken." During his career Hardeen would replicate many of his brother's feats but leave nothing like his mark.

Houdinis sprouted back home too. "[Y]our success in Europe is the talk of Vaudeville America," Martin Beck wrote to him. "Everybody envies you." Houdini learned that Middleton's dime museum—where he had struggled himself—was exhibiting two handcuff workers, billing one as "Houdini's Only Rival" and the other as "greater than the great HOUDINI." The American imitators included, if he can be called one, Jacob Hyman, the friend from the neckwear-cutting firm with whom Houdini had launched the Brothers Houdini. Hyman was still performing in the Northeast as "The Great Houdini, King of Handcuffs," getting modest notices for slipping manacles in fifty-five seconds at police stations. A New York theatrical paper, the *Dramatic Mirror*, wondered how "Houdini, King of Handcuffs" could be simultaneously in England and in Massachusetts: "What 'Houdini' Is This?" Hyman wrote in, giving a history of the Brothers Houdini. In dissolving the act, he explained, he had never agreed to give up the name, and had as much right to it as his ex-partner.

"Perhaps he has," Houdini said, "but he has no honor." Enraged, he cabled the *Dramatic Mirror*, appealing to managers not to advertise Hyman: "If he has brains enough to act, let him make a name for himself." Probably at his request, his brother Leo (now a physician) turned up onstage at a performance of Hyman's in Springfield, Massachusetts, an attorney in tow. Asserting that only Harry could legitimately be called Houdini, he challenged Hyman to escape some cuffs he had brought, then snapped him into a crabbed pair that stayed put. "If any one ever deserved to have a name," Houdini wrote a few weeks later, "that has been myself. I have spent thousands advertising my name have broken out of 15 jails, and now this man claims he has as much right to use Houdini as myself."

Houdini spawned not only imitators, but also a bull market for his secrets. Magic shops offered his escape act, or something like it, to the whole fraternity. The English dealer Ellis Stanyon (1870–1951) advertised for one guinea or five dollars, "THE GREAT HANDCUFF RELEASE As performed by Houdini at the Alhambra Theatre." In his journal *Magic* he published a method for getting out of packing boxes, involving the use of thin, greased nails that could be easily forced out. Houdini accused Stanyon of having posted a bounty of several pounds for his secrets. But even ordinary lay newspapers such as the *Southeastern Herald* advertised for sale "the secret of the handcuff release," price five shillings, "guaranteed genuine, and the same as performed by Houdini."

Houdini dismissed the methods purveyed by Stanyon and others as being nothing like his own, "puny attempts at duplication." In exasperation, however, he tried for a while to set himself off from the legion of Handcuff Kings by appearing as HOUDINI THE JAIL BREAKER. Useless. "I changed my billing to 'Jail Breaker,'" he groaned, "and they all took that title, too." Stanyon sold jail-escape techniques as well, for instance advising wannabe Jailbreak Kings that while examining the cell beforehand, they could hide its key somewhere inside. "Yes, *if* you *can*," Houdini scoffed. "You are to accept for granted that it is all plain sailing and that the prison wardens will stand by like fools." Stanyon also described methods of concealing keys while nude, clearly referring to Houdini:

> I have it on good authority that one of the numerous Handcuff "Kings" who prides himself on being able to accomplish all his business under "test conditions" i.e. after being examined nude, also prides himself on the smallness of his keys, each of which he has fitted into a little celluloid tube properly made and shaped, that it may, without injury to the parts, be passed into the anus and thus concealed.

In this case the decorous Houdini denounced Stanyon as a man "compelled to drag his pen through mire." But he did not deny what Stanyon said, and in fact his surviving apparatus includes a pill-sized metal capsule, of brass or perhaps even gold.

Houdini did not just suffer his army of copycats or denounce them in writing. Sometimes he made war on the stage. One battle involved an escape artist named Mysto, who challenged all comers to handcuff him for a twenty-five-pound prize. In Salford, a division of industrial Manchester, Houdini found himself booked at the same time as Mysto, at a rival music hall. Annoyed to have another sham Handcuff King next door—"all the world knows," he said, "Houdini is the recognized King of Handcuffs"— he also resented comments by the rival theater manager that Mysto brought more money to his hall than Houdini could, for about one-fifteenth the salary, and escaped from a sealed coffin, as Houdini could not. Ordinarily Houdini might have only lashed out in the press. But Mysto's coffin release smacked of his own Packing Box Escape, recently introduced.

On the stage of the Salford Regent Theatre, Houdini duplicated and then, outrageously, exposed Mysto's method. He began by addressing the audience:

> Ladies and Gentlemen, I sincerely apologize for bringing a coffin on the stage. I think it is entirely out of place, and I sincerely trust that when I have finished tonight's exposure, no coffin will ever again be used as an accessory to a public amusement, or manipulated to deceive anybody.

This said, Houdini lay down fully clothed in the black-painted coffin, constructed by the same mortuarist who had built Mysto's. (The "gruesome sight," as a Salford paper called it, was relieved by a gallery wit dolorously calling "good-bye.") The coffinmaker drove home six long screws into the coffin lid, sealing the boreholes with wax. From inside, Houdini extended his hands through two holes in the lid, where they were locked in regulation cuffs. A screen was positioned around the coffin, and to the bewilderment of the audience Houdini calmly strode forth less than two minutes later.

Then Houdini explained the entire effect. He showed that the cuffs were gaffed, and came off easily when he contracted his wrists. He told how the long screws holding the head end of the coffin had been replaced before the performance by much shorter screws, so that the endpiece gave easily to pressure. All he had to do was pop the cuffs and push out the weak panel, then crawl out of the coffin and reattach the endpiece, using the original long screws so that the box could be examined.

In divulging another magician's secrets, Houdini committed high treason. Illustrated magazines of the period often ran picture exposés of card palming and the like; photos of Houdini himself appeared in the English *Royal Magazine* and *New Penny Magazine* disclosing crimps, second deals, and other cardsharking techniques, and standard apparatus such as the vanishing lamp. Just the same, for most magicians the first rule of the art was, and still is: Don't Expose. An English magician sent a report on the "despicable" Salford exposure to the American magic journal *Sphinx*, and called on the Society of American Magicians to rebuke Houdini for "this most flagrant breach of the cardinal principle of their society." Houdini claimed he was fighting not Mysto but the rival theater manager. Whomever he meant to crush, the episode dramatizes his blindness to boundaries in getting at his competitors.

Foreign theater managers, Houdini learned, knew something about hurting the competition too. Having canceled his contract with Martin Beck, he was on his own in dealing with English and continental managers. Overrun with offers, and truculent to begin with, he was in no mood to take anything from them. "They have tried to dictate to me," he said, "and those days are long gone past 'Thank God.'" He bitched often: at being asked side money for some service ("I raised hell"); to get his photograph placed on the advertising curtain; over his position on the bill ("So I answered him back in a loud tone of voice, 'Well if you don't change the program you will have no Houdini tonight.' And off I walks"). Probably to gain more control over his performances, he briefly turned manager himself. While in England he put together and starred in a ten-turn show—"the largest that has ever travelled in the Provinces," he claimed—taking 60 percent of the gross. It did "enourmous [*sic*]" business, but too much kept him hopping, "my time filled before I even get to the city we are booked in."

Houdini's hard learning about foreign managers came at the hands of the Moss Empires chain. Founded by Horace Edward Moss, later Sir Edward Moss, Empires was the largest, most successful variety circuit in the world, embracing thirty-three music halls in England and Scotland, including the London Hippodrome. Late in 1902 Houdini signed a contract to play Moss theaters for twenty weeks, at a salary of £100 weekly, about $500. The contract gave Moss the option of renewing him for another twenty weeks, which the management decided to do early in 1904. Houdini, however, had agreed to appear that spring at the Glasgow Zoo-Hippodrome—site of his great packing-box success—run by the rapidly expanding Barrasford Tour, which also signed him for various shorter engagements at £125 weekly, about $625.

Unwilling to work for less money than he could make elsewhere, Houdini told the Moss representatives that they could not use their option if he received a better offer. Rejecting this as "utter nonsense," they sought an order from a Glasgow court interdicting his appearance at the Zoo-Hipp, and forcing him to perform for them under the terms of the option. The court found for Houdini, however, ruling that although the option committed him to working twenty weeks on the Moss tour, it did not specify when, during the year, the dates were to be filled, leaving him free to work for the Barrasford chain. The Moss management did not give up. They went into a London court to prevent Houdini from appearing in Liverpool, but lost again. They then offered him a new contract for a salary equal to what he was getting from Barrasford's—which he spurned.

In return for his defying and defeating them, Houdini believed, the Moss management set out to ruin his reputation and career. To do the dirty work they engaged for their tour another escape artist, Frank Hilbert. In Newcastle, Leeds, and other towns he not only got out of handcuffs but also explained how, displaying the picks and other instruments concealed in his clothing. Houdini viewed Hilbert as an agent provocateur, sent out by Moss Empires to lose him his audience: "when a manager grows jealous there is no telling what he will do. . . . if they can't secure a performer they will spoil his show, so that when he does appear he will not be the wonder that he is billed as being." Publicly he denied any resemblance between the methods Hilbert exposed and his own. But he considered Hilbert a threat: "The very managers that I have made thousands of pounds for are now trying to ruin the act for England."

Rather than be ruined, Houdini decided to ruin Hilbert first. "Houdini never forgets," a friend reported him saying; "he might forgive but never forgets." His chance came near the end of his overseas stay, in April 1905, when he arrived in Cardiff, Wales, for an engagement at the King's Theatre. He found the city posted with bills for Hilbert at the Cardiff Empire, a Moss theater. Moss officials anticipated trouble, and sent a message to the regional manager directing him to eject Houdini should he appear at the theater and "attempt to create disorder."

Houdini did some anticipating of his own. He hired a hairdresser to gray his hair and reshape his nose with wax. Adding a walking stick, spectacles, and a gray mustache, he hobbled into Hilbert's evening performances on April 10 and, a lame old man, took a sixpenny seat. He always prized loyalty, especially from his family, a close and mutually protective lot. Bess bought a ticket for the stalls, together with Houdini's thick-spectacled sister, Gladys, then visiting from the States. Hardeen, who had played the Cardiff Empire, came along too. His emergence as a successful escape artist had done nothing to change his mind about the advice he once gave a nephew: "if you are in a fight hit the other guy first." In his touring he had collected a scratched face and shiner from a fistfight in Germany, and had flattened a man with a punch to the eye aboard a ship.

The mayhem at the Moss Empire that night survives in conflicting stories from Houdini, from the Cardiff press, and from the theater manager, constables, and other witnesses called to the resulting trial for assault. In his own rendition Houdini cast off the geezer disguise once Hilbert began his escape act. He stood up and called out a challenge: "I have a pair here that you can't open." At this he was set on by three constables, four theater officials, and the Moss regional manager, Lea, who grabbed him by the throat. "Ladies and gentlemen," Houdini said he cried out, "see how they are treating me." Lea threw him against one of the constables, who kneed him in the ribs, carried him out on Lea's orders, and dumped him into the stone alley. He dropped four feet down some steps into a muddy passageway. Unable to walk or even stand, he believed his leg was broken. As he tried to get up, Lea kicked him, and he lay in the alley until Hardeen put him into a cab.

Theater officials and the police denied manhandling Houdini and accused him of faking a broken leg for publicity. In their version, when Houdini rose in the theater he hollered at Hilbert, "You're a fraud; you're a d—— fraud." A bobby asked him to leave quietly, but he put his legs between the policeman's, threw him, and began swinging a walking stick. He was hurried out of the theater and set down "carefully" in the alley, no more battered than that "his collar was all awry." This point Hardeen disputed during the assault trial. He swore that when he saw Houdini in the passageway, his collar and tie were "torn up" and he looked "as if he had been through a thrashing machine." A physician who examined Houdini testified that he had a discolored lip, abrasions on one leg, and sprained muscles in the other.

Houdini's family stuck by him during the uproar. According to the *Cardiff Western Mail*, Bess jumped up from her seat in the stalls waving a second pair of handcuffs for Hilbert to open, and had to be escorted from the Empire with Gladys, "screaming loudly." Hardeen approached Lea menacingly until a policeman stood between them; in the presence of a police inspector and four constables he threatened to show up at the hall every night and create a disturbance. He accompanied his brother in the hansom to King's Theatre, where Houdini was scheduled to go on at ten that night. When they arrived Houdini rushed onstage—hair disheveled, collar unbuttoned—and addressed the audience hoarsely: "Ladies and gentlemen—I must apologize for appearing like this, but I have been thrown out of the other theatre. . . . They have nearly broken my leg." The announcement brought cries of "Shame, shame" and, by one newspaper account, "thunderous cheers." He managed to do only half his act, the injured leg forcing him to omit his barrel-and-jail-cell escape.

In the next days Houdini obtained a summons for assault against the management of the Cardiff Empire. They may have found some pleasure in the fact that the case came to court but was dismissed. Houdini found satisfaction himself, however. His attack on arrogant managers and a too-presumptuous Handcuff King paid off in the ways that mattered to him most. "Went to Empire and raised a rumpus against Hilbert," he wrote in his diary. "Raised hell in the streets. This helped my business. Papers full of account."

SOCIAL, DOMESTIC, AND LITERARY LIFE

Houdini hugely enjoyed England, and over his long stay became more popular there than in the United States: "if I had my choice," he told a British reporter, "I should prefer to be a native of this country. The people here are very kind to me." He was not a political creature. Although he arrived in England during the last year of Victoria's long reign, and played through the early years of King Edward's rule, he said nothing about the labor unrest of the time or the controversies over imperialism and Britain's inglorious war in South Africa. "I hope to keep out of politics," he once said, "for that is a game in which most of us are defeated before we even get into."

By contrast Houdini often commented on British show business. In touring the music halls he was struck by the popularity of black performers, with whom he sometimes shared a bill. "The colored race over here have made a great big hit, and certainly are making good with their ability," he wrote. "The color line is unknown . . . and many a team have I seen in which the man is colored and his partner white." Houdini rarely used such epithets as 'nigger' and 'sheeny'—unlike many others in his time—and then to indicate social class much more than race or ethnicity. He appreciated the superiority of British racial attitudes to American, blacks being "all looked upon here just as amiably as if they were white"; "were I a colored man," he said, "I would never leave this country." On the other hand, with few exceptions he had little good to say about the English provincial cities he toured, finding them all alike and dead on Sundays: "You can't even spend your money." The cities being distributed "zigzag fashion," too, a twenty-five-mile journey might involve two changes of trains. And he generally found the connections bad, the trains slow and ill equipped for "seeing the man." Luckily, where vaudeville circuit dates in the States might be hundreds of miles apart, his jumps in England were often only eight or ten.

Houdini enjoyed British sporting life. He befriended the big-race jockey Jim Morgan, attended the national championship for the hundred-yard dash, hosted a supper for the champion Oldham footballers ("Made a great Fair Play speech to team. Best speech I ever spoke"). The world of strenuosity and victory returned his interest. He was often interviewed in health and sporting journals, such as the *Illustrated Sporting and Dramatic News*, the *Mirror of Life*, and *Health and Strength*, which published a photograph of him *au naturel* but for a jockstrap. He evidently gave them some fine yarns to go with it. "He is one of a family of athletes," *Health and Strength* reported. "At cross-country racing he was considered one of the best men in America." Always curious about feats of strength—"I have made it a point," he wrote, "to come in contact with the most powerful human beings in my generation"—he became pals with the "Russian Lion" George Hackenschmidt, "positively the greatest wrestler in the world to-day."

A heavyweight with a fifty-two-inch chest, although only about five foot six, Hackenschmidt had never been thrown. Houdini kept close watch on the championship shaping up in London in the spring of 1904 between Hackenschmidt and the giant Turkish wrestler Nouriah, for a purse of ten thousand dollars. After the fight, which did not last long, Hackenschmidt gave him the details: "He told me that his idea was to throw the Turk as quickly as possible, and when he managed to get what he calls the 'death grip' the Turk jabbed both his fingers up 'Hack's' nose." Despite the sneak attack on his mucous membranes, Hackenschmidt pinned Nouriah's neck to the mat, taking the heavyweight crown and purse in forty-four seconds.

Not one to be outdone, Houdini threw Hackenschmidt. Like Sandow and other strongmen, Hackenschmidt had a popular music-hall turn, exhibiting his build in attitudes meant to recall classical statues. He and Houdini often compared receipts, Hack conceding that the boxoffice record of 210 pounds he set at Sheffield had been overcome only by Houdini, at

300. Houdini discussed with him the possibility of copromoting a top-rank wrestling match, and hoped to bring him to the United States, presumably as his manager, to star in vaudeville. They chummed around London together, Houdini joking that he traveled with Hackenschmidt "to protect me." And Hackenschmidt seems to have entertained Houdini and Bess when they took a break from the provinces: "Be so kind to come with your darling bubbie wife to London for Sunday," he wrote Houdini on one occasion, "you can sleep with me in one bed till Monday. I cannot do more for you."

Bess still sometimes assisted Houdini, quick-changing with him in Metamorphosis or standing by the cabinet curtain as he dealt with cuffs inside—"two young? people," Houdini said, "roaming around trying to make an honest million." But now and later most intimate details of their life together went unrecorded. A secret-keeper by profession, Houdini was usually mum about his private affairs too. Yet many people who saw them together said that he seemed devoted to her. The impression is confirmed by the lifelong stream of notes he left her in their flats and hotel rooms, addressed "Darling One and Only," "Precious Lump of Sweetness," "Sweetie Wifie, Mine," affectionately signed "Ehrich," "Houdinsky," "your popsy." One from 1899 is typical, arranged by Houdini to look something like verse:

> *Adorable*
> *Sun Shine*
> *of my Life*
> *I have had my coffee,*
> *   have washed out this glass,*
> *   and am on my way to business.*
> *Houdini*
> *"My darling I love you"*

Unvarying from this tone of joshing puppy-love, the fifty or so notes that survive leave a faintly hollow impression, more of joy in feeling love than of pleasure in loving. Bess nevertheless spoke of them as tributes of tenderness. "Every morning," she wrote on one of his notes, "I would find a dear funny little Message like [this], on my pillow."

However prized she felt by Houdini's peppy ardor, Bess at some depth also registered the guardedness that underlay it and the rest of his personality. Excitable, like him, she often had attacks of nerves, became cross and sulky, contracted colds, sometimes with complications that curtailed their touring. Skilled at sewing and embroidery, she loved to make clothes—and to buy them. Houdini perhaps put it more truthfully than he intended in telling a friend she was "busy shopping, so as to be happy though married." Flush now, he could afford to buy her bracelets and other gifts; she accumulated diamonds as well. But he did not always indulge her purchases without muted reproach, as once when giving her an extra twenty dollars. "I suppose you had a lot of things to buy that had looked temptingly out at you from the shop windows," he questioned in a note. "Or did my little baby buy things to eat. Never mind."

The couple remained childless. "[M]y wife says she wishes she could raise children and stop working," he told a friend in 1903, "and perhaps in 1905 we may rest long enough to raise one of them things called children ourselves." He shared Bess's longings, and their barrenness pained him. "We have been married for 10 years and all we have is a 'dog.'" How sorely Bess and Houdini both wanted children is reflected in the near-parental concern they invested in pets. They carried with them in touring a small white dog, Charlie, sometimes smuggling him across national borders by using one of Ching Ling Foo's conjuring methods (although, Houdini said, "scared to death for fear of detection"). When the animal died, after eight years with them, Houdini filled his diary with little other news. "Charlie, our dog, dying," one entry goes. "Have taken him away from Surgeon Thompson so he can die at home. Bess crying. I don't feel any too good." And again, "Poor, dear little Charlie dog died. He is out of misery. Has been our only pet and earned our love." Bess reacted no less vehemently to later finding a pet parrot dead. "Bess very ill and breaks down re Polly."

Houdini socialized much with other magicians, generally a colorful bunch. He had tea with David Devant (David Wighton, 1868–1941), inventor of the Vanishing Motorcycle; passed a Christmas night at the Keppel Street boardinghouse with Howard Thurston, the Ohio card king who made selected cards float up from the deck to his outstretched hand; and got to know Chung Ling Soo (William Robinson, 1861–1918), a New York–born imitator of Ching Ling Foo who was world famous in his own right. Squat and muscular, Soo worked in Chinese garb, producing large water bowls filled with goldfish and blowing smoke and sparks from his mouth (the chemicals involved eventually destroyed his teeth). Houdini talked magic hours on end with his friend T. Nelson Downs (1867–1938), renowned for his palming—"one of the Historical lights of magic," Houdini called him. It was Downs who pioneered the magic specialty act, snatching silver from thin air as King of Koins. A midwesterner by birth, Downs like several other magicians had matured on the shady side of the law. According to Houdini, he had run a "fake Magic Shop," worked for a "fake spiritualist," and been wanted by the federal government for a "swindle."

Houdini stayed friendly with these and many other magicians. But except in Downs's case, a globe-covering sense of rivalry usually led him to belittle them in private. He reminded himself in his diary of what happened when he took a box seat for a show by Chung Ling Soo: "The crowd kept yelling '*Houdini*' and when Soo calls for a committee they yell 'Houdini on the stage.' " He kept an eye on Thurston, who after laboring hard and borrowing money was about to open an opulent illusion show. He watched out too for the ever-more-popular Horace Goldin (Hyman Goldstein, 1873–1939). Goldin, who had left Russia as a boy, started out like Houdini in American dime museums, where they first met. Criticized for his heavy accent, he began performing silently and introduced a whirlwind trick-a-minute style that remains influential to this day. Houdini confided that although many considered Goldin the leading British magician, "that has to be proven to me." And Goldin had a case of "swelled-headology, but not as bad as H. Thirston [*sic*]."

With his theatrical dreams being realized, Houdini took time to reclaim a piece of his past. However poorly educated, the rabbi's son respected learning. "We have records for five generations," he boasted, "that my direct fore-fathers were students and teachers of the Bible and recognized as among the leading bibliographers of their times." He let it be known that his father bequeathed to him all of his books, and that he vividly remembered his father's writing. (Asked by an interviewer, "Who is your favorite author?" he replied, "My dad.") He carried a typewriter with him on the road and sometime spent whole days writing letters. He claimed he could pound away at eighty words a minute, and was "more accurate than high price stenographers." Maybe, but it does not show. His letters are wonders of in-and-out margins, irregular spacings between words and within them, commas and periods mis-hit for letters, xxx-ings out—an everything-botched typing as distinctive as most other people's handwriting.

Houdini wrote but did not publish a manuscript entitled "The Art of

Escape," filled with unusually open reflections on handcuffs, lockpicks, and the like, and nuts-and-bolts advice. Spit on your wrists before being bound, as a help in slipping off chains and ropes; wear gaiter (laceless) shoes: "These can be easily kicked off. Carry keys and picks in the shoes." He did publish the first of the dozen or so short stories he would write, entitled "A One-Night Engagement." Printed in the British monthly *Wide World*, it told how during his medicine-show days two gamblers shot him in the hand after he refused to crack a gambling-joint safe. An eighty-word-a-minute whopper, surely, to embellish his legend.

Trying out journalism, Houdini wrote as European correspondent for two publications, the monthly magic journal *Mahatma* and the theatrical paper *Dramatic Mirror*. In *Mahatma*, official organ of the Society of American Magicians, his column appeared under the name "N. Osey," ostensibly a traveling German reporting on magicians abroad. He kept up the persona by elaborate internal ruses:

> I have a little news, and that is regarding the man calling himself Theo Hardeen, who is at the present time in England, and claims to be a brother to Harry Houdini, and wonder if it is true. A friend of mine in London tells me that he looks very much like Houdini. Should this, however, be true, how did he get hold of the act? . . . Should this meet the eye of Houdini, I trust he will investigate. . . .

Houdini had fun with the literary ventriloquizing, and its cover allowed him to dish his contemporaries publicly. One exemplary bit reads: "Thurston, the Card King, is in Copenhagen, Denmark, and has made the biggest hit that has ever been made there. I know this to be authentic, as I read a letter that he wrote to a manager." Houdini's lengthy *Dramatic Mirror* reports offered inside dope on the whole range of show business abroad, for the use of American acts headed there: efforts to form theatrical unions, baggage restrictions, the triumphs and bombs of plate destroyers, strong-hair men, ice-bear wrestlers, and soap-bubble jugglers, as well as Isadora Duncan, Buffalo Bill, and other stars. The reports are entertainingly racy, enough to make one wonder how much of the language is Houdini's and how much an editor's.

More ambitiously, Houdini began gathering material for a book. He grandly envisioned it as the "biography, incidents, etc of every magician, from the time of Moses to the present year." It would be a corrective to

Thomas Frost's classic *Lives of the Conjurors* (1876), which, he said, "I am going to prove full of false statements, and dates." While touring he took notes, checked facts, and queried living relatives of magicians of the past. He sought out, among others, the nephew of Signor Blitz Jr. (active in the 1820s) to ascertain whether Blitz had ever, as Frost claimed, caught with his bare hand a marked bullet fired from a gun (he had). The nephew gave him not only information but also rare clippings, photographs, and play-bills of Blitz, which Houdini meticulously mounted on the clothlike pages of two immense looseleaf books. The research merged with a more general desire to amass a library of works on magic, which he began buying up and shipping to New York. His purchases opened a new field of competition. In 1903 he declared that he possessed "the most expensive collection of books on the Art of Practicable magic"—a brag ambiguous enough to be in some limited sense true.

A bonanza for Houdini's research, and the foundation of his library, came unexpectedly in the spring of 1904, during his twelve-day illness following the Mirror Cuff Escape. A note arrived from someone who said he collected magic memorabilia that might interest Houdini. Invited to his hotel room, the sender turned out to be a bent, bewhiskered old man in a raincoat, so shabby that the porter had refused to let him up. He said he had brought along only a few of his treasures. But he started showing Houdini virtually unobtainable playbills, advertisements, and lithographs of magicians going back to Isaac Fawkes in the early eighteenth century. Houdini felt as if he "had been dazzled by a sudden shower of diamonds." Ill or not, he made an appointment to see the whole collection the next morning. Bundled in a taxi, he was taken to a musty basement room where the old man made him tea on a "pathetically small stove." Houdini stayed until past three in the morning, by his telling, when Hardeen and a physician appeared and dragged him back to his sickbed.

The man was Henry Evans Evanion (1832–1905)—"The absolute greatest collector of magicians' material," Houdini called him, "that ever lived!" Formerly a professional magician, Evanion had inherited some of his rarities from his father and grandfather, and for fifty years had compiled information on the history of magic at the British Museum. He had sold the museum some of his priceless holdings; bit by bit Houdini bought what he considered the choicest that remained. In the process he grew fond of Evanion, who wakened memories of the also needy and scholarly Mayer

Samuel Weiss. "I treated the old man," Houdini wrote, "as if he had been a father." In June 1905, when he received word in Wigan that Evanion was dying, he rushed after his show to Lambeth Infirmary, finding Evanion barely able to speak, from cancer of the neck and throat. "But he brightened up when he saw me. I told him I only came to London to see him. He was greatly surprised to think I thought so much of him. 'Did you come here only to see me? God bless you, Houdini,' he said 'God bless you.'"

Houdini recorded the hospital visit in his diary, but without mentioning an episode that he highlighted in published accounts a few years after. The omission casts some doubt on whether the dramatic moment occurred as and when he said. As a gift in parting, Houdini later wrote, Evanion presented to him his treasure of treasures, an irreplaceable book of exceedingly rare programs of Houdini's progenitor Robert-Houdin, magician of magicians—the "central jewel in my collection," Houdini called the book. However the visit concluded, it was the last time he saw Evanion, who died just days later. Houdini paid for the funeral carriages, and stayed in touch with Evanion's nephew, who sent him pages-full of information about the history of magic, and about the latest English locks.

FOUR

1900–1904

GERMANY: THE BERLIN POLIZEIPRÄSIDIUM; THE COLOGNE SLANDER TRIAL

HOUDINI ALTERNATED his circuits of British music halls with tours on the Continent, mostly in Germany. He played throughout the country, from Hamburg in the north to Munich in the Bavarian south, from Rhenish Cologne through the coal and iron districts of the Ruhr in the west, in Dresden, Frankfurt, Hannover, Leipzig, and a dozen smaller cities and towns. Audiences knew him as *Ausbrecherkönig* (escape king), *das unaufgeklärte Räthsel* (the unexplained riddle), *der Unfesselbare* (the unshackleable)—or simply and most often, *König der Handschellen* (king of handcuffs).

Before and after starting out, though, Houdini had to be cleared by the German police. In September 1900, two months after opening at the London Alhambra, he brought his basic handcuff-subtrunk act to the Dresden Central Theater. Scheduled to go on to the prestigious Berlin Wintergarten, he received what he called a " 'command' " to appear before Berlin police officials, without whose approval he would not be allowed to continue in Germany. This meant facing Big Brother. With much of Europe committed to representative government, the Second German Empire remained an authoritarian state. Under Emperor Wilhelm II police oversaw the sale of provisions, inspected lodging houses, and framed regulations for public behavior. They also supervised the censorship of entertainment, to silence onstage criticism of the empire's institutions and ideology. "Every singer and vaudeville comedian," Houdini observed, "must submit his entire act, in typewritten form, to the police fourteen days before date of opening. The police look the matter over, and if there is anything about it that they don't like, such material is promptly cut out."

Houdini's "command," moreover, came during a wave of police prosecutions against frauds of all sorts. These included what he termed "Spoof shows," acts that made bogus claims—such as his own might be thought to do. Authorities investigated a theatrical horse named Kluger Hans, for instance, to test its advertised ability to add and tell time without secret cues from a trainer. The sweep extended to mediums. Police prosecuted the noted Spiritualist Anna Rothe, who claimed a gift for materializing rare flowers from the air. Houdini attended the proceedings, though it meant lining up at the courtroom at eight in the morning and paying ten marks on the side for standing room. After awaiting trial in jail more than ten months, Rothe was convicted of fraud, fined five hundred marks, and sentenced to another eight months.

In this menacing atmosphere Houdini came to Berlin, residence of the kaiser—a city of nearly two million inhabitants, divided into 102 police districts. His examination took place at the newly built Polizeipräsidium (police headquarters) on the Alexanderplatz, site of the massive Grand Hotel. Just after noon on September 20, he was stripped naked and faced a crowd of three hundred policemen, headed by Meerscheidt-Hüllessem, police president of Berlin. Houdini's arms were tightly clamped behind his back with thumbscrews, finger locks, and five different hand and elbow irons. Mouth bandaged, he was allowed to work under a blanket. He unhooped himself in about six minutes and laid the test gear on a table, neatly.

For satisfying his inquisitors, Houdini received an official endorsement from Police President Hüllessem. "At this time," it cautiously declared, "we are unable to explain the way in which the locks are opened and remain undamaged." The statement did not concede much, but it was enough, bearing the "highest signature in Germany bar *the Kaisers*," Houdini noted. He spoke of it as unprecedented, and advertised himself as "the only artist in the history of Europe to whom the German police have given the

Imperial certificates." (To a friend he wryly added that he intended to be examined before the kaiser himself and become official conjurer to the imperial court: "That will look very nice on paper, Hofkinstler [*sic*] Houdini.")

The certifying opened the way for Houdini's debut at the Wintergarten, and then his entry into the rest of Germany. But he managed to stay out of the police line-of-sight only about nine months, when troubles with them brought on two trials that spread over a full year. He came into police view again in towery Cologne, where the *Rheinische Zeitung* published an article entitled "*Die Entlarvung Houdinis*" (The Unmasking of Houdini). It told a complicated tale that in essence accused Houdini of two crimes: trying to bribe a policeman into arranging a fraudulent escape at the Cologne police station; and paying off a civilian police employee for helping him put on another phony escape, at a public performance. Houdini treated the article as a crude payback, "an open case of conspiracy against me. The German police do not like the manner in which Houdini so openly defies them, and they thought they would put a stop to me." He hired a well regarded German lawyer named Schreiber and sued the newspaper editor and the policeman for slander.

In Wilhelm's iron domain, the allegations against Houdini were serious. But were they true? Yes more likely than no. Houdini understood that one did not fool with the German police. They wore the uniform of the kaiser, carried large swords, and looked "fierce, as if hunting for trouble." That did not stop him from approaching the police chief of Bremen, at the man's home, to ask help in stirring up local interest, and providing front-row tickets for him and his daughter. According to his friend T. Nelson Downs, Houdini once remarked, "If I find a lock or a jail I can't spiritualize I must fix or arrange a way out." The trial that arose from Houdini's slander suit may well contain clues to some of his secrets.

After a postponement, the proceedings began in Cologne on February 19, 1902, with lengthy morning and afternoon sessions over two days. The many columns of press coverage unfortunately give no sense of the witnesses' appearance or personality. But they do fully lay out their two opposed versions of Houdini's alleged bribe attempt and bribe. The main defendant was Werner Graff, a patrolman (*Schutzmann*)—the lowest rank in the German police. He swore that he owned a handcrafted lock, which Houdini had heard about from another escape artist. Houdini came to the station house, Graff said, and asked to speak with him privately. When they were alone, Houdini explained that he wished to use the unique lock in a nude demonstration before the chief of police. He asked the patrolman for a duplicate key, to hide in his anus. "That way we both could make a lot of money," Graff quoted him saying. "But I mustn't betray the plan." Houdini offered him twenty marks, with the promise of more later. Graff refused, and the demonstration never came off.

Sometime later, Graff continued, he challenged Houdini to escape from a chain hitched by his lock, this time at a theater. Houdini accepted, but again intending a fraud. He approached a civilian police employee named Lott, offered him the twenty-mark bribe, and "begged" him to supply a duplicate chain. During the performance, Houdini escaped after eighteen minutes—by deceiving the "innocent" public, Graff testified. He simply filed through the original chain, left it in his cabinet, and brought out the uncut duplicate to show the audience.

In presenting his case for slander, Houdini gave a vastly different account of the two events. The first, he testified, never happened. On arriving in Cologne he asked to give a demonstration at the police department but was turned down. Period. The second did not happen the way Graff described. After Graff challenged him to escape, he said, Lott advised him not to accept. Lott warned him that at the performance Graff planned to switch the special lock for a "dead lock" (*todtes Schloss*) that could be closed but not reopened. Lott was right, as Houdini discovered when being trussed onstage. Thinking quickly, he decided to expose the switch to the audience. He did so by asking Graff momentarily to reopen the (dead) lock, knowing that was impossible. Graff protested that he had lost the key. Houdini then declared to the audience, "I think I have the right to get free however I can." Returning to his cabinet he simply broke the lock. He did not deny giving money to Lott, but testified that he did so after the show, in appreciation for Lott's warning: "You're a good guy," he said he told Lott. "May I give you a little something?" ("*Sie sind ein braver Kerl, darf ich Ihnen eine Kleinigkeit geben?*")

The two parties having given their conflicting stories, some twenty-five witnesses took the stand to support one or the other. Too voluminous to summarize here, their testimony came down to a swearing contest. Lott, for instance, testified that Houdini had in fact tried to bribe him. But Houdini's lawyer brought forth a merchant from Essen who swore that Lott had told him he received no money from Houdini. Likewise, the creator of Graff's special lock, a Cologne mechanic, testified that the lock Houdini used for the challenge was the one he had made—openable, and not a dead lock. But Bess swore that she saw Graff take a dead lock from his pocket during the show; when she told Houdini, he said aloud: "This officer is a common liar. He has changed the locks." (Graff's attorney agreed with Bess's account of what Houdini said, if on nothing else, and brought a countersuit against Houdini for publicly insulting an officer.)

In the end Houdini himself won the case for Houdini, at the cost of painful self-betrayal. With dozens of charges, rebuttals, and surrebuttals before the court, the chairman asked Graff to explain how Houdini could have obtained a file and, hands locked, used it to cut through the chains. Graff replied that Houdini doubtless had a file in his cabinet, which he used by sticking it in the floor or in a box for stability. Lott added that Houdini told him that he carried a file and pliers in a concealed tool belt. The chairman asked Houdini to demonstrate that he could indeed have opened Graff's lock without such instruments. Graff had brought the device to court, or so he said. Houdini insisted it was not the original lock. Nevertheless he took it in hand and began smacking it against a metal plate he had fastened below his knee. After several minutes, its spring weakened by the blows, the lock came open. Houdini also allowed himself to be chained and locked. Taking the judge with him into a corner of the courtroom—where the judge, but not the spectators, could see what he was doing—he slipped out fast.

It is unclear which of these proofs, perhaps both, Houdini had in mind when he later said that to win his suit he had been "compelled to expose my secret." That was not easy to do. "Just imagine," he wrote to a friend, "in order to save my honor I had to show how I did it."

The court ordered Graff to pay two hundred marks for slander, and exacted fifty marks from the *Rheinische Zeitung* for having published what he said. The puny fines amounted to only about forty and ten dollars, respectively, in addition to which the court fined Houdini three marks for publicly insulting the patrolman. More valuable to him, the newspaper ran a retraction: "we feel obliged to confess that we did Mr. Houdini an injustice without knowing it. We express today our deepest regrets that we had by publishing this notice insulted him and damaged his business."

Far from damaged, of course. "This case has filled all the papers," Houdini wrote, and "has given me a great deal of prominence." He got even more, for Graff did not quit. The patrolman appealed the judgment to a higher court, which met in Cologne at the end of July. The new trial went late into the night. This time around Graff brought as witnesses a police inspector, two commissioners, and about twenty regular police officers; Houdini imported some of his witnesses from as far as London and Vilna. But the large new cast offered no new evidence. Again the court put Houdini to the test of opening one of Graff's prepared locks, which he did in four minutes. Graff should have known when to stop. He lost again, and was ordered to pay court costs that now included the travel expenses of many witnesses and to pay Houdini several hundred dollars for lost bookings.

Exultant, Houdini widely distributed a broadside announcing the outcome of his long days in court:

OFFICIAL POLICE NEWS FROM GERMANY!
HARRY HOUDINI THE AMERICAN HANDCUFF KING
SUES THE COLOGNE POLICE FOR LIBEL AND WINS
In the highest court . . . Police officer Werner Graff was found guilty of slandering Harry Houdini, and was heavily fined, he must pay all costs, and insert an advertisement in all of the Cologne Newspapers, proclaiming his punishment, at the same time, "IN THE NAME OF THE KING" openly apologize to Houdini for insulting him.

This open apology is the severest punishment that can be given to a Royal official, and as the lawsuit has been running over a year, the costs will run into the THOUSANDS OF MARKS. . . .

The battle gave him, he wrote, "the singular pleasure of defeating the Police in their own court. . . . I made them look like a lot of DIRTY MEN." He referred to the victory as "the greatest feat I ever accomplished." This was becoming standard: whatever feat made a loud buzz, he called his greatest ever. On the other hand, he *had* faced down the enforcers of Kaiser Wilhelm, swords and all: "the people over here . . . fear the Police so much, in fact the Police are all Mighty, and I am the first man that has ever dared them."

AROUND GERMANY

Wherever he performed in Germany, Houdini spoke his patter in German. He had grown up hearing the language at home, and read and wrote it decently enough to correspond a bit in it and comprehendingly underline his hundreds of reviews. But he spoke at best what one listener called a "*drollige[r] Kauderwelsch von amerikanischem Englisch und Berliner Deutsch*"—"a droll gibberish of American English and Berlin German." Reporters exercised themselves trying to reproduce his faulty accent, grammatical gaffes, and failure to pronounce *w* as *v*: "*Sie musse endschuldige mein slechte Sprack, aber es is der beste, das ich hab.*" Very roughly this reads: You gotta eggscuse my turrible speak, but it iss the bess I got. Yet whatever the defects of his broken German, Houdini's efforts to perform in their language enhanced what the press called his "obliging demeanor" ("*verbindliches Wesen*"), and audiences were charmed: "it makes them all friendly with me," he said, "before I have performed a single trick."

Houdini became a special favorite in industrial Essen, an urban forest of fuming smokestacks dominated by the 220-foot chimney and fifty-ton steam hammer of the Krupp Steel Works. In repeated reengagements and prolongations at the Essen Colosseum, he premiered his Packing Box Escape; opened a Reichsbank lock designed to secure the kaiser's own funds; played himself in a skit entitled "Adventure at the Düsseldorf Exhibition" (inspiring the headline "*Houdini als Schauspieler*"—Houdini as actor); and underwent some Hodgson-level ordeals. In May 1901, a "Mr. Smart Man" from Krupp challenged him to slip a homemade pair of cuffs that took twenty minutes to lock. The cuffs gave, and could be narrowed by screws to squeeze the wrist: "and the Krupp man screwed it down until it touched the bone," Houdini related, "and imigane [sic] the pain that caused me." He could not get out fast enough: "I was in that dam (excuse the dam but I said worse than that when I was in the cabinet) . . . I was in that cuff half an hour and it seemed like an eternity." The ordeal "maimed" him, he said, leaving his right wrist so sore and puffed up that he could not put on cuffs for a week.

During a Colosseum performance the next year, a challenger named Kinsky roped Houdini in a way the local *Volksfreund* called "simply inhuman." As King of Handcuffs, Houdini did not often do rope escapes, although they had a long history in spirit-medium demonstrations. In an article for the *San Francisco Examiner*, a few months before leaving the United States, he even divulged some escape techniques for use when roped into a chair:

> The whole secret is in getting the first hand free; after that it is all plain sailing. The quickness with which one gets out depends upon how much one can get a little slack in the rope. When I am about to be tied I always sit a little forward from the back of the chair; the people tying me do not notice this. If my feet and legs are to be tied to the chair, then I sit so that my knees are at least one-quarter of an inch from the chair leg. . . . One cannot be tied so that they cannot get some slack in the rope when they want it; if by no other means they can secure it by expanding the chest while being tied.

The article probably contains some disinformation, and its methods may not have come into play in Essen, where no chair seems to have been used. Instead Kinsky simply hauled away on Houdini's body. "Sometimes it was disgusting to see how he tightened the rope," the *Volksfreund* continued. "[He] tied the American as you would tie a piece of cattle." Houdini's escape after seventeen minutes brought "ongoing, never-ending applause and calls of Bravo," which did not cease until he appeared for six curtain calls. But afterward he had to pack icebags on his hands, they were so bruised and swollen.

Off and on, for several months, Houdini performed in the Circus Busch and the Circus Corty-Althoff. Two of the most distinguished circuses in Europe, they little resembled the ten-cent roadshows of his apprenticeship. Corty-Althoff gave its summer season under a tent that seated 3,5oo spectators. Busch had permanent buildings in Hamburg, Berlin, Vienna, and elsewhere—arabesque pavilions that were as "warm and comfortable," Houdini said, "as any variety house in America, and a good deal better than some that I know." Merging circus and music hall fare, they offered not only a hundred prancing horses and ponies, but also leading variety acts and showy spectacles. Working again in a familiar milieu, Houdini shared in concern that the horses had developed *Rotz Krankheit* (a nasal disease) and lamented the death, in Teplitz, of his exhibition-platform friend the Transparent Ossified Man; "A special coffin had to be built for him," he noted, "and the poor fellow was buried in a sitting position."

Whether in variety theater, pavilion, or tent, Houdini everywhere ran up against Houginis and Coutinis, Harry Rudinis and Harry Mourdinis— *die Herren Copisten*, the Mr. Copyists. They included a portly Fräulein who worked as "Miss Lincoln die weibliche Houdini." Though performing in bloomers, she filched his trademark bowed-down-by-cuffs-and-chains pose for her advertising cards (one of which he inscribed to Bess: "My Dear little Popsy Wopsy. What do you think of this???"). As he did in England, he sometimes dealt with parasites by squashing them. A Kleppini, for instance, advertised that he had escaped after being handcuffed by Houdini himself. That was more than enough to send Houdini after him at a circus in Dortmund, in mustache and tinted glasses. Kleppini appeared in the arena and repeated his boast to the audience. Houdini, as he told it, "took a flying leap of twenty-two feet downwards to the centre of the ring . . . and cried . . . Well, look! I am Houdini!" He slapped Kleppini into "a simple French police cuff," in which Kleppini gave himself the lie by failing to escape. "[T]he German performers are, without a doubt," Houdini decided, "the greatest brain thieves that ever existed."

Houdini had many such clashes in Germany, none more revealing than that with "Hilmar the Uncuffable." The others are known mostly through newspaper articles; that is, from outside. But Houdini wrote a private, unpublished account of his run-in with Hilmar. It alone shows the savage contempt he felt toward those who traded on his achievements and presumed to duplicate them. In front of about four thousand people packed into Berlin's cavernous Winter Garden, Hilmar mounted the stage to challenge him. Houdini snapped his alter ego into a pair of Berlin handirons— double-locking cuffs requiring two keys to open. The Uncuffable exited the cabinet after seven minutes, still cuffed and "red as a lobster," Houdini said.

Houdini's personal account of what he did next to shame Hilmar reads like a sadistic fantasy of merciless tables-turned revenge, cackling with bitter glory:

> I grabbed him by the arm and took him to the footlights and said, "Now, tell the audience you could not and can't get out of the cuffs."
>
> He refused to do so, so I said, "All right, you need not, but I will not unlock you. Take the cuffs as a souvenir of Houdini and go. Go to a locksmith, as I refuse to unlock you."
>
> He then showed his cur spirit and cried like a spanked babe. He cringed and fawned like a dog and begged me to unlock him. I refused, but he cried so much the audience felt sorry and cried out, "He is beaten enough. Please release him."

So I released him and said, "Do you wish to try the cuffs locked in front?" He drew back and the audience rose and shouted, "Throw the imitator out! Don't let him try anymore! Out with him! Out with him!" He finally had to leave the building.

So much for this jackal, "Mr. Slob E. Hiller," as Houdini called him, "a certain beer saloon waiter . . . who cleans the spittoons, washes windows and runs errands for a cigar store."

Whatever his mood, for German audiences Houdini could do no wrong. From the time of his first dates in Berlin, his press notices struck a single note: "No superlatives can express the excitement this uncanny man produced." The management of the Essen Colosseum awarded him a three-foot-high silver loving cup inlaid with six hundred marks in three- and five-mark pieces, for pulling in the largest boxoffice receipts in the theater's history. Postcards of him in chains were sold around Germany. Other artistes referred to him in their acts. A Scots performer quipped, in German, that Houdini did not ask the Winter Garden for a fee; he just asked to sleep the night in the room where they kept their safe. The Schwartz Brothers ended their turn with a burlesque of Metamorphosis, using the magic word "Ha-Houdini!" "Now, in Berlin," Houdini reported, "when someone meets you and tenders you some news, instead of saying 'Is that so?' the exclamation of the listener is 'Ha-Houdini!' "

Houdini was treated as far more than an entertainer. Intellectuals compared him to Faust in his defiance of limitation, dubbing him "the Symbol of Freedom" (*"Symbol der Freiheit"*). Some social commentators regarded him as a cutting-edge criminologist, an instructor to the kaiser's constabulary. As a Dresden columnist wrote: "It is not without significance for the criminal police to know what level of skill can be attained in opening all kinds of locks without the use of any sort of tool or perceptible external force. In criminal investigation . . . such a science can be of great value." But the crime world was equally interested. According to a Danzig newspaper, burglars followed Houdini's exploits closely: "These are skills that every burglar would give his life to learn. The Berlin heavies (*"schweren Jungen"*) are said to have approached Houdini repeatedly, respectfully asking for private lessons in the art of escape."

Germans speculated wildly, too, about Houdini's methods. With Spiritualism flourishing in the country, many attributed his abilities to supernormal gifts. Baffled by Metamorphosis, a Düsseldorf newspaper decided that he must harness "astral powers":

> In dematerialization, or the phenomenon of self-dissolving, the force of attraction and cohesion between molecules is overcome. As has been proven through innumerable examples, every body can in this way be brought in an aetheric condition and therefore, with the help of an astral stream, be transported from one place to another with incredible speed. In the same instant the power used for the dematerialization is retrieved; the aetheric pressure again shows the molecules, which again take on their original locale and former shape.

Only astral power, the writer concluded, made it possible for Bess and Houdini to dissolve themselves and penetrate the bag and the trunk, "so that the lady can take his place and Houdini can take hers."

In notices and interviews the press gave Houdini acres of free publicity. "*Der Napoleon der Reklame*," a German newspaper called him (the Napoleon of advertising). With advertising creating a vivid new world of images, signs, and symbols at the turn of the century, and becoming a source of entertainment itself, Houdini studied the trade closely. He owned a copy of Henry Sampson's *History of Advertising from the Earliest Times* (1875), and befriended the press agent Kit Clarke, said to be the inventor of the alliterative advertising paragraph; he also kept a filebox labeled "Advertising Schemes" and doodled out such "Advert. Stunts" as a booklet entitled "How to bring up children" ("Bring them up," it reads when opened, "to see Houdini performance [sic]"). He learned much as well from the practice of promotion by inundation—"mammoth advertising," he called it—used by nineteenth-century circuses and medicine shows, which sometimes plastered a town with thousands of posters. He got up colorful lithographs vaunting his triumph at the Werner Graff trial. They depicted him, handcuffed, facing five robed judges, a bust of the kaiser looking down on the proceedings under the slogan *Ehrenerklärung!*—Apology! In Dortmund alone he distributed two hundred copies. During a later tour of England he used, in seven months, more than thirty-six-thousand advertising sheets. Nelson Downs accounted for a large part of Houdini's success in calling him "the P. T. Barnum of today."

However well known, Houdini tried without letup to become better known. While sowing posters and photographs throughout Germany, and wherever else he went, he ran fullpage ads that howled his name in bold-face capitals, with single and double underlinings, double and triple exclamation points. He constructed eyecatching lobby exhibits, including a board display of famous handcuffs. He issued a promotional booklet in the shape of a lock; a HOUDINI MASCOT for children; a large decal of him-self in white tie, to be wetted and transferred to a pane of glass. At the end of 1903 he put together a twelve-page pitchbook entitled *America's Sensational Perplexer*, describing the crowds he had drawn in place after place, to demonstrate how he had "positively created the Biggest Sensa-tion, and broke more records for drawing paid Admissions than any other act in the annals of Show History." In England he sold the books for a penny, but gave away thousands when he came to a new town, ordering extras in lots of twenty-five thousand. He would issue several revised editions under varying titles, until by 1922, according to his count, six million copies had been circulated. To appeal to the chapped of hand he even endorsed a lotion, Zam-Buk—"Houdini uses Zam-Buk for cuts, bruises, and sores."

What with making headlines, getting talked about, and tooting his own horn, Houdini was, he said, "the best advertised man that ever crossed the vaudeville stage in Europe."

HOUDINI ON GERMANY; HEINBERGER AND FRIKELL

Houdini found Germany comfortable—the cooking "second to none"—and considered it "the greatest country in the world for performers." In some cities one could play for up to ten weeks, while in England, at least in the provinces, three weeks was extraordinary. In the United States, too, per-formers hustled from city to city on some midnight express, week after week, and remained strangers to each other. But in Germany, and Europe generally, the long engagements made for socializing. "You stay in town long enough to become acquainted, you meet your fellow artists in the *cafés*, you are welcome all over, and you are treated like a friend instead of a 'barnstormer.'" No friend to managers, however, he was involved in efforts of German variety acts to form a quasi-union, an "Artist Loge," to oppose the Managers' Association. He joined the lodge and attended meetings, where contracts and such matters were discussed in Spanish, Italian,

French, German, and English. All in all, he said, "the European artist's life is far ahead of the American's."

At the same time, like many other proper Americans, Houdini found much to offend his morals, his wallet, and his democratic sense. A non-smoker and teetotaler, he disapproved the beer-guzzling from one-liter mugs in Munich and elsewhere: "the first thing they do in the morning, after opening their eyes, is to ask 'how is the beer to-day?'" In the same city he happened to enter a store to buy picture postcards. The "saintly looking" saleswoman showed him some that made him blush and hurry out— "after I had purchased all I wanted, that is, I did not want them, but simply bought them to show how wicked are the pictorial cards in Munchen. . . . No wonder this city is known for its 'Art.'" Other customs of the country surprised him: women in evening dress at the Dresden Opera, calmly eating sandwiches from newspapers; women at the other end of the social scale toiling as street sweepers and hod carriers. Few practices irked him more than that of the hands ever outstretched for tips, especially in rows when he left his hotel after an engagement: "They will wish you God Speed, Safe Journey and quick return, but while they say this, their eyes are saying, 'Well come on, shell out, are you blind, dont you see that we want money, and want it quick.'. . . the game over here is 'Skin the Americans' and they all play this great game." He particularly disapproved of the compulsory military service. Much as he liked Germany, he said, "I would never live in a country where your right is not your own."

At times Houdini felt homesick. Passing an Independence Day in Essen, he missed the firecrackers and the noise, making it "a very dreary Fourth for me." Especially he missed his mother. In his broken German he remarked to a reporter: "*Ach, man kann night aben eine bessere Mutterchen, wie ich. . . . Meine Mjutterchen is meine Liebste auf die Welt*" (No one in the world could have a better mother than I do, and my mother is the dearest person on earth to me). That was a fact, confirmed by his behavior. He was now supporting Cecilia Weiss, more than fulfilling the promise he had made to his father that she would "not want for anything." He wished for her to recognize and share in the success that made the support possible, and sometimes "fixed it" with a cable operator to send her wires from abroad signed by some country's king and queen—"and she honestly believed it," he said. She well might have, for the joke fell little short of his real longings for distinction. When he brought Cecilia to Germany for the summer of 1901, he reportedly bought her a dress that had been made for the recently deceased Queen Victoria.

Houdini took time off to pursue his literary and historical interests. In Dresden he bought for his budding library a rare fifteenth-century German manuscript of *Albumasia Sive*, a work by the Arabian astronomer Albumazar. Actively researching his encyclopedia of magic, he looked up two noted German magicians of the past. He traveled by express train from Cologne to Münster to interview Alexander Heinberger (or Heimbürger, 1819–1909), a stooped eighty-four-year-old with a snowy beard, so hard of hearing that he "fairly trumpeted" at him. But a half century earlier, famous as Alexander the Conjurer, Heinberger had become the first magician to perform at the White House (for President James Polk) and, better still, the only one to be mentioned in *Moby-Dick*. And he had known Robert-Houdin, John Henry Anderson, and P. T. Barnum. Seeing Heinberger's letters, playbills, and scrapbooks, Houdini said, "was like having the history of magic unrolled before my eager eyes."

From Cologne, Houdini tried to contact the elderly Wiljalba Frikell (1816–1903), who had retired to Kötchenbroda, a small town near Dresden. He hoped to meet Frikell for two reasons. Having been in magic for longer than sixty years, Frikell probably had given more performances than any other magician and was a living historical archive. More than that Houdini "had heard," as he put it, that Frikell was the first modern magician, a place usually given to Robert-Houdin. It was Frikell, and not Robert-Houdin, who first rejected the conventional pompous robes, flowing draperies, and bulky apparatus, and performed in everyday clothes on a simplified stage using ordinary objects. Houdini does not mention where he "heard" this. But Frikell's priority as a radical innovator was pointed out by Thomas Frost in his *Lives of the Conjurors*, the very history of magic Houdini condemned as error-ridden and meant to supplant. In his research as in his performances, Houdini's tactic with competitors was to obliterate them.

As Houdini told the story, he wrote Frikell asking for an interview, but received only the curt note *"Herr verreist"*—the master is on tour. Skeptical—Frikell was, after all, eighty-seven—he went to Kötchenbroda uninvited, only to be told by Frikell's wife that the old man had gone away. Still doubting, and determined to make something of his visit, he hired a photographer to stand across the street and snap Frikell should he step out of his house. The photographer waited all morning as Houdini pleaded with Frikell's wife, urging on her the debt her husband owed to the literature of magic, "which he could pay by giving me such direct information as I needed for my historical work." Finally exhausted, Houdini left. In time he learned, however, why Frikell had stayed hidden in his house: as a young man Frikell had fathered an illegitimate son. Looking through the shutters, he got it into his head that Houdini was the son's son, come to "claim recognition."

After several more aborted attempts to meet Frikell, Houdini was at last invited to Kötchenbroda on the afternoon of October 8, 1903. A woman greeted him at the door, he remembered, with the words, "You are being waited for." Inside, things had been arranged for his visit—research material brought forth; the walls hung with photographs of Frikell, orders presented him by royalty, recently cleaned gold medals. But the old man, struck by a heart attack two hours earlier, was dead, laid out in the dress suit he had donned in Houdini's honor. His face was still wet where his wife, hoping to revive him, had splashed cologne. "There we stood together," as Houdini remembered the scene, "the woman who had loved the dear old wizard for years and the young magician who had been so willing to love him had he been allowed to know him." She disclosed later that his expected visit had overcome Frikell's dislike of strangers and revived his hospitality. "If you knew," she said, "with what yearning my dear dear Frikell had expected you that day."

Houdini often recalled the spooky encounter. It made him, he said, "believe there must be something in 'fatality.'" The feeling of being driven cannot have been unfamiliar. In seeking out elderly, forgotten men such as Evanion, Heinberger, and Frikell he honored and recharged the memory of his father, his mission to cheer them in their obscurity and rescue them from oblivion. Mrs. Frikell made him a present of her husband's wand, but what Houdini had come for, Frikell had taken with him. He retained all his life a small scrap of paper found in Frikell's dress suit, on which the revolutionary magician had written his last words, in pencil, illegibly.

PARIS, BLOIS, *MERVEILLEUX EXPLOITS DU CÉLÈBRE HOUDINI*

Houdini claimed that during his tour abroad he performed in five languages. As *"Koning der Uitbrekers"* he got up enough "hollandish" to deliver his patter in Dutch, escaping nude from an Amsterdam jail cell and conquering unusual bolted cuffs, horseshoe-shaped, that fettered his crossed hands. His Danish, however, nearly misled his Copenhagen audience into taking him for a comedian: "they laugh," he winced, "as if I were doing a monologue act." Scheduled to open at the Folies-Bergère in December 1901, and anxious to make a hit in Paris, he went a month early to spend time practicing his French. He and Bess took a flat at 32, rue Bellefond, "a little home of our own."

But as happened in London and Berlin, Houdini got off to a bad start in Paris. On reaching the city he learned that the proprietor of the Folies had been "taken to the Insane Asylum" and the theater sold to two Algerian-born Jewish magicians, the Isolas, owners of the Paris Olympia. After buying the Folies they canceled existing contracts and offered the performers new ones at less money. Houdini proudly held out, meanwhile giving a demonstration at the newspaper offices of *Le Journal*. The show reportedly brought "explosive oohs and aahs of wondering admiration" and persuaded the Isolas to make him a "magnificent offer." He opened at the Olympia in early December, headlining twelve acts and, despite his stumbling French, managing to enlist for a challenge the chiefs of the Sûreté and the *police municipal*, as well as the *préfet de police*. Engaged with top billing for a two-month run, he hired seven baldheaded men and painted on the dome of each a single letter of his name. They would sit in a row at Paris cafés, bow their heads, and doff their hats one at a time until their hairless skulls spelled HOUDINI. This Barnumesque teaser, Houdini bragged, "positively stopped traffic." But he came to consider it *de trop*, his one publicity stunt that made him "look sheepishly at myself."

Although featured on the front page of the French magic journal *L'Illusionniste*, Houdini as "*Le Roi des Menottes*" never had the success he hoped for in Paris. His reviews were superlative, but relatively few and brief. He offered to break out of the cage on Devil's Island that had held Capt. Alfred Dreyfus. But military authorities refused—afraid, he said, of stirring up the social conflicts already released by *l'affaire*. Nor did he ever take to the city. Paris ushers, he learned, "will not let you alone unless you hand them a few sous." And even the "finest" people patronized risqué revues that reminded him of "old-time Bowery resorts," seated as they were to be able to look up into lingerie—"and nothing is said."

From Paris, Houdini made a pilgrimage to the town of Blois, on the Loire, birthplace of Robert-Houdin. Before leaving, he wrote to his namesake's daughter-in-law, asking permission to place a wreath on the master's grave and to thank her in person. She said no to both. Houdini made the four-hour journey anyway, by a "stuffy" train. He does not mention whether he got into Robert-Houdin's house, but it would have been a treat. The ingenious conjurer had rigged the place with such gadgets as an electrified feeder that distributed oats to horses in the stable at scheduled hours, and a swinging kitchen door that, as servants passed in and out, wound up a clockwork dinner bell in the cockloft. Houdini did speak with a son-in-law, who showed him much of Robert-Houdin's apparatus and hinted that although Madame had denied him permission to pay tribute at the grave, there was no law against it.

"I therefore went to the quiet cemetery," Houdini wrote, "and for fully half an hour I stood with my hat in my hat [*sic*] at the tomb of Robert Houdin, and with all the reverence and homage with which I respect his memory." He also laid on the grave a huge floral wreath—made of glass beads, following French custom—inscribed, "Honor and respect to Robert Houdin from the Magicians of America." The emotional journey meant so much to him that he sent himself a postcard from Blois "to remember the date"—January 28, 1902—and kept a piece of stationery from the town's Grand Hotel, on which he typed: "Hotel I stoped [*sic*] at during my visit to Blois France, visiting the grave of Robert Houdin." For all the nostalgia, the visit was more pregnant with the future than Houdini knew. He "had heard" things about Wiljalba Frikell that would lead him to see Robert-Houdin differently. Within a half dozen years he would set out, in the name not of the magicians of the United States but of himself, to crucify Robert-Houdin and destroy his reputation.

During one or another engagement in Paris, Houdini made his first, although brief, motion picture. The date is uncertain, as early as 1901 or late as 1905. But even in 1901 films were beginning to invade, and would soon compete with, vaudeville theaters and music halls. The Olympia program during Houdini's debut performances already included motion pictures of Sarah Bernhardt. Many turn-of-the-century magicians worked with or as filmmakers, movie magic at first being closely tied to stage magic. David Devant showed "animated photographs" as part of his performances in 1896, and went into film production himself. The French film pioneer Georges Méliès (1861–1938) was a skilled magician, and made many short cinematograph pictures using trick photography to perform vanishes, transformations, decapitations, and similar conjuring effects.

Houdini met him around 1901 in Paris, where Méliès owned and ran the Théâtre Robert-Houdin.

Produced by Pathé-Frères, Houdini's film was entitled *Merveilleux Exploits du Célèbre Houdini à Paris*. No complete copy seems to have survived, although the original was probably not much longer than the three and a quarter minutes that remain. Houdini in a light suit and black fedora is strolling with Bess along a Paris street. They come upon some helmeted *flics* tussling with a drunk. Deploring their brutality, Houdini tries to break up the fray; the police chase him. Knowingly he sends Bess off, then allows himself to be captured and taken to the station. Stripped to trousers and shirtsleeves, he is thrown in a bare stone cell. Six mustached cops wrestle him into a waist-length straitjacket, then leave. But the story-board announces that Houdini "snaps his fingers" at the police. He escapes the jacket, hurls it to the floor, scornfully stomps on it. The *flics* reenter the cell, astonished to find him free. They lock him in several pairs of handcuffs and leave again. Houdini bangs the cuffs on the floor, opening at least some of them, and kicks off his shoes. One of them conceals a door key, which he uses to open the cell. As he flees past a guard outside the police station, the available film breaks off.

Merveilleux Exploits illustrates Houdini's lifelong attempt to stay current, in this case by exploring a new medium of entertainment. It also attests to his habit of keeping and revamping what works. So far he had done the Straitjacket Escape inside his cabinet, unseen by the audience. Far more effectively he began presenting it in full view, so that his gyrations could be seen. The film candidly shows his frantic-looking struggle to get out: he crouches, kneels, twists, hops, trying to bring in front of him the strap that connects the long arms of the jacket behind his back. Then, still lying on the ground, he sets both feet on the strap, stirrup-style. Violently he arches back and forth as if astride a haywire rowing machine or lunatic rocking horse, *pushing* the strap down with his legs until the jacket begins skinning off his body. After seventy-five seconds he is out, shirt mussed, hair wild. Journalists vied with one another trying to describe his eely flipflopping: "He pulled and hauled, jerked and jumped, rolled and wriggled," one wrote. "He wriggles and squirms," another said, "humps and writhes, slips his head under his arm, skates along on one shoulder, chews a buckle or two, and peels off his crazy house trappings as a boy does his bathing suit."

Were all the jumpingbean antics always necessary? A difficult jacket strapped with chest-crushing tightness can take away one's breath and call for joint-wrenching contortions. An easier, looser jacket can be slipped quite easily, the challenge to the performer lying in how to convince the audience that the escape has been difficult. "Here is where Houdini's genius really showed," a pupil of Hardeen's remarked, "he could make it look extremely tough!!"

RUSSIA

A Russian theatrical agent saw Houdini's act in Paris, and after much haggling arranged for him to appear in Moscow in the spring of 1903. Houdini felt uneasy about playing Russia, and stayed so during the five or so months he spent there. Under Nicholas II and his wife, Alexandra, Russia seemed a mysterious place to Westerners, vast, isolated, and out of step with the world despite a population not much less than that of England, France, and Germany combined, mostly peasants. Omnipresent police executed the czar's will, controlling movement in the country through an internal passport system. The regime was not unresisted, however, and events during the year of Houdini's entry hinted of things to come. An industrial strike in the south was joined by workers in mines, ports, railways, and oilfields. A general strike was declared in July, with demands for the calling of a constituent assembly.

Houdini found Russia forbidding from the start, and "about as difficult to get into as Heaven." He departed Berlin on the evening of May 2. Before entering Russia, the train was stopped by Russian border guards, who took away his passport, books, and newspapers. They also ransacked his baggage, including the "desk-trunk" containing his typewriter, correspondence, and research material. Told that his papers would be detained for inspection by a censor, he shipped the trunk back to Berlin instead. The officials would have sent him back too, he believed, on discovering his kit of "burglar tools," except that he had obtained a permit to bring it in. On top of these affronts the customs officials soaked him, charging duty on "old stuff and props" he had used for years. Apparently transferring to a Russian train at the border, he was shocked by the crowding in its third-class carriages: "a butcher in America," he wrote, "would hesitate before he would ship his cattle in one."

Houdini disdained playing the nightclub-like Moscow "cabinets," and was booked in the more theater-like Yar. This noted Moscow restaurant offered private dining rooms and a main room with a stage for variety performances. Much patronized by the city's high society, it later became the scene of a notorious incident in which Rasputin, drunk and lecherous, exposed himself. As a Moscow journalist described the restaurant's luxe, somewhat decadent atmosphere, "If you would like to see the most exquisite dress and the most expensive diamonds go to the Yar. If you would like to taste the best food go to the Yar. There you will meet Moscow millionaires surrounded by hangers-on who can get money from them." The entertainment began at eleven—just after dark during the short summer nights—and ended at one. Houdini went on stage at about twelve-thirty. Whether he performed in Russian is uncertain. A city newspaper said that he "speaks nothing but English," but he wrote a friend that "I am speaking my full act in Russian." More likely he was helped out, as he admitted, by his little German and less French, one or the other of which was familiar to "all the better class of people."

The Moscow press rated Houdini the "main attraction" at Yar. "The performance starts," the *Moscow Gazeta* observed, "but nobody is interested in dancers and singers. Everybody is waiting for Mr. Houdini to appear on the stage." Reviewers often appraised not his act, however, but the tensions in Russian society it brought out. A cartoon in the magazine *Alarm Clock* depicted the top-hatted and ostrich-plumed diners at Yar, and quoted remarks made at a contrasting table of "Losers": "the trick is not bad, but if we knew Houdini's secret of opening locks we could break into safes and good positions without needing to have pull to open the door for us." Satirizing the split between Eastern orthodoxy and Western modernity, the *Gazeta* reported a conversation between two patrons from the outskirts of Moscow: "Is it a sin, Vassily, to watch him perform?," the woman asks. "What if he's using evil powers to do all those tricks?" "He's a foreigner," her companion replies, "and all these foreigners are trained in mechanics. This is civilization for you. Even in Russia right now, everyone wants to be a mechanic. Civilization is the word." Houdini understood: he found his audiences certain that he possessed supernatural powers, the Russians in general superstitious and backward, " '200-years-behind-the-time' folks."

Some of his observations Houdini reported to vaudevillians in the States, through his column in the *Dramatic Mirror*. But Russian censorship constrained him from saying much about the police. Their control over the variety stage, and over the population generally, appalled him. "I am keeping my eyes open," he alerted his readers, "so that I can explain things well after we depart from Russia." He was able to send a few warnings just the same. The police could stop any performance they wished, and recently had banned the "Seven Florida Creole Girls" for cakewalking. The Moscow chief of police read all advertising copy, and "should he take a dislike to you he can compel you to leave Moscow inside of twenty-four hours, and there will be no questions asked." Performers had to buy expensive tax stamps to legalize contracts, even to receive their salaries. If they deposited money with the police they rarely got it back.

As had not happened even in absolutist Germany, Houdini felt that *"spy detectives"* kept him under surveillance at all times. To practice delivering his patter in Russian, he went to a deserted racetrack and declaimed his lines loudly to an imaginary audience. They included, "I defy the police departments of the world to hold me," and, "I challenge any police official to handcuff me." Police surrounded him, he said, in twenty minutes. "If any country ever was police-ruled," he summed up, "why that country is Russia." Glimpses of the Russian penal system left him still more jittery: defendants standing hours in court awaiting arraignment, denied chairs; convicts being marched through the streets carrying their black bread and a pot for tea; the "awful" Russian prisons, the worst he had ever seen. Photographed by the police on the chance that he might do something criminal, he worried about making some misstep for which he could be charged, arrested, and sent to Siberia.

In his abhorrence of the Russian police, Houdini had special satisfaction in escaping a "Siberian Transport Cell or Carette." Unfortunately this legendary feat is poorly documented. No photographs of it exist, nor even any accounts in the Moscow press. According to Houdini, reporters were barred because "Mr. Russian Spy" feared spreading the news that "a young American named Houdini escaped from their dreaded cell." Instead he performed "for the edification of the secret police only." The only non-official eyewitness to the scene was his assistant, a mustachioed German named Franz Kukol. He had hired Kukol to help with his ever more trunkfuls of apparatus, advertising, and personal papers, and to fill in for Bess. Three years younger than Houdini, this multitalented assistant also served as his personal photographer. But Kukol apparently left no account of the escape either. Nothing remains but Houdini's boastful, questionable retellings, and a poster he later produced in Leipzig, picturing the scene.

As Houdini described the escape to an English journalist, after arriving at the Moscow prison with Kukol he was stripped and gone over by three of the secret police, rigorously: "I was laid on a table and one man started from my head, and searched down to my feet, while another man started at my feet and worked up to my head. I was then turned round and about, being rather roughly handled." (As he more colorfully put it to an American friend, "talk about getting the finger, well I received it three times.") Marched into the cold prison yard, he saw the horse-drawn carette, used for dragging prisoners to Siberia. It struck him as "a large, somber looking wagon . . . very like a large safe on wheels."

The Leipzig poster depicts the drama in the cobblestone yard, hemmed in by high prison walls broken by rows of crossbarred windows. Houdini stands naked, his parts hidden by his manacles. From each wide cuff hangs an iron weight the size of a coffeepot. The cuffs are joined, dumbell-like, by an iron rod, itself chained to foot fetters being clasped on him by a kneeling officer. The cuffing is watched by two guards in sentry boxes and a dozen other police in uniform: small-visored pillbox caps, belted brown jackets, gray trousers tucked into glossy boots. Several epauletted senior officials stand by, smoke rising from the cigarettes in their white-gloved hands.

Locked into the vault-shaped carette, Houdini was told about its security system—"no doubt with the idea of giving me confidence." One key locked the door, but a different key opened it. And the key that could let him out was held by the governor of the notorious prison camp at Sakhalin Island, off Siberia, a twenty-day journey from Moscow. Houdini had stipulated that to allow him to work in secret, the carette must be backed against a wall, covering the "slit" in the door. What shows in the poster as a slit, however, was rather, in Houdini's account, a window about six inches square, divided in four by iron bars. He later learned that the police chief sent men with binoculars to an adjacent building, from which they tried to peer in at him through the aperture. They might have learned something, for it was through this slit or window, Houdini claimed, that he worked on the keyhole, set some thirty inches below. After about forty-five minutes he swung open the steel door, "pouring down with perspiration" despite the cold. He expected applause. Instead the police again searched him and the carette, then collared Franz Kukol, took off his clothes, and searched him too.

Houdini's accounts give little ground for speculating on his method of escape. He later said it was simple. But in his many retellings the duration of the escape also shrank, to twenty-eight minutes, twenty, or even "less than twelve." If he picked the lock or somehow got a duplicate opening key (the Russian police were famously bribable), he would have needed an extension device, given the two and a half feet between the small window and the keyhole. But his nude body offered such an object no obvious place to hide. Maybe the fully clothed Kukol passed it to him or planted it in the carette (in the circumstances, a life-threatening gamble). However managed, Houdini's against-all-odds escape miffed the police. They withheld a certificate they had promised him if he succeeded, though he applied for it several times. Yet despite this and the press blackout, he said, news spread throughout Russia that he had beaten a despair-inspiring Siberian carette, making "the biggest sensation that has ever been up here."

Houdini notched two lesser victories during his run at the Yar. In June he gave a private performance, including needle swallowing, for Grand Duke Sergei Aleksandrovich and the grand duchess at Palace Kleinmichel. The duke awarded him an ornamental champagne ladle worth, he estimated, more than a thousand rubles (five hundred dollars). As a trophy he rated it with the silver bowl he had won in Essen. On behalf of Kirhoff Brothers, the leading Russian lockmakers, he also opened a safe that had stubbornly stayed shut for years. According to *Encore*, an English theatrical journal, every safecracking means had been tried short of dynamite, which might break and scatter the contents—seventy thousand pounds' worth of jewelry. Houdini reportedly opened the safe in nine hours (reportedly).

After his engagement in Moscow, Houdini tried to tour elsewhere in Russia. At the U.S. consulate he signed a two-month contract—drawn up in elegant copperplate hand—with an impresario named Igor Timofayevich Kuznetsov. Kuznetsov booked him to perform "magic with chains and trunk—in theatres, gatherings, outdoor arenas, clubs, restaurants, private homes and anywhere I find it suitable." Houdini would receive four thousand rubles a month, plus a percentage. By early August he was ready to leave for St. Petersburg, home of the czar, but the trip never came off. In one of several explanations he gave, an elderly manager named Walkofsky—whom he may have confused with Kuznetsov—gave him a "marvellous" deal to work in St. Petersburg, sealed it with a champagne supper, then disappeared. Houdini started a lawsuit but learned that Walkofsky-Kuznetsov, his variety days behind him, had grown senile and now ran a milk shop: "whenever he had a flush of his old-time managerial blood run through his veins he would engage artists for vast amounts and then forget all about the contract."

Houdini did get to the renowned annual fair at Nizhni-Novgorod, a picturesque port on the Volga, eleven hours from Moscow by express. A microcosm of the rich diversity of Russia, its three-thousand-shop covered markets offered profusions of silk, goldwork, clocks, and knickknacks, surrounded by another mart of four thousand huts where merchants of every ethnic type—Chinese, Turks, Persians, Armenians—displayed their glassware, pelts, teas, chests. For all its exotic brilliance, however, Houdini found the place repellent. Hired as a special attraction during the two-month-long fair, he discovered that female performers were barred from its variety stages. To obtain permission for Bess to assist him, he had to give a trial show for the police. And the police were everywhere, always ready to demand a passport: "Every day I see a bunch of people marching along being returned to where they came from, as they have no passports. Imagine being arrested for not having your passport." Prostitutes on the streets and an air of anything-goes made the slums of England and Europe look, he said, "like orphan asylums."

Houdini found not much else in Russia to like. He thought the country's magical life dead—"only poor magicians, and nothing worth mentioning." The situation of Russia's five million Jews shocked and offended him. The same Grand Duke Sergei Aleksandrovich he entertained by swallowing needles had marked his appointment as governor-general of Moscow in 1891–1892 by ousting twenty thousand Jews from the city. Houdini had assimilated to Christian America, not only in marrying a Gentile: the meaningful holidays to him were the Fourth of July and Christmas. He had his own brand of Jewish anti-Semitism, too, which could be hard to tell from other varieties. An entry in his 1904 diary reads: "Some Jew tried to get out of the handcuffs to gain the £100. He failed." Still, even with his stage name he made no secret of his roots: "I never was ashamed to acknowledge that I was a Jew, and never will be." He saved newspaper clippings bearing on the fate of Jews in the world: "Attacks on Jews Renewed in Hungary," "JEWS IN FINLAND," "A Jewish Theatre for London." And no matter where his schedule landed him on October 5, the anniversary of his father's death, he located a synagogue where he could recite the ritual prayer of mourning. Many such annual entries punctuate his diary: "I went to Manchester [England] to a temple early at 6 o clock and said Kaddish. One man gave me a tallis and placed it on my shoulder."

Even before going to Russia, Houdini had been surprised to find "a secret feeling among the Europeans against Jews." In his *Dramatic Mirror* column he related several anecdotes about "Antisimets [*sic*]." The police in Vienna forbade the appearance of two troupes of Polish Jewish singers, on the trumped-up excuse that "as they sang in the Polish language no one could understand them"; a German comedian in Hannover was hissed off the stage for telling an anti-Semitic joke, unaware that most in the audience were Jewish. When Houdini himself was not taken for Jewish, as often happened, bigots sometimes opened up in his presence, woundingly: "it is awful what I hear from people that are Jew Haters," he wrote from Munich, "and do not know that I am a Sheeney. But the H— with them (excuse my warm language) it takes all kinds of people to make a world."

But none of this prepared Houdini for the vicious anti-Semitism in Russia. How he managed to find work in the country is itself a mystery. Jews were not allowed to enter Moscow, and by a recent police decree Russian theater managers could not hire Jewish performers or musicians. (By one account he identified himself on his passport as a Catholic.) Not only were Moscow and all its theaters closed to Jews, but the city's "3,000 churches, and more coming" included not one synagogue. "It has even gone so far," Houdini wrote, "that they will not allow a Jew to turn Christian, for it has become a known fact that a Jew will turn 'in name only' so as to be able to enter Moscow."

As it chanced, Houdini arrived in Russia during a surge of anti-Semitic violence. On April 6, 1903, Easter, it struck Kishinev, in Bessarabia, a city of about 150,000, of whom a third were Jews. Over a two-day blood spree, inflamed by rumors that the czar had ordered a Jew-slaughter, a mob that included peasants and thugs from outside Kishinev killed forty-seven Jews and wounded nearly five hundred. Houdini visited the scene of murder, torture, and looting, "horrified," according to an American press report; "nothing like it," he commented, "could occur in any country but Russia." Through his *Dramatic Mirror* column he told American readers of another massacre of Jews in a town called Glischnick, and efforts to censor foreign newspapers coming into Russia that contained reports of it. "There is an awful state of affairs in some of the cities," he wrote, "but it has been like this for years."

Houdini left Russia with a feeling of relief and liberation, looking back on the country as "some sort of a mild prison" from which he had "managed to escape." After much red tape and passport searching at the frontier, the police allowed him, Bess, and Kukol to leave the Russian train and return to Germany via Warsaw, "thankful to think," he said, "that nothing had happened to transport us to Siberia." The five-month stay improved his bank account, his reputation, and his language: he could "talk Russian like a Turk!" But what he had seen there continued to oppress him. Somewhere or other he picked up a Russian edition of *The Protocols of the Elders of Zion*, published in St. Petersburg. And he later entered in his scrapbook newspaper photos of the Grand Duke Sergei, published when a bomb thrown into the ex-governor-general's carriage by the Socialist Revolutionary Party literally blew him to pieces.

"The sun shines for me every day," the Handcuff King wrote, mightily pleased, overall, with his transatlantic success. Photographs of the period show him decked out in a velvet-collared coat, a walking stick in his gloved hand—mirror of fashion, star—or duster-clad in an automobile, one of several he owned or rented although, oddly, he would never feel comfortable at the wheel and avoided driving. He kept accounts of the receipts he commanded, one hanging-from-the-rafters record after another: "Packed Houses . . . Packed jamed [sic] houses. . . . Thousands turned away. Police refuse to allow any more to enter. Manager afraid to pack them in. . . . Seats sold on stage. . . . Breaking records for paid admissions. . . . Crowds so big it became unmanageable. Broke into theater without paying." Having started out in London making about $300 a week, by the end of his first overseas expedition, in 1905, he was earning in England and Germany around $1,000, "not an excellent salary," he said, "but an '*exhorbiant*' [sic] or newspaper salary." During one bustout week in England he earned $2,150, his highest salary ever ("*not* so bad," he said). And he was booked through 1907. "Pretty good," he told his diary, "for Dime Museum Houdini."

If the exhibition platform remained a reference point for Houdini, so too did Ehrich Weiss at the Pastime Athletic Club. Writing to a boyhood New York pal, Bill Mulhane, he enclosed a new cabinet photo of himself, nattily dressed: "Ready, SET, Go," he penned across it, "and Weiss is in the Lead." With his taste for overchewed imagery and sentiment, he often spoke of his career and of life as a race, rule number one being: Take the Lead.

Typically, he advised other magicians not to spite superior performers, but outrun them: "buckle up your courage and start in the race with him; if you persistently stick to your work, you will soon have the grim satisfaction of passing by him."

Grim satisfaction: Houdini's satisfaction in victory would always have a touch of grim. The stress of his difficult escapes, with the always-near possibility of losing a challenge, often got to him. "You know for the last 11 years Ive had the same strain over & over day in & day out," he confided to a physician friend in the spring of 1901: "my nerves are all run down and I am not well as the *prepetual* [sic] worry and excitement is beginning to tell on me and I am afraid that if I don't take a rest soon Ill be all done up."

Madness fascinated Houdini. As if being strapped into a straitjacket twice a week were not enough, he occasionally visited insane asylums. He outlined the plot for something to be titled "The Monster," in which a deranged scientist transplants the brain of a dog into the head of a foundling, who acquires the dog's habits and desires. At times he feared becoming dogbrained himself. While performing in Hannover, he drew up a testament directing that the money he had banked in Berlin was to be divided between Bess and Hardeen, should he suffer any "sickness which may hurt my mind," or "should anything happen to me, that will make me uncapable of judging my own mind."

Houdini's satisfaction was troubled, too, by a sense of impermanence: "we can never tell," he often said, "what is likely to happen." Anxious to provide against whatever might come, he cut corners and tried to save. For all his fat salaries, photos at the time show him leaning from the window of third-class train cars. Part of what he earned he sent to the United States to be banked, "enough to buy *a few* umbrellas for rainy days." Walking in Liverpool one day he looked into a pawnshop and spotted a medal that he realized had a distinguished history. Depicting an American eagle, it had been awarded, a quarter-century earlier, to the famous minstrel man Sam Hague. While living, Hague had refused to part with it; now his widow had been forced to sell it. The chunk of hard luck made Houdini recall a certain pawnshop in New York's Bowery, its window filled with presentation cups, loving chains, championship prizes of all sorts. He had walked by "[m]any a time" he reflected, "and looked at the silent remembrances of past favorites and never have I forgotten the fact that 'life is but an empty dream.'"

To Houdini the victorious finish line always seemed just around the corner from the dime museum, the rainy day, the hockshop, the "empty dream." His memory contained no more painful reminder, however, than the example of Mayer Samuel Weiss, to whom his thoughts also often returned. On a train once he indited eleven stanzas, in imitation of some limping poetry by a versifier named Elizabeth Akers Allen. She began: "Backward, turn backward, O Time, in your flight,/ Make me a child again, just for to-night!" Houdini closely copied her lines, but addressed his to his father:

> *Backward Turn backward o Time in your flight*
> *Bring me my childhood just for a night*
> *Father come back from the Echoless shore*
> *And be in the midst of those you adore.*
>
> . . . .
>
> *Hardship those days held us in her grasp*
> *"Money-less" the name of the lock on the hasp*
> *Old age preventing your fingers too weak and too sore*
> *To even provide for the clothes that we wore.*

Houdini's two stanzas make a curious pair. The first expresses a longing to revisit his childhood. But the other describes his childhood as a time of decline, unsuccess, and misery. Why long for it, and want to return?

The answer comes in the final lines of Houdini's poem. Grim as the past had been, they reveal, it furnished a hovering warmth that, even amid success, weighed on him as missing and beyond recovery:

> *. . . I have wandered wide and far*
> *On ocean wave and whirling car*
> *But in my memory your image is engraven deep*
> *"TADA"—come back and rock me to sleep.*

Like his ill-made stanzas, Houdini's victories, his Take-the-Lead velvet collars and bookings through 1907, would always be overcast by a perturbing nostalgia, where phantoms of the comfort that had gone melted into shapes of the oblivion that might come.

FIVE

1905−1909

RETURN TO THE UNITED STATES; 278

Except that he missed his family, Houdini was in no hurry to get back to the United States. "I don't like America so well, although I am a full-blooded American," he told a reporter. "When I reach England I know it isn't America, because there isn't graft there." Shakedowns aside, Keith's vaudeville circuit would not meet the thousand dollars a week he now demanded. A representative wrote to him in Germany explaining that Keith's currently used not one feature on a bill, but four or five, so his asked-for salary was "quite prohibitive." And they could not count on his promotional stunts to drum up extra business: "*It is absolutely impossible for us,*" the representative emphasized, "*to get the co-operation of the police force in tests and experiments in connection with your work, and therefore secure the valuable advertising which you are able to do in the west and in Europe.*" Keith's offered five hundred dollars if he returned, but Houdini held out for double that: "I have no desire at all to play America, unless I am worth *that money* to the managers." He said he might "NEVER" play the States again.

During his four and a half years abroad, Houdini returned home only twice—briefly in the spring of 1902, and for an eleven-week summer vacation two years later. Both times he sailed second class and, a rotten sailor, became woozy, rubber legged, and worse. The earlier jaunt was unhappy. He wept on arrival to think that his father would not be there to meet him. He found his mother in poor health and his sister, Gladys, needing surgery to drain "PUS in her head," the by-product of a cold. His trip in 1904, however, was restorative, "a great thing for my nerves." On reaching New York he stayed up all night talking with his brothers, then for a few days did nothing but visit friends. In July, leaving Bess in the city, he set out with Hardeen on a sentimental journey to the Midwest.

The brothers stopped in Milwaukee to see several elderly women they had known in their shoeshining days, as well as Dollie Patterson (now Brown), who had been the wife of their half-brother Herman. Traveling a hundred miles north and twenty years back in time, they revisited Appleton. "The handcuff king still claims Appleton as his home," the local *Daily Post* recorded, "and has advertised the city more than any other person living or dead." They had their picture taken in the park where, Houdini recalled, Mayer and Cecilia had often sat. Harry drank once again from the spring there, and even sent some of the water back to New York. On the return trip the brothers ate at a kosher restaurant in Chicago with their brother Nat, who saw them off on the Twentieth Century Limited—a treat in itself. Houdini shared the new era's enthusiasm for speed and speed records, and marveled at the eighty-mile-an-hour bursts that hurtled them to Manhattan in less than twenty hours: "a swell train," he decided.

When Houdini came to America again the following summer, 1905, he planned to work for six weeks, return to Europe for a final tour, and then quit show business, "pleased to retire on what I have managed to collect." Instead he signed with Keith's for an Orpheum tour, presumably at his asking price, and re-signed for another thirty-five weeks, so that he stayed three years, until the fall of 1908.

Houdini's announcements of his imminent retirement would become frequent. Although never fully carried out, they expressed real longings to get off his high-pressure schedule and have time for himself. Well-heeled from victories abroad, he bought a seven-acre farm in Stamford, Connecticut. Once the property of a man fittingly named Triumphant Lockwood, it had substantial buildings, with fields, gardens, livestock, and an orchard locally celebrated for its cider. The site, called Web Hill, became known as Weiss Hill. Houdini spent the summer there with Bess before beginning his tour, picking fruit and berries, and relaxing—or trying to.

He felled twenty trees to clear a road, he told a reporter, and moved some two- to three-hundred-pound boulders, unassisted, onto a wagon and carted them off.

For life in town, Houdini also laid out twenty-five thousand dollars for an elegant brownstone at 278 West 113th Street in Manhattan. Spacious enough for a star, it enclosed behind its respectable lace curtains a dozen rooms on three floors, with several fireplaces, baths, and kitchens, plus a cellar and basement. Located across Morningside Park from Columbia University, it was one of many handsome new town houses and small apartment buildings in Harlem that beckoned to successful Jewish immigrants, who moved there in droves. By 1910 Harlem housed the second largest concentration of East European Jews in America, to whom a private home in the area signified prestige. Measuring how far he had come himself, Houdini dropped by the working-class tenement on East 75th Street where he and his family had survived when they first came to New York. "I'd hate to live there now," he wrote in his diary. "Niggers and Cubans now reign supreme in that street." The comment was no less ironic than ugly, for at the same time that well-off immigrant Jews were settling in lower Harlem, the African-American community that would replace them was being established a mile north.

Too often on the road to use 278 as more than a rest stop and mailing address, Houdini turned over his brownstone to the Weiss family. His mother and sister moved in, as for a while did his brother Bill, thirty-three, preparing to marry, and often enough flushed with drink to be nicknamed "Lobster Bill." A German servant, Anna Aulbach, looked after them. The head of the household was Houdini's twenty-five-year-old brother Leopold. American-born, Leo had graduated from Bellevue Hospital Medical College in 1899 and was doing well in the new field of X-ray medicine. He had become a consulting roentgenologist at a New York hospital and had published an article, "The Use of X Ray in the Exact Localization of a Foreign Body." He hung his shingle in a first-floor window at 278 and set up X-ray apparatus in an office inside. A bespectacled, intellectual-looking young man with a pointed beard and lively wit, he enjoyed the success of his older brother, "that illustrious man, Handcuff Houdini." A bachelor and ladies' man too, he liked bussing Bess and visiting the Gaiety Girls when Houdini owned the company, "to look at the nice padded shapes of those beautiful burlesquers." Houdini took enough pride in his brother's superior education, unique in the Weiss family, to retain throughout his life the invitation to attend Leo's medical-school graduation exercises.

Whatever else Houdini felt about returning to America, to be once again with his mother was a pleasure and a relief. In their sharp facial features, he and Cecilia resembled each other. But she was now nearly sixty-five, a squat, somber-looking, gray-haired widow. Her advancing age worried him. After having himself photographed with Cecilia and Bess, he wrote in his diary, "I hope *not* the last time together." He felt guilty over having stayed so long away from her. At least he implied as much in "Bahl Yahn the Strong Man," a short story he published in the *New York Sunday World*. It tells how the father of a circus Hercules made his son promise to "always take care of your mother if anything happens to me." Bahl Yahn obeys, carrying her on his back in a seat "like a queen." But success in another country makes the strongman "stop worrying about his poor mother." In time the sight of an aged woman with her young grandson reminds Bahl Yahn of his oath. He returns to his own country to resume his obligations, once more carrying his mother regally on his back.

Bahl Yahn-Houdini did better than that. Making up for his long absence abroad, he brought Cecilia to his performances, went marketing with her ("to buy up all the goose grease"), watched her as she read the German newspapers, got her shoes and clothing, took her to the drugstore for hot chocolate or on outings to Atlantic City or Coney Island (where they met Mrs. General Tom Thumb). A diary entry of January 1908 records, by projection, the fervor of his devotion to her. Having bought his mother a train ticket and berth to visit him in Cincinnati, where he was playing, he noted that on her arrival "Charlie the dog went wild for thirty minutes with joy."

THE MILK-CAN ESCAPE; THE MANACLED BRIDGE JUMP; HOUDINI VS. HARDEEN

Houdini's new, three-year tour on the Keith circuit took him across the country, from Boston and Washington to Pittsburgh, New Orleans, and San Francisco. His earlier performances in such cities counted little in making a hit now. Almost five years had gone by; both he and his audience had changed. To a Cleveland reporter his stage speech seemed to have "the precise manner of a German speaking academic English." Many vaudeville-goers knew him only as a name or photograph in rapt accounts from foreign countries.

On the other hand Houdini had learned how to keep an audience on his side. Highly conscious of his stage manner, he thought out his own version of Robert-Houdin's much quoted dictum that a magician is but an actor playing the part of a magician. He distinguished between opposing styles of presentation that he termed "mechanical perfection" and "self-exploitation." Most magicians strive for the first, relying on the effect to sell itself: "Here is a bowl of rice," he parodied them, "and here is a bowl of water and now you see a bowl of rice and water." He contrasted this with the magician whose presence sells the effect, who dramatizes it "through the medium of his personality." To this slight-seeming but all-important difference he attributed half his power to spellbind.

The "Emperor of Sympathy-Enlisters," as one reviewer called him, Houdini made his voice carry loud and clear throughout the house from the moment he stepped onstage. "I . . . walk down to the footlights," he explained, "actually put one foot over the electric globes as if I were going to spring among the people, and then hurl my voice, saying 'L a d i e s a n d G e n t l e m e n.'" He complimented the audience on its kindness and fair play. He flashed his contagious smile, to show his pleasure in performing for them. Often he broke the tension of his escapes with gags. Before climbing into a packing case in Bremen, for instance, he quipped, *"Gelingt es mir, dann ist es ein feiner Trick, gelingt es nicht, dann ist es eine gute Kiste!"* (If I succeed, it's a fine trick; if I don't, it's a good chest!) Houdini's studied geniality figured no less than his locksmithing knowhow or athletic prowess in convincing audiences that he worked miracles. As Bess acutely remarked, "it was Houdini himself that was the secret."

In trying to reestablish his American reputation, Houdini took his escapes up a notch. The new height of imagination and daring drew larger crowds than had ever seen him before. Having always relied on his early training as a runner and acrobat, he now recovered another athletic skill he once had. As a boy he had swum strenuously in the Fox River in Appleton, and later the East River in New York. He picked swimming up again, taking lessons in lifesaving and practicing where he could—rivers, the ocean at Atlantic City, bathhouses, YMCAs, athletic clubs—going long distances to build stamina. In one workout he accompanied a pair of world-champion swimmers, the Mackay sisters. He dived too, and once battered his head on the bottom of a concrete pool, being "nearly knocked senseless."

Still more arduously Houdini disciplined himself to endure cold water, and to hold his breath while submerged. Getting up at seven in the morning, he headed straight for the bath, presumably the large sunken tub he installed at 278 for the purpose. There he subjected himself to ever colder water and ever longer submersion. He chilled the bathwater with ice, bringing its temperature down, in one trial or another, to fifty-two, fifty-one, forty-nine, forty-eight degrees (when a doctor stopped him); several times down to forty-five; and at least twice down to thirty-six degrees, barely above freezing. After a while he got used to being bone-cold: "It is getting to be a habit," he noted in his diary. "Only feel good after one of those baths."

Houdini also practiced staying immersed in the tub, covered by water at normal temperature. With Bess sometimes clocking him on a stopwatch, he reached two and a half minutes—impressive, but way below the personal record he set at the age of eighteen, so he said, of an awesome three minutes, forty-five seconds. He decided to do some running to strengthen his lungs. He also practiced swimming underwater (attaining fifty yards in forty-nine seconds) and simply holding his breath (once, in his dressing room, for three minutes). Occasionally at least, he combined the two grueling exercises. He would then practice staying underwater in an ice bath. Once he held out for thirty-eight seconds.

This suffocating hypothermic regime served as preparation for two thrilling new escapes. "I am submerged in a large can, that has been filled with water"—as he described the first of them—"and the lid is placed on, and locked with 6 padlocks, and in 3 minutes I am free. It is a fine looking trick, and almost defies detection." The can resembled a galvanized commercial milk can of the period, though large enough to hold someone Houdini's size, cramped in fetal position. Six hasps on the cover fitted over staples on the neck, so that the top could be padlocked.

In performance Houdini poked and pounded the can to demonstrate its solidity. When he walked offstage a moment, stagehands filled it to overflowing with twenty or so pails of water. Returning in a bathing suit, he first invited the audience to experience what long submersion might be like. He asked them to time themselves while holding their breath. Then he squeezed himself into the can, the displaced water splashing onto the stage. Long before a minute elapsed, most spectators gave up, gasping. Houdini, however, stepped out of the can, smiling, to perform the actual test.

Kukol appeared onstage with an ax. Houdini explained that if something went wrong, Franz would after a certain time smash the milk can open. Now handcuffed, he again folded himself inside. This time the steel cover was slammed on, the hasps latched, the cover padlocked. The ghost house was pulled forward to surround the can. The audience waited nervously, watches in hand, Kukol standing ready to hack. After little more than two minutes Houdini walked from the cabinet, dripping, puffing, blowing, breathless. The ghost house was withdrawn, revealing the milk can with its six padlocks still closed and in place.

As usual Houdini called his scary new escape "the best that I have ever invented." But restless to outdo himself, also as usual, he varied and refined its presentation. Over the next few years he had the can padlocked and set in an iron-bound wooden chest, also padlocked, and escaped from both in about three minutes. Or he had the can filled with beer, bringing many mutually-profitable challenges from local brewers, happy to publicize Lieber's Special or Royal Pilsen. He also tried to work out, but never performed, an escape in which the locked milk can would be inserted upside down into a larger can, also filled with water and locked. So that the entire audience could see the time ominously tick away, he built for the stage "the largest stop-watch in the world." In another superb touch he advertised that spectators could bring their own padlocks and use them to lock the milk can.

They could do so because although the escape seems impossible, its method is elegantly simple. Getting out requires no concealed tools, and the apparatus can be examined quite closely without giving up its secret. Houdini referred to it as "the first challenge he has ever presented that was mechanical." This is not to say the escape is easy. It is frightening. Immersed in the can, the performer hears through the water an amplified racket of hasping and locking, and knows the blackness of darkness. He feels pressed in by the steel walls. The crouched, kneehugging position makes it difficult for him to hold his breath so that his lungs seem bursting.

In the second of his thrilling underwater escapes, Houdini made a suicidal-looking leap from a high city bridge into a river—*manacled*. He knew all about the risk. In unpublished notes he classed the Underwater Handcuff Release in "the high school of escapes," requiring "extreme carefullness." Apart from having big lungs and knowing no fear, a performer had to be able to slip the irons fast. Houdini warned novices not to try the escape, "unless you resort to fixed cuffs, which require only a pull to open, and even these might go wrong with disastrous results." For himself, he added, "I have never used fixed manacles in any of my stunts." He sometimes used his own rather than borrowed cuffs, but only for their extra weight, to "sink quickly to the bottom and out of sight of my audience, so that they might not inspect my method of releasing myself." Whatever the restraints, he said, undoing them underwater was "dangerous business at the best."

Actually the spring locks of ordinary handcuffs—designed for quick fastening—are simpler and more vulnerable than the pin-tumbler or wafer locks used in homes and businesses. As Houdini put it, "a handcuff is not a strong iron, a Yale lock or even a cheap trunk lock is safer; it is strong, but its mechanism is less complicated." Standard cuffs can be picked by a hairpin, paper clip, or piano wire, or opened by a simulated key, fashioned for instance from a ballpoint-pen cartridge. But add to that the dangers of plunging into deep water, from a high perch, stropped hand and foot. Would not even Houdini, in those conditions, have gaffed the cuffs? Among many other methods, filing down the ratchet will make cuffs slide open without resistance. Hardeen, who later performed the feat himself, wrote that he had two pair of regulation English police irons "'fixed' for jumping." For most of Houdini's imitators the problem was not how to slip the cuffs after jumping, but how to keep them from falling off before.

Houdini's own presentation is documented in a surviving film of his promotional jump from the Weighlock Bridge in Rochester, New York, on May 6, 1907. The dark industrial setting was not typical, however: blackened factory buildings, a grimy steel bridge spanning a sooty canal. A crowd estimated at ten thousand collected two hours before the twelve-thirty performance. Mostly men and boys in dark clothing and caps—as they appear in the film—they jam the towpath alongside the canal. Some youngsters have scrambled into the undergirdings of the bridge for a closeup view, lying on struts and diagonals. Attended by Franz Kukol—a gentleman's gentleman in derby hat and wing collar—Houdini removes his coat and vest, strips his suspenders and pleated dress shirt, peels off his trousers and stockings. Clad only in long white undershorts, he poses a moment for the movie camera. After a policeman locks him into two pairs of cuffs, he climbs to the topmost truss of the bridge, barechested, holds up his shackled wrists to the crowd, shouts to them ("Good-bye"), and jumps straight down toward the canal. As the plummeting feetfirst white blur splashes into the inky water, one pair of cuffs flies off. In fifteen seconds Houdini bobs up, the other pair dangling from one wrist; he sinks again, then surfaces with both cuffs unlocked, waving them above his head as he swims to the towpath.

In November of that year Houdini made a more picturesque jump at New Orleans, where a noontime crowd of ten thousand stood in driving rain on a slippery levee to see him challenge the Mississippi River. No canal this: boarding the upper deck of the steamer *J.S.*, Houdini took soundings and found enough water, he said, for "a family of whales." The manacling was on a Mississippian scale too. Houdini was handcuffed behind his back, his elbows drawn together by a pair of irons chained to the cuffs. A judge draped another chain around his neck, crossed it on his chest, brought it behind him to bind his wrists to his back, then padlocked the ends around his throat. Chains clinking, Houdini descended to the lower deck and out to the end of a carpeted gangplank. On his appearance, according to the *New Orleans Picayune*, the crowd "vented a gasp that sounded like a long-drawn sigh."

Standing at the edge of the plank, Houdini called to Kukol, who was manning a small skiff, and instructed him to keep the boat close. With a steamy mist rising from the rolling flood, he shouted "Goodbye, boys!," thrust his head forward, and plunged in. "A subdued murmur came from the wharf," the *Picayune* reported. "Some of the throng said nothing, only gazing with white-drawn faces at the place where Houdini had disappeared. The seconds slowly began to pile up." After half a minute a bare arm appeared clutching a mass of chains and opened locks, followed by Houdini's head, shaking the water from his hair. He threw the irons into Kukol's skiff and swam in long strokes to a platform moored at the wharf, where he was helped out. Afterward he admitted that the pull of the Mississippi's current had unnerved him: "That's an awful river. . . . And the further down I went the colder and darker it became."

Other manacled promotional jumps on his return to the United States equally tested Houdini's endurance of freezing airless depths. He leaped from the Belle Isle Bridge into the icy Detroit River twenty-five feet below, shivering in the raw wind; from the railing of the Seventh Street Bridge in Pittsburgh into the Allegheny River; and from the Harvard Bridge into the cold early-spring water of a Charles River channel, so many boats

Houdini's half-brother, Herman Weiss.
(Library of Congress)

Rabbi Mayer Samuel Weiss in Appleton.
*(Boldt Collection, Houdini Historical Center,
Appleton, Wisconsin)*

week of Oct 23 - 1893

At the new State Street Globe Dime museum, near Van Buren street, Kohl & Middleton will present during the coming week, the Houdini Brothers, wonderful wizards; Miss Cozart, the long haired lady; Oklahoma Bill, the scout, and his prairie wife; Fannie Burdette, the tiny midget, and the great Prof. King; while in the three theaters there will be stage shows every hour by Goggin and Davis' comedians, Durant and Howell's first prize Ideals and the Midway Comedy company,

Probably the first ad for Houdini, at a Chicago dime museum, 1893.
(Jacob Hyman Collection, Houdini Historical Center, Appleton, Wisconsin)

Harry and Bess as the Rahners, 1894. *(Library of Congress)*

The Houdinis with the Welsh Brothers circus, 1896. Two of the Bard Brothers appear
in the top row *(right)*. *(Museum of the City of New York)*

my first book. Houdini

Mysterious
HARRY HOUDINI.

signed may 29/1921

Published as near as I can remember

about 1894 — Remembered 1894

/TRICKS.
Requiring no practice or special apparatus.
Price 25 Cents.

Printed in Chicago. HH

Houdini's first pitch book, ca. 1894. *(Theatre Arts Collection, Harry Ransom Humanities Research Center, University of Texas at Austin)*

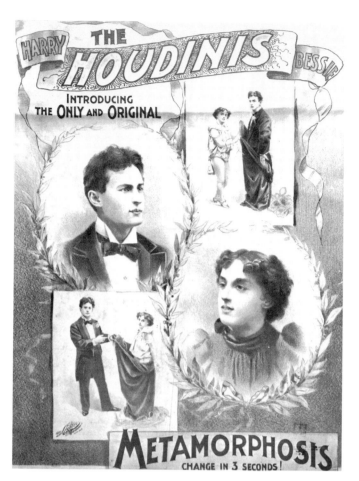

Poster for Metamorphosis.
(*Morris Young Collection*)

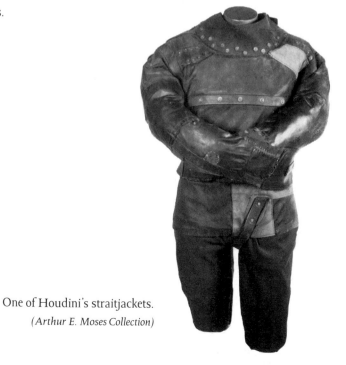

One of Houdini's straitjackets.
(*Arthur E. Moses Collection*)

Needle Swallowing, 1924. *(Library of Congress)*

A Nude Jail Cell Escape. *(Morris Young Collection)*

A Sandowesque moment. *(Morris Young Collection)*

Demonstration of back-palming for his brothers Theo (*left*) and Nat.
(Theatre Arts Collection, Harry Ransom Humanities Research Center, University of Texas at Austin)

The Davenport Brothers (*rear*) inside their cabinet. *(Bill McIlhany Collection)*

Under Martin Beck's management, ca. 1900. *(Museum of the City of New York)*

1903

(Morris Young Collection)

HARRY HOUDINI.

(Sidney H. Radner Collection, Houdini Historical Center, Appleton, Wisconsin)

(Theatre Arts Collection, Harry Ransom Humanities Research Center, University of Texas at Austin)

(Sidney H. Radner Collection, Houdini Historical Center, Appleton, Wisconsin)

Contemplating a silver facsimile of the
Mirror Cuffs. *(Morris Young Collection)*

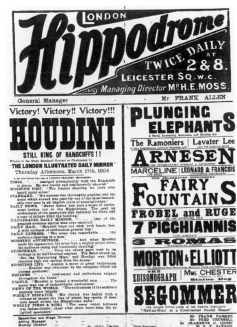

Victory in the Mirror Cuff Escape.
(Harvard Theatre Collection)

Trying the wheel, England, 1900. *(Museum of the City of New York)*

Studios 22, Bedford Street. -Strand- London.

Hana LTD.

With T. Nelson Downs, King of Koins. *(Theatre Arts Collection, Harry Ransom Humanities Research Center, University of Texas at Austin)*

With brother Theo (Hardeen) in Paris, 1901. *(Library of Congress)*

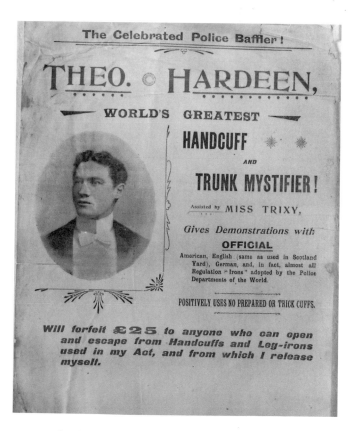

Advertising handbill for Hardeen. *(Author's collection)*

With brother Leo. *(Arthur E. Moses Collection)*

With Cecilia Weiss and Bess. *(Theatre Arts Collection,
Harry Ransom Humanities Research Center, University of Texas at Austin)*

Harry and Bess in Dortmund, Germany, 1901.
(Ed Hill Collection)

ABOVE LEFT: Poster announcing Houdini's first Packing Box Escape, at the Essen Colosseum, July 31, 1902. *(Harvard Theatre Collection)*

ABOVE RIGHT: Playing Holland, 1903. *(Harvard Theatre Collection)*

Lithographic poster declaring Houdini's victory in his suit for slander at Cologne, 1902. *(Museum of the City of New York)*

At the Circus Busch. *(Sidney H. Radner Collection, Houdini Historical Center, Appleton, Wisconsin)*

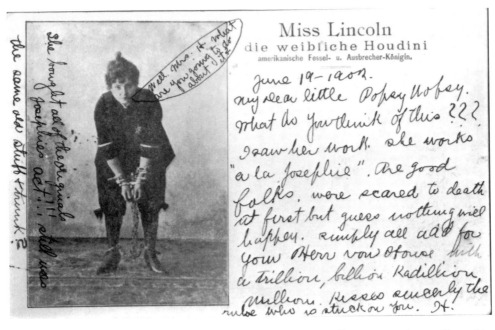

(Theatre Arts Collection, Harry Ransom Humanities
Research Center, University of Texas at Austin)

ABOVE AND BELOW: Two Houdini-ettes.

(Volker Huber Collection)

Wiljalba Frikell and his wife. *(Theatre Arts Collection, Harry Ransom Humanities Research Center, University of Texas at Austin)*

 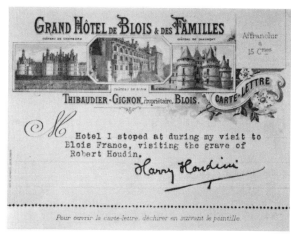

Mementos of the visit to Robert-Houdin's grave, 1902. *(Theatre Arts Collection, Harry Ransom Humanities Research Center, University of Texas at Austin)*

At the Yar. *(Harvard Theatre Collection)*

New York, 1904. *(Ken Trombly Collection)*

Back home, 1908. Houdini's sister, Gladys, appears in the second row, to the right of Cecilia Weiss. *(Jacob Hyman Collection, Houdini Historical Center, Appleton, Wisconsin)*

In Delavan, Wisconsin, visiting the Flitcrofts, who had taken in Ehrich Weiss as a runaway boy. *(Library of Congress)*

Bussing his mother. *(Library of Congress)*

The Milk-Can Escape. *(Morris Young Collection)*

The can padlocked. *(Robert Lund Collection; Photo: David Odette)*

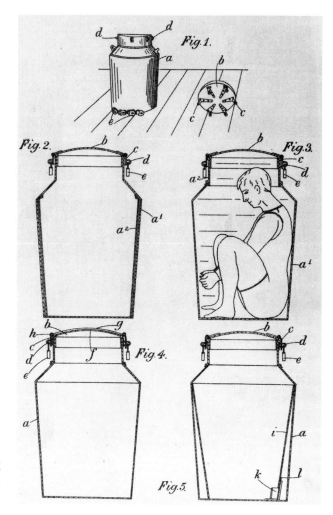

Diagrams accompanying British patent for the Milk-Can Escape. *(New York Public Library)*

Poster for Milk-Can Escape inside a locked box. *(Billy Rose Theatre Collection, New York Public Library for the Performing Arts)*

Underwater Handcuff Escape. *(Sidney H. Radner Collection, Houdini Historical Center, Appleton, Wisconsin)*

ABOVE AND BELOW: Manacled Bridge Jump, Boston. *(Library of Congress)*

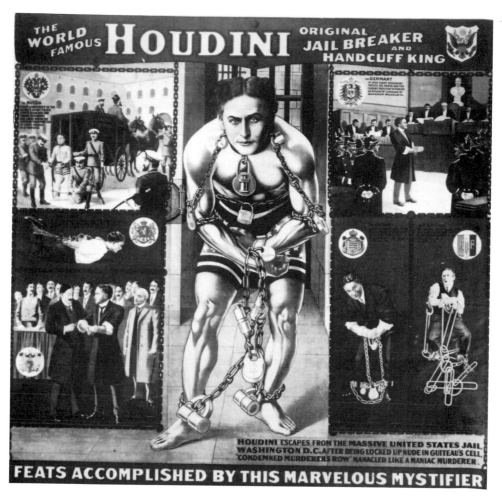

Lithographic poster featuring Houdini's 1906 escape from the jail cell of Charles Guiteau. *(Museum of the City of New York)*

The Weed Tire Chain Grip Escape, 1908. *(David Copperfield Collection)*

Houdini as author, holding a copy of *The Unmasking of Robert-Houdin*.
(Sidney H. Radner Collection, Houdini Historical Center, Appleton, Wisconsin)

minutes. In another twenty, still naked, he had opened the cells of the other prisoners, somehow persuaded them to exchange cells with one another, then relocked the doors, dressed himself, and appeared again in the main hall. "When the officials found what he had done with their prisoners," the *Post* reported, "their amazement passed all bounds." The jail superintendent gave him a certificate attesting to the penological value of his escape, "in that the department has been instructed as to the adoption of further security."

"Houdini," a friend once said, "would murder his grandmother for publicity." As if staying under, jumping in, and breaking out were not enough to get attention, he also enlisted Hardeen in staging a fratricidal war. Returning from Europe after a seven-year stay, Hardeen was booked for an American tour—on Houdini's recommendation—by the Klaw-Erlanger vaudeville circuit, rivals to Keith. A New York paper reported that Houdini suspected his brother "was coming from Europe to drive him from the stage." He boarded a revenue cutter and made for Hardeen's White Star liner even before it could dock, "to meet him and learn his intentions." After a long conference on deck they decided to have peace. "I was very much alarmed to learn that my brother was coming," Houdini told reporters later. "He says that he will not antagonize me . . . I guess the country is big enough for both of us."

Yet the stories Houdini planted in the press were not very far from his actual feelings. Just two days after Hardeen's arrival he wrote to a friend, this time in earnest: "I don't think that I have anything to fear, as I am the originator, and he is like the rest of my imitators, with the exception that he is my brother (and a dam [*sic*] good brother at that)." "I don't think" here sounds much like 'I hope I don't.' In fact, given Hardeen's success abroad, Houdini had reason to think of him as a rival. "Last night I was carried home," he wrote Houdini from England, "and thousands followed me to the house cheering all the way." A few reviewers even preferred Hardeen to the older brother who had invented him. He "outdoes his prototype," one commented, after Hardeen had shed a dozen handcuffs and leg-irons. "Instead of taking an age to do it he goes through at top speed."

Houdini perhaps had grounds for envy as well. He could be tough and pragmatic, but Hardeen was tougher and cynical. To slip out of a contracted booking in Aberdeen, Hardeen obtained a phony statement from a physician saying he was too ill to appear. He was spotted a few days after, addressing a meeting of striking music hall workers. Also no doubt with a cheating heart, he later acquired a phony elementary school diploma and a phony birth certificate. And unlike the childless Houdini, Hardeen was raising a Hardeen-like son, "a great big fellow," he told his brother, "as he has an awful broad back and big chest. And he is all mussel [*sic*]." When Hardeen cabled further news of his potency sometime later, Houdini triple-exclaimed: "he has another son born!!!" Hardeen knew something about inner strain himself, let it be added. He suffered bile problems, piles, and such severe ulcer attacks that on one trip, an assistant recalled, he had to eat cream every hour.

With real rivalry at play beneath the cooked-up one, the pretend grudge-fight got off to a nasty start. Hardeen told reporters he so much admired Houdini that he was willing to hire him as an assistant. The wise-crack got into print, which was its purpose. But Houdini found it genuinely insulting. It "got Harry on my neck," Hardeen recalled, "and there was nothing synthetic about his anger." He promised his brother "never to do that particular thing again." The fake slugfest continued. When Houdini and Hardeen appeared the same week at rival vaudeville houses in Kansas City, the local press printed their jabs at each other's bridge jumps:

> "Bah! An imitator, that's all. Why, just two weeks ago I jumped off the Otto Fisher bridge in Louisville, sixty-five feet high, into five and a half feet of water, and rock bottom at that," Hardeen said last night. "And I challenge the world to duplicate my 5-mile swim up the Thames River from Kew bridge to Tower bridge in London, handcuffed. . . . Houdini can't do it. He isn't strong enough."

Following this the paper printed Houdini's counterpunch:

> An imitator—just an imitator. These fellows that imitate me won't tackle my hard tricks. They don't go into ice water with hands and feet shackled. On December 2, last year, I jumped the Belle Isle bridge at Detroit and there was ice in the river, too. I crawled up the iron arm of a dredge boat in San Francisco, carried seventy-five pounds of iron on my hands and feet and dived forty feet with it. I'd like to see Hardeen do that. He can't.

Hardeen, at least, relished the whole business, "the newspapers having us cutting each other's throats—and just two loving brothers living off the fat of the land."

THE OPEN CHALLENGES

If Houdini needed more to regain his American audience, he got it through a series of electrifying no-holds-barred challenges. In essence, he offered to escape from anything whatsoever. For each new heartstopper he printed new broadsides and posters proclaiming its terms in block capitals on pink or yellow sheets and shouting its significance: "HOUDINI'S World-wide reputation is at Stake." Some challenges were twists on proven escapes. Instead of a packing case, for instance, he used a zinc-lined, screwed-down piano crate, or a box fastened by "toe nailing," that is, by hundreds of nails driven in at different angles. Some other challenges relied on principles he had used before, but in appearance were radically new. In Rochester, New York, he was nailed to a door, face down, his hands and legs outstretched, chains passed through holes bored in the door around his wrists, ankles, and neck, then secured by locks and handcuffs.

Most of the challenges, however, were unique chefs d'oeuvre requiring much extra care, as if a pianist prepared a different concerto for every performance. Usually done inside his cabinet, they involved a product manufactured by some company. He accepted a challenge from the Pittsburgh Auto Vise and Tool Company to escape from four of their vises, advertised as the largest and strongest ever built, designed for holding the heaviest machinery. A Chicago envelope company put him into the world's largest envelope, 150 inches high and 54 inches wide, made from 16,000 square inches of their heaviest rope-fiber manila stock, the sides riveted with tension fasteners, the whole roped and sealed. He escaped a giant football manufactured by the A. J. Reach Company, carried onto the stage of a Philadelphia theater by the University of Pennsylvania football team, which laced him in with a brass chain. One challenge that he repeated several times saw him stuffed in a standard U.S. Postal Service mailbag, the top folded over and cinched by a heavy leather strap and rotary lock (he escaped in twenty-one minutes, while the band played "My Country 'Tis of Thee").

Onstage the freak objects created a visual shock, none more so than the surreal junkpile hauled to Keith's 125th Street theater in New York on

April 10, 1908. The Weed Tire Chain Grip Company challenged Houdini to be enmeshed in and escape from their product—heavy automobile chains used to prevent skids on slippery roads. Loops of the chains were drawn over his head, arms, and legs, and across and around his body—tightly enough to leave red indents. Then, laid out mummy-bound on the stage, he was hooped within two steel-rimmed automobile wheels. These too were wound in chain grips and padlocked. Through the steel tangle he was also handcuffed. In photographs of the escape he appears ridiculously encoiled and helpless, the skewer in a shishkebab of tires and chains, a machine-age Laocoön. Moved into the ghost house—the audience growing more and more excited—he worked loose after nineteen minutes: "he could not speak," one newspaper reported, "and reeled off the stage, with an attendant holding him up."

The open challenges brought Houdini even more bizarre offers, which he turned down as moonstruck or as deathtraps. By his account, a sea captain proposed throwing him into thirty fathoms of water locked in a lead-booted diving suit, from which he must get free without getting wet. Employees of an electric company wanted to blow a human-sized incandescent bulb around him, from which he must escape without breaking the glass. Ironworkers volunteered to padlock him to the bottom of their triphammer, from which he must detach himself before it struck its five-ton blow, as it did twice a second. A plumber offered to encapsulate him between two bathtubs, spiked together; a builder wanted to construct a house onstage and brick him in ("He thought the audience would wait"). Others bade him enter a cannon, whose mouth they would heat and pinch closed with a mammoth press, or dared him to exit a sheetiron coffin, seamed with plaster of Paris, clinched with a hundred bolts and nuts, banded with steel, and set in a lime kiln.

Houdini's fiendish catalog sounds at least in part invented, although the actual challenges he overcame were stupendous enough to draw wall-to-wall raving houses. The press spoke repeatedly of his turning audiences into a "yelling, cheering mob," of spectators becoming "frenzied" or driven to "a pitch of excitement bordering on hysteria." The highvoltage impact his challenges generated came in part from their cumulative and escalating difficulty, as if he could tolerate not even himself as a rival. His determination to top himself again and again appears especially in two incredible engagements at Keith's Boston theater, early in 1906 and 1907.

Like Essen, Boston was a special city for Houdini, where he had a devoted following he went out of his way to please—"Houdinites," the *Boston Post* called them. He particularly liked the local Keith's, too, which advertised itself as the "most elaborately decorated, and most sumptuously appointed amusement establishment on the face of the earth." It may well have been. A lofty entrance, under a huge transom of opalescent glass, led into lobbies and a main foyer aglow with softly shaded lamps and Siena marble, featuring leather-upholstered tête-à-têtes, writing desks stocked with monogrammed paper and gold pens, choice flowers arranged in ornamental jardinieres, china cabinets, tiled fireplaces, dainty boudoirs. Seventy-five employees did nothing but clean the place uninterruptedly night and day. The Boston Keith's assured its patrons that they were not mere vaudeville-goers but guests estimable enough for admission to the lair of Commodore Vanderbilt. To appear at this "million dollar theatre," as Houdini called it, was itself a distinction: "the engineer appears in dress suit," he wrote.

During his two runs at Keith's, Houdini orchestrated a crescendo of ever-more-fantastic escapes that engaged the entire city of Boston, piling climax on climax to ignite a wild enthusiasm. On March 9, 1906—three hundred overflow spectators having been granted standing room on the stage—he was triple-handcuffed and confined in a locally manufactured hamper made of close-woven rattan, impervious, presumably, to wires, blades, or similar tools. The cover was locked in five places, the keyholes sealed with Japanese wafers signed by members of the committee. With Houdini inside, the hamper was chained and roped tight. The difficult escape took him an hour and two minutes, and he reappeared with traces of blood on his hands; the locks and signed seals were, however, intact. The next week, stripped and handcuffed, he beat the city jail on Somerset Street. Bafflingly, its three exits—through a jail office, the courthouse, and police headquarters—remained guarded. He got out of his handcuffs; opened first his own cell and then another in which his clothes were locked; dressed; slipped past police waiting at the three known exits; somehow found a passage through the snow-covered prison yard; jumped its outer wall; climbed into a waiting car; and drove off to Keith's, where he telephoned the police to announce his escape—all in twenty-three minutes.

In a special performance at Harvard a few days later—the room so packed that some students sat in the fireplaces—Houdini escaped in twelve minutes after two undergraduates tied him with sixty feet of rope. Only days later, at Keith's, he was chained and padlocked inside an antique prison restraint known as a "Witch's Chair," something like an iron outhouse; he released himself in an hour and a half. The following week he demonstrated needle swallowing to an invited audience of Boston physicians. In his museum days he had learned how to push a needle through skin without harm. To convince the physicians that he smuggled no extra needles in or out of his mouth, he invited them to sew it shut. They declined the elective surgery, but agreed to examine his mouth with professional thoroughness. Even so he disgorged the needles strung nearly equidistant from one another on two feet of white thread. For a fillip he pinned one needle through a fold of his cheek.

Each successive stunt made news, even outside Boston. The *Washington Times* reported that "the people of [Boston] and, indeed, of the surrounding towns for miles around were fairly wild with excitement over the wonderful escapades of the jail-breaker and seeking to find some means of thwarting him." A Boston–New York–Chicago music publisher issued a piano piece called the "Houdini March Two-Step"; another Boston company awarded him a gold medal in the form of a roped packing case; the *Boston American* sponsored a Houdini Day for limericks:

> *Of Houdini we all have heard tell,*
> *He escapes from locked handcuffs and cell,*
> *He's a wonder, no doubt*
> *But let's see him get out*
> *Of a six p.m. train on the "El."*

With Houdinites attending his every performance, the entire city, another newspaper reported, had "really been seized with a fever for this wonderful mysteryist. . . .'How many times have you seen him?' was sufficient introduction for hundreds of his admirers to open conversation."

Bostonians remembered Houdini's 1906 run when he returned the following year, opening at Keith's on January 7. "Audience applauded me for fully five minutes," he recorded in his diary. "Makes me feel proud to be so well liked. And Bess my darling is all swelled over it." The applause continued so long he had to make a speech in response. Nor did he disappoint his fans. His ads promised a "special sensational stunt at every performance," and he offered over the month, inside his cabinet, a well-attested but almost unbelievable series of escapes from:

- a roped paper box, while triple-handcuffed (escape time twenty minutes)
- a screwed-down coffin (perforated with airholes), handcuffed and leg-ironed (fifty-eight minutes)
- a long ladder, to which he was locked and chained by a five-man committee, his feet shackled to one end, his neck to the other, his hands secured crosswise between the rungs and behind his back, making it impossible for him to reach the fastenings at either end (seven minutes)
- a snug-fitting leather bag manufactured by a local shoe company, a heavy chain drawn through twelve large eyelets on each side and padlocked together with three Yale and three Corbin locks (twenty-three minutes)
- a roped and padlocked case nested within another locked and padlocked case
- a glass box, roughly a three-foot cube, made of three-eighth-inch-thick panels bolted together, the inside bolt heads countersunk so they could not be nipped off, the outside bolts gripped by nuts and drilled through near the ends so they could be doubly secured with small, two-tumbler padlocks (thirty-six minutes, after being searched by a committee of twelve)
- a body-girdling web of heavy woven cord and waxed fishing line, the challenger using a marlin spike to tighten the knots and separately tying each one of Houdini's fingers to the next.

There is no record of how long it took Houdini to pick apart the web, but the tying onstage lasted an hour and forty-five minutes. Working without the cabinet, he labored a half-hour to free his fingers alone, the effort mangling his fingernails.

These wonders were just warmups for Houdini's prodigious escape at Keith's, on February 12, from an iron boiler—into which he was riveted in full view of the audience. He performed at ten-thirty at night, having released himself at a matinee that same day from a door to which he was handcuffed and nailed. The boiler, made as a challenge by employees of the

Riverside Boiler Works of Cambridge, was a regulation hotwater tank nearly five feet high and two feet in diameter. Like several other devices put forward by Houdini's challengers, it was placed on public display in front of Keith's to advertise the test. Houdini examined the boiler himself and announced, as he sometimes did with very difficult escapes, that he might possibly fail to get free. In handcuffs and ankle chains, he was helped to crawl feet first inside the boiler, which lay on its side. Workmen fitted on and secured the boiler's cap. Through the flanges they inserted two long bolts, at right angles to each other, and riveted the protruding ends.

Houdini entered the boiler at ten-thirty-five; he swung aside the curtain of his cabinet at eleven-thirty. His dress suit was torn and soiled, his hands bruised, his face bloody. One reporter described him as "pale, weak, and trembling. . . . hardly able to stand erect." The boilermakers cut off the riveted heads of the bolts in order to open the tank and satisfy themselves that it did not contain anything or anyone, perhaps a Houdini double. It did not. With a wave of the hand, the one and only Houdini ambled into the wings, and only two days later defeated the Derby Desk Company by liberating himself from inside one of their locked six-foot rolltops.

How could Houdini have opened and reriveted the boiler? In 1950, a mechanic named Bert Clark revealed Houdini's secret—convincingly—in a Providence, Rhode Island, newspaper. Since the method has appeared in public print and no modern escape artist is likely to attempt the feat, the information can be repeated here. Houdini knew many ironworkers, cabinetmakers, and locksmiths, and he brought Clark to Boston to examine the boiler. Clark measured the tank carefully and in consultation with Houdini made exact duplicates of the long bolts, but incised screw threads on the ends where the original bolts would be riveted. He also machined two nuts in the form of the rivetheads. Houdini hid the special bolts and fake rivets in the hollow legs of his ghost cabinet. Clark also tooled a tiny pipe cutter that could be disassembled, whose parts Houdini hid on himself. The night of the performance at Keith's, Clark stood in the wings with Franz Kukol, looking on as Houdini was eased into the boiler, the genuine bolts inserted crosswise and riveted. Inside, Houdini planned to assemble his pipe cutter, cut the bolts, knock them through, lift the cap, and climb out. Then he would insert the faked bolts through the cap and tank, tightly screwing the faked rivets to their ends. Concealing his cutter and the original hardware, he would emerge.

Using this no-nonsense method, Houdini expected to be out quickly. That did not happen. Although the audience never realized it, an unanticipated problem kept him locked inside the pitchblack tank. Houdini and Clark had failed to consider that where the pipe cutter sliced through the bolts it left a small, raised curl of metal. These protrusions stuck in the holes of the cover as Houdini tried to push the bolts through. Perspiring heavily, he worked the bolts over for fifteen minutes but still failed to force the metal lips past the holes. As time dragged on and he failed to appear, the band replayed its music, then replayed it again, Clark and Kukol watching nervously from the wings.

Houdini's resourcefulness saved him. It occurred to him to disassemble the pipe cutter and use one piece as a spike, set onto the end of a bolt. Using another piece of the cutter as a hammer, he tapped the bolts out one by one. As a Boston newspaper headlined his escape the next day: HOUDINI VICTOR IN SUPREME TEST. He agreed. "This challenge is the limit," he jotted in his diary. "Greatest test I ever did." To mark his spectacular engagement, B. F. Keith tendered a dinner in Houdini's honor at the Boston Athletic Association, with many prominent Bostonians among the seventy-five invited guests.

CONJURERS' MONTHLY; THE UNMASKING

Resettled in the United States, Houdini got down to making his mark as a literary man. He published one of his occasional short stories, "Dan Cupid—Magician," the tale of a poor young sorcerer who wins as his bride the fiancée of an English earl and becomes "the fashionable world's new-found idol." Like his imposing brownstone, it suggests aspirations for social rank. (Reaching for a new realm of taste, too, he visited the Metropolitan Museum of Art.) He also published *The Right Way To Do Wrong* (Boston, 1906), a ninety-six-page exposé of second-story men, professional beggars, bunco artists, and similar crooks. With its crime-does-not-pay tone, *The Right Way* belongs to the muckraking literature of the period, designed to root out social exploitation and corruption. But the prose is too slickly professional to be the work of a barely educated amateur like Houdini, and the cagey opening statement does not inspire confidence that he wrote much of the monograph himself: "I was almost too busy to write this book, although I have been collecting the material for a long time. But now I am pleased it is written."

Houdini's hand appears more clearly in his two main literary ventures at this time. In September 1906 he brought out the first issue of *Conjurers' Monthly Magazine*, a journal for the magic fraternity priced at ten cents a copy. Too often on the road to compile every issue himself, he had his brothers Nat, Bill, and Leo help out, Hardeen serving as "English representative." Where most magic journals feature explanations of new tricks and illusions, he concentrated on historical articles, drawing much of the information, photos, and playbills from his encyclopedia research. In all other ways too the magazine reflects his unicorn personality. The many typos, misspellings, and grammatical errors are Houdini, as are the ads solicited from detectives, scalp experts, and razor-strop manufacturers; the charitable appeals to help ill or impoverished magicians; the scorching book review section ("Reading and Rubbish"); and the columns filled with praise of Houdini, by himself and others.

Houdini particularly used *Conjurers' Monthly* to demolish imitators, detractors, and enemies. "[T]he surest method of finding out if you are a success," he wrote in one editorial, "is to find out how much jealousy and malice your success may have aroused in the beings who are the milestones of the worst kind of life's failures." Smalltimers had always plagued him, of course, and now he no sooner introduced something new than it was stolen. By 1910 the Mysto Magic company was selling "Houdini's Milk Can Escape" for thirty-five dollars. The shameless mimic Oudini published an eighty-page booklet disclosing secrets of escape from most of Houdini's ingenious challenges—"Iron Boiler Mail Bag Glass Case Iron Box Coffin Band Box Paper Bag Iron Bottle Rope Chair Tramp Chair." Houdini stabbed back in *Conjurers' Monthly*, for instance when the escape artist Brindamour claimed that he had performed the coldest and the longest manacled dives in history: through a hole chopped into the ice-covered St. Lawrence River, and from a Pennsylvania bridge into water 117 feet below. Over several issues of *Conjurers'*, Houdini exposed him as not only a liar but also a crossdresser. He had met this clone several years before, he said, performing as a ballerina. As proof he reproduced in the magazine one of Brindamour's old business cards: "Professor of Legerdemain/Teacher of Fancy Dancing."

With its medicine-show self-promotion and streetfighter taunts, *Conjurers' Monthly* was bound to offend, and did. Houdini got into an editorial war-of-words with the leading American magic journal, *The Sphinx*, published in Kansas City by Dr. A. M. Wilson (1854–1930). Had they not been competitors, Houdini might have enjoyed knowing Wilson, another of those Evanion-like genteel codgers with a long life in magic behind him. A thin, balding man with large eyeglasses, frosty mustache, and a benign countenance, Wilson had first appeared onstage before the Civil War, with Robert Heller. He entered the Methodist ministry, and through his work with the oppressed grew interested in medicine, becoming a practicing physician and a teacher in the Kansas City University Medical College. But he remained active in magic as publisher of *The Sphinx*, where he dispensed the eccentric sayings he called "Wilsonisms."

Even before becoming a magic editor himself, Houdini had reasons for resenting Wilson. *The Sphinx* rarely mentioned him, and once printed his name as "Haudini." At the same time it praised his copyists and applauded Howard Thurston for giving "the greatest magic show ever seen on the American stage." Houdini waited no longer than his second issue to take revenge. He related editorially that a New York magic dealer had told him he had sold twice as many copies of *Conjurers'* as of all the other magic journals combined. "Think of it," Houdini crowed to his readers, "the Baby Edition, the newest arrival, at one clean jump, should become the foremost paper of its class in the world." Wilson refused to be provoked into a public quarrel, but to colleagues he speculated on what had set Houdini off. He must have riled Houdini, he believed, in turning down his request to appear on the cover of *The Sphinx*. He dismissed him as someone "absolutely void of education and mental training," out just to gain attention and cash in: "he would betray his best friend for money or a page in a daily newspaper."

However closely magicians may guard secrets, many are quick to betray confidences, and the magic grapevine works fast. Wilson's private comments got back to Houdini and stung. As he usually did when someone questioned his goodheartedness, he replied in venom laced with schmaltz: "certain people state that I do all my good work for the advertisement that I may obtain out of it," he told a friend. "I know in my *heart of hearts* whatever good deeds I do is simply to help along people and poor unfortunates that I may meet in my life's journey."

Fuming already, Houdini exploded when Wilson published a letter from a Milwaukee reader, innocent-seeming but to him outrageous. The correspondent predicted that on the western vaudeville circuit, handcuff acts would soon be confined to the ten-cent houses. The remark only stated what many magicians were saying, that the handcuff escape had been cheapened by imitation and worn out by repetition. But Houdini took it to mean that he himself was on the skids, headed back to dime shows. In a lead editorial he blasted the elderly Wilson as a "dog in the manger," his retort smacking of nagging guilt about sons outstripping fathers:

> A man of middle or old age, with the beautiful calling that gives
> him the knowledge to render succor to the sick, helpless and dying
> ought not to allow envy and jealousy to stir him to besmirch his
> conscience and defile manhood and family in a useless endeavor to
> heap calumny upon the character of those of younger blood whom
> he sees passing him by with giant strides.

Understandably insulted, Wilson replied, in the next *Sphinx*, that he had thought nothing of printing the letter about ten-cent western theaters. Although Houdini took it as "a personal allusion to himself" it referred to no one in particular. "I am sorry for him that money has become his god," Wilson added, "and self-conceit has caused him to idolize himself."

Wilson was not alone in this view. The Belgian magician Servais Le Roy (1865–1953) remarked that Houdini's "ego bordered on the incredible and was a source of wonderment." Reviewers had pounced on it from the beginning of Houdini's career, and still did: he "makes an introductory speech telling how good he is," the *New York Telegraph* complained, "and you wonder why he doesn't . . . get on about his business of breaking out of handcuffs." A crude self-infatuation had become evident in Houdini's personal life too. Now or not long after, he embossed his personal checks and some of his stationery with a profile portrait of himself. His signature was embroidered on his laundry bag. He named one of his dogs Eric, another Charlie Houdini, and a pet canary simply Houdini. (Franz Kukol got the point, naming his son Harry Houdini Kukol—as Houdini recorded in his diary.) The initials H or HH adorned his cufflinks, calling-card case, belt buckle, pajamas, and bathroom tiles. On some notes for tricks he drew out the meaning of the initials, writing beside them "Champion of the World."

But Wilson's view of Houdini's self-worship left out part of the picture. In the escape business, as the Amazing Randi put it, "if you are not an egotist, you are a failure." What but a megalomaniacal brassballed self-assurance could have dragged Houdini inside a riveted boiler or to the depths of the Mississippi River? His grandiosity was necessary to his success in another way as well, putting him mentally beyond reach of the youthful poverty and failure that kept threatening to pull him back into its orbit. And he could be playful about it, as he was in answering the questionnaire in an autograph book of Bess's:

> *What characteristic do you admire most in a man?*
> Bashfulness
> *What do you consider, is your best quality?*
> My hatred for Publicity

"[I]t wasn't an unpleasant ego," a friend remarked. "It wasn't at all, because he saw through it himself." Depending on the circumstances, Houdini's I-Am-Who-Am could be vicious or self-mocking. Or mystifyingly both: one hardly knows which way to read his statement that "with due modesty, I can say that I recognize no one as my peer."

The editorial war between *Conjurers'* and *The Sphinx* continued. Ex-Methodist minister Wilson told other magicians that Houdini went around calling him an SOB and saying he had a little black book listing three hundred married women with whom he, the minister, "was holding criminal relations as an adulterer and fornicator." Wilson also warned the secretary of the Society of American Magicians (SAM) that, in having undertaken some work for the group, Houdini was scheming to lure the society into declaring *Conjurers'* its official journal. He may have been right. Houdini recorded in his diary that during a "very stormy" meeting of the SAM, he asked the members to do just that. The unexpected rebuff made him groan: "not one stood up for me." He announced his response in the next issue of his magazine, in one icy sentence: "Harry Houdini has resigned from the Society of American Magicians, and is no longer a member."

The SAM's lack of support may have influenced Houdini's decision to suspend *Conjurers' Monthly* in August 1908, after two years of publication; he was scheduled to return abroad at the same time. Wilson's *Sphinx* exulted, calling the demise "inevitable," since *Conjurers'* "was intended primarily as an advertisement for the owner." As usual Houdini did not forget. With the suspension of his magazine, he no longer asked magicians to choose between *Conjurers'* and *The Sphinx*. But he made it clear that they must choose now and forever between him and Wilson. When Thurston asked for a $250 loan, Houdini reminded him that when they were both playing Chicago, Thurston had invited Wilson to his show: "I informed him to go to Wilson for the money." He also told off the Viennese magic teacher Ottokar Fischer, an old friend who dared to publish an article in *The Sphinx*. "I wrote you that a certain Dr. Wilson was a bitter enemy of mine," he said. "As you have seen fit to accept his friendship by writing for his paper . . . you can consider our years of friendship at an end and I trust you will have the good sense NEVER TO WRITE TO ME OR APPROACH ME IN CASE I PLAY YOUR CITY."

Conjurers' Monthly figured in a weightier event than Houdini's scrap with Wilson. As the lead article in his first issue, Houdini published an essay he wrote entitled "Unknown Facts Concerning Robert Houdin [*sic*]." It argued that Robert-Houdin "was not original" and was "only a little above the average entertainer." Houdini expanded his charge into a pro-fusely-illustrated book, *The Unmasking of Robert-Houdin* (1908). This was the final form taken by the encyclopedia of magicians he had been planning since at least 1902. Initially he had conceived the book as a corrective to Thomas Frost's *Lives of the Conjurors*. But over the last few years he had come to see Robert-Houdin as the greater villain in falsifying the historical record of magic.

Robert-Houdin's fame rested in part on his use of electricity, mag-netism, and other technological means to produce some of the most cele-brated effects in magic history. He described many of them in his also celebrated *Memoirs of Robert-Houdin: Ambassador, Author, and Conjurer*—"the Shakespeare of Magic," Houdini called it. They included such classics as his flourishing orange tree, into one of whose mysteriously blooming fruits he sent a handkerchief that had been borrowed and van-ished; and his ethereal suspension, in which he levitated his six-year-old-son horizontally, supported by nothing more than a thin pole beneath the boy's bent elbow. In *The Unmasking*, Houdini denied Robert-Houdin any claim to have devised these and other effects identified with him. In chapter after chapter he traced their invention back to earlier magicians. By doing so he believed he had restored rightful credit to the originators, changed the outlines of the development of western conjuring, and uncloaked Robert-Houdin as "a mere pretender, a man who waxed great on the brainwork of others."

Houdini challenged his namesake's fatherhood on another basic ground as well, the style of his performance. In a section of his *Memoirs* entitled "My proposed Reforms," Robert-Houdin described the changes he had wrought in presentation practices of his day, substituting gas jets for candles, evening dress for eccentric costumes, bare Louis XV wood consoles for the floor-length tablecloths that invariably raised suspicions of a hidden assistant. These and other reforms, he wrote, constituted "a complete regeneration in the art of conjuring." But Houdini had learned otherwise. "The credit for this revolution in conjuring," he declared in *The Unmasking*, "belonged to Wiljalba Frikell." On this important point too, he believed he had transformed the historical record, moving the map of magic from Blois to Kötchenbroda. As a result of his research, he announced, "The master-magician, unmasked, stands forth in all the hideous nakedness of historical proof, the prince of pilferers."

Houdini was not through. He attacked Robert-Houdin also for lacking finesse in sleight-of-hand, for giving incorrect explanations of other performers' tricks, for failing to mention P. T. Barnum. And more. Robert-Houdin's "supreme egotism," he said, led him to give overblown paraphrases of his newspaper reviews and to falsify the story of his life in order to make it picturesque. The Frenchman's *Memoirs* was no more than a "volume of fiction"—and written not even by Robert-Houdin but by a Paris journalist.

This skinning-alive was for many magicians a sacrilege. David Devant protested to Houdini that he had "not only unmasked Houdin but . . . torn every rag from his back." Others objected that Houdini ignored Robert-Houdin's major improvements on earlier effects and overlooked his contributions to the psychology of deception. For many French magicians, Houdini's assault amounted to a national insult. The editor of the journal *L'Illusionniste* ridiculed his primitive knowledge of French, his use of "documents more or less apocryphal," his know-it-all Yankee tone: "I prostrate myself. I crawl before this American swaggerer who knows how to attain the truth no matter where."

While denying priority to Robert-Houdin, Houdini garlanded himself with it. In print, correspondence, and inscriptions on gift copies of *The Unmasking*, he again and again called his book "The First Authentic History of Magic Ever Published"—often doubly or triply underscoring the word "First." He saw it as a torchbearer, "a book with a mission," and lowered the price from $2 to $1, absorbing the loss so that he might reach "the great reading public." The dethronement of Robert-Houdin was his "sacred duty," so he paid to have the book translated into French and continued his research, intending to issue a revised edition "and prove my case 'still stronger.'" ("The older I get," he said ten years later, "the more I know Houdin never invented his feats.") As if *The Unmasking* were one of his inimitable escapes, he offered a challenge of $250 to anyone who could adduce its peer, "a book which has taken so much time, energy, travel and money, with such authentic data regarding real magical inventions."

Through "with," this was a safe bet. The King of Handcuffs had a rabbinic love of learning: "If his attention," a friend wrote, "had early been turned in the direction of scholarship, he would have achieved fame as a scholar." With a real scholar's curiosity and *Sitzfleisch*, Houdini peered and toiled to establish the facts about Robert-Houdin, traveling far to see a tombstone, buying up playbills, staying up until three in the morning writing. But he did so with no understanding of how scholars assemble, judge, and organize evidence. He worked from mounds of clippings and hundreds of bits of paper on which he (or his brother Leo) had jotted information and queries. He accepted as true most of what he found in print, and often paraphrased his sources inaccurately, garbled quotations, and cited wrong page numbers.

For establishing the priority of Robert-Houdin's effects, actually, few other human beings could have been worse suited than Houdini. His indifference to dates and facts encompassed virtually all but family anniversaries and house receipts. Photographs of himself that he dated 1901, for example, can be shown to have been taken in 1908. On various passport applications he completed for his tours of Europe and Russia, he gave his height hit-or-miss as five-four, five-five-and-a-quarter, five-six, or five-seven; his eyes diversely as brown, blue, and gray; his complexion as dark or fair; his year of birth as 1873 or 1874 (for the 1920 census he decided on 1876). Almost no date he supplied in a letter or newspaper article can be trusted.

Debate over *The Unmasking* continues to the present. Some magicians damn the book; others accept or reject its arguments piecemeal; none endorses it whole. Too many issues are involved to examine here, but it can be said at least that the book suffers from divided intentions and a shaky premise. Houdini began the work as an encyclopedia of magicians, and only later began taking aim at "the prince of pilferers." As a result, *The Unmasking* discusses dozens of conjurers who had nothing to do with Robert-Houdin, and seems to be always going off the subject. Houdini came to recognize that it hauled in two different directions: "The only mistake I made," he conceded, "was in calling my Book Houdin Unmasked. It ought to have been history of magic." His conclusion that Robert-Houdin's effects were "not original," moreover, is mostly hollow. It debunks what Robert-Houdin never boasted, at least not in his *Memoirs,* where the matter occupies maybe 4 pages spread across 436. On the more general question of whether Robert-Houdin was the first magician to modernize his appearance and stage settings, if he was not *the* first—as he may have been—he was certainly among the first. And even if he may be said to have claimed too much, Houdini allowed him nothing at all.

Clearly Houdini turned on Robert-Houdin the contempt he felt toward those who tried to expose or exploit himself. His very title seems shadowed by the headline of the Cologne newspaper article that reported his alleged police bribes: *"Die Entlarvung Houdinis,"* The Unmasking of Houdini. He also distinctly wrote the book as "THE CREATOR OF THE HANDCUFF SHOW," as he now sometimes signed himself. Early in his career he claimed no more than to be the first escape artist who challenged the police or sprang jail cells naked. But now he had come to regard himself as the originator of the handcuff act itself. "I created a *new line*," he said. "No one had ever trod the path of Escape until I cut the pathway to fame." In *The Unmasking* he cast Robert-Houdin as another Hilmar, Kleppini, or Brindamour, one of a historic breed who grew great by sniffing after pathbreakers and filching their inventions.

The enormity of Houdini's ego needs no further measuring here. But given his need to outpace all competitors, it seems no accident that he launched his quasi-parricide at a time when he had won a success that left no other rival than "the Father of Modern Magic." *The Unmasking* brought his ego into play on a new field as well, as if in the literary realm too the King of Handcuffs must win at least a fiefdom. His amassment of historical material, he felt no reluctance to admit, was "THE GREATEST COLECTION [*sic*] IN THE ENTIRE WORLD." He drew up for the preface a statement explaining that if he had committed some errors, well, Shakespeare made his Anglo-Saxon chieftain King Lear mention spectacles, and Tintoretto painted the biblical Children of Israel carrying guns. "Do not for a single second think," he added, "that I am egostical [*sic*] enough to class myself in the category of these celebrated men. My only object in quoting their various mistakes is to show that if the 'Great' can stumble, I as a new aspirant in the world of literature should not be judged too harshly for mistakes." He omitted the statement from the published book, remarkably though it managed to transform self-deprecation itself into personal glory. Other magnificos to whom he at one time or another compared himself include Alexander the Great, Galileo, and "in my poor little way, Columbus."

Finally, as to Houdini's slap that Robert-Houdin's "supreme egotism" led him to make his *Memoirs* "picturesque and interesting rather than historically correct," Houdini was right to the extent that some of the adventures Robert-Houdin recounts are sheer fictions. But he was even righter about Houdini. Now actively redesigning his past, he freely invented facts about his own origins. He began a sketch of himself in the 1909–10 *Magician Annual* with the statement, "My birth occurred April 6th, 1874, in the small town of Appleton, in the State of Wisconsin, U.S.A." He was born, of course, on March 24, 1874, in Budapest. But over the last few years he had been giving out the newly invented time and place, on his passports and elsewhere, both to honor his mother (who for some obscure reason observed his birthday on the sixth) and to shuck his immigrant past. Ever eager to link himself with celebrated persons and events, he later gave the date of the family's arrival in New York—July 3, 1878—as "on or about" the Fourth of July. In dedicating *The Unmasking* to his father, he identified him as "Rev. M.S. Weiss, Ph.D., LL.D.," awarding the rabbinic jack-of-all-trades learned degrees as so many fake medals for his academic tanktop.

Once, in writing a letter, Houdini wonderfully mistitled his book "Robert Houdini Unmasked." Indeed, with its many anecdotes illustrative of the author's selfless truth seeking, *The Unmasking* is a strangely self-condemning performance, unaware of its self-fawning and regicidal intent, haunted throughout by its own conclusion: "The master-magician, unmasked, stands forth in all the hideous nakedness of historical proof."

THE UPSIDE DOWN

Every conjurer who has in him, as all conjurers should have, the creative instinct of the artist, and aims therefore at putting something of himself into his work, must of necessity be to some small extent an amateur mechanic.

—PROFESSOR HOFFMANN, *Latest Magic*, 2ND ED. (1918)

All the achievements of the artist, his creations, etc., are in fact roundabout ways of conquering human objects —i.e. people—without admitting that this is his real aim. In order to save their self-esteem most artists pretend that their main aim is creation, and not the winning of applause, of consideration, of appreciation.

—MICHAEL BALINT, *Thrills and Regressions* (1959)

The first thing for the performer to ascertain is, if any member of the committee has followed the sea. . . .

—HOUDINI, *Magical Rope Ties and Escapes* (1921)

SIX

JANUARY–JUNE 1910

THE *MALWA*

Aboard the Peninsular & Oriental steamer *Malwa* in January 1910, the "Whistling Coon Contest" was held as follows. A lady was given an envelope containing a piece of paper with the name of a tune written on it. A gentleman across the deck raced toward her. He tore the envelope open, read the name, and whistled the tune in her ear. She wrote down the name as he raced back. Whoever finished first, won.

The draw of the game chose Houdini to whistle "Home Sweet Home," and he beat his partner, he said, "easily." That may have been consoling, for he had begun the voyage lying seasick all day on a deck chair, confirming what he always knew: "I am not even a fair weather sailor." Except during a smooth passage through the Suez Canal, he slept badly the whole trip. And as the *Malwa* bucked rough ocean off Ceylon, he still had two weeks to go before reaching western Australia, after a voyage of ten thousand statute miles from Marseilles.

Houdini had arrived on the *Malwa* unexpectedly. For sixteen months he had toured music halls, variety theaters, and circuses around Britain and the Continent, mostly offering an act stripped to two strong escapes, the straitjacket and the Milk Can. He had little reason to seek out Australia. His reappearance in England had been greeted as a return of the native—

"Houdini Home Again," the *Manchester Chronicle* announced—and rewarded with ecstatic notices acclaiming him the "greatest sensation of modern times." Moreover he had said publicly that he would never perform in Australia: should anything happen to his mother, it would take too long to return to her. On that ground even England was too far off. He brought Cecilia and Bess's mother there for two months, paying their passage and expenses, giving them each a five-dollar-a-day allowance, and getting idolatry in return: "The two mothers and Bess," he noted after a performance at Plymouth, "hear 'em cheer me for ten minutes."

Three considerations enough overcame Houdini's reluctance to bring him to the deck of the *Malwa*. The first was an offer from a leading Australian theatrical manager, Harry Rickards, under whose sponsorship Sandow had established schools of physical culture in Perth and Adelaide. In June 1909 Rickards offered Houdini twelve weeks' work in Australia, and agreed to pay him at booking-rate for the long time spent merely in travel. For someone who delighted, as Houdini recently had, in obtaining second-class French railroad tickets at third-class fares, the offer could not be refused. "I RECEIVE FULL SALARY WHILE ON BOARD THE STEAMER," he whooped to a friend, asking him to spread the news. Adding together what Rickards would pay him for performing and for traveling, he figured that for his twelve weeks onstage he would be making better than two thousand dollars a week, "the biggest salary he has ever paid to anyone so far." In reality Houdini was being paid a less-than-usual thousand a week for his time; or, if being paid two thousand a week for his work, in reality he was not being paid for his months of travel. But he saw the situation in terms of screwing a manager. The arrangement, he gloated, made Rickards pay him for "twelve weeks doing nothing."

A need to slow down also moved Houdini to endure the long, sick-making ocean journey. His two-escape act was compact but also draining, "the hardest on my body that I have ever attempted." And outside the theater he had brought English and continental audiences the manacled bridge jump he had introduced in America: handcuffed behind his back, he leaped from the balustrade of Berlin's Friedrichs Bridge into the dirty water of the Spree Canal, landing deep in mud; arms chained to his neck, plunged through stormy wind into the cold harbor of Aberdeen; double-cuffed, threw himself into the Seine from the roof of the Paris morgue. At times he felt as much burnt-out as tired. Returning to his hotel after a three-set New

Year's Eve performance, he found scant welcome: "poor old deaf landlady had a very bad meal," he recorded in his diary. "Went to bed after eating an apple and whatever was fit to eat left from tea." There were anxious moments too: he was present one night in a Paris theatrical office when an employee pulled a gun. Amid the cries and hysteria, he pushed the intended victim out of the room, at the risk of making himself the gunman's target. "Good thing he did not point it at me," he wrote later, "for I might have become real angry and might have got shot."

Houdini seems to have felt restless as well, if that is one meaning of his several shopping sprees. In his recent enthusiasm for paintings, he visited not only art galleries and museums but also major London and Paris auction houses, such as Christie's, bidding on important canvases that usually sold for much more than he was willing to pay. Although he acquired works by Teniers and Hogarth, he was no connoisseur. From a Brussels dealer he bought at one swoop fifteen oil paintings, unidentified but framed. Fancying the works of a ninety-year-old British academic painter, W. P. Frith, he bought two and visited the old man at his home. When Frith denied having painted them, Houdini allowed him to destroy the canvases by cutting the female subjects' throats. He also bought himself an expensive eighteen-carat gold chain and, for Bess, a gold thimble and solid silver case, to complement her ever-increasing dresses and hats. "Her trunks full to overflowing," he noted in Paris. "She has no worries."

Whatever its price in seasickness, life on the *Malwa* gave Houdini a change of routine and new things to see. Stopping in Port Said, putting up at the Continental Hotel, and getting himself a white tropical suit—"my Ice Scream suit," he nicely said—he went to see street magicians perform cups and balls, one of the oldest effects in magic, and among the most difficult to do well. To his disappointment, the Egyptians worked "very raw," stealing loads from their loose blouses with a liberty no European magician would be allowed. Worse, they all used the same cups, spoke the same English patter, and produced the same chicks for a finale: "I believe they have one school and all go there." Back on the *Malwa*, crossing the Indian Ocean, he and Bess danced at a costume ball, Bess as a fairy queen. For the first time in their marriage, she fainted. He picked her up and carried her to bed: "she danced with the Captain," he explained later, venting what sounds like jealousy, "who danced only one way." When the *Malwa* touched Colombo, Ceylon, they got off and hired a native-drawn rickshaw to see the sights, which included another dress for Bess to buy.

The *Malwa* itself carried the most compelling reason for Houdini's trip. Boxed in its hold lay an even more luxurious purchase than his gold chain and fifteen framed paintings. It was a Voisin biplane with a sixty-horse-power ENV engine, in which he intended to become the first person in Australia to fly.

Unlike his dabbling at art collecting, aviation was for Houdini a made-for-each-other passion. His career coincided with the technological and commercial revolution of the late-nineteenth and early-twentieth centuries, a career inconceivable without the modern corporation, the transcontinental railway system and vestibule passenger train; the mass-circulation newspaper; the new automobile, linotype machine, moving picture, and typewriter; not to mention the Bean Giant handcuff and the organized urban police department. For him, escapable milk cans belonged in part to this world of scientific breakthrough and amazing invention. He often advertised himself as an inventor, working on locks and handcuffs as tirelessly, he said, "as Stephenson building the first locomotive, as Edison bringing to view the telephone, as Marconi revealing the wireless telegraph." Among such innovations, nothing seemed more astounding than the new ability to fly. Aviation held for Houdini the allure not only of risk, competition, and prestige, but of miracle. There was for him, as he wrote, "magic in flight."

Houdini's firsthand introduction to aeronautics seems to have come in 1909, an *annus mirabilis* that saw the first powered ascents in Canada, Austria, Sweden, Rumania, Turkey, Portugal, and Russia. He was in England on July 25, when Louis Blériot made the first flight across the English Channel, without compass or instruments—a feat of aviation unrivaled in public excitement until Lindbergh crossed the Atlantic eighteen years later. "It was the talk of the world," Houdini wrote, "and made history." He claimed to have been present at the first great international air meet, held at Rheims from August 22 to 29. The claim may have amounted to no more than arriving in America "on or about" July 4, since in order to attend the meet he would have had to make a quick trip between engagements in England—possible, but a rush. If he did go, he witnessed such pioneer aviators as Henri Farman and Glenn Curtiss setting then breaking new records every day for speed, distance, and endurance. Financed by the great champagne houses of the region, the meet put on more than thirteen hundred flights. The final day drew two hundred thousand paid entries to the aerodrome, an estimated one hundred thousand more spectators looking skyward from hills outside the course. These and many other landmark events in 1909–10—the first flights by night, through snowstorms, with several passengers, across the Alps—confirmed worldwide expectations that the airplane would soon transform human life.

How and when Houdini purchased the Voisin biplane he was bringing with him to Australia is uncertain. As usual he told the story several ways. In one he said he bought the plane during the Rheims meet, after seeing the racing-car driver Henri Rougier pilot it effortlessly. He had come near getting a Curtiss biplane, of the kind in which Curtiss won the twenty-five-thousand-franc Rheims award for speed (47.1 miles per hour). But the Curtiss seemed less safe than Rougier's Voisin, and, Houdini said, "I was but a timid bird, and I wanted to take no chances at the start." So he bought the Voisin, and with it hired the winner of the mechanics' race at Rheims, a Frenchman named Antonio Brassac, "the greatest mechanic on the field." In a contrary story, however, he placed the purchase in Hamburg, after seeing a flight by the German aviation pioneer Hans Grade, who in 1909 carried the world's first piece of airmail. Inspired to have his own flying machine, Houdini bought the Voisin in Hamburg for five thousand dollars, he said, as being "the only purchasable airplane on the continent." What is certain is that he did somewhere hire Brassac, and bring him along on board the *Malwa*, and that in Hamburg he took his first lessons on the biplane.

Houdini's introduction to flying proved difficult and frustrating. Performing twice nightly during a two-month stay at Hamburg's cabaretlike Hansa Theater, he went mornings to an army parade ground outside the city, where his Voisin sat in a rented shed. Taxis to the place were hard to find and, edgy perhaps, he nearly got into a fistfight with a cabdriver who insulted him, whom he ended up suing. He was in some pain, too, having just undergone minor surgery. Years of yanking the lower strap of a straitjacket through his crotch had left a "bad spot" on his backside that had to be cut open. And when he finally assembled the Voisin, its engine quit. A day or so later, when he got the engine running, brisk November winds made flying impossible. One clear, windless morning he piloted the biplane up several feet, but it nosed down, and the propeller broke "all to hell." He waited two weeks for a replacement from Paris, which arrived in more bad weather. When he did at last make a flight, on November 26, it apparently lasted a minute and a half at most, barely long enough for the fifty or so spectators to notice the name painted in block capitals on sidepanels of the wings and tail: HOUDINI.

Houdini continued his flying education when he reached Paris just after New Year's Day 1910, readying himself for the trip to Australia. With Brassac he toured the Voisin factory on January 3, viewed the latest improvements and bought extra parts for the plane and its motor. Next day he visited the aviation grounds at Chalon, where he watched admiringly as passengers were taken aloft by two leading French aviators: Hubert Latham, a risk-all chainsmoker who had recently completed the first overland flight in Germany; and Henri Farman, who won the endurance prize at Rheims by staying airborne just over three hours. "They certainly are fliers," he told his diary. Chalon provided some sobering sights as well: Houdini saw a female pilot, Madame Laroche, smash up her Voisin by flying it into a tree. He met the prize-winning Belgian pilot Charles Van den Born, who the following year would make the first flight in Asia. "He is going to Australia with a machine," Houdini recorded. "Is a bit sore on me, looks on me as a rival." Perhaps inspired or worried, he set out next day to practice taxiing his Voisin at a field used by Latham and Farman, but was fogged in.

On January 6 Houdini left for Marseilles, where he planned to haul his plane in large crates aboard the *Malwa*, bound with stops at Port Said, Colombo, and the Fiji Islands for the Antipodes. Brassac reached the train only thirty seconds before it left, and forgot to bring a spare part that was packed and ready to be taken along. "I gave him hell," Houdini noted. Considering that Houdini was not well trained, and was entering a race in which the competition was practiced, intense, and no less daring than he, there was more to worry about than spare parts. He acquired (and presumably read) a pamphlet entitled "Rigid Stable Aeroplanes," and he took out a twenty-five-thousand-dollar life insurance policy—the first, he claimed, ever written for an airplane accident. "Hope," he wrote in his diary, "all will be well with me and my machine."

DIGGERS REST

On February 6 the *Malwa* reached Australia, a sunlit continent, not yet developed. After docking in Adelaide, Houdini, Bess, and Brassac took a train for the four-hundred-mile trip to Melbourne, then a city of broad streets and flat uninhabited spaces, with a population of six hundred thousand. Setting up the Voisin proved costly and troublesome. To his annoyance, Houdini had to put up a duty of about $750 on the plane, refundable when he left. Then the machine had to be borne to the aviation ground at Diggers Rest, some twenty miles from the city. He bought a forty-foot-square tent to house it, and motored out from Melbourne over the next weeks as Brassac began unpacking and assembling the parts and testing the engine, in brainbaking heat. "Hottest day I ever lived," Houdini wrote on February 20. "Must have been 119 in the shade and the wind was scorching. Drank enough water to float a rowboat." He discovered that he had a rival at Diggers Rest—not the Belgian Van den Born but a Melbourne garage owner, Ralph Banks. Banks had imported a plane built by the Wright brothers, installed it in another tent on the field, and was also planning to attempt the first flight in Australia.

While readying the Voisin, Houdini performed in Melbourne. He promoted his Australian debut by leaping from the city's Queens Bridge into the Yarra River, bringing out a crowd estimated at twenty thousand. Several people were nearly killed by a taxicab, and in the crush of straw-hatted men and sunbonneted women straining to see over the bridge, many fell—a "terrible mob," Houdini called it. Clad in a bright blue bathing costume and twenty-five pounds of chain and padlocks, he dived twenty feet from the parapet, head first, into the muddy Yarra, his eyes open all the time to watch for sharks. Billed as "the Great Mysteriarch," he drew large crowds also to the opera house, where he did his straitjacket–Milk-Can turn and revived Metamorphosis. In trying to protect the Milk-Can Escape, he had taken out a British patent on the effect, with diagrams for four different methods. Yet when he passed through Paris en route to Marseilles, he saw his pirated invention performed at a circus. And he no sooner arrived down under than he learned, joltingly, that an Australian bandit was doing it in Sydney.

More important at the moment was the new title Houdini aimed at and held in view. "I stand a chance," he wrote home, "of being the *First Flier* in this country." Once the Voisin was set up at Diggers Rest, and the ground cleared of stones and other obstacles, he kept to a fatiguing schedule of car trips there before and after his performances. Early morning was the best time for practices, the air calm and interruptions unlikely. Sometimes he left

Melbourne around four in the morning to get to the field early. Other times he left the city near midnight, then put up at the field in his tent or under the Wright machine. One night it rained so hard that he did not arrive at Diggers Rest until two, and then the car became mired. He hired a chauffeur named Jordan to transport him in a four-cylinder Enfield. To redeem the time he tried once more, under Jordan's instruction, to learn how to drive. He succeeded at least once in cranking the automobile to a start ("I never could do it before"), and once in driving almost the whole distance from Melbourne and back.

Conditions at the airfield worked on Houdini's nerves too. One night a poisonous tiger snake turned up near where he slept, and had to be killed with a stick. He woke at all hours, and felt the effects: "My eyes are getting weak, think from loss of sleep." Because of strong winds at the field, practices sometimes had to be canceled and were often brief. When his rival, Ralph Banks, attempted an early-morning flight despite vigorous gusts, on March 1, the Wright plane rose twelve or fifteen feet, swerved, and crashed, flipping over. Banks survived with a black eye and torn lips. Houdini helped pick up what remained of the plane, hoisting a long piece over his shoulder. "I sincerely hope," he wrote that day, "to make the flight inside of a week."

Houdini's hopes much depended on Antonio Brassac. Armed with oilcan and spanner, mechanics looked after such essential tasks as cleaning valves, changing spark plugs, and starting the engine. Although Brassac's name does not appear in the standard histories of early flight, Houdini attributed a distinguished history to him: instructor of Farman, builder of Blériot's Channel-crossing plane, mechanic to Rougier (allegedly the Voisin's previous owner). He prized Brassac's help and gave him a hefty "bribe" to keep him from returning to Europe. "No mother," Houdini was reported saying, "could tend her child more tenderly than Brassac does my machine." In fact Brassac lived in the tent with the Voisin, and may have built the plane himself. In surviving photographs he appears in grease-monkey's coveralls, a serious, dark-haired young man with a dark mustache, shorter even than Houdini, perhaps no more than five four. His temper, on the other hand, was said to be colossal. In French or his limited English he cursed the Australian winds nonstop, muttering, "*Beaucoup de vent*" or shouting "*Cabre, cabre!*"—the motion of a dangerously rearing horse that, in a windtossed airplane, might mean disaster.

On March 18, after more than a month's tinkering, the Voisin stood ready to explore the mysteries of air. Simple in basic design, it can be visualized as a familiar biplane, except that the long, square-tipped wings were joined at the ends and near the cockpit by vertical cloth-on-wood panels. The uncovered, skeletal wood fuselage between the wings extended to the tail, similar in design to the wings. Technically this kind of biplane construction was "cellular." The tail consisted of one, and the wings of four, rectangular cells or boxes, much like box kites, covered with sheeting used in hotair balloons. The wings rested on two bicycle wheels, with strong springs to minimize the shock of landing; the tail on two smaller wheels; with a still smaller guard wheel in front so that if the plane nosed to earth it might roll instead of smashing. The slightly arched, ribbed wings seem to have been thirty-three and a half feet long and six and a half wide, with a gap between them of around five feet. The plane was driven by an eight-cylinder, sixty-horsepower ENV engine and an eight-foot aluminum propeller capable of twelve hundred revolutions per minute. ("ENV," a corruption of *en V*, merely meant V-shaped.) The Voisin weighed some twelve-hundred pounds. With its boxy double wings connected to its boxy tail by a fragile-looking open framework, it seemed, when aloft, both lumbering and spidery.

The plane worked fairly simply. The pilot sat upright between the wingstruts, the propeller and engine behind him, a driving wheel in front. Pushing or pulling the wheel governed a simple elevator—a horizontal slat on the nose that lifted or lowered the plane. Turning the wheel pulled cords that moved a stiff canvas rudder in the tail, for going left or right. As the author of a 1910 book on aviation summed up the operation: "The pilot of a Voisin flyer has only to do two things, change the angle of the horizontal rudder to rise or fall, and incline the vertical rudder in the tail to make a turn." In starting up, the plane was secured to a post or held down by a squad of helpers. The propeller was turned over by hand to draw fuel into the cylinders. Then, with the throttle open, the propeller was whirled again, blasting the engine alive with a great roar and explosion of grayblue smoke. The plane strained and vibrated as the dynamometer approached the 160 kilos necessary to fly. When the rope was unmoored or the helpers let go, holding their caps to their heads, the shaking junglegym of sticks, cloth, and piano-wire bounded off as if unleashed.

Aviators considered the Voisin a stable plane, at least in calm skies. But it allowed the pilot to maneuver little more than up and down, and beyond moving the rudder, no way of righting the wings in a gust. Its heavy weight made for relatively slow ascents, jerky descents, and ponderous turns. With airplane design changing rapidly, it was becoming obsolete, and within a year or so would be discontinued. And it was liable to every kind of aviating mischance that could mean serious injury or death, and often did—the propeller might snap, the engine might fail, a sharp turn might collapse a wing, the pilot might lose control.

Houdini made three flights in the Voisin on the morning of March 18, a Friday. How he dressed for the event is unknown, but in photographs taken at Diggers Rest he sometimes wears a business suit and leather pilot's cap with goggles (the plane having no windshield), sometimes a fashionable outfit of golf knickers and tweed cap, visor turned rakishly backward. Shortly before eight o'clock, the plane was taken out of its tent onto the field, a shallow basin offering, in Houdini's description, "at least five miles circular to move about in and only two trees in the whole spot"—although he favored taking off from a far slope in order to clear them. His first spin was simply a test of the wings. Taxiing around the field before about a dozen spectators, he noticed a problem with the elevator, which Brassac corrected by adjusting the rudder.

With Houdini back in the pilot's seat Brassac counted, "*Un, deux, trois,*" and twisted the propeller. The engine growling, Houdini released the clutch, setting the plane rolling at just over thirty miles an hour. When he had traveled forty or fifty yards he raised the elevator, sending the gawky machine, for the first time, about twenty-five feet into the air of Australia. Sweeping around in a narrow circle, he lowered the elevator and touched ground again, smoothly, in a minute. By one account Brassac became so excited that "he forgot to speak French, and rattled off English terms of endearment to the great bird."

The follow-up trial went less smoothly. Houdini made a complete turn of the field, covering a mile or two. But in landing he forgot to straighten the elevator. The plane would have crashed except for the guard wheel, which touched down first so that the plane ran along the ground for a distance on its nose, tail in the air, Houdini partly out of his seat, ready to jump out from in front of the screaming propeller. But he straightened the elevator, bringing the plane on its wheels again, when helpers pulled it to.

Houdini's third flight on the eighteenth was perfect, and it lasted about three and a half minutes. As the plane lifted it passed over rises and stone fences, making a circle of more than two miles and reaching an altitude of about a hundred feet—a height he later said he did not notice in concentrating on the position of the elevator. Gliding down, he came to rest again within twenty feet of the starting point. His forehead, by one account, was beaded with perspiration, his hands wet.

But Houdini left Diggers Rest elated. To testify formally to his record-making flights, he secured a statement signed by Brassac; Ralph Banks; the chauffeur, Jordan; and several others. A reporter who accompanied him on the drive back to Melbourne asked what he felt during the trials. Houdini revealed that when taxiing his every muscle felt taut, but that as soon as he was aloft, the tension vanished and he felt a sense of ease. ("Never in any fear and never in any danger," he recorded later in his diary.) When he landed on the nose wheel, his only conscious thought had been whether or not to jump. He leveled off the plane without thinking—unconsciously, as one righted a bicycle: "You've got to do it," he had learned, "before it happens." But what he felt most of all was the high of the new century's new magic. "I know what it is to fly in real earnest," he said, delighted. "I can fly now."

Under such headlines as HOUDINI FLIES, the Melbourne press ran photographs of Houdini's ascents, calling them "a red letter day in the history of aviation in Australia." But like many other 'firsts' in the history of aviation, including that of the Wright brothers, Houdini's first-flight-in-Australia was not clearcut. Five hundred miles to the northwest, near Sydney, a twenty-year-old automobile racer named Fred Custance had taken up a Blériot monoplane on Thursday, March 17—one day before Houdini's trials in the Voisin. Lifting off in the darkness of 5 A.M., Custance made three one-mile circles in five and a half minutes, at an altitude, however, of only about a dozen feet. With daylight he took off again, hoping to establish a height record. But he lost control of the plane at fifty feet and crashed, smashing the undercarriage and breaking the propeller. Whether this qualiifies as 'flight' is arguable. Custance was not a trained pilot and may not have flown so much as hopped. Moreover, the Federation Aéronautique Internationale (FAI)—a world regulating and licensing organization set up in 1909—had established rules for officially recording flights that included codified witnessing procedures. Houdini's witnessed and attested flights met the FAI's criteria; Custance's did not. No photos, either, were taken at any time during Custance's attempt.

For Houdini, of course, matters of priority counted not much less than living and dying. "I want to be first," he told a reporter in Australia, "I vehemently want to be first . . . it is all I ask." But how much and how soon he knew about Custance is unclear. Several Australian newspapers reported the young man's flights, and some of Houdini's private comments indicate that he may have read the accounts. "I am the first aviator in Australia," he wrote to a friend, but then added, in French, a sort of 'at least': "*Sans contest, je suis la premier prestidigitateur qui vole*" (I am, uncontestably, the first magician who flies). In his diary he wrote, in block capitals: "FIRST REAL FLIGHT IN AUSTRALIA"—perhaps an acknowledgment that Custance had flown before him, but not really.

What most vividly suggests that Houdini suspected his claim might be tainted is his hectic determination to reinforce it. On March 19, only one day after his ascents, he returned to Diggers Rest to fly again. Owing to wind and minor engine problems he managed to get up for only twenty seconds. He returned again the next day. News of his exploits had spread, and he was met by sixteen cars bringing spectators from Melbourne, by country folks on horseback and in buggies, and by others drifting to the field. This time more than a hundred people witnessed his trials. A man named McCracken was also present to act as timekeeper, stopwatch in hand, recording the duration of the flight and calling it out in minutes to the onlookers.

The morning was cloudy. Brassac considered the breeze too strong for flying. But Houdini defiantly rolled again to the farther slope of the Diggers Rest basin, rose, bounced down on a hop, then sailed a few hundred yards close to the ground and stopped, airborne just twenty-six seconds. No giving in. He took off again from the same slope, quickly rising to forty feet. In taking its first corner the plane was shaken by a puff of wind, but completed its first circle, to applause (which Houdini afterward said he had not been able to hear). In making a second circle the Voisin tilted tail-down to a nearly vertical position—Brassac's dreaded "*Cabre, cabre!*" As the *Argus* reported the moment:

> "Ah! the danger," murmured Brassac. But his troubled face soon cleared as Houdini righted the plane and sailed on serenely.
> "Two minutes," counted Mr. A. M'Cracken. . . . Houdini came round in beautiful style to commence his third circle.

"Look out for the tree!" came a warning shout from a spot in the centre of the basin, where half the crowd had gathered beneath another tree. . . . The flying man did not hear the shout, but he saw the tree, and he soared up to a height of some 70 ft. . . . Then it was seen that the plane was about to take the ground. It came down in a long, swift glide, and just as it reached the earth, a treacherous gust canted up the right wing. The point of the left wing grazed the earth, and threw up a little cloud of dust. A big "Ah!" went up, but Houdini straightened the plane, and in two seconds was afoot, bowing acknowledgment of congratulations. Mr. M'Cracken's timing of the flight (3 min. 45½ sec.) was confirmed by several other gentlemen who had motored to the field.

The flight of nearly four minutes was, Houdini said, "undoubtedly the best that I have made." He later admitted he had wanted to stay up longer, but the engine seemed powerless to churn through the wind. After replacing one or two wires that had broken in the shock of landing, he and his crew set to work tuning up the engine, intending to fly again later in the day. Some yachtsmen who arrived, however, predicted increasingly strong winds, and the plane was shut down.

But only for a day. With his first-flight record in doubt, Houdini tried the following morning, a Monday, for a distance and endurance record. Taking off almost at the stroke of seven, before some thirty spectators and a timekeeper, the plane fought tricky winds throughout. Just the same, halfway into his second circle of the airground, Houdini went for broke. So far he had kept within the basin. But now he sailed off into the open countryside, swooping over walls, fences, trees, and housing tents, then sweeping back over the waterhole near the flying ground, the plane wavering and then tilting slightly, but dangerously, upward in the crosscurrents. Brassac began waving a red flag to bring Houdini down. But the Voisin seesawed on in the wind, rising to a hundred feet then dropping in long swoops to twenty or thirty. Houdini made a fine landing, however, sliding down in a series of slants and coming to rest, lightly, almost where he had taken off.

Houdini had covered about six miles in seven minutes, thirty-seven seconds, rising higher, going farther, and staying up longer than he ever had before. It was not enough for him. When the handshakes and congratulations ended, he had the Voisin's engine ignited again, "Just for a little practice in rising and descending," he said. This time he took the plane up fast to well above one hundred feet, making one faultless circle in a minute and a half before coming down, "never slewing or canting an inch," one newspaper reported, so that "it was impossible to tell when flying ended and rolling began." Upon landing he announced that on the first calm day he would try to stay aloft for half an hour. The day's work, the *Argus* commented, "fully established his claim to be considered the first successful aviator in Australia."

ROSEHILL

With its grimy, narrow, wandering streets, Sydney resembled Manchester and the many other manufacturing cities Houdini had played in the north of England. Opening there on March 28 for a six-week engagement, he gave a short speech at the theater, saying he planned to retire in two years and probably devote himself to aviation. The audience cheered his announcement that he planned to make an ascent in Sydney. And they loudly applauded when he added the hope that after his reputation as the Handcuff King had been forgotten, he would be remembered in Australian history as "the first man to fly there in a machine heavier than air."

But the most enduring impression Houdini left on Sydney may well have been that of his near-disasters. The first came with his promotional jump into the municipal bathing area of Woolloomoolo Bay. Cuffed and chained, he attempted the feat after climbing a ladder to the second platform of a high-dive tower, where he stood thirty-one feet above eighteen-foot-deep water. (He later gave the height as eighty-six feet.) Motioning to an assistant in a punt below, he joshed, "If I don't come up in two minutes, come down for me," then stepped to the edge of the platform. After taking a half dozen deep breaths he bent slightly forward and leaped outward. But instead of plummeting feet first, as always, he was angled forward by a strong wind, a human "*Cabre, cabre!*" He came down face first. "When he hit the water," the *Sydney Herald* reported, "his face appeared to strike the surface a terrific blow." He came up after forty-five seconds holding the unlocked fetters before the yelling crowd, and managing to conceal his pain, at least from the *News* reporter, who said he "did not appear to be in the least distressed." In fact the whop gave him two black eyes and knocked teeth loose.

Houdini's mishaps in the Voisin, however, were visible to all. Horseracing in Australia being virtually a national sport, he rented a suitable flying field at Sydney's Rosehill racetrack. Although he built a special straightaway for takeoffs, this was a working course surrounded by a wooden rail, with fences and water jumps for steeplechase racing. He made his first attempt on April 18, a windless day with a morning frost still on the ground. Attendants holding the tail fell down as the throbbing Voisin shot from their hands up the prepared track. The plane rose, pitched violently left, righted itself, then descended again after making only a few hundred yards. It was taken back to the starting point and set out again on its takeoff, but refused to lift. In making a third attempt the Voisin bounced ominously, like a stone skimming the water, took off, again lurched violently left, righted itself, lurched left again, and came down in a rush. The left side of the elevator hit the ground so hard that Houdini was thrown from his seat, landing a distance away on his hands and knees.

Hundreds of spectators showed up at Rosehill for Houdini's follow-up efforts over the next few days. But strong winds and then horse-training sessions kept the Voisin grounded. Probably fearing the delays would cost him his audience, Houdini advertised his trials in the press, with an extra come-on: "Afternoon tea for the ladies will be served in the Pavilion by the hostess, Mrs. Houdini." The jamboree kept Bess and her assistants busy pouring tea, distributing food from hampers, and washing countless dishes. But the plane now developed serious engine trouble, refusing to pull the critical 160 kilos. One day, as Brassac worked on the cooling system, some connecting tubes slipped off, spurting boiling water that scalded his shoulder and thigh. And when Houdini made a new attempt on Friday morning, April 22, he got up to about 100 feet but floundered in turbulence and fell rapidly, the Voisin smacking on rough ground that broke off one of its wheels—justifying his care in having brought spare parts from the Voisin factory in Paris. With his remaining time in Australia running out, the engine trouble defied the efforts of five men working on it for a full week, "until I almost gave up in despair."

When the engine was finally repaired, it provided, during a flight of only two and three-quarter miles, a stomachturning airborne rollercoaster. On Sunday, May 1, some five hundred spectators showed up at Rosehill, watching as Houdini took a drink of tea and milk and climbed into the Voisin. The engine may have been restored to better-than-new working order, for one paper compared its roar to the sound of "a thousand maniacs released." The plane leaped to 20 feet, then suddenly dipped, speeding groundward at close to forty miles an hour. "The public gasped," according to the *Morning Herald*, "for it seemed as if the aviator were rushing to certain destruction." Houdini managed to rise, soaring to an altitude of 150 feet. But here, side-on crosscurrents threw the Voisin on a sensational tilt. Climbing almost perpendicularly, Houdini gunned the plane out of the danger zone and, turning into the wind, stabilized the wings. But as he continued his tour of the track, a gust tossed the plane downward until, as spectators gasped, it came within 3 feet of some tents on the field.

Gathering speed, Houdini slowly rose again and, after another circuit of the field, started down. As he touched ground and cut off the ignition, he found the Voisin rolling fast toward a racing hurdle that had accidentally been left on the course. Raising the elevator, he caused the shut-down plane, astonishingly, to bound over the hurdle. And somehow he was able in about a dozen more yards to halt. Some of the crowd rushed him, lifted him on their shoulders, and brought him to Brassac, who called the flight "the most sensational" he had seen. As reported in the gaudiest account of the test, "Men tossed up their hats; women grew hysterical and wept for sheer excitement . . . mid deafening cheers and salvos." The death-defying loop-the-loop pleased Houdini no less: "I made the flight of my life."

Measured by the current state of aviation, Houdini's achievements were unremarkable. By the time he flew in Melbourne, the world altitude record stood at more than four thousand feet, and Farman had stayed in the air longer than four hours, covering 144 miles. Still, in his overweight and underpowered Voisin, Houdini had performed aeromagic for thousands, probably, of Australians, who for the first time saw a human being ride the sky, a prince of the air. His efforts were honored in a ceremony at the Sydney Town Hall, where the Australian Aerial League awarded him a trophy depicting Australia and two eagles. The chairman roused three cheers for him as the first person to fly on the continent. No one referred to young Custance, whose claims, Houdini wrote a few months later, were "proven untrue." So he could take for himself "the glory of having been the first successful Australian aviator." With the small qualification—"successful"—that seems just.

Instead of clinching Houdini's right to the title, the trophy further confuses it. The date inscribed is March 16, one day before Custance's flight and two days before Houdini's. Houdini may have had the date engraved later, falsifying it in order to establish his priority. Or the Aerial League may simply have misdated his flight. An Adelaide newspaper complained that the league gave the trophy to the wrong person, but newspapers in Sydney, where Custance's flight had occurred, granted Custance no claim and described Houdini's flights as firsts, without question. The Aerial League published a photograph of Houdini with the Voisin in their pamphlet "Wanted at once! An Aerial Defence Fleet for Australia," above the caption, "The Birth of Flight in Australia." And one of the important early books on aviation, Claude Grahame-White's *The Aeroplane: Past, Present, and Future* (1911), does not mention Custance but names Houdini in its list of "The World's Airmen," identifying him as "Music-hall artiste. Bought a Voisin biplane, and has made flights upon it."

Houdini's schedule in Sydney left little time for sightseeing or social life, but he did get to meet two men he admired. A lifelong boxing fan, he enjoyed being prominent enough to be introduced at ringside when he attended a fight. And over the years he noted in his diary when pugs such as Kid McCoy, a world-class light heavyweight, attended his shows. He sometimes bet on fights, too, and collected forty dollars when middleweight champion Stanley Ketchell, the savage "Michigan Assassin," won a record-book thirty-two-round rematch against the former champion, Joe Thomas. In Sydney, Houdini got to speak for two hours in his dressing room with Bob Fitzsimmons, a hard-punching old ring warrior, raised in New Zealand, who fought his last match at the age of fifty-two. Fitzsimmons told him that when he lost his heavyweight title to brawny Jim Jeffries at Coney Island in 1899, someone had drugged his bottles of White Rock water, so that he could not remember the second round. He also confided "a lot of dope" about James Corbett, and, with Bess present, reenacted how he knocked out Gentleman Jim for the heavyweight title in 1897. "Fitz rose and was going to land on me," Houdini recorded, "and Bess thought he was going to hit me and she screamed!!!"

In Sydney, Houdini also met William Fay, former manager and partner of the always-to-be-honored Davenport Brothers—in Houdini's view, his true progenitors. He was curious to know whether such once-famous men, in old age, had drifted into poverty, like Mayer Samuel Weiss, or prospered. Fay, he learned, had been with the Davenports in their rich heyday, had invested soundly in Australian real estate, and was now wealthy. Houdini got firsthand information about the brothers, planning to include "the real account" in a new book, tentatively titled "History Makers in the World of Magic." He hunted up the grave of William Davenport, who had died and been buried in Australia in 1877. It was badly neglected, and in his running battle with oblivion Houdini paid to have the stonework repaired and the grave planted with flowers.

Houdini made his last trip to Rosehill on May 3, not to fly but to watch the Voisin being crated. "Let Brassac cut it in half," he noted, puzzlingly, "so that it will pack smaller." He sent the machine for storage to England, having announced that he would fly there from city to city along his next music hall tour. Meanwhile he and Bess were scheduled to sail on May 11 from Brisbane back to the United States. "Pity I can't carry enough petrol to fly home with my good wife," he reflected. Aboard the *Malwa* he had lost more than twenty-five pounds to seasickness, so he said. And although he hated small ships his return passage was booked aboard the Canadian Pacific Line's *Manuka*, a "miserable wretched looking steamer" of only 4,500 tons. "I am certain that I will break all records for being sea sick," he wrote on the fourth. "I saw the steamer yesterday and am sick already." At least the *Manuka* was bound direct for the United States, by way of Vancouver; returning by way of England would drag out the ordeal another four weeks. And this way he could spend an extra month with his mother and family.

It was time to go home. What with the 3 A.M. awakenings, temperamental engines, and unseen hurdles, Houdini had not relaxed as he needed to. "Health in bad condition," he noted near the end of his stay in Sydney, "not having had much sleep for the past two months." Still up much of the night, he felt relieved to have the Voisin packed and out of the way, "else it would have given me nervous prostration." And all that on top of the challenges and manacled high dives, the daily grappling with straitjackets, locks, and chains. He gave the *Sydney Daily Telegraph* a glum reckoning of what he had accomplished in Australia: "I have done things which I rightly could not do, because I said to myself, 'you must'; and now I am old at 36."

Maybe, but in essence Houdini remained Houdini undiminished. Before leaving, he tossed his manager, Harry Rickards, for thirty pounds toward the cost of a berth, and won. Seventeen days out aboard the crowded *Manuka*, he joined in some deck games, entering the results in his diary at unusual length. He won the Swinging the Monkey game. He won the Skipping Rope contest too, having at it until a handkerchief tied to his ankle came loose, got entangled with the rope, and made him miss—but only after a prizewinning 439 successive jumps. Going three-for-three, he also won the appallingly-named "Whistling Coon Contest"—not surprising, since on the *Malwa* too he had easily raced across the deck before his partner-opponent could write down "Home Sweet Home." His diary does not mention which tune the draw of the game chose for him on the return trip. But it does contentedly declare the outcome: "I beat Bess out of her prize."

The voyage proved satisfying in another way as well, bringing the Birdman and the Aerial League trophy to New York in time to celebrate his mother's sixty-ninth birthday at a family kaffeeklatsch.

SEVEN

1910 — 1913

THE UNDERWATER BOX ESCAPE; THE CRAZY-CRIB AND WET SHEET ESCAPES; NEW CHALLENGES

H OUDINI CRISSCROSSED the Atlantic over the next three years, playing two nine-month tours of Great Britain and the Continent, broken by a yearlong tour and more relaxed summers in the States. In an ironic turn of his career, he made a selling-point out of not performing the feat that first made him famous. "NO HANDCUFFS," he advertised. The mushroom Handcuff Kings could go on sweating off armfuls of Plug 8s and Berliners. For himself, he let it be known, such escapes had become too easy. "I never do handcuffs," he said now, "always something ELSE."

But in leaving the field to his former rivals, Houdini tried to burn it down first. Copying his copyists, becoming as it were Hilmar's Hilmar, he exposed their techniques in a 110-page illustrated book entitled *Handcuff Secrets* (1910). This get-even volume appeared in U.S., British, and German editions, under the imprint of commercial publishing houses. In addressing the lay public, Houdini obviously hoped to demystify the handcuff escape act and destroy what audience remained for his clones. So that his readers could become "adepts in entertaining and mystifying their friends," he offered to teach them "the methods that can be, and have been, used to imitate my performances." At the same time he made it clear that Houdini's own secrets would remain unfathomed: "I shall not delve into the very deep intricacies of some of the great modern feats of handcuff manipulations, and jail-breaking, as accomplished by myself." Whatever its effect on the stage, the book made a stir with the law. German police forbade reproduction of Houdini's illustrations of lockpicks, as being helpful to burglars. The London *Times* reported that a copy of *Handcuff Secrets* was found at the home of two brothers who had broken into a laundry. The prosecutor at their trial observed that Houdini explained how to make skeleton keys: "I can hardly understand how such a book can be published by such well-known publishers as Messrs. Routledge," he protested. "It is a book on technical education in the art of thieving." The court deplored the release of *Handcuff Secrets* as "a wrong to the community."

Houdini had no trouble replacing handcuff escapes. Consider his clothing. "Houdini No Beau Brummel," one interviewer wrote, having found him in a shabby felt hat, "a large grease spot on the lapel of his coat and tiny hole in the knee of his trousers." In photographs of him taken off-stage, his readymade suits often seem wrong-sized, baggy, and creased; bits of string droop from his bulging pockets, his shirts are crumpled and stained, his fingernails dirty. His first biographer, Harold Kellock, wrote in cooperation with Bess herself, and reported that she had to steal his soiled underwear in the night to get him to change it.

Houdini's sloppiness was likely the outward expression of his inner distracted brooding on magic and escapes. Like Michelangelo, Beethoven, and some other slovenly geniuses of greater arts, his mind hummed with problems and solutions. "I have tried through many a sleepless night," he wrote, "to invent schemes to make an audience appreciate some worthy effort of mine." His eternal preoccupation is evident not only in his always-changing stage performances but also in his extensive memorandums and illustrations for routines, gags, new effects. A notion for an improvement:

> In fixing the self-tie rope, have one knot in it as a guide that goes on the left hand side. . . . When self-tie is on, put left hand in so that the knot is on top of left wrist. For self-tie, the left wrist must be tied with a slip rope.

A reminder of a suggestive possibility:

EVERY PACKAGE OF CORN FLAKES COMES WRAPPED IN A WAX
PAPER AND BEARS THE SIGNATURE OF W. E. KELLOGG

A piece of business, headed "Big Laugh":

> Plant in box, man and woman. Houdini asks committee to come
> on stage. Man starts to get up, woman pulls him back. Woman of a
> chatterbox type. Have the man try to get up two or three times, the
> woman scolding. If you wish to see this to a finish, have the man
> finally come up and the woman leave the theater.

Hundreds of such notes survive—written, typed, or scribbled in every
phase of thoughtful design and sudden inspiration on scraps of paper,
folded sheets, stationery from steamships, businesses, hotels in Des
Moines, Chicago, Savannah. In diagram after diagram, too, Houdini
sketched the mechanism of some new unthinkable escape: from a zinc-lined
box, soldered; a galvanized coffin filled with water; a nailed packing case
thrown over Niagara Falls.

None of these escapes ever got performed, although Houdini enough
developed a few to apply for patents on them. In 1912 he sought German
patents for a watertight chest on four legs, which would be locked and then
lowered into a larger chest, which would be filled with water and locked
too. The performer would thus be islanded, dry, inside the smaller chest,
but surrounded on all sides by the water in the outer box. Houdini's design
allowed him to escape from both boxes without damaging the locks—and
without becoming wet. He also applied for a patent on a sort of theatrical
deepfreeze (*Gefriervorführungsapparat*), a device by which he could be
frozen inside a block of ice yet walk away leaving the block whole—a miracle he would try to work out his entire life.

For his no-handcuffs tours at home and abroad Houdini devised and
introduced several major new escapes. In effect combining the underwater
manacle-release and the packing box, he got out of a wooden box while it
was submerged. He scheduled the premiere performance for Sunday
morning, July 7, 1912, at New York's East River. The pier was crowded to
suffocation—groups of boys clinging to piles, enough reporters present,
according to the *New York Times*, "to get out any New York daily." Houdini
and the box stood aboard a barge towed by a tugboat, accompanied by

assistants and by his brother Leo, carrying a just-in-case medical satchel. But the police refused to let the show go on, by one account because the city's blue laws forbade performances on Sunday. As he did with most other things that stood in his way, Houdini fixed that. He told the tug pilot to make for Governors Island in New York Harbor—federal property, lying outside the city's jurisdiction. As the barge pulled away, to "howls of disappointment from the shore," he began stripping down to a spotless white bathing suit.

With the tug moored at the island, a committee checked the box for secret springs or panels, and searched Houdini for tools. Spectators had been invited to bring their own restraints, and some double-lock, double-ratchet handcuffs and leg-irons were passed around to reporters for examination. With a movie cameraman filming the scene, Houdini was shackled and placed in the thick pine box. Measuring forty inches long, twenty-two wide, and twenty-four high, it was perforated with quarter-size holes that allowed air to enter, as well as water. It offered barely enough room for him in a sitting position, knees raised. The lid was stuck shut by thirty-six wire nails, the box bundled with heavy rope and nailed-on metal bands, export-packing style. Sewer pipes loaded with iron sash weights, some two hundred pounds' worth, were hung from the box to make it sink. With Houdini scrunched inside, the weird human package was shoved out onto some planks extending from the barge, and dumped into the harbor. Filling rapidly, it sank to the level of the sea, where it lay all but submerged, rocking, the lid showing occasionally in the gentle swells. The tug meanwhile had lowered a lifeboat, in which Houdini's assistants gripped a safety-rope that kept the box from floating away in the outgoing tide.

About a minute later, in a small splash beside the box, Houdini bobbed up. He was smiling, to applause from thousands of passengers aboard three ferryboats and the toots of two nearby tugs. Swimming back to the barge, he climbed into it up a rope, hand over hand. The box was hauled aboard with the aid of a spar and examined again, still girt by ropes and bands, the lid still nailed, the double-lock shackles lying inside, sprung open. The *Times* and other papers reported Houdini's new escape in huge headlines; *Scientific American* pronounced it, not unreasonably, "one of the most remarkable tricks ever performed."

When Houdini repeated this wonder off the Battery, in 1914, he turned it into a civic spectacle. At the announced time, four automobiles set off from the uptown theater district along Broadway for Lower New York, distributing handbills as they went. Houdini may have learned something from his chauffeur in Australia for, in his bathing suit and accompanied by Hardeen, he himself drove a sixty-horsepower racing car. Cheered all along the three-and-a-half-mile route, this time he found New York Harbor filled with small craft, as many as one hundred thousand spectators gaping from the windows of downtown skyscrapers. His brother Bill came to see the performance, but could not get through the throng lining the wharves and docks along Battery Park. Police reserves had to be called to keep people on the fringe from toppling over the seawall into the bay. It was, one newspaper said, "the biggest free show ever seen in New York or anywhere else." When Houdini popped up, in about fifty seconds, the "shrieks of tugs and steamers and the applause of the multitude were deafening."

From Houdini's busy brain also came an escape from a so-called crazy-crib, a strong, light bedstead used in hospitals and insane asylums to restrain exceptionally violent patients. In performance he lay down on the spring mattress, wearing a broad leather band around his midsection that was strapped to the sides of the bed. Then his ankles and thighs were bound to the crazy-crib by straps and leather anklets. After his arms were crossed over his chest and hard-belted together, his wrists were strapped to the frame, pulling the arms in opposite directions. Finally his neck was held down by a leather collar, also yoked to the bed. In full view of the audience, he managed first to stretch one hand to his throat to loosen the collar, then unhitch the wrist straps with his fingers and teeth, freeing his hands to do the rest. As a London newspaper described the fierce agon, he "wriggled" fully twenty minutes,

> his hands blue, his face livid, and everybody thought the task impossible. The next moment and the bed slipped from its position, and Houdini, all but choked to death, had to gasp for the bed to be replaced in its original position. Then started an awesome struggle for supremacy. At twenty-five minutes, by almost a superhuman effort, he got the neck collar adrift, and writhing like a snake, opened the buckles of the wristlets with his teeth, and in five minutes later he was entirely free, very nearly exhausted, and with his evening clothes, from his shirt to his trousers, literally torn in ribbons, he walked down the stage.

The audience, the account concluded, "became quite hysterical, and it was quite ten minutes before the curtain was lowered."

In a related escape, hospital orderlies or insane asylum attendants rolled Houdini in sheets, mummy fashion, leaving only his head uncovered. After tying him to an iron hospital bed, they poured over him fifteen to twenty buckets of hot water, which made the sheets and knots shrink. As with the Crazy-Crib, he performed this escape without the cabinet, so that the audience could see his corkscrewing conniptions. Although he considered it the "most releastic [*sic*] challenge I ever presented," the feat had problems. For one, the release demanded muscle-wrenching turning and squirming to loosen the skintight sheets: "Dangerous to health," Houdini noted. For another, as most magicians realize, difficulty has no relation to impact. Many knucklebusting card tricks, for instance, are dull; many mindbenders virtually work themselves. "The audience never knows," Houdini wrote, "whether the stunt is hard or easy." Despite the everything-you-got effort, the Wet Sheet Escape did not have the wallop of the Milk-Can or many other far easier escapes. Because of the difficulty or the uncertain reception, Houdini did not perform it often.

During this same period he extended the list of his once-only open challenges. Knowledge of them comes almost entirely from journalists, who in reporting the escapes from a lay point of view failed to mention—and probably never noticed—maneuvers essential to their success. The accounts record what an untrained eye thought it saw, but no clue to Houdini's methods. In brief, Houdini at this time escaped after being chained, spreadeagled, to the chassis of a Marmon 32 automobile, and being roped to a girder on the roof of the under-construction Heidelberg Tower in New York, overlooking a three-hundred-foot drop into Forty-second Street. He also got out of one sheet-iron cylinder bolted inside another; a stifling high-pressure diving suit and steel diver's helmet, in which he was cuffed behind his back and ankle-ironed; a sea bag, an outmoded sailcloth-and-leather device once used to restrain mutineers or wildly drunk sailors on the high seas, by enclosing the prisoner neck to foot; and a black hole for the condemned in an eighteenth-century convict ship, chained to ringbolts behind a six-inch-thick door eight feet below the waterline (once released, he dived through an upper porthole into the harbor).

Maritime people, who know knots and ropes, figured in two stunning challenges Houdini undertook in 1911. In Chatham, England, four naval officers proposed sliding a rifle barrel under his arms behind his back, tying his hands in front, and roping his feet to an iron ring nailed to the floor. In this tethered position he would be lashed in front of a loaded cannon, timed to discharge in twenty minutes and puree him. Local authorities would not allow the fuse to be lit, but he released himself in just twelve minutes, kicking off his shoes and undoing some knots with his toes. At the Boston Keith's, he played Jonah to a prehistoric-looking sea beast that had been caught by some Cape Cod fishermen. One Boston newspaper described it as a "big turtle-tortoise-fish," or simply a "What-is-it?" The creature, perhaps an elephant seal, was hauled to the stage by a dozen men and laid on its back. The sliced-open stomach had been sutured with steel chains run through metal eyelets. With the chains slack, Houdini crawled inside, sprinkling perfume where he was about to lay his head. After manacling his hands and feet, the committee drew the chains taut, passed them around the creature's back, and locked them. Concealed by screens while the orchestra entertained, Houdini came forth from the belly of the acrid corpse in fifteen minutes, greasy but grinning.

TORTURE ESCAPES AND THE CHINESE WATER TORTURE CELL

With their bondage and writhing, these and many of Houdini's other escapes smacked of torture and sadomasochistic display. That was part of their fascination, and reflected his own curiosity about human deformity and mutilation. Perhaps trying to confront some underlying horror of annihilation, he collected articles about an armless artist who could paint with his teeth, a Cannon Ball King whose cannon misfired, crushing his legs. He pasted in his diary a grisly photo of pirates decapitated by Chinese officials, the cutoff heads strewn on the ground like cabbages. In an envelope labeled "Chinese Tortures" he kept a set of revolting snuff snapshots that showed chunks of flesh being hacked from a woman tied to a stake, her gouged-out breasts and thighs pouring blood. He tried to look for himself, too. Touring the Midwest in 1908, he took a side trip to see the remains of some children who had been incinerated in a schoolhouse fire: "awful looking spectacle," he recorded. "Poor kid's head, arms, and legs burnt off."

Houdini brought some of his lurid imagining onstage. In 1908, he had accepted (arranged?) a challenge in London from several Cantonese seamen, who dared him to escape a rack used for punishing criminals in

China, known as a sanguaw. It resembled the triangular shafts of a cart, standing narrow end downward on a wooden base, with a crossbeam at the top. All around the instrument hung straps and chains. London newspapers referred to it as a "torture machine," and represented Houdini as "a student of Chinese torture schemes." He fed the suspense by insisting that two physicians be present to see that he stood in no danger of strangulation and was not in fact being tortured.

Houdini met the challenge at London's Oxford Music Hall, noted for its plush stalls and glowing decor of gold, electric blue, and pale pink. On November 20 the rack was carried to the stage by four Chinese men wearing Western-style clothes but in pigtails. First they crossed Houdini's ankles and bound them into a sort of dog collar, the strap fastened to chains nailed to the base of the sanguaw. Chains were wound around his neck and nailed to the crossbeam. His hands were belted and chained to the sloping side-supports. The result was to draw out his body at once upward, downward, and laterally, forcing him to stand on tiptoe to avoid strangulation. "His position was that of a criminal," one newspaper reported, "who cannot stand because his feet are crossed and chained, who cannot sit because the chain round his neck, nailed to a beam over his head, prevents stooping, and who has to depend for support on his manacled wrists."

Pulled and stretched taut, his gullet pressing the choking chin chains, Houdini bit by bit managed to force off his left laced shoe and free a foot— "with a strain," one reporter wrote, "which must have been agony"—then to free both feet from the chains. Reverting to his circus days on the horizontal bar, he laboriously lifted himself by his strapped wrists and executed something like half a back-somersault, throwing his legs in the air and wrapping them around the crossbar. In this underslung position he began nipping open the wrist-straps with his teeth. He released one hand, then the other, and at last unwound his neck chains, so that in fifteen minutes he had stepped free to the front of the sanguaw. When the wildly rooting audience demanded a speech he merely said, "When there is no more left of Houdini you may think of me as having done something to entertain you."

The following year Houdini overcame a gibbet, reconstructed by some Glasgow smiths after a device formerly used in Scotland to suspend criminals in midair until death. This "instrument of punishment" consisted of a cage of steel bands to encase the body—in appearance a sort of latticework mummy case—with a separate steel tube to encircle the head. Houdini acquired at least two other, authentic torment contraptions. He bought at auction the electric chair that had been used at New York's Auburn prison in 1890 to execute the first American criminal sentenced to die by electrocution. He considered having himself strapped in, onstage, and bounding out just as the current began crackling. In Germany he bought an antique iron maiden torture chest—an airtight box porcupined inside with some six hundred deadly-sharp (*haarscharfe*) nails that made movement unbearable and ensured a quick and bloody death. He escaped from it at the Circus Corty-Althoff.

These were but preliminaries to Houdini's greatest mechanical escape, some would say his greatest escape—the Chinese Water Torture Cell. The basic apparatus consisted of a cabinet about five and a half feet tall, in appearance much like a small glass phonebooth, filled with water. Houdini was locked in upside down, hanging by his ankles from a stock, covered by a locked steel lid. In letters and conversation he usually referred to the escape as "the Upside Down" or "USD."

Houdini experimented three or more years before performing the USD publicly, and elaborately guarded its secret. Having learned that patents failed to stop would-be Houdinis, he had grown interested in protecting his effects by copyright. He saw no difference, he said, "between a creative magician and a dramatist, poet or composer." So he registered the escape in England as a one-act play, entitled *Houdini Upside Down*. To secure his claims, he gave the play a one-time production in Southampton, before a one-man audience. On the basis of this pseudo-performance, he notified managers throughout the United Kingdom of his copyright, by registered mail. He also issued warnings to the theatrical profession generally that he had a "SPECIAL LICENCE FROM THE LORD CHAMBERLAIN" for his play, and "I will certainly stop anyone infringing on my rights."

But copyists were less likely to be scared off by Houdini's threats than by the Upside Down itself, which was not easy to duplicate, much less to use. According to Hardeen, the cell, built in England, cost more than ten thousand dollars. The frame was of mahogany and nickel-plated steel, the side panels of half-inch-thick tempered glass, held by watertight rubber seals. Houdini had to carry extra glass panels as well; one broke during a performance—because the water was too hot, he believed. Packed with its pulleys, ropes, clamps, and other essentials into four traveling cases and three crates, the apparatus weighed around three-quarters of a ton.

Performing the USD required toilsome arrangements, too. The water had to be kept temperate. Some was poured from four brass tubs on the stage, filled with 100 gallons of boiling water. Another 150 gallons came from a long fire hose pipelined to the wings, and had to be run off first until it cleared, so the audience could see Houdini inside the cell. A large tarpaulin was laid out underneath, which after the show had to be flown backstage on a strong batten to dry. The cell water had to be drained off afterward, which meant cutting an eight-inch-square trap in the stage and installing a chute. An offstage winch was needed to raise Houdini to the tank and lower him inside. Since he usually invited a large committee to the stage, several small tables also had to be provided, and as many as eighteen chairs. Setting up the USD seems to have been hardly less troublesome than assembling the Voisin. And, according to Houdini, escaping from it was little less dangerous: "flying," he wrote, "is child's play in comparison."

Houdini introduced the Water Torture Cell in Germany, eighteen months after his mock playlet in England. He first presented it at the Circus Busch in Berlin, as the *Wasserfolterzelle*, on September 21, 1912. In a typical performance, the curtain rose slowly on an eerily handsome setting: three assistants outfitted in gold-laced purple; four brass water buckets; the glass-and-burnished-brass cell on its waterproof sheet, surrounded by a cloth-of-gold cabinet; a felling-ax stuck in a heavy woodblock, gleaming with menace. Entering in evening dress, Houdini began by saying:

> Ladies and gentlemen in introducing my original invention the Water Torture cell, although there is nothing supernatural about it, I am willing to forfeit the sum of $1,000 to anyone who can prove that it is possible to obtain air inside of the Torture Cell when I am locked up in it in the regulation manner after it has been filled with water.

As can be heard in the wax-cylinder recording Houdini made of this patter in 1914, he delivered the lines loudly and slowly—in his "Emperor of Sympathy-Enlisters" voice. A New York theatrical newspaper tried to render his enunciation: "Lay-dees and gentle-men, introducing my or-rig-inal invention. . . ."

Houdini explained that the stock fit snugly into the top of the cell, and locked in such a way that it could not be opened from inside even if unlocked. His assistants knew how long he could live without air, he said:

> . . . one of them watches through the curtains ready in case of emergency with an axe, to rush in, demolishing the glass, allowing the water to flow out in order to save my life. I positively and honestly do not expect any accident to happen, but we all know accidents *will* happen and when least expected.

With that, Houdini invited the large committee onstage to examine the cell. He sometimes covered the stage-wait by throwing in his Needle Swallowing, but otherwise dashed into the wings, stripping off his dress coat as he went. His assistants, now wearing fishermen's oilskins and Wellington boots, mounted brass-bound stepladders, climbed to the top of the cell, and began filling it from the buckets and the high-pressure hose. Before they had finished, Houdini reappeared, drawing a robe over, now, his blue bathing suit.

Before being sunk into the cell, Houdini demonstrated the thick stock. He had an assistant swing open the jawlike device along its heavy hinge and clamp the halves over one of his bare feet—size seven and a half, he noted. This showed that the opening cinctured his ankle firmly, so that he could not extricate his foot without unlocking the stock. He lay down on a mat while his assistants and some committee members locked-in both his ankles. They passed over his body a steel reinforcing frame slightly larger than the stock, in which the stock nested. Ropes lowered from flies were hooked to steel rings on corners of the frame. Then a windlass in the wings began slowly raising the stock and frame off the mat, and Houdini's legs with it. This maneuver, seemingly of no moment, was delicate and dangerous. A sudden sway could break Houdini's ankles. The winching continued until he hung directly over the cell, head down. Taking deep breaths, he clapped his hands as a signal to lower. As his assistants guided him in, overflow water showered down on the tarp.

How did it feel? "Imagine yourself jammed head foremost in a Cell filled with water," Houdini wrote, "your hands and feet unable to move, and your shoulders tightly lodged in this imprisonment." "Tightly" is right. Seen from the audience upside down through glass and water, Houdini seemed to fill the tank—arms folded across his chest, cheeks billowing like a blowfish as he held his breath, head touching the cell floor, his hair swirling like seaweed. Looking out at the audience he could have seen only a watery blur of color and lights; he would feel his chest tighten as his air ran out. To perfect his constriction, a steel lid was squeezed down flush over the cell and padlocked, enclosing the stock but leaving his bare feet exposed, soles up. The cabinet was quickly drawn around the cell, an assistant standing by with the emergency ax. The orchestra began playing, menacingly too, "Asleep in the Deep."

The Upside Down was not as fast as the three-second Metamorphosis, but it was startlingly fast. Depending on the performance, Houdini left his still locked and waterfilled torture cell behind him and burst from the cabinet, drenched, after two minutes, one minute, even thirty seconds.

Its novel apparatus, ominous presentation, and impenetrable method made the USD a showstopping escape. "To say the applause was deafening is putting it too mildly," a London reviewer wrote. "The audience seemingly rose in a body and cannonaded with their expressions of approval." The *Stuttgart Neues Tageblatt* called it "uncommonly astonishing and awe-inspiring. . . . A trick of incredible cunning." For some spectators there was no question of trickery, release under such conditions being possible only by supernatural means. J. Hewat McKenzie, a well-known Spiritualist, served on Houdini's committee during one performance, standing close to the cell. He said he experienced there a "great loss of physical energy" as Houdini used his "powers of dematerialization" to pass through the glass and transport his inchoate self to the back of the stage, where he rematerialized and returned to the stage front dripping with water. "This startling manifestation of one of nature's profoundest miracles," McKenzie added, "was probably regarded by most of the audience as a very clever trick."

Houdini was no less enthusiastic about the escape than were his other admirers. "I believe it is the climax of all my studies and labors" he wrote. "Never will I be able to construct anything that will be more dangerous or difficult for me to do." The USD was more than another *miracle du jour*, for he would feature his "*Stagerer*" the rest of his career.

Only a month or two after Houdini introduced the escape in Berlin, however, a Miss Undina began presenting a facsimile. He got a temporary injunction from the German courts, blocking her use of it until the case could be decided. To combat Miss Undina he shrewdly created a Miss Undina-ette to compete with her. He taught the escape to a German artiste named Wanda Timm, apparently gave her a duplicate cell, and paid her a salary of 150 marks a month (and third-class railroad fare) to perform the Upside Down as "Miss Trixy." He retained the right to cancel the contract should she be unable to perform the feat "because of loss of nerve, anxiety, insecurity," and swore her to secrecy concerning its method. As things turned out, he won his court case against Miss Undina, and Miss Trixy seems to have kept her word. Even today the secret of the Water Torture Cell is known to perhaps only a dozen people.

THE MAGICIANS' CLUB; THE WEISS FAMILY; IRA DAVENPORT; AVIATION IN AMERICA

During his overseas tours, Houdini spent another eighteen months in Great Britain. For the first time he played Ireland, his debut in Belfast bringing out such crowds that police and detectives had to be called to turn them away after standing room was exhausted. The long stay left him feeling more than ever as much an English as an American magician. "I know England," he said, "better than I do America."

Houdini leased or bought a London flat, at 84 Bedford Court Mansions, and assumed a leading role in English magical life. Having resigned from the Society of American Magicians, he led an attempt to organize a comparable English society, with the help of his sometime-friend Will Goldston (Wolf Goldstein, 1878–1948), a leading London magic dealer. Many prominent British magicians attended the planning session, held at a London restaurant in May 1911. Acting as chairman, Houdini sketched for them his vision of a fully-staffed palatial clubhouse modeled on the most select English clubs, with workshops and trained mechanics to produce or mend apparatus. The organization came into existence in 1913 as the Magicians' Club, with Houdini as president. Not surprising: in addition to being, as the members acknowledged, the "heart and soul" of the movement to found the club, he paid its first six months' rent, donated other money to its fund for indigent colleagues, and was, after all, Houdini. Above the door of the bar was hung a portrait of him, furnished by him.

Houdini made a dynamic president, with a talent for organization. For the first annual dinner he personally oversaw the guest list, the favors for ladies (small dolls, sewn partly by Bess), even the printing of programs— not surprising either, since the cover too featured his portrait. Having put his name and reputation behind the club, he meant to make such gatherings distinguished, "like a London event," and splashy. "I believe it is absolutely essential to have some of the leading London papers representatives at the dinner," he told Goldston. "It is not whether we can afford it but is a case that we must have them there." He urged Goldston to set up a press table and invite for the feed a dozen well-placed journalists, "at the very least."

Houdini recognized that staying abroad too long might sap some vital, national element of his personality. He felt that he needed to return home for a year about every three years, "so that I will get back the American atmosphere, for eventually one sinks slowly into the habits of the country in which one lives and I know my work suffers." But in bringing Houdini home, the need to get back in touch with the "American push" counted less than did his family. Hardeen had bought a new home, in Flatbush, Brooklyn; Nat a new business on Sixth Avenue in Manhattan. Gladys (Gittle, by her Yiddish nickname) had turned her poor eyesight to some advantage in helping to edit a newspaper printed in Braille. Leo had left Houdini's Harlem brownstone and opened an office on fashionable Central Park South. The *New York Times* mentioned him as the X-ray specialist brought in for some experimental brain surgery that restored vision to a boy who had been blinded half his life by a brain tumor.

Yet Houdini's enjoyment of his family, like the pleasure he took in his own success, was troubled by a sense of fatality: "In our journey through life we ought to keep our dear ones in mind all the time," he wrote to Bess, "for as we pass along, the mile stones turn into Tomb stones marking the resting place of some beloved one." His brother Bill and his mother seemed headed down such a dark road. Only about a year after marrying, Bill was diagnosed as tubercular and went off to a sanatorium, where Houdini visited him (nearly getting in a fistfight with the "insulting" barber there). Cecilia, now about seventy-two, was having stomach trouble, sometimes crying out in pain to her doctor son, "*Leopold, rette mich*"—save me. Worried about her health, Houdini sent her to the Catskills, about a hundred miles north of Manhattan, for the salubrious mountain air. When his mother was in town, he as usual plied her with money and took her shopping.

From New York City, Houdini paid a memorable visit, in July 1910, to Ira Davenport, the surviving brother of William. The trip, at Ira's invitation, involved eight hundred miles of travel, to and from the region of giant lakes outside Buffalo, in western New York state. But it represented for

Houdini a chance to meet and speak with his artistic father. Ira had settled with his daughter and second wife in Mayville, a village near Lily Dale, the famous colony of Spiritualist mediums. Met by Ira at the train station, Houdini found a shrunken old man coping with throat cancer, his drooping James Brothers mustache turned white. In Houdini's account of the meeting, they sat talking into the night on the open porch of Ira's small frame house. He took notes as Ira described the "trials, battles, praise and applause" of the Davenport Brothers' career. His own familiarity with it so much impressed Ira, he said, that the old man remarked, "you positively know more about the real facts than I, who was the principal actor."

As Houdini sat, notebook in hand, Ira took a long piece of rope and divulged to him, thrillingly, perhaps the best-kept secret in Western magic. He explained the Davenport Rope-Tie, which had enabled the brothers to bang tambourines and strum guitars while knotted inside their spirit cabinet, by instantly slipping in and out of the tightest fastenings. According to Houdini, Ira said to him, smiling, "Houdini—we started it, and you finish it." Despite his age Ira had toured as recently as four years before, giving his last performance for an American regiment near Santiago de Cuba. He suggested to Houdini that they undertake an international tour, offering a "mystery entertainment" as partners. "By combining his reputation and my knowledge and experience," Houdini felt, "we would have been able to set the world agog." Their show was never to be, for Ira died a year later. Just the same Houdini left Mayville with privileged knowledge. "I believe I am the only human," he said, "who can rightfully answer all questions regarding the ability of the . . . Davenport Brothers."

While in the States, Houdini had a chance to observe the progress of American aviation, which awed and also discouraged him. At Mineola, Long Island, he watched some flights by Charles K. Hamilton, a former trick bicycle-rider who in 1910 flew from New York to Philadelphia and back in a day. Recalling the interminable waits in Australia for calm days, it "amazed" him, he said, to see Hamilton take off in "any wind," without even testing the pull of his propeller. What he witnessed during an international meet in Chicago impressed him still more: four Wright machines leaving the ground at three in the afternoon and cruising until dark; a biplane doing eighty miles an hour for two hours; seven pilots reaching altitudes above five thousand feet. "I never before saw such wonderful sights," he wrote to Bess.

The aviators included Lincoln Beachey, probably the world's boldest stunt pilot, known for diving from five thousand feet with his motor shut off, and landing where he chose. Houdini saw him dive from three thousand feet but mistook the stunt for a calamity—"grew weak in the knees," he said—and felt relieved that Beachey had been "saved." A genuine accident made him more than a gulping bystander. A flyer named St. Croix Johnstone, who currently held the American long-distance record of 176 miles, was killed when his plane came apart at six hundred feet. After the meet the other aviators held a benefit exhibition for Johnstone's widow. Houdini volunteered to have himself shackled hand and foot and taken up over Lake Michigan. As the plane skimmed the water at fifty feet, he jumped out, arose from the lake with his limbs free, and swam ashore.

During the meet Houdini spoke with two monumental figures in American aviation. They were Orville Wright, who had made the enshrined twelve-second flight at Kitty Hawk lying face down on the lower wing of his and his brother's biplane; and Glenn Curtiss, whose touchdown the year before in New York City after a flight from Albany—the first long-distance flight in the Western Hemisphere—had been greeted by more than a million people. With Wright and Curtiss, Houdini had the rare experience of meeting two people who were better known to him than he to them. They "seem to know me as an Australian flyer," he told Bess, "and want to know all about my country." His tone leaves it uncertain whether he felt honored or miffed at being taken for Houdini the pilot. Either way, sometime later he had himself photographed with Curtiss, and Wright went to see him perform, onstage.

Houdini made no impression at all on another pilot, the flamboyant John B. Moisant. Creator of the barnstorming flying circus, Moisant sported a diamond stickpin and had worked as a machine-gunning soldier of fortune for revolutionaries in El Salvador. In 1910 he entered a Paris-to-London air race, with stops, against the Frenchman Hubert Latham. Moisant showed his disdain for the competition by taking up with him his mechanic, Fileux, and a kitten, Mademoiselle Paree. In the States his progress made frontpage news for several days, especially after he landed in Dover; the press proclaimed that it had fallen to an American to make the first flight from Paris to English shores. When Moisant was only about forty miles from London, however, an exhaust valve in his engine broke, forcing him down. He made a fresh start but was forced down again, splintering his propeller. Newspapers revealed that his monoplane was marooned in a garden in Kent, thirty-nine miles from London, waiting for spare parts.

Learning of Moisant's situation, it occurred to Houdini that he could help. His Voisin and several thousand dollars' worth of parts lay in storage in London, together with all sizes of wires and two propellers for an ENV motor. He telegraphed Moisant offering the whole lot—"GRATIS my entire Bi-plane." He even offered to bring the equipment to him, "so that you can complete your journey." But Moisant did not answer. Houdini cabled the postmaster to ask whether the message had been delivered. When he learned that it had been put into the hands of Fileux himself, he blow-torched Moisant a letter:

> I believe that there is a little Courtesy due me from you. It makes no difference whether you were able to make use of my offer or any part of my Bi-plane or not—you could at least have made use of my pre-paid message to thank me or decline my offer. But perhaps you are in the habit of receiving GRATIS things pertaining to your Bi-plane worth Five to Eight Hundred Dollars—? . . . I think either an explanation or an apology is due.

Moisant seems to have made Houdini some sort of reply, and in just under three weeks did reach London. A few months later a gust upended the tail of his plane during a landing in New Orleans, and he was killed.

Whether treated as champ or chump, Houdini was losing interest in flying, if not in aviation. He had seen that without spending much more time, money, and energy he could not compete with aviators who stayed air-borne several hundred miles and reached heights of better than a mile. He (or a ghostwriter) now and then contributed a letter or short article to the *National Aeronautic Association Review* or *The Aeroplane*. But in 1913 he sold his all-but-obsolete Voisin and gave up piloting. In his you-pick-'em style, he gave a range of reasons. "I stopped flying because it became too common," he wrote, "and did not require the ability or courage which I thought it required." Contrarily, a German newspaper reported that "the whole thing appeared to him to be a little too dangerous [*etwas zu gefährlich*]." The likeliest explanation is the one he gave at the very end of his life: "I had had my adventure in the air."

MORE STRAIN, NEW ASSISTANTS

Houdini had left Australia feeling exhausted, and his new tours did nothing to revive him. "NO HANDCUFFS" turned out to mean No Letup, and his incessant presentation of new effects kept him tired. "Harry is worked to death," Bess wrote in 1911, "he looks so old, he is quite gray." Newspapers too began to comment, for the first time, on the silver in his hair. Publicly he repeatedly announced his retirement, while privately he moaned into his diaries and letters: "Gee but its hard to keep at it all the time. . . . Very hard job. Must invent some new means of enlightening my labors." He tried to ease up by including "animated pictures" in his act, showing his audiences films of himself piloting the Voisin or jumping a bridge in Paris. But not all managers appreciated the switch. "I want a performance by you," a British manager wired him, "not a cinematograph act."

Unwilling to concede that he could never race fast enough to beat himself, Houdini was repaid by greater strain and conflict. Over the years he had often been hurt during performances, but in November 1911 he suffered his first lasting injury. It came from what he called "a most peculiar accident." While playing in Detroit, he accepted a challenge to escape a large strapped bag. By his standards that sounds routine. Yet the straps were unusual, being round, and the challengers, a "gang of longshoremen," tightened them But Good. For two weeks after, Houdini urinated blood. He ignored the condition, moving on for engagements in Pittsburgh. There the pain got so bad that he saw a doctor, who told him that a blood vessel in one of his kidneys had ruptured. The physician ordered several months' rest, and reportedly added that unless he gave up his more gutbusting escapes he would be dead within a year.

Keeping the information from Bess and from his mother, who were with him in Pittsburgh, Houdini completed the three remaining days of his run, canceled bookings for the next two weeks, and went back to 278 to rest in bed. "I am taking a vacation," he wrote to Will Goldston, "laying on the broad of my back and doing some thinking." The bleeding having stopped, he went on to the Columbus, Ohio, Keith's, where in short order he got out of a packing case, a mailbag, and a beer-filled milk can. But his kidney ached constantly; he was depressed and concerned that it might become a "permanent worry." Making things worse, while walking down an icy street he fell and reinjured the kidney. A few months later, during one of his everything-straining wet-sheet escapes, he tore a ligament in his side. The kidney continued to pain him for the next few years, and possibly longer. In 1913 a physician in England described it as having "a considerably greater inspiratory lunge than normal"—a now-discarded notion that movement of the kidneys could cause their blood vessels to kink. He recommended a spring truss to ease the pain. Houdini of course continued offering his body to be stretched, crunched, and winched, although by one account he always slept with a pillow under his side to protect the kidney area from pressure.

At the same time Houdini found more than ever to squabble about with front-office people. He broke a contract with the Circus Busch management, was sued by the American agent Jennie Jacobs for $2,250 in allegedly unpaid commissions, was canceled by the manager of Keith's Washington for not keeping Hardeen out of an opposition theater there at the same time. Affronts like the last were "a hard blow to my pride and dignity," he said, and he enjoyed getting even: "I have raised Cain in thousands of theatres." To spite the Keith's manager, he bought out the opposing theater for a week and played there himself, netting $4,300. He raised more Cain at an Empire theater in England, after the management failed to notify ticket buyers that, by mutual agreement, he would not be appearing for two of his matinee performances. During the first matinee, he stalked onstage just as a new act was about to appear. He egged on the audience to get their money back or stay in their seats all day until they could see him at the evening show, which half the crowd did even though police were called in to expel them.

The most hellbent of Houdini's revenges ended in his arrest. After his last performance at the Colonial Theatre in Norfolk, Virginia, he got into a contract dispute backstage with the manager, who on instructions from the New York office withheld four hundred dollars of his salary. The amount represented a fine for his having complained about the management directly to the audience, much as he did in England. He learned of the fine just as the closing act went off and the sheet was dropped to display some moving pictures. Still in his bathrobe, he rushed onstage into the glaring projection beam and shouted "I want my money. These people won't give me my salary." The stage manager tried to drag him behind the scenes, but Houdini resisted. Police arrested him for disorderly conduct and put him in a patrol car, before a large crowd gathered outside the theater. Taken to the station house, he was released on fifty dollars' bail, paid by another performer. "I will admit that I became excited," he told a reporter afterward, "but who wouldn't cry for $400—even make a bigger fuss than I did."

Transportation and logistics were becoming a major fuss too. When starting out in show business, Houdini could probably pack his entire act in the Metamorphosis trunk. Now, with his milk cans, underwater boxes, Water Torture Cell and the rest, he was lugging around well over a ton of equipment, which had to be moved in and out of railroad cars several times a month, and brought back and forth to the theater to be unpacked and repacked.

To handle it all, Houdini took on several new assistants, in addition to Franz Kukol. Some he hired and let go, but one who remained with him permanently was Jim Collins, a dapper, somewhat cadaverous-looking young Irishman. Houdini often quarreled with his assistants (and often quickly made up), even with the dependable, easygoing Collins. Yet Collins thought him "a good boss and a fair one." His assistants being vital to his own success, Houdini also paid them well, as Collins recalled: "Many times, when there was no need for it, as I was on regular salary, he gave me substantial presents and bonuses to show his appreciation. . . . as far as I know no magician has ever paid an assistant what Houdini was generous enough to pay me." (Collins's salary at this time is unknown, but in 1924 he received $50 a week in and around New York, $60 en route, and half those amounts during layoffs.)

Houdini boasted that he chose his assistants on hunches, "simply walked among the applicants, looked 'em over, said 'I'd like to see you for a moment,' and then let the mob go, picking one man only. Never made a mistake." But he knew what he wanted, loyalty above all. His assistants would have access to secrets that millions of people wanted to know. As he also did with the plumbers and tinsmiths who built his milk cans and other apparatus, he routinely had them sign a formal oath, sometimes deposed in a lawyer's office, swearing to never reveal what they learned. Many of these documents survive, such as the oath Houdini drew up in Bremen in 1912 for a temporary German assistant, Josef Zwettler:

> I hereby swear by God the Almighty, not to reveal in any manner to anyone, no matter who it might be, nor even to give the smallest hint, of the secrets, instructions, plans, apparatus, constructions you have confided in me in reference to the execution of your numbers.
>
> Should I any manner directly or indirectly act against this oath you will have the right at any time to begin court action against me

for perjury. In addition, the above mentioned oath above also refers
to the following: that even should I leave my position with you, I
will nowhere and never permit myself to copy any of your numbers
. . . or even work as an assistant in [an act] similar to yours.

Houdini extracted such oaths like a feudal lord, and in fact inspired a sort
of fealty. The son of one assistant recalled that his father, having pledged
absolute fidelity to Houdini, refused to teach him any tricks at all. Even so
Houdini took no chances. None of his assistants, he claimed, knew all the
workings of any of his escapes. "Each one has his special duty to perform,"
he said, "but none of them understands the whole of the business."

Until the end of Houdini's career, all of his assistants (Bess excepted)
were males, and for obvious reasons he looked for them to have mechanical
skill, especially in cabinetry. Collins was an accomplished carpenter who
also made bookcases for his boss, and one Christmas gave him a Nest of
Boxes—a classic effect in which a borrowed watch or ring vanishes, and
reappears in the last of three nested boxes, each locked. The delicate, invisible mechanisms built into the boxes require fine workmanship, and Collins
made the exquisite set himself. Since the assistants appeared onstage, in
goldlaced uniforms, Houdini also required that they be good-looking. His
ideal assistant, in sum, was a loyal, handsome cabinetmaker.

Houdini's helpers took over most of the headaches of dealing with his
evergrowing equipment. A photo of him and Bess with assistants at
Charing Cross Station in November 1909—before he introduced the
USD—shows them with eight trunks and two large hampers. Three years
later he was saying that he now carried forty pieces of baggage. They held
not only his apparatus but also books for his ongoing research, stacks of
advertising, wardrobe for himself and four assistants, and the toolshop that
his once-sufficient burglars' kit had become—loads of wrenches, mallets,
files, awls, leather punches, bandsaws, oilcans, hanks of wire. To store it all
he hired masons to break into the front wall of 278 and make a large trap
door so that he could get his baggage from the street into the cellar. He kept
separate storage facilities in London, on two floors of a building at 54A
Little George Street, Hampstead Road.

Houdini's 1911 inventory of his London warehouse runs to fifteen
pages. The items on a single page give some idea of the mountain of equipment he now depended on (the spelling is typical Houdini):

1 Iron Cage for can made in Dundee
1 Iron Gibet
2 Boxes of Metal types for Right
    Way to do Wrong
1 Euston Challenge Can
1 Electric Chair
1 Basket open with handles—Glas
    clock
1 Challenge Wood Barrell
1 New Barrell lid
1 Original Oceana Barrell
1 Improved   "   "
1 Automatic Figur bought from Verli
1 Oblong Box for Novel Autom.
    Figur

1 Hatbox tray full of books. Mrs. H.
1 Gamage Can
1 Can 1910 unprepared
1 Australian Straightjacket
    (Sceleton)
1 Can wooden crate empty
1 Foundation for Sung-war [i.e., the
    Sanguaw]
1 Parrot cage
1 Dressmaking form
1 Wooden pail crate empty
1 black trunk Linen Mrs. H.
1 old trunk, kitchen things etc. etc.
    Mrs. H.
4 Packing Cases

Other pages list, in addition, needles, stencils, hatboxes, zinc tubs, airplane parts, canvas bags, cabinet cloth, boiler ends, bathing trunks, files of correspondence, a pistol, a bed, an emery wheel, and on and on. He seems to have thrown nothing away. The inventory includes old boots, "old Tricks," even "old J[ock] straps."

In Houdini's mind only one thing justified this unwieldy one-man bazaar: "I want my show to be the best of its kind whilst I am alive. When I am dead there will not be another like it."

EIGHT

1913–1915

DEATH OF CECILIA WEISS; THE "GRAND MAGICAL REVUE"; THEODORE ROOSEVELT

WHEN HE TYPED UP his recollections of those three awful weeks in July 1913, Houdini began with the events of the sixth. He was about to sail abroad again. As his mother always did when that happened, she asked to go with him to Cypress Hills, for a farewell visit to the grave of Mayer Samuel Weiss. He had bought a family plot at the cemetery, to which he had moved the bodies of his half brother and Rabbi Weiss. ("Saw what was left of poor father and Herman," he recorded, fascinated by the exhumation. "Nothing but skull and bones. Herman's teeth were in splendid condition.")

Cecilia was proud of the Weiss plot at Machpelah, as Cypress Hills was also known. She often visited it herself, praying for her deceased husband's blessing on their children. On the sixth, a Thursday, Houdini hired a car and driver to take Cecilia, Hardeen, and brother Nat with him to the cemetery, in the borough of Queens. When they got there he announced that he was going to lie down on his father's grave—so that he could say he lay there before Cecilia did. Obviously he meant to show that his mother's life meant more to him than his own, but Hardeen stopped him from making the morbid tribute. Afterward Houdini had the driver take the group to a tea company, where he made good on some money that his brother Bill owed the firm. Cecilia kissed him and said, as he transcribed her words, "*Nu, wirdst du mehr gluck haben*"—"Well, now you'll have more luck."

For Houdini this was to be no average overseas tour. He was scheduled to give a command performance for the king of Sweden, at the palace in Stockholm. He also planned to revisit Budapest, his birthplace. And for the first time in his career he would appear under his real name. He had petitioned the courts for a name-change, which would go into effect during his Atlantic crossing. Ehrich Weiss would then legally become Harry Houdini.

Houdini recalled that on the day of his sailing he got up early. His mother had spent part of the evening at 278 lying on the couch downstairs before going to bed, a sign, he thought, that she was "getting wise" and taking some rest. In retrospect he realized that she was growing weaker: "The Great Dissolution was gradually taking place." Again having hired a chauffeur, he took Cecilia, Bill, Bess, and Bess's mother across the Hudson River to the Hoboken docks, where he was booked into room fifteen of the *Kronprinzessin Cecilie*. Some of the group felt upset about a girl servant who had recently left the household. "Not the usual good feeling," Houdini recalled, "that we had for the past sailings." Just the same he was the last passenger to embark. "Ma was worried and told me to remain on board," he wrote, "but I kept coming back and embracing her and kissing her goodbye."

As Houdini hugged her, his mother looked at him and said, "*Ehrich, vielleicht bin ich nicht da wenn du zuruck kommst [sic]*"—"Ehrich, perhaps I won't be here when you return." He tried to "jolly" her, reminding her that she had said the same thing at his other departures. When he gave her a farewell kiss she said, "*Geh doch in Gott's nahmen*"—"Get along, in God's name." He turned to some people on the pier and said, "Look, ladies and gentlemen, *Mein Mutter stosst mich fort von Ihr*"—"My mother is pushing me away from her." She waved off his kidding with a "*Nein, nein, nicht so,*" prodding him to board now and return to her in good health. When he reached the deck, his mother called for him to bring her back a pair of warm woolen slippers, size six. He said, "Alright Mama."

A photo that Houdini took of his departure confirms his recollection that it was clouded by "bad feeling." The *Crown Princess Cecilia* was a big, fast ship—twenty thousand tons, run at 23.5 knots. Houdini had crossed on it before, favoring the technologically-advanced liners of the North German Lloyd company and also, surely, the ship's name. The picture, snapped as the *Cecilie* pulled away, shows the party at dockside in a festive tangle of paper streamers. Jowly, silver-haired Mrs. Rahner appears glum; Bill in his bowtie and straw boater seems frail and bony; squat Cecilia in her Old World, funereally dark gloves, hat, and dress looks aged and tightlipped, staring fiercely at nothing.

Landing in Hamburg about a week later, Houdini and Bess got a midnight train to Copenhagen. They arrived in midmorning and were met by his assistants. Franz had a cable for him but did not present it until after Houdini and Bess had settled in their hotel room. Houdini noticed that it came from Asbury Park, a New Jersey seaside resort where Hardeen was working and had taken Cecilia along for a vacation. Thinking the cable was a welcoming message from "the folks," Houdini delayed opening it until he arrived at the Circus Beketow, where he was scheduled to perform. "It was a cable from Brother Doc," he wrote later, "telling me that Mother was stricken and that there was no hope." A cable from Hardeen was also waiting, undelivered, at the post office. It said that if he wanted to see Cecilia alive he had to catch the first steamer to America. He immediately canceled his engagements, booked passage on the *Cecilie*'s return voyage, and hurried back to Germany for the departure.

In recounting these Copenhagen events, Houdini left out the most dramatic moments. They may have been too bitter, or only too embarrassing, to describe. On her first night in Asbury Park, Cecilia had been paralyzed by a stroke that left her unable to speak; she died on July 17, just past midnight. According to the best available information, Houdini received news of her death later the same day, after performing, in Danish, before a circus audience that included the princes of the royal family. He opened the cable during a press reception, fainted upon reading it, and when he came to began weeping. The same night his ailing kidney gave him so much pain that a physician was called, who pressed him to enter the hospital immediately. Instead he cabled Hardeen to postpone the funeral. The Danish physician accompanied him on a train to the German border, where a substitute physician took over and looked after him until he reached the ship.

Houdini's account resumes with his entry to the parlor of 278, three weeks after his downhearted sendoff from the United States. Cecilia's corpse had been laid out for burial—against all tradition, for Jewish law requires interment within a day or two after death. Her preservation implies that he cabled home strong demands to see her one last time. He noticed that she had a spot on her cheek, and she seemed to him "dainty," even smaller in death than she had been in life. With these impressions came two thoughts. First, in the service of her children she had expended a great loving energy: "I gaze upon her features so still and quiet, resting for the first time in 'Her Earthy Career,' " he wrote. "Her work was never finished. Night simply interrupted her work, but now as I always told Her she would 'Rest for Ever.' "

The second thought was of her closeness to his father. It came tinged with jealous rivalry. Something she had said to him during his teens had stayed with him: upon Mayer Samuel's death he had told her not to weep, but she replied, "*Wenn du hast ein hüml 28 yehr, wurdst du auch weinen*"—"If you had had a heaven for twenty-eight years you would cry too." Her loyalty to his father's memory had made him feel, he confessed, "insignificiant [*sic*]." Viewing her corpse, he recalled that one of her favorite sayings had been, "*Gibts nichts nur mann and frau*"—"Nothing matters but husband and wife." And he envisioned her laid beside Mayer Samuel, "Her best friend, one for whom she mourned ever since he obeyed the mighty command. . . . one who loved Her best of all." His parents might even then be reuniting above, he reflected, to his loss and their delight: "I know if there is a Meeting Place Both are Happy in this event, which leaves all us children miserable." He brought a chair from Cecilia's room and stayed by her body all night. In his flight from Denmark he had not neglected to buy, he claimed, the size six woolen slippers she had asked for on the dock at Hoboken: "That was her last request, and I obeyed her." He put them in her coffin before she was buried beside his father at Cypress Hills, the next day.

"I who have laughed at the terrors of death, who have smilingly leaped from high bridges," Houdini wrote, "received a shock from which I do not think recovery is possible." In fact he would brood over Cecilia's death the rest of his life. A friend of his last years remarked, with some annoyance: "I have never spoken to Harry Houdini when he didn't say something about that mother." In the weeks after the funeral he rarely left the house except to visit Machpelah, "bowed down with grief." And for the next three years he lived the emotional equivalent of "*Cabre, cabre!*," trying to stay aloft but nearly out of control.

That his mother's death should so destabilize a world-famous thirty-nine-year-old superman seems all too human. But the irony is too teasing to pass by without speculating on something of what Cecilia's death meant for Houdini's career, and on his resources for overcoming it: "I am what would be called a Mothers-boy," he admitted. "[I]f I do anything, I say to myself I wonder if Ma would want me to do this?" That applied as much onstage as off. He had often brought Cecilia to watch him perform, of course, no time more revealingly than when he made his first manacled bridge jump, in Rochester in 1907. He wanted her to see it, he said, because "I thought something might happen." It is a remarkable reason, as if by plunging into the grimy canal he could rouse her concern for his welfare and in that command her attention. More remarkable still, considering that he might have killed himself, after the performance he wrote proudly in his diary, "Ma saw me jump!" Houdini needed no king of Sweden to see him work. The royal box in his mental theater was occupied by Cecilia, watching him outshine Bill, Nat, Leo, Hardeen, and especially Mayer Samuel. The extraordinary exclamation identifies probably his sharpest secret spur to applause-getting: "Ma saw me jump!"

The loss of his regal cheering-section made a large part of the "shock," as Houdini called it, "from which I do not think recovery is possible." To counter it he could call on the Boosterism he had always cultivated to fight off his tendency to melancholy. Throughout his career he preached self-improving vim and saved countless thumbs-up maxims from such journals as *Mind Power Plus*: "To be so strong that nothing can disturb your peace of mind. . . . To talk health, happiness and prosperity to every person you meet." In his scrapbooks he amassed an anthology of the most insipid newspaper verse of his time, whatever preached the Optimist's Credo:

> *I sing a song to the optimist,*
> *To the man who is brave and strong,*
> *Who keeps his head when things go right*
> *And smiles when things go wrong.*

Rotary Club watchwords could not have taken Houdini far in overcoming the shock of his mother's death. But they were backed by his deep reserves of élan, by his greasestained absorption in magic and escapes, and by a cre-ative will driven by God-only-knows what kind of striving, in addition to oedipal conquest. Probably every kind—immigrant grasping for material success, the spur of fame, a lifetime habit of hard work, celebrity status-seeking, animal fear of annihilation, romantic longing for transcendence, athletic record-keeping, American expansionism, overcompensation for a dismal past, a feeling that nothing he could do was good enough, counterphobic risktaking, exhibitionism, narcissism. Whatever motives propelled his will—and all the above seem in some degree present—his every performance was a demonstration that he could and would not be hindered. In getting free now from despair, he could summon up the same sense of himself he advertised to the world on one of his first posters: "Nothing on Earth Can Hold HOUDINI a Prisoner!!!"

At the time of Cecilia's death Houdini had been booked abroad for the next three years. On the last day of August he sailed from New York for Hamburg. For the rest of his life he retained his boarding pass, on which he wrote: "after loss of mother." His mood as he again left for Europe he revealed in a shipboard letter to Hardeen: "As big as this steamer really is my heart hangs over its sides and reaches and ever will reach Cypress Hill." As he moved with the Circus Corty-Althoff into Nuremberg, a city he had never played before, he began collecting his "Sainted Mother's" letters to him. He had them transcribed in "good German," typed out, and put in book form so he could read them easily. Each letter, he observed in his diary, was "a love story, a prayer to God to protect her children, a plea that we should be good human beings." In gathering and reading them he shed, he said, "many a bitter tear."

Houdini returned to the stage roiled by conflict between dedication to his work and torment over Cecilia. "Act works beautifully," he wrote of one Nuremberg performance, then: "Had a terrible spell after show on account of my darling Mother." While playing the medieval-looking city he once again landed in a German court, this time as farce. He announced that to prove he had no access to air inside the Water Torture Cell, he would stay underwater while chained in Lake Dutzend, part of a pleasureground outside Nuremberg. He did the stunt despite an injunction against it by the city's police senate. Thousands of spectators watched from the bank, surrounding the lake in crowded rows as he sprang, heavily chained, from a boat. Also watching were an army of police, who prosecuted him in civil court for having flouted the senate's ruling.

Nurembergers sided with Houdini, whose exhibition released much resentment against police overzealousness: "Our police can show incredible energy," the *Nordbayerische Zeitung* said, "when matters concern these kinds of trifles." The trial became an occasion for satire. Testimony revealed that as the city police were spreading out to capture Houdini at the lake, the municipal streetcar administration was placing additional trams in service in order to bring as many Nurembergers as possible to see him. Here, one newspaper commented, "the disgrace to the police would seem to have been large enough, but it gets better." It turned out that the police commissioner, one Schlumberger, had not notified Houdini of the injunction until the day *after* his jump. Trying to salvage the honor of the kaiser's finest, the prosecuting attorney asked the court to penalize Houdini 210 marks for bathing in a public place. But the judge declared Houdini's muddy September dunking no bath, and acquitted him. To the police, commented the *Tagespost*, the affair brought new glory "in the domain of imbecility [*dem Gebiete der Schildbürgerei*]."

The ludicrous trial was visited in progress by idle lawyers and court officials, who joined in the merriment. Which Houdini did not. As one newspaper put it, "the accused sinner was the only one in the courtroom who remained serious and did not laugh along with the rest." What Houdini was thinking and feeling can be surmised from the letters he wrote from Nuremberg to Hardeen, on the black-bordered mourning stationery he now used exclusively. He felt bewildered, he said, "so lonely that I don't know what to do properly." He longed for some end to his grief, he said, but saw no possibility of it. "Am hoping that eventually I will have my burning tears run dry, but know that my Heart will ALWAYS ACHE FOR OUR DARLING MOTHER." He had always known too that he loved their mother greatly, but her death had brought him the unexpected knowledge that he had also depended on her: "my very Existence seems to have expired with HER," he told his brother. "My brain works naturally, and I try and scheme ahead as in the Past, but I seem to have lost all ambition."

In October, Houdini moved with Corty-Althoff to Berlin and then to Stuttgart. While headlining a bill that included "Konsul Patsy," the world's best-dressed chimpanzee, he ruminated on illusion. Since his mother's death he saw existence differently, he wrote to a cousin, in German; he had come to understand "*dass die ganze Welt fast ein Drama ist*"—"that the whole world is just a play." But a night or two later he was part of the play himself, a broomstick tied behind his knees, his hands knotted to the ends, left like an overturned tortoise, in which position he was laid on a plank and roped to it ankles and neck. On the evening of October 28, Pierre Althoff, director of the circus, hosted a gala marking Houdini's thirtieth year as a performer, since 1883—counting the time, as Houdini did himself, from his appearances as the nine-year-old trapeze artist Ehrich Prince of the Air. The affectionate public sent flowers, Houdini's assistants gave him an engraved punchbowl, Althoff presented him with a massive silver wreath as the *perpétuel évadé*, "eternal evader." Houdini introduced Bess to the audience, remarking that for thirty years he had eluded every chain but one, and far from complaining always congratulated himself on the "solidity and inalterability of the conjugal link." Actually, Bess had become unwell, perhaps from worry over his condition, he thought. He needed to pull himself together for her sake too, he realized: "Must try and cheer up and be a man."

During November, Houdini moved back into variety, at the Paris Alhambra. He found some satisfaction in doing "very big," but it did not last long. "Dash its TOUGH," he wrote his brother from France, "and I cant seem to get *over it*. Some times I feel alright, but when a calm moment arrives I am as bad as ever." Cecilia's passing had brought forth a mystery that oppressed him on its own. He learned that despite the stroke that left her speechless, she had tried to convey to those around her a message for him. Its substance remains unknown, but reportedly was meant to shield him from information that would have embittered him toward some close relative or friend. He seems to have learned enough of it to have it gnaw at him. "Time heals all Wounds," he told Dash, "but a long time will have to pass before it will heal the terrible blow which MOTHER tried to save me from knowing."

In a rare move Houdini canceled his last engagements in Paris and took Bess for a vacation to the Riviera. He won two thousand francs gambling at Monte Carlo. But in his black mourning suit, black bowtie, and black porkpie hat he could not have passed for a tourist on a spree. Several times he visited a cemetery reserved for plungers who had gone broke at the gaming tables and then committed suicide. "A terrible feeling pervades the first time one sees the graves," he wrote, "and thinks of the human beings who finish their lives in this manner." The necropolis of suicides fascinated him. Depressed himself, he recorded in his diary some of what he learned about the victims. More had killed themselves in winter than in summer; their bodies were buried for seven years, then exhumed, boxed, and saved in case relatives wanted to rebury them; the casinos, hoping "to keep things

quiet," stuffed money in the corpses' pockets to suggest they had not murdered themselves over gambling losses. Bess had continued unwell—
"Maybe she is sick???," he wondered—and in his diary he wrote: "Saw
grave of man and wife who committed suicide together."

Returning to England to begin five months of contracts there, Houdini
spent Christmas Day in London. He had often done so with pleasure, but
he passed this Christmas with "a soul of pain." The thought of Hardeen in
New York with his sons stirred up old sorrow about his own childlessness,
and with that the memory of Cecilia's wishes for him. "God has seen fit not
to Bless Bess and myself with children even though Ma prayed for it." In a
letter to Hardeen he described a recent dream: he was back in Appleton,
where he saw his mother and father having coffee under trees in the park,
"so calmly drinking and chatting as they did when you and I were romping
kids." He ran to get his camera. Although he knew in the dream that he had
not owned a camera in Appleton, he searched for it, stopping once in a
while to "feats [feast] my eyes on both our Parents"—the voyeuristic scene
suggesting some childhood witnessing of their sexual activity. "I feared
they would note by my actions," he said, "that I was excited." Writing to
Hardeen brought home to him that for more than six months his correspondence, like everything else, had become obsessed with what willy-nilly kept
invading his consciousness. "I can write alright when I keep away from that
heart rendering subject," he told Dash, "so will try and avoid it, if possible.
But I have to write to my brothers once in a while about HER whom we miss
and for HER with whom I feel as if my heart of hearts went with HER."

Feeling done-in, Houdini was again tempted to quit show business. The
theatrical press reported that on returning to London he canceled his English
bookings, "with the intention of retiring from the stage," but was persuaded
to resume them. Setting out for the provinces early in the new year, 1914, he
once more shuttled around Barrow-in-Furness, Dover, Nottingham. In the
spring he launched a brand-new show consisting entirely of magic, a "Grand
Magical Revue." He seems to have been planning the revue for months
before he left the States, trying once again to get away from the mental and
physical strain of his escapes, this time by dropping them altogether. To
equip himself he went on one of his buying binges, purchasing old and new
apparatus in France and England from magicians, dealers, and inventors,
including the "Cremation of a Living Woman" and the rest of the show of the
nineteenth-century illusionist Dr. Lynn (Hugh Simmons [1831–99]).

The revue proved short-lived, and only a few sketchy accounts of it remain. Houdini varied the length of the show, which ran an hour at most. The parting curtains revealed a glass casket, about the size of a large box of candy, hanging from cords at stage center. Houdini took eight coins one by one from a stand and threw them toward the suspended box. Vanishing as they left his hand, the coins could be seen and heard falling into the closed casket. In Houdini's hands this pretty opening effect was psychologically equivalent to a blood-rite, to some primitive hunter's gorging on his slain wolf to ingest its power. For the glass case Houdini used was a replica of the famed Crystal Casket invented by Robert-Houdin, the powerful predecessor he had recently brought to earth as "the prince of pilferers." Grief may have left him feeling shot, but his chutzpah remained in good repair.

Among the other tricks and illusions in the revue was Calico Conjuring, in which Houdini cut or burned and then magically restored a long strip of cloth. In Money for Nothing, he went into the audience to produce hundreds of coins from thin air—his version of the classic Miser's Dream perfected by T. Nelson Downs. The large illusions included the appearance and disappearance of various assistants from cabinets, and Lady Godiva, the vanish of a pony and rider. The show ended with a revival of Metamorphosis, featuring Bess. She performed "magnificently," he noted, "as though she had never retired." In the circumstances he seems to have found comfort in working with her again. He passed his fortieth birthday, in Edinburgh, with a lament: "Alas, my darling Mother not here with us to wish me birthday greetings."

For some performances Houdini added one of the most ingenious, and vexed, effects in the history of magic, an illusion he advertised as "de Kolta's Marvellous Cube." It was the creation of a bearded, baggy-eyed French magician named Buatier de Kolta (1847–1903)—"my ideal magician," Houdini called him, "the Master Brain of Magic." An epitome of the turn-of-century magician-mechanic, de Kolta invented some of the most popular effects in modern magic, including the Vanishing Bird Cage. His Expanding Die—Houdini's Marvellous Cube—consisted of a bare platform about four feet square and eighteen inches high, on four legs. The magician opened a satchel and took from it a spotted die about six inches on a side. Inside it, he announced, was his wife. He placed the die on the platform, arranging two large open fans at the back. At his touch the die visibly burgeoned, dots and all, springing out to a two-and-a-half-foot cube. Lifting the cube from the platform, he revealed—just as promised—his wife sitting there, cross-legged.

Brilliant though it was, the Expanding Die gave Houdini trouble. He bought the illusion from Will Goldston (who had acquired it from de Kolta's mistress), together with Goldston's "word of honor" that he would not sell another. But duplicates or at least copies of the complex apparatus existed, one of them owned by Houdini's friend Chung Ling Soo (Billy Robinson). At least in his own mind, Houdini had purchased exclusive performance rights to the illusion and had made Soo promise not to present it. When he heard it rumored that Soo was about to do so, he wrote him by registered mail, reminding him of his pledge. Surprised, Robinson replied from Wales that Houdini was "labouring under a delusion." As he recalled their conversation, he had on the contrary told Houdini that he intended to put the die into his show right away.

Given Houdini's emotional state, he may well have misunderstood or just forgotten what Soo told him. In any case Soo was no Houdini-ette but a first-rank magician, best known for allowing two examined and marked bullets to be fired directly at him by two guns, and catching the slugs on a plate. He did not flinch before Houdini: "If you think you are going to brow beat or bully me or intimidate me into not continuing to do it, you have made a big mistake," he wrote back. "I am not jealous of you neither do I fear you." He also pointed out, devastatingly, that Goldston had published construction plans for the die, for anyone to build. It was therefore "foolish" for someone of Houdini's "presumed bright intellect" to "give up a big sum for sole rights of a thing *after* it had been given to the public for a Guinea." Mechanically the die was a headache anyway, and Houdini fiddled for months to "get it into shape." The inner works were such a mess of wires, rods, and springs that he had to take instruction in handling the illusion. And de Kolta's original action made the cube expand sluggishly: "the wire he used for springs may have been good enough for him," Houdini said, "but not speedy enough for me." In the end he probably performed it publicly only once or twice.

With or without the die, the revue seemed to Houdini the "Best show I ever presented." Managers did not think so. They wanted the escapes he alone could perform, not bulky boxes or coin effects that many other magicians could do as well or better. The production was burdensome to transport and expensive to mount, too, including liability payments to an insurance company and eight hundred pounds in wages for six assistants.

Although Houdini perhaps presented his Grand Magical Revue no more than ten times, he brought plans for a new illusion with him to America when he left England. He sailed on the *Imperator*. Resigned to winning "all the sea-sick medals on board of *all* ships," he was pleased by the big new liner's steadiness. And the voyage afforded him, after a year of misery, a moment of real pleasure—the unalloyed egotistic sublime. As he often did, he gave a show during the crossing. The select audience included former president Theodore Roosevelt, with his often-caricatured squeaky voice, thick eyeglasses, and Chiclet teeth. In overcoming his boyhood asthma, Roosevelt had made himself into a horseman, rower, and boxer. Recently he had taken one of his wilderness expeditions, to map the unexplored River of Doubt in the Amazon rain forest. Hacking his way through jungle, he had been bitten by fire-ants and become delirious after contracting malaria. For Houdini no audience could be more welcome. He craved acceptance by the worldly great, and he practiced the muscular manliness Roosevelt had recommended to the nation as "the Strenuous Life."

Reaching back to the spirit-medium bunkum of his medicine-show days, Houdini pulled off a dumbfounding mystery. For one trick he prepared beforehand two schoolroom slates. Apparently blank, they would be tied together to receive a message from the 'spirits.' When separated again, the slates would display a chalk map of South America indicating Roosevelt's travels. In presenting a preliminary trick during the performance, Houdini had Roosevelt write a question on a slip of paper, then fold the slip to conceal what it said. He had planned to give Roosevelt a mediumistic reply, verbally. But on secretly gaining a look at Roosevelt's question, he discovered it to be, "Where was I last Christmas?" The answer was the very map of South America he had drawn on the slate, for use in a different trick. "It was only by the greatest coincidence that this happened," Houdini wrote.

When heaven grants magicians such gifts, as on rare occasions happens, they try to parlay them into holy miracles, as Houdini did. Amazingly, he revealed on the slates the map the spirits had drawn in reply to Roosevelt's still concealed question. He later felt some gleeful twinge of guilt in having created a whizbang effect by doing not much: "It was a shame the way I had to fool him," he wrote. But baffling a former president was worth it. When they took a constitutional on deck the next morning, he said, Roosevelt put an arm around him and asked, "man to man," whether he had produced the map by "genuine Spiritualism." "No Colonel," Houdini said he answered, "it was hokus pokus."

The day before landing in New York, Houdini produced another miracle, of sorts. He was photographed standing on deck next to Roosevelt beside some funnels, in a group of eight men. Next day he sent a copy of the picture from the fogbound liner to his brother Bill, to show him, he said, "that T. Roosevelt and your bro are Pals." To show the world as well, after he got home he had the six other men in the group airbrushed out of the picture. Hokus pokus, he alone seemed to be standing on deck with Theodore Roosevelt. He copyrighted the flattering fake and over the years sent and gave out hundreds, perhaps thousands, of copies.

WALKING THROUGH A BRICK WALL; THE SUSPENDED STRAITJACKET ESCAPE

Back in New York City, Houdini often visited Cypress Hills Cemetery. Sometimes he went with his brothers or Bess, sometimes alone, sometimes to mark his birthday or a religious holiday such as Tisha b'Av, more often simply because he felt the need. Entering each trip in his diary, he also calculated the passage of time: "I go alone to Cypress Hills. . . . Bleak and windy. It is sixteen months and five days since Mother went to sleep. I certainly feel lonely." He felt worse than lonely—forsaken, stranded "high and dry" in "the desert of Life," abandoned like a child who had been taken to a railroad depot by his mother and had watched her depart without him. "Here I am left alone on the station, bewildered and not knowing when the next train comes along *so that I can join my mother*."

Places associated with Cecilia took on a different meaning for Houdini. Leo drove him and Hardeen to Asbury Park, to photograph the scene of her death—room eighteen, he recorded, Imperial Hotel: "things have never been the same, since," he wrote afterward, "and I know that they can never be the same again." Appleton lost its attraction for him. He had often revisited the town in the past, and then delighted in telling his mother what he had seen. But now "the link with the past is severed, and the charm of going to my home town is gone for ever." Nor could he tolerate any longer living in the splendid Harlem brownstone he had bought in the first flush of success and shared with his mother over the last ten years: "the Home is a

Home no longer for me," he decided, "and must be disposed of." In August 1914 he advertised the place for sale "at a sacrifice," asking eighteen thousand dollars, two thousand dollars less than he had paid for it, not to mention the automatic hot-water plant and other improvements he had installed. Either because he had no buyers or, more likely, because he reconsidered selling, he instead leased the house to a fraternity from nearby Columbia University.

Two months after returning to New York, he and Bess packed their personal things and went to live, "for a year at least," with Hardeen, his wife, and two children in Brooklyn, in a house at 394 West Twenty-first Street, Flatbush—cable address applicable to them both: "Handcuff, Brooklyn."

In dozens of small ways Houdini kept Cecilia ever present. He went back over entries about her in his diaries and wrote brief comments on some, as if drawing out significances hidden at the time. Next to an earlier entry that some buttermilk had spoiled her stomach, he wrote, "Mamma did not want to die. She suffered very much." He printed up in quantity and mailed out a black-bordered mourning card with an engraving of Cecilia and the inscription IF GOD IN HIS GREATNESS EVER SENT AN ANGEL ON EARTH IN HUMAN FORM, IT WAS MY MOTHER. Turning Mother's Day into one of the high holidays, he wrote to Anna Jarvis, daughter of the woman who had founded the commemoration; sent flowers on one Mother's Day to "all Mothers graves I knew"; drew up a collection of Mother's Day sentiments, beginning, "Every day is mother's day for me"; and began a Mother's and Father's Day scrapbook. He filled it with pictures of himself, Bess, and Cecilia, and verselets entitled "Today is Mother's Day," "My Father's Voice," "Just An Old Woman," "When Pa is Sick," "Only a Baby Small." He pasted in pertinent newspaper articles. One item, headed "Dies at Mother's Burial," concerned a mourner at a New York cemetery who collapsed beside his mother's open grave and dropped dead in the arms of his wife.

On the inside front cover of this breviary of mother-worship Houdini wrote: "Live with your friends. . . . remembering they may one day be your enemies." Considering the mushy content of the scrapbook, the hardbitten epigraph stands out with the ill grace of a spittoon. But trustworthiness was what Houdini saw in Cecilia as unique. It set her apart from the world of bodysnatchers against whom he must defend himself by exacting promises, patents, oaths: "I . . . swear never to betray Houdini," he had a new assistant vow. "So help me God almighty and may he keep me stead-fast." In fact, except for Cecilia, Bess, and a few others, Houdini had little faith in people: "the pain will ever be there," he felt, "for . . . real loyal friends are scarce in this world."

Houdini's future in entertainment still seemed fuzzy to him: "this is the first time in my life where I have had time, wherein I need not hurry or worry, for the world looks and feels different since my Mother joined Her Best Friend and Sweetheart my Father." To make things even more uncertain, just four days after he returned to the United States came the political murders of the heir to the throne of the Austro-Hungarian Empire, Archduke Franz Ferdinand, and his wife. Over the next two months Czar Nicholas II had mobilized his army, Germany had declared war on France and invaded Belgium, and Britain in response had declared war on Germany. Houdini had been booked in Germany for annual three-month engagements over the next five years. These were canceled as Allied and German armies began fighting along the Western Front.

Houdini did not lack offers to perform away from the erupting war in Europe. One theatrical paper reported that he was going to Japan; he had in fact looked into the possibility of playing Tokyo and other cities in the Orient, but the idea came to nothing. Insistent offers came for a three- to four-month tour of South Africa. A Cape Town agent named Harry Hanson wrote him half a dozen times promising that "there is money in this country for you"—and few expenses beyond two pounds a week to buy drinks for reporters. He also held out the lure of vanquishing a popular South African imitator, or in this case impostor, who actually appeared under the name Houdini. "If I could induce you to come out with a small company," Hanson wrote, "it would be a splendid boom and advertisement to bill you as the 'Real and out [sic] and only Houdini.' " Houdini learned that "Houdini," in actuality Abraham Beresford, was a genuine bad egg who had served twelve months' hard labor for shopbreaking and theft, and one month for battering his illegitimate son with a rope. Houdini kept the prospect of a tour in South Africa alive (but never went there), meanwhile granting Hanson power of attorney to get an injunction prohibiting Beresford from using his name.

In the fall of 1914, still rather drifting, Houdini fulfilled an earlier contract to appear at Hammerstein's Roof Garden in New York, then accepted an offer to once again play the Keith and Orpheum vaudeville houses, mostly out west. His touring over the next sixteen months or so first took him east to Boston and north to upstate New York and Canada; then into Chicago, Toledo, and elsewhere in the Midwest; from there to California and Colorado; and finally to Texas, Tennessee, and Louisiana before he returned east and settled again in New York in the early spring of 1916.

As though picking up the pieces of his failed revue, Houdini led off with a new illusion he had bought in England but not yet shown. As "Walking Through a Steel Wall," its invention was claimed by S. E. Josolyne (1892–1965), a British magician who sold Houdini the secret and performance rights, without any apparatus. Houdini reworked Josolyne's idea, and presented it as "Walking Through a Brick Wall." To forestall thievery he again copyrighted the effect as a playlet, in this case the story of a father who in wishing to deny his daughter's hand to a suitor—the son of his worst enemy—sets the young man the impossible task of walking through the brick wall in his garden, which the youth of course does. Working on the stage until four in the morning to set up the illusion, Houdini presented it first at Hammerstein's, and after that at the Boston Keith's.

As seen by the audience, a large brick-and-mortar wall was erected, running from the front of the stage to the rear so that both sides could be viewed. The wall was genuine; in Boston it was put up by members of Bricklayers Union No. 34. With a large stage committee grouped around the sides of the wall in semicircles—making a sort of human parenthesis about the structure—Houdini stood facing the middle of one side. A six-foot-high screen was placed around him, its twin set in the same position on the other side of the wall. The *Boston Globe* described what happened next:

> Houdini's hands wave above the screen. "Here I am!" he cries. "Now I'm gone."
>
> Immediately the screen which covered Houdini is taken away. The prisoner is not there. Immediately the screen on the opposite side of the wall is taken away. There stands Houdini, smiling serenely at the mystification of the clever ones.

The magician's seconds-only flight from one side of the wall to the other, his apparent passage through solid brick, was visually astonishing. Houdini no sooner presented the illusion, however, than the prolific British illusion-builder P. T. Selbit (Percy Thomas Tibbles [1881–1938]), claimed it as his invention, not Josolyne's, embroiling Houdini in their dispute. Magic dealers in New York and Indianapolis began offering blueprints of the effect for only fifty cents. Probably also because of the effort involved in building and tearing down a brick wall twice a day, Houdini performed the illusion only a very few times before turning it over to Hardeen.

Houdini's new tour produced three lesser wonders, and one masterpiece. In Fort Worth he donned a quilted overall and Eskimo-style hood to protect his head. Hands tied behind his back, he allowed himself to be dragged down Main Street roped behind the motorcycle of Ormer Locklear, a local hill-climbing stair-bumping daredevil. Jounced a short distance, Houdini freed himself before the cycle attained real speed. At the Washington, D.C., Keith's, he notched another president when Woodrow Wilson saw him do the Water Torture Cell. By his account Wilson said to him afterward, "I envy you your ability of escaping out of tight places. Sometimes I wish I were able to do the same." A further lift awaited him when he visited the Senate gallery the next day. After several legislators recognized him and waved greetings from the floor, he was invited to the room of Vice President Thomas Marshall, where he did an impromptu turn for a crowd of politicians. He called the overlapping events "the proudest day of my life." In Los Angeles he risked an escape after being literally buried alive, manacled. His attempt is not well documented, but he reportedly experimented first by having himself shackled and buried at shallow depths, clawing his way out of one or two feet of sandy soil. When fully six feet under, however, he tired fast from trying to clear the suffocating ceiling of earth. For a moment, by this account, he panicked. Breath running out, he tried to holler, clogging his mouth and nose with sand. But, calming himself down, he found he strength to dig through, "completely exhausted."

Houdini's tour brought forth the image by which he remains most often visualized: a man in white shirtsleeves and dark trousers dangling upside down from a tall building, arms outstretched in a pose of inverted crucifixion. He seems first to have attempted his "outside stunt"—as he called the Suspended Straitjacket Escape—hanging forty-five feet from the office building of the *Minneapolis Evening Tribune* on September 29, 1915. Over the next three years he performed it almost anytime he opened in an American city large and modern enough to have skyscrapers. From Denver and Omaha to San Antonio and New Orleans, Cleveland and Pittsburgh to

New York and Providence, the "outside stunt" became frontpage news, the enormous crowds drawing teams of reporters, photographers, and cameramen who made it the most fully recorded of all his escapes.

A typical newsreel of Houdini's performance opens on a broad avenue or public square in the city's business district, usually before the multistory office building of a newspaper. He cannot be seen for the dun-colored sea of bobbing straw hats, caps, and derbies, a shoulder-to-shoulder human horde, mostly men and boys, packing the place in numbers up to a hundred thousand. Traffic has frozen, although the milling police try to clear an aisle through which here and there a streetcar, automobile, or horse carriage barely creeps, engulfed by spectators who fill the avenue for a quarter mile or more, pressed even into sidestreets from which nothing can be seen. Work has stopped too. Thousands jam the balconies of surrounding office buildings, lean from open windows, roost on ledges and rooftops straining for a look. Dozens more swarm over the fenders and roofs of cars, wrap themselves around telephone poles, watch from scaffoldings. Some in the distance raise binoculars. The crowd is so tightly squeezed together that it seems to move as one, an agitated amorphous blob.

Houdini stands on the platform of a horse-drawn wagon, parked against the sidewalk. A breeze lifting both strands of his short necktie, he addresses the throng through a giant megaphone. When he waves his fedora in greeting, many take off their hats and wave back. His curly graying hair, parted as always in the middle, is slicked down. He takes off his necktie, laughing and joking with those nearest the platform, and slips his arms into the camisole, of leather or canvas, held out to him by two or three volunteers—policemen or insane-asylum attendants. One embraces him in a bear hug while another buckles him in, sticking a knee in the small of his back for purchase. Grimacing, Houdini braces his feet as the attendants draw and pushpull the straps, the trio staggering about like dancing drunks.

In his tight cocoon Houdini lies down on the platform. Collins wraps padded cloth around his ankles and carefully ties them together by drawing in and around them figure-eights of heavy rope, which he attaches to the hook of a windlass. Above, a beam projects from a window at the top story of the building, with a block and tackle. Collins and some others raise Houdini's legs toward the rigging, as workmen draw the rope steadily through the pulleys. Head downward, he is hoisted toward the beam, slowly jerked upward in short fits and starts, higher and higher, swaying and bouncing slightly, passing windows filled with onlookers, faces in the crowd turning upward with his ascent. The hauling stops when he dangles nine stories or more above the street. For a moment he is still.

Then, suddenly, the struggle begins. Houdini all in one moment thrashes, twists, arches, swells and contracts, his neck tendons bulging. Bending and unbending from the waist, he flaps his torso as if doing high-speed situps, spinning on the rope that whips around above him. Arms still encased, he forces one then the other canvas sleeve over his head to work at the buckles on his back. Some of his white shirt is showing, the jacket having loosened and slipped down his trunk. His paroxysms seem epileptic. He frees the strap connecting the long sleeves. He flips the strap over his shoe soles and tugs on it violently, a crazed weightlifter stooping to lift himself by his own feet. In three minutes or less, body flexed like a bow, he shucks the jacket off his head. He grabs it with one hand, holds it out, then drops it from the height to the platform below. His figure starkly visible in his contrasting white shirt and dark trousers, he flings his freed arms to the side to signify his triumph.

Houdini is lowered swiftly to the ground, still upside down, arms still outstretched. At street level his body is gently passed along on upraised hands to the platform, and carefully helped to a standing position by Collins. Shirttails out, hair snicksnarled, broadly smiling, Houdini bows to the applauding crowd. Beaming still, he knots up his tie, kibitzes with spectators pressing to the edge of the platform. The applause continues, and he acknowledges it by applauding back, hands raised high.

Houdini's new escape was no less chancy than spectacular. He had noodled out of straitjackets hundreds of times, of course, and had often hung from his ankles in the Water Torture Cell. Combining them, in effect, offered the (small) advantage that the torso lengthens when suspended upside down, producing some extra slack inside the jacket. But the several-story haul on pulley ropes and the midair convulsions in getting free painfully strain the ankles, however well-padded and securely tied. When Houdini did the escape in Oakland, the ropes intertwined so that he could not be lowered to the ground. A window cleaner finally leaned out and drew him to safety with a couple of towels, but only after he had been hanging some eighteen minutes. The ordeal left his ankles in "pretty bad shape," he said. He soon adopted a new ankle harness made of strong bands of webbing with the ropes attached to them, and added a safety wire to one ankle so that he could be fished in if the pulley failed. Because the ankle tying was crucial, he entrusted it only to Collins and his other assistants, as he did the still-more-critical moment when he was lifted by hand toward the rigging, held by the shoulders and steadied as the pulley began to lift. Here a wrong move could fracture his neck.

For the rest no one could help. To be run up into the air head over heels on a block and tackle drains blood into the brain, dizzyingly. At about 30 feet the rope begins twisting. Seen from 150 or more feet, upside down, the masses of people and concrete sidewalk below seem the maw of the grim reaper: "The whole town of Boston whirled around me," Houdini remarked of one performance. "My eye was the axis of the town."

There is always danger, too, of catching in overhead wires or hitting the building wall, always close by. (Several performers have been killed trying the Suspended Straitjacket Escape.) Houdini himself once cut his head, apparently on a window ledge. But as everyone realizes, he wrote, "the easiest way to attract a crowd is to let it be known that at a given time and a given place some one is going to attempt something that in the event of failure will mean sudden death."

The crowds did of course come, the largest that had ever seen him or anyone else perform. Newspapers in city after city tried to gauge their unprecedented size: "There has not been such a crowd of people gathered around a newspaper office in Baltimore since the time of Cleveland's first election, back in 1884"; "Never has Providence seen such a gathering"; "it was the biggest crowd ever assembled in Washington at one place except for the inauguration of a President." Photographs and films of these gasping and screaming assemblies record how much of his success Houdini owed to the mass culture of the new century. The impersonal newspaper offices or bank buildings from which he dangled made a stage on which he could be seen for blocks, playing out a personal drama before a corporate background that he transformed into a spellbinding civic theater of thrills.

JACK AND CHARMIAN LONDON; JESS WILLARD

The final months of Houdini's Keith-Orpheum tour brought him two unusual encounters—one gratifying and fateful, the other bizarre but a boost. While performing in Oakland, late in November 1915, he met the novelist Jack London and his second wife, Charmian. Houdini sought and enjoyed the company of literary people. Over the years he had met or corre-sponded with the poets-of-sorts Edwin Markham and Edgar A. Guest, and the minor novelist Edna Ferber (like Houdini, a Jew who had grown up in Appleton). But Jack London was in a different league. A Californian fired up with frontier rebelliousness, he had been an oyster-pirate, boy socialist, Klondike gold prospector, railroad tramp, and newsman, but was famous as the author of vastly popular novels about the tooth-and-nail Struggle for Survival, such as *The Call of the Wild* (1903) and *The Sea-Wolf* (1904). He surely knew of Houdini before they met; the hero of his then-most-recent novel, *The Star Rover* (1915), undergoes "Post graduate courses of strait-jacketing" while awaiting execution at San Quentin. Adventurous and impulsive, London found in Charmian a formidable "Mate-woman," as he liked to call his wife, an outdoors-loving writer and musician, liberated, vivacious, and seductive.

From their nearby ranch at Glen Ellen, the Londons went to see Houdini perform at the Oakland Orpheum. Great theater and vaudeville fans, they visited him backstage after a matinee and took him to a favorite restaurant for dinner. They so much enjoyed the meeting that they returned to see him again the next day. Jack had spent five hours in a dentist's chair, but gamely went onstage as part of the committee when some stevedores trussed Hou-dini in a challenge tie. Again they dined out after the show, this time joined by Bess, and the next day, Thanksgiving, the Houdinis gave a dinner for Jack and Charmian in their hotel room. Hardeen was present too. Still playing out the cooked-up feud with his brother, he happened to be appearing in Oakland at the rival Pantages theater. Evidently Houdini already considered the Londons special friends, for he or Hardeen let them know that the 'feud' was a publicity gimmick. At the dinner or before, Hou-dini had photographs taken of himself and Bess with the Londons, and of himself alone with Jack—a new T. R.—copies of which he sent to friends.

Houdini was scheduled to leave for Los Angeles, but the couples made plans to meet again in the future. Charmian sent the Houdinis a copy of *The Log of the Snark* (1915), her narrative of the Londons' attempted round-the-world voyage in a fifty-foot ketch designed by Jack. She inset a photo-graph of herself, in a towering bonnet, and Jack, in his union suit, resting against the *Snark*'s lifeboat. Her page-covering inscription looked forward to a reunion, hoping "we may all gather in the Valley of the Moon some not far distant day. . . . Yours for Adventure." But in addressing the copy to her new friends she miswrote the word 'wife': "Dear Harry Houdini and Harry Houdini's dear with." Whether or not the slip can be read as a wish to make Bess disappear, Charmian was attracted. "Charming Houdini," she recorded in her diary. "Shall never forget him." In fact, neither of them would forget.

By the time Houdini received the book in Los Angeles, he was bursting with news for the Londons—and for everyone else. He sent off a letter to Jack: "What a scene you could have written, had you been present and witnessed the battle." The "battle" was fought at the Los Angeles Orpheum on the evening of November 30. Houdini had called for a committee of ten to certify the conditions for some escape, but only seven volunteered. He therefore stepped to the footlights, smiled, and made, as he recounted his words, a graceful appeal:

> I said that I would be highly honoured, and I thought the audience would likewise, if instead of three men, one who was equal to three would come up. "I refer to Mr. Jess Willard, our champion, who, I hear, is in the house."

Surprised into silence a moment by the announcement, the audience broke out into gusty applause. Jess Willard was the heavyweight champion of the world. He had won his title seven months earlier by knocking out Jack Johnson in twenty-six rounds under brutal sun in Havana. Houdini looked toward the first balcony, where Willard was seated—a six-foot seven-inch giant whose top fighting weight was 265. For a ring aficionado such as Houdini, the heavyweight champion was in a class of celebrity not much less exalted than Roosevelt and Wilson. "Those who are in favour of having Mr. Willard on the stage," he continued, "please signify by applauding." The audience clapped tumultuously.

Willard's reply was not what Houdini, or the two thousand ticket-holders, expected. "Aw, g'wan with your act," he groused. "I paid for my seat here." Houdini started to get out some answer, but Willard went on: "Give me the same wages you pay those other fellows and I'll come down." Ironically Willard's grumbling may have been nothing more than a cover for stage fright. Although he had once killed another fighter, Bull Young, in the ring, he was known to have a peaceable disposition and to be embarrassed by his awesome size. Some even thought he lacked fighting spirit, and that the aging Jack Johnson, certain he could not beat the "White Hope," had reposed on the canvas for the count.

The audience, sensing something unusual, became quiet. But Houdini tasted blood. He had often before kicked up a fuss onstage, and was not about to be humbled now. He said he would be happy to pay Willard what he paid the rest of the committee, i.e., nothing. He repeated his invitation, with a bite: "Don't crawfish. Kindly step right downstairs and come on stage."

Rising out of his seat this time, Willard called out, "Go on wid the show, you faker, you four-flusher. Everyone knows you're a four-flusher." As the audience began hissing Willard, Houdini strode to the footlights, "white with rage" by his account, and let him have it:

> Look here, you. I don't care how big you are or who you are. I paid you a compliment when I asked you to be one of the committee. You have the right to refuse, but you have no right to slur my reputation. . . . let me tell you one thing, and don't forget this, that I WILL BE HARRY HOUDINI WHEN YOU ARE NOT THE HEAVYWEIGHT CHAMPION OF THE WORLD.

Willard's swearing and cursing in reply was drowned out by the yelling din of the audience, who all turned on him and, the *Los Angeles Record* reported, "hissed him from the house." As Houdini described the scene in a letter to his sister Gladys, "nothing like this howling mob of refined ladies and gentlemen ever crossed my vision of success. . . . Instead of a place of entertainment, it was a seething, roaring furnace."

The uproar got frontpage photos and headlines in Los Angeles and New York: HOUDINI MAKES MONKEY OUT OF JESS WILLARD; CHAMPION DRIVEN FROM THE THEATER BY HOOTS AND CALLS; WILLARD LEAVES TOWN. The story stayed alive for days in follow-up accounts of Willard's secret departure from Los Angeles, criticism of him by his friend Jack Jeffries (JEFF MAY PART WITH WILLARD), and Houdini's afterthoughts. The last took rise partly from an event abroad, the deaths of 128 Americans in the torpedoing of the British liner *Lusitania* by a German submarine. Sharing in the upswell of patriotism that resulted, Houdini told a reporter: "I am an American and am more proud of that fact than anything else. That's why it hurt me so to realize that Jess Willard, whom I regarded as OUR champion, would act as he did."

For all his public indignation, Houdini was privately delighted. "I have received at least a million dollars' advertising space from this fray," he wrote Gladys. He had acted out his million-dollar fantasy too, his treasured scenario of triumphant displacement. He had not merely taken on and stared down Jess Willard, but overthrown him, "struck him a blow that knocked him out of the theatre," he said, "knocked him down and out of the hearts of hundreds of thousands of his admirers." The rumpus did him good. After so long a spell of listlessness and grief, it made him feel a bit like Houdini again. "I am greeted on the streets as 'Hello, Champion' and 'How is the Champion?'"

NINE

1916–1917

HOUDINI IN 1916

I've about reached the limit," Houdini told a reporter in the spring of 1916, before being hoisted to still another roof. "Hereafter I intend to work entirely with my brain." The world had often heard this swan song, of course. But the "outside stunt" turned out to be the last escape Houdini invented. Between 1916 and 1919, entering his mid-forties, he began remaking his life and career, channeling much of his imagination and energy away from vaudeville and variety into other interests.

At this moment of middle-aged metamorphosis, Houdini found that his escapes had earned him a degree of fame beyond which celebrity, the adoration of the moment, passes into mythology, celebrity etherealized by historical memory. Taking on the lineaments of a fictional character, he appeared in Germany as the co-hero of a thirty-two-page dime novel, *Auf den Spuren Houdinis* (Trailing Houdini), published also in Danish and French editions. Here a trio of envious Handcuff Kings tries to eliminate him by pouring sulfuric acid into his Milk Can. He is rescued by none other than the admiring Sherlock Holmes. The press often coupled the two men as opposite-but-equal forces, Holmes able to penetrate all secrets, Houdini possessing secrets that cannot be penetrated. In 1920 Houdini also starred as the hero of "Houdini's Schooldays," a six-month series in *Merry and*

Bright, an English comic book for boys. Depicted in Eton collar and straw boater, he cavorts as a fifteen-year-old student at Rathgar College, learning Latin and mastering Euclid with the rest, but on the side thrashing school bullies and picking a locked classroom door with a penknife. Political cartoons often compared his knack for getting out of a tight spot with the government's immobility in some predicament. In one of dozens, a worried-looking Uncle Sam appears inside a chained submarine labeled "U-Boat Crisis," thinking, "If I could only find a way out o' this," while the tagline says, "But Your Uncle is Not a Houdini."

Houdini was no less illustrious among his peers than with the public. The *Celebrated Actor Folks' Cookeries* (1916), a cookbook, offered in addition to recipes-with-photographs from such other stars as Enrico Caruso, Theda Bara, and Charlie Chaplin, one supposedly from Houdini for "Bread-and-Butter Custard," an abomination of sugary custard poured over buttered white bread, then baked. ("I happen to have a weakness for sweets," the book quotes him as saying.) Over the years he had worked with or gotten to know the leading variety performers of the period, among them Fannie Brice, Al Jolson, Eddie Cantor, the Keatons, Sir Harry Lauder, George M. Cohan, and W. C. Fields. Even in the face of such competition, his friend Will Rogers, the lariat-twirling cowboy satirist, called him "the greatest showman of our time by far." The theatrical newspaper *Billboard* went perhaps even further in rating him "the greatest showman on earth."

Debuting in the 1918–19 edition, Houdini was listed in *Who's Who* regularly throughout his lifetime. A Pittsburgh newspaper reported that his salary was "nearly double that of the President of the United States." Magicians of the period named tricks after him, such as "the Houdini Cards," in which a selected card 'escapes' from a deck bound with rubber bands. Ministers of different sects preached on "Life's Straightjackets [*sic*]," on "Houdini and the Art of Getting Out of Things," or against drink: "When whiskey ties you up you STAY tied." News was made by a horse named Houdini, which came in first at a New Orleans track, a twenty-to-one shot; by a rodeo cowpuncher who dived into the Harlem River on his horse, also named Houdini; by a farmer who went looking for his runaway four-foot-long alligator, named Houdini too.

In fact "Houdini" was passing into the language. "The name of Houdini has now become accepted everywhere as an adjective," the *Columbus Dispatch* noted. "Everywhere newspaper paragraphers, editorial writers, cartoonists and even lexicographers are using the name of the celebrated escapist." As a noun "Houdini" stood for an expert at extrication; adjectivally it signified "elusive"; in verb forms it meant to make a getaway. Houdini himself observed to the wife of a prominent dictionary publisher, Mrs. Mable Wagnalls, that a Scottish murderer who sold his victims for dissection had entered the dictionary as "burke"—a verb meaning to dispose of something quietly. Might not a "respectable young man," he suggested to her, "eventually get into the dictionary some time"? Mrs. Wagnalls took the hint. In its 1920 edition, Funk & Wagnalls' popular dictionary included the verb "hou´di-nize"—"To release or extricate oneself from (confinement, bonds, or the like), as by wriggling out."

In having become universalized into a human type and a mode of action, Houdini realized something of his lifelong desire to be considered unique. And following such singularly famous personages of his time as Chaplin or Pavlova—and many others in history—he wished to be thought of by a single name only. "I would like to be known as Houdini, not Harry Houdini," he wrote, "It sounds better, looks better, and is better." He sent out Christmas cards that caricatured him sitting at his desk, behind a sign reading DON'T CALL ME MR. HOUDINI—JUST SAY "HOUDINI." Being addressed any other way riled him: "I am called Harry on legal documents and by my enemies." There was, after all, no Mr. Alexander the Great or Harry Columbus.

Much of what had brought Houdini to this height he was now preparing to downplay or abandon. By the 1920s he would seem a different sort of public figure altogether, less easy to define as "to release or extricate oneself," but no less clever, fiery, and entertaining.

THE FDC; DRAMA COLLECTING

Houdini's withdrawal was timely, for vaudeville was being challenged as the major form of popular entertainment. Phonographs and, soon, radios, were bringing music and song directly into people's homes. Within four years of the opening of the first American motion picture theater—in McKeesport, Pennsylvania, in 1905—eight thousand more opened. By 1915 movies offered such serious competition that the vaudeville impresario E. F. Albee threatened to cut the pay of, or blackball, acts that appeared in them. He warned Houdini personally: "your value in vaudeville would be very much lessened on account of your name being advertised as extensively as it would be in motion picture houses." Just the same, many big-name acts went into movies, and the rewards were great: *Billboard* reported that Chaplin, at one time a music hall performer, received a $150,000 bonus for signing on with the Mutual Film Corporation, at a weekly salary of $10,000.

Houdini was interested, and already had some motion picture experience. The short straitjacket-escape film he made in Paris had been shown here and there; movies of his bridge jump or Underwater Box Escape now took up ten minutes or so of his thirty-minute turn; and he had served as a special-effects consultant on the 1916 Pathé thriller *The Mysteries of Myra*, devising a whirling-mirror gadget supposedly capable of inducing hypnosis. Around the same time he got an offer to appear in a full-length feature. As originally proposed, he would be Captain Nemo in a screen version of *Twenty Thousand Leagues Under the Sea*, a prospect he faced with both confidence and amused uncertainty, "as I am an adept swimmer, a good actor(?)." The young producers, the Williamson brothers, had invented devices for submarine photography, and Houdini looked forward to recording one of his underwater escapes in front of the camera, for once leaving no doubt about its authenticity. Publicity releases went out in the fall of 1916 that he was looking to buy a five-hundred-pound man-eating shark, to fight to the death underwater, wielding a knife. You bet. The story idea changed in the planning to an international land-sea-air "Epic of the Elements." But the underwater escape remained: he would be shown freeing himself from a sort of bathysphere, a steel chamber with a window two inches thick and five and a half feet in diameter.

Houdini was playing recreational tennis and golf, and had stayed trim. With the old boyish eagerness, he once again began tough training for swimming and staying underwater. He found his breath-holding skill not only unimpaired but improved, "positively BETTER than ever. . . . Two minutes is only a cantor [*sic*] for me, and three is just a bit of a struggle"—a payoff, he believed, for his good habits, "the fact that I do not drink, smoke or keep late hours." Shooting was planned for the Bahamas, where he thought he would also check the possibility of performing for the first time in Havana. But film producers proved no more reliable than theater managers. Like many movie deals, this one went little further than brainstorming. Having been hired for the largest sum, reportedly, ever paid one performer for a single motion picture, Houdini ended up suing the

Williamson brothers for back salary, contending that they never exercised their right under his contract. (He eventually recovered $2,500.)

But the possibility of a new career in movies took hold. Anything but discouraged, Houdini wrote and copyrighted a treatment for a film that would display his talents dazzlingly. Entitled "The Marvelous Adventures of Houdini The Justly Celebrated Elusive American," its thrill-a-minute plot, a harbinger of rockem-sockem action pictures, provided for him to write a code message by a pencil gripped between his toes; wrestle a thug to the death, underwater; climb a wall human-fly fashion; get fired from the torpedo tube of a submarine; and escape from, among other things, a strait-jacket suspended from a ship's yardarm, a steel submarine net, and a burning warehouse in which he sat roped to a chair.

This Ma-saw-me-jump epic also did not get made. But Houdini found a different entry into the profitable movie business. In the spring of 1916 he began organizing the Film Development Corporation. Although automatic film-processing already existed, most developing was still done by hand-dipping racks of exposed film into tanks of solution. Houdini's Film Development Corporation promised a faster, cheaper process using machinery and chemicals worked out by an aniline dye expert named Gustav Dietz. Dried and polished film could be turned out at the rate of eight thousand feet an hour, more in one day, Houdini boasted, "than any 20 human beings can in a week with their present methods." Some of his high hopes were built on ignorance, for instance a belief that the quality of the developed film did not depend on "how badly or *goodly* they are taken." Nevertheless, in September he wrote out a check for $4,900 and signed contracts that brought the Film Developing Company into existence. With himself as president and Dietz as treasurer, the FDC opened an office at 1790 Broadway and leased a sizable factory at 216–222 Weehawken Street, in West Hoboken, New Jersey, where mechanics began putting together the processor and installing equipment.

Houdini also invested long hours in becoming a serious book collector. The effort was linked in his mind with the past, with "my beloved father, selling his library in his old age." He managed to buy back some of the Hebrew works his father had been forced to sell, but did much more than restore what had been lost. Although his magic library had swollen over the years into the largest in America, at least, he advertised in the *New York Evening Post* to increase his holdings:

As I possess the largest collection (private or public) in the world of material regarding magic, magicians, books, scripts, programmes, spiritualistic effects, documents, steel engravings, catalogues, letters, clippings, automata, am still looking for anything that would embellish my collection on the subject of magic or mysteries. HOUDINI, 394 E. 21 St., Brooklyn, N.Y.

Once settled in Flatbush, he had Collins, Kukol, and two other assistants classify his magic collection and arrange his programs and clippings in chronological order; the task took seven weeks.

Set on being more than Dime Museum Harry, here as elsewhere, Houdini considered extending his collecting to drama and the theater in general. He felt unequal to it, however, for the field was "stupendous." He bought two important letters by Edwin Booth, the outstanding American Shakespearean actor of the nineteenth century, and brother of Abraham Lincoln's assassin. But when he learned of the Booth material owned by the eminent Boston collector Robert Gould Shaw, he said, "I felt my feet grow cold." He doubted, too, whether he could afford to tie up the small fortune required to build a major collection. And he realized that because he had concentrated on magic items, he had thrown away many chances to collect while abroad. In all, he felt at first that he would have to stay with what he had: "I have no complaints to make, but could not compete with the big men in Drama."

But of course The Big Men had never stopped Houdini before (MAKES MONKEY OUT OF JESS WILLARD!). He rationalized becoming a drama collector by deciding that his past work as an actor entitled him to become one: "I had forgotten myself that I played parts years ago." As he reasoned it out with a friend, only half kiddingly, in his roadshow days he had done many farces and burlesques, and in Essen had taken the part of himself in a play about the Düsseldorf Fair. "As the house was packed that night, I can take my stand with the other Drama 'guys' and so . . . I am almost fit to be in the Drama collection." *In* the Drama collection is right. On top of undertaking to build a distinguished drama library, Houdini had begun envisioning the even larger respectability of making himself a place in the history of drama.

One of the first "Drama 'guys'" Houdini sought out was Robert Gould Shaw himself, whose private library became the basis of the Harvard University theater collection. He viewed Shaw as the bookman's Houdini—someone who had beaten out all competitors and stood unrivaled: "Mr. Shaw can wade through his material," he said, "and know that no one in the world can possibly duplicate his collection." He visited Shaw in Cambridge and then sent rare magic books and programs to fill out the conjuring section of the Harvard library, often receiving rare playbills from Shaw in return. At first he felt out of his depth with Shaw and tried to impress him. He opined, for instance, about the nationalistic rivalry between the leading American tragedian, Edwin Forrest, and the English actor William Charles Macready, which ultimately left twenty-two dead and thirty wounded in the infamous Astor Place riot of 1849. "I herewith place myself on record as Pro-Forrest," he wrote to Shaw, "as from the data in my collection"—data which cannot have made much of a pile.

Shaw stood for a different Boston from the one Houdini knew intimately. He represented not the snazzy dress-suited engineers of Keith's flagship vaudeville house but the elite reserve of the Athenaeum. Boston Brahmanism both impressed Houdini and offended him. The mix shows through his (presumptuous) advice to Shaw on snobbism and democracy:

> I hope you will accept my suggestion of having a separate list of *"Incomparable Items"* in your collection, from which you could eventually have a book published, & thus spread history in an accessible manner, as all roads do not lead to Boston (though all cultured Roads do) and by having a book published every John Doe in "4 Corners" may be able to read a few things regarding your collection.

Uneasy as the class difference made him feel, Houdini kept up an active correspondence with Shaw, invited him to visit in New York, and gave him tickets when he played Boston. Not least, he sent memorabilia about his own career, seeing in this major collector and in the rising Harvard theater library a pathway to immortality and legitimacy: "Enclosing you newspapers for your Houdini material," he once wrote, "which may some day be useful."

Houdini corresponded too with George Pierce Baker, mentor of Eugene O'Neill and creator of the Yale School of Drama. He also cultivated the friendship of Brander Matthews, professor of drama at Columbia University, and author of such highly-regarded books on the subject as *The Development of the Drama* (1903). He went to hear Matthews lecture on Shakespeare, but halfway through the talk fell asleep, "was so tired after my work." (His boxoffice instinct stayed awake: "not a big crowd," he noted.) He chatted with Matthews afterward, however, and later invited him to Flatbush to see his magic collection—"which I have all reason to believe is second to none"—as well as a so-called extra-illustrated edition he had purchased of one of Matthews's own works, *Actors and Actresses of Great Britain and the United States.* Published in five volumes, the set had been disbound and extended to fully twenty-seven volumes by inlaying four thousand illustrations, portraits, and letters relating to the various players—a serious and expensive acquisition.

It was not Houdini's only one. In his new drama collectors' race he quickly took some gold medals. In March 1917 he purchased from a London dealer several letters of Edmund Kean, the ideal of the Romantic actor; a collection of the personal papers of the popular English comedian Charles Mathews; and a true treasure—a thirty-page manuscript diary of a journey to Paris written by perhaps the most influential actor in the history of the British theater, David Garrick. Just four months later Houdini took on, as he put it, another "*big contract.*" He located and bought eight folio volumes, the entire set, of Kean's programs, including the actor's first appearance at Covent Garden—"the most wonderful Kean collection in the WORLD," he exulted, "some of the bills are NOT in the British Museum."

As a sideline to his drama collecting, Houdini also began buying general Americana. In his earliest touring days with Bess, he had taken time to visit places with historical associations, for instance the house of John Brown in Kansas or of Barbara Frietchie in Maryland. Now he acquired a run of presidents' autographs from Washington to Woodrow Wilson, some of them scarce, including a war letter of Ulysses S. Grant. With more than a little assassin in his own nature, he gathered letters of every member of the Booth family. Naturally it intrigued him to learn too, that "the first thing Edwin Booth did, upon hearing that his brother had assassinated Lincoln, was to secretly visit his mother." Curiosity about his purchases led him to do some small research and writing. He gleaned details about O. Henry's three years in prison for embezzlement from the prison physician, "a lot of information that never will or ought to be published." After buying a manuscript song of Stephen Foster's—a "great gem"—he spoke with an elderly newspaperman who had supposedly roomed with the composer and found him where he had slipped and mortally fractured his skull. Houdini swallowed this yarn and wrote it (had it written) up for *Etude*, a popular music magazine, where it was published as "The Last Days of Stephen Foster." It may have been around this time that he also bought a portable writing desk alleged to have belonged to Edgar Allan Poe.

Houdini made literary capital out of his still-growing magic collection as well. He was preparing a revised edition of *The Unmasking of Robert-Houdin*. Errors had crept into the original, he said, because he had had to proofread the galleys on trains; by now he had gathered twelve whole sheets of corrections. He gave up his in-progress "History Makers in the World of Magic" but turned over what he had done so far to Henry Ridgely Evans (1861–1949), a Baltimore journalist and magic historian who had been writing a similar book of his own. Apparently trusting Evans to make good use of his research, he toasted him: "Let OUR TIME *start the accurate magic age.*" But the new age began and ended, predictably, with Houdini virtually taking over the writing of Evans's history. He sometime stayed up half the night to read the chapters Evans sent for comment, and often sent back a writer's nightmare of uncushioned slams: "some of the material must be eliminated"; "chapters are dull and you must have gone into them whilst you were tired"; "there is a great deal WRONG" (or "wrong very wrong") (or "great great many corrections").

In the end Houdini poured so much of his own material into the history, he said, and spent so much time correcting the drafts, that he all but demanded an equal place on the title page. He proposed that the book appear "as originally planned by Harry Houdini & Henry R. Evans."

GOOD WORKS; THE SAM

With his film and collecting interests already diverting his energy, Houdini offered some more of it to charity, or at least to doing without pay what he considered Good Works. His magic and escapes over the years, he told a reporter, had served the selfish purpose of "building up my own reputation." Now he wanted to turn his ingenuity to some public good: "it is only right that what brain and gifts I have should benefit humanity in some other way than merely entertaining the people." Actually, for all his penny-pinching on small matters, his generosity on large ones was prodigal and already well-known. He often handed gold pieces to the down-and-out and sent checks to "folks in need." Not only checks: he gave many benefit performances at charity hospitals and orphan asylums. A recurrent sort of entry in his diaries reads: "Toronto. Sheas Theatre. I asked Jerry Shea to give 100 old men of the Poor Institution a free show." ("My sympathies," he said, "always go out to the old and helpless.") By one story, true in spirit if not in fact, after seeing shoeless children on the streets of Edinburgh, he bought three hundred pairs of shoes at a bootmaker's and invited the children into the theater to have them fitted.

Houdini's Good Works at this time brought him not only satisfaction but also much publicity, and some new authority. At the end of 1916 the actor John Drew presented a statuette of herself to Sarah Bernhardt, on behalf of the Actors of America. Sculpted in Paris, of bronze, it showed her seated on a throne, as the queen in Victor Hugo's *Ruy Blas*. In addition, it had not been paid for. When Bernhardt received a bill for $350, she returned the piece. Houdini heard about this affront to the world's most admired actress and paid for the statuette himself, with barely credible results. According to *Variety* his generosity begot more than 3,500 newspaper stories. Bernhardt showed her gratitude by giving him the statuette. Still touring although her leg had been amputated the year before in an operation for blood poisoning, she also went to see him do a suspended straitjacket escape in Boston. Houdini told the press that as they drove back to her hotel in a limousine, she asked whether he could restore her missing limb: "She honestly thought I was superhuman." A New Orleans newspaper protested that Bernhardt was too intelligent to ask such a silly thing. But Houdini insisted that she was superstitious and that—talk about barely credible—"I have never in my life sent a misleading story."

Houdini's goodwill went out not only to the disabled and the famous. At the end of 1915 he did needle swallowing before seventeen hundred inmates in the prison yard at San Quentin, and the next fall gave a free show for the warden and some fifteen hundred prisoners at Sing Sing. He had always felt that he himself had the makings of a menace. "Had I been born of different parentage," he often told interviewers, "I might have developed into a very dangerous criminal." At Sing Sing he gave a three-hour show—an unprecedented length for him or any other magician—reviving his handcuff escapes, getting out of a packing box built onstage by convicts, doing magic tricks, projecting a half-hour of his movies, and making a speech in which he urged the men to be "loyal" to Warden Osborne. Obviously sympathizing with the inmates, he reported that when he broke open a loaf of bread to produce a borrowed and vanished watch, some grabbed the bread and ate it "as if it were the finest cake possible. It was white bread, and I think they get grey or black."

In trying to do good, Houdini also devised and patented a new kind of diving suit—"a wonderful thing for me," he wrote, "as it is a boon to mankind." The first diving suit had been created in the eighteenth century, a leather garment with a spherical helmet that received fresh air through a tube, from an above-water bellows. Houdini's suit improved on earlier models by allowing the diver to put it on without assistance and, in an emergency, shed it underwater in forty-five seconds. Houdini achieved this by dividing the suit in two at the waist, where it could be disconnected by pulling a lever. The diver stepped out of the lower-body section, which dropped down, and pulled the upper section over his head like a sweater. Preparing detailed drawings, Houdini secured patents in both England and the United States. He believed he had helped prevent some of the many drownings among divers, the suit being to them, he said, "what Lord Kelvin's safety lamp is to the miner."

Houdini asked and received no money for his Good Works. But one beneficiary of them left him a fortune, at least on paper. The bequest came from the mother of Washington Irving Bishop (1856–1889), a brilliant young American magician who had billed himself as the "World's First Mind Reader." While blindfolded under layers of cotton padding and cloth bags, Bishop was able to find hidden objects, drive a team of horses, and play on the piano a piece of music merely thought of by the audience. His fate, however, was to undergo the most grotesque death in magic history. A sufferer from catalepsy, he collapsed in a trance after a performance at the Lambs Club in New York. Physicians pronounced him dead. And then, believing that its configuration might reveal the secrets of his feats, they removed his apparently still-living brain.

Bishop's mother, Eleanor, had written to Houdini from upstate New York in 1915, begging a loan in memory of her "angel boy." A onetime actress, she had married the grandson of Czar Nicholas I, who abandoned her. She styled herself "HRH Princess Alexandra Nicholas." (She also claimed to have been a friend of Lincoln and a cousin of Gladstone.) With her appeal to Houdini came a hellish tale of woe, perhaps clinically paranoid. She said she was starving, subjected to insult, going blind, unable to walk, about to be kidnapped. The very lives of herself, her maid, and her companion were in danger: "loaded guns were pointed at our heads 3 weeks ago by our landlady's daughter-in-law. She threw a lighted lamp at her mother in law's head—kicked her babies out doors—the grand mother driven to suicide hung herself in this cellar—and the grandson was drownd in the lake." She frantically called on Houdini to protect her and lend her enough money to get to New York City. Houdini sent the money, and in thanks got much of her son's memorabilia for his magic collection.

That was, relatively, nothing. Upon her death, Bishop left Houdini no less than $30 million. The fixed-for-life bequest made headlines, but he wisely told reporters he had no hope of cashing in. What the tormented woman left him, it turned out, consisted of one-third of the claim she believed she had against the government of Denmark, with interest.

Houdini particularly extended himself on behalf of magicians, through the Society of American Magicians. Founded in 1902 (and continuing to the present), the SAM was a fraternal organization centered in New York City. It published a monthly magazine, *M-U-M* (Magic, Unity, Might), and held meetings and staged shows at Martinka's magic shop, where local magicians, many of them amateurs, could try out and exchange tricks. Houdini's relations with the group had run hot and cold. He had resigned in 1908, but four years later the members had voted to recognize his contribution to magic by making him an honorary member. In its present form he considered the SAM parochial and drab, and now devoted still another large chunk of his time to making it a truly national body, in the public eye.

To help him rejuvenate the organization, Houdini enlisted its aging past president Oscar Teale (1847 or 1848–1934), another Mayer Samuel Weiss stand-in. A severe-looking, old-school eccentric who wore small eyeglasses and a high collar, Teale had worked long before as a semi-professional magician called Ottilidio, the name being, he pointed out in his Tealesque way, "an amalgamation of certain vowel and certain consonant sounds to be found in his legitimate name." He wrote a scholarly but weird treatise on magical aesthetics entitled *Higher Magic: Magic for the Artist* (1920). With much pseudo-psychologizing, gaudy variation in typefaces, and grammatical error, it proposed, in nine "Stages," a more aesthetic or "Higher" form of conjuring. This amounted to not much more than substituting the elevated word "problem" for "trick" and keeping one's dressing-room neat as "a veritable Boudoir." The son of a blacksmith—or,

Tealesquely, his "paternal progenitor having been a satellite of Vulcan"—
he yet had studied architecture at Cooper Union and was currently an
instructor in the subject at Teachers College, Columbia University.

Houdini stayed in constant touch with Teale as, during a new western
tour, he tried to bring local, unaffiliated magic clubs into the SAM. Teale
was enthusiastic about Houdini's vision of creating a large, unified,
national network of professional and amateur magicians, and enjoyed the
contact with his vitality: "Between us, *you* and *I*," he wrote to Houdini,
"we will stir things up." Wherever he played, Houdini delivered a lengthy
formal address to the local magic club—making speeches, he said, "is one
of my favourite pastimes"—and usually threw a banquet for the members
at his own expense. Regaling the Buffalo Magician's Club in October 1916,
for instance, he began by trying to allay the fears of many such groups that
in merging with the SAM they would lose their identity as the Demon
Club, the Houdin Club, or the like: "The Magicians Clubs as a rule are
small; they are weak . . . but if we were amalgamated into one big body the
society would be stronger, and it would mean making the small clubs powerful and worth while." He described such other benefits of union as the
"free Masonry" of SAM members finding a welcome wherever they happened to be and, conversely, the safeguard of a city-to-city hotline to track
exposers and other undesirables ("Links & Blinks are coming to Buffalo,"
he imagined the alert going out. "Give them a hot reception. Do what you
can to discredit them.")

As had happened in London, Houdini persuaded many magicians to go
along with him. The Buffalo club joined as the first branch (later
"Assembly") of the Society. With Teale preparing application blanks and
sending him information and contacts by letter and telegram, Houdini dined
with, addressed, and got pledges from similar clubs in Detroit, Rochester,
Pittsburgh, Kansas City, Cincinnati, and elsewhere. "Twill be a grand association if we get 'em all," he wrote Teale. "This is the biggest movement ever
in the history of magic." In places where no clubs existed, he rounded up
individual magicians, introduced them to each other, and urged them into
the fold. "You certainly go on record as the PRIZE WINNER," Teale wrote to
him, in an idiom much to Houdini's taste. "No man could have done more
than you are doing." By the end of 1916, magicians' clubs in San Francisco
and other cities that Houdini had not visited were swamping Teale with correspondence, unsolicited, offering to become assemblies.

The reward for Houdini's efforts came on June 2, 1917, when he was nominated and, unopposed, elected president of the Society of American Magicians, with Teale as secretary. He deserved the distinction. Not only was he the most prominent American magician but also in effect he had created the longest-surviving organization of magicians, which now embraces more than 250 assemblies worldwide.

As with everything else, Houdini did not so much take up the presidency as plunge into it. His first known official act was to call for the creation of a council to investigate the entry "Conjuring" in the latest edition of the *Encyclopaedia Britannica,* which he said contained inaccuracies (and which failed to mention any American magician, himself included). He immediately got the group noticed by organizing a bash at the McAlpin Hotel that was covered by the New York press: MAGICIANS, AT ANNUAL FEAST, FOOL ONE ANOTHER. Soon he was presiding at meetings, overseeing publication of *M-U-M,* looking into ties with the London Magicians Club, getting the members to reserve their much-loved but overworked Battery Salute for important occasions only. The presidency had social advantages too. He was able to freely invite friends and people of influence to the shows and dinners as guests of honor, among them Brander Matthews and Robert Gould Shaw.

THE EXEDRA; THE WEISS FAMILY IN 1916; HOUDINI AND BESS

Chatting with Houdini into the night over coffee and blackberries-and-cream, Oscar Teale became something like his confidant, private secretary, and factotum. Houdini often called on Teale's presumed skill in writing and real ability in architecture, asking him to revise rough drafts of articles he sent for publication, and to oversee the paperhanging and chimneysweeping involved in leasing the Harlem brownstone. He entrusted to Teale an even larger, precious task: designing and superintending the construction of a massive monument for Cecilia Weiss.

Houdini's stop-and-go emotional turmoil had subsided. But mourning had become a constant of his inner life. "I feel her loss," he wrote in the spring of 1916, "more and more as time goes on." He no sooner returned to Flatbush from performing out of town than he visited Machpelah Cemetery; during layoffs he went frequently and even bought a bicycle to ride out there. He returned to Cecilia's grave on symbolic occasions too—the anniversary of her death (when he made a midnight pilgrimage), his own birthday, her birthday—which he honored by having the body of her mother disinterred and reburied near her, to "make Her a birthday present." His grief seemed to be there for good, as though, he said, it would "never be over while the light of Memory is clear." He brooded on the last kiss she had given him, on the dock at Hoboken ("the feeling comes back to me, and I get melancoly [*sic*] moods"); the silk socks and cookies she would mail him at Christmas, to all parts of the world; the letter she had sent his father in 1863 accepting his proposal of marriage, a "sacred possession." In her memory he equipped or donated a hospital ward, designated on a plaque "The Cecilia Weiss Ward. Furnished by Her Devoted Son Mr. Harry Houdini."

Thoughts of Cecilia called up sad recollections of others as well. He nearly cried when, in a subway station, he ran into Mrs. Loeffler, the boardinghouse owner with whom he and his father had first lived in New York. He had been thirteen then, she was now nearly eighty, "the only one left of the Old Guard." He kept a picture of Rabbi Weiss on his dressing-room table; recorded some of his poems on a wax cylinder, in German; stood half an hour in front of the Sixty-ninth Street tenement from which he had been removed for burial, twenty-four years earlier. He took the volume of children's stories, *Our Boys Chatterbox*, he had received at Christmas 1884, when he was ten, and wrote in it: "This book given to me by my Brother Herman & his wife. The only thing I have left of the days of long ago." Others must call him "Houdini," but at such times he saw himself differently. He signed the remark, "Harry Houdini (Ehrich Weiss)."

Suffused with remembrance, Houdini had Teale design a fitting memorial for Cecilia within a monument for the entire Weiss family, including himself. The monument was cut from a thousand tons of Vermont granite, ornamented with figures hewn from Italian marble, at a princely cost of about forty thousand dollars. Teale created it in the form of a Greek exedra (resting place), essentially consisting of a long, curved, high-backed bench and dais on a stone pedestal. Being a monument and not a mausoleum, it did not violate Jewish law, although such theatrical shrines to the dead are distasteful to Jewish custom. While Houdini was on the road, Teale oversaw the labor, which went on for a year in frustrating difficulty and delay. The contractors deviated from Teale's model, a marble seat developed a crack, cement plugged a water-sluice, faulty drilling broke large slabs of stone, which had to be replaced.

The exedra was dedicated, impressively, on October 1, 1916, a Sunday. Houdini hired a scribe to fill in the names on the engraved invitations. About 250 people attended the ceremony, many of the men in tall silk hats, Houdini in mourning clothes. Reported in newspapers as far off as Pittsburgh, the proceedings were conducted by Rabbi Bernard Drachman, who had bar-mitzvahed Houdini, and Rabbi A. B. Tintner, whose father had married him and Bess. The outward display did not make for internal difference, however; six months later Houdini was still lamenting that he had "lost the guiding beacon of my life."

How much solace Houdini found in living family members is uncertain—as he would have wanted it to be. For all his brashness, friends and associates found him reserved, guarded about his personal affairs. E. F. Albee, who signed him to contracts on the Keith circuit for thirty years, remarked: "I never knew him intimately and I never met anyone who did, except his wife." Houdini's move to the Brooklyn home of Hardeen and his wife, Elsie, to judge from his few cryptic references about it, turned out uncomfortable. "I do not like the atmosphere re certain things in Flatbush," he wrote to Teale, with no further explanation. Strain feels present, too, in Houdini's curt diary entry concerning an SAM banquet at which he was to be honored: "Dash and Elsie did not wish to go." If living at close quarters made for friction between Houdini and Hardeen, it is no wonder, since professionally they were miles apart. As president of SAM, Houdini signed his younger brother into admission as but another member. And he had always considered Hardeen a kind of hand-me-down: "if you want to see my old time feats performed," he told a friend, "drop in and get acquainted with him." Whatever the "certain things" he found irritating in Flatbush, he was thinking of moving back to the Harlem brownstone, or trading it for a house in the suburbs.

The lives of Houdini's other brothers were rocky at this time, which disturbed him. Bill, an accountant, hemorrhaged internally in the spring of 1916, a sign that his tuberculosis was advancing. Houdini saw a divorce coming for Nat, the businessman, who was having marital problems. But he does not seem to have been prepared for the shock the divorce brought with it, ten days after. Nat's ex-wife, Sadie Glantz, married Leopold Weiss, Nat's own brother—and Houdini's. Sealed by Pennsylvania law until the next century, the divorce papers may or may not show whether Leo, growing wealthy from his medical practice beside the Plaza Hotel, had carried on with his brother's wife before the divorce, as seems likely. Houdini saw the situation, adulterous or not, as a family disgrace. He connected it with the mysterious secret his mother had alluded to in her dying words, and came to feel that Leopold's betrayal had contributed to her death. He nursed a lifelong wrath toward Sadie, and at some time took a family group-photograph and cut Leo's head out of the picture.

Houdini's own marriage, by most appearances at least, gave him little reason to think of straying. He still found Bess young-looking and spirited: "She is forty-four," he noted on one birthday. "Looks and acts like 24." Although they had a Scots maid they had brought from Glasgow, Bess liked to cook. He appreciated the "fruit-served Breakfast" she readied for his early rising before going to sleep herself, the bar mitzvah spread she prepared for Bill's son, to feed sixty guests. His idea of comfort, he said, was to be sitting in an armchair in his library, "hearing Mrs. Houdini call up 'Young man your lunch is ready.'" He appreciated her Cecilia-like loyalty too: "all my fights when she thinks I am right she is alongside, helping me load the machine guns." He showed his pleasure and gratitude with flowers, shopping checks (a thousand dollars on her forty-fifth birthday), and the lovenotes he continued to send from the road or leave around the house for her to discover. He addressed them to "BEATRICE BEAUTIFUL HOUDINI," "Darling-Darling Darling," or "Winsome Wilhelmina," and closed with some version of "a trillion, billion Kadillion million, Kisses sincerely the rube who is stuck on you." Bess preserved the notes, and later spoke of his having shown her "the greatest tenderness imaginable."

On the other hand, more than twenty years of marriage to Bess had done little to wean Houdini from his mother. On a photograph of himself between the two women, an arm around each, he wrote, "My two Sweethearts." When giving Bess a luxuriously-bound copy of *The Cambridge Book of Poetry and Song* (1882) as an anniversary gift, he recommended that she read first of all Poe's "To My Mother." With what smiles, sighs, or scowls Bess treated this division of her husband's affections is unknown. But Houdini felt some need to justify it. In a letter to her about two years before Cecilia's death, he tried to explain that "the two loves do not conflict," differing as husband from son:

> I love you as I shall never again love any woman, but the love for a
> mother is a love that only a true mother ought to possess, for she

loved me before I was born, loved me as I was born and naturally will love me until one or the other passes away into the Great Beyond, not passing away but simply let us say "gone on ahead."

Despite Houdini's sudsy reasoning, in his affections he had always ranked his mother on a level with his wife, expected Bess to accept the fact, and even in some degree confused her with Cecilia. In one of his unpublished short stories, "Blood Brothers," he named his hero Haddon Harcourt— HH—and gave Bess's middle name, Beatrice, to HH's mother.

In some degree Houdini gave Bess the role of mother in real life too. Despite her elfin girlishness, he often referred to her as "the Boss" and played gee-whillikers Huck Finn to her rule-wielding Aunt Polly. Seeing her as a monitor to his sloppiness, he sent a photograph of himself neatly groomed, inscribed: "You will kindly observe that 'we' have on a nice clean collar and a new tie—as 'we' know you like to see 'us' that way." Before a large audience he once turned to her and said, "Am I a good boy?" He wanted to stay a good boy, too, and not antagonize her: "in home life I make as much noise as a church mouse." The exceptions enough upset him that in his sparse diaries and notes he recorded times when she became "sore," "very mad," or "very angry" with him, and might "give me the dickens" or "get a 'tantrum' and give me hell." Casting Bess as a scolding parent, for all their closeness he was glad at times to be on his own. "Mrs. H has gone to her mothers (good)," he wrote during a week off, "and I am now a grass widower (Great)." What darker thoughts came to him can only be guessed, but he did collect some peculiar newspaper clippings on marriage: "Hubby's Right To Spank Wife Is Upheld by Court," "Polygamy After the War," "Hitched Wife to Plow; Gets 30-Day Sentence."

One fear in relation to Bess particularly troubled Houdini. In trying to do "all that is humanly possible to fortify your future," as he put it, he took out a fifty-thousand-dollar insurance policy payable to her, and transferred the Harlem brownstone to her name. Added to the rest of the money and goods he had acquired, it made a large inheritance, and he worried that after his death Bess might give it away or be cheated out of it. He prepared "important instructions" for her to keep in mind should he die before her. By far the most important was that if she remarried she must obtain an ironclad prenuptial agreement retaining to herself the sole right to what he had left her: "Make who ever it is *sign away his marriage right in every-*

thing, otherwise do not marry him." The possibility of ending up a failure-after-the-fact, of losing to some second-best fortune hunter all that he had earned in his rise from obscurity, struck him with such horror that he repeated the commandment to her in a half dozen other emphatic forms:

> Under no circumstances what so ever, marry any one who will not sign away the marriage potion [*sic*], as they will have half of every-thing I worked and slaved for, suffered and went hungry and sleep-less nights to earn. *Dont marry* if the whoever he may be man will not sign away his marriage right.

He told her to save his instructions and consult them if someone proposed marriage. He read them over periodically himself over the next ten years to see if they needed correction. But each time he found them "to my desire."

Whatever the strains, Bess and Houdini enjoyed each other's company and had a life together. They saw the 1916 Ziegfeld Follies, went dancing. Both of them were astounded to read of the death, in California, of their recently-met friend Jack London, his body poisoned by years of heavy drinking and smoking, drug-addicted from trying to cure his lethal kidney disease. They cabled Charmian London to ask "if this shocking informa-tion is founded on facts."

WAR; HARRY KELLAR; THE VANISHING ELEPHANT

Houdini's new rhythm—"I only work about 7 months a year," he said—was further altered by world events. Since 1914 the United States had maintained neutrality toward the war in Europe, which by the end of 1916 had heaped up more than a million casualties. But after a break in diplo-matic relations with Germany in February 1917, and the sinking of four American vessels by U-boats in March, Congress declared that a state of war had been "thrust upon the United States." By June, General John J. Pershing had arrived in France with his staff, and the first numbers had been drawn in the draft.

Houdini registered for military service the same month—"HURRAH, now I am one of the boys"—but at forty-three years old was passed over. He had felt at home in Germany, and was so much admired there as to inspire a rumor abroad that he was a German spy. But now he distanced himself from the Second German Empire, very publicly. He told the press that he had become an advocate of war with at least part of Germany during his first European tour. Although he had had his first flying lessons in Hamburg, in speaking to reporters he now assigned them to Australia. He destroyed photographs that showed him seated in Hamburg at the wheel of his Voisin, with German officers grouped around the plane. He dusted off the story of his prosecution by Schutzmann Werner Graff in the German courts (HARRY HOUDINI TELLS/OF KAISER'S APOLOGY). At the same time the outbreak of war deprived him of Franz Kukol, his assistant for fourteen years. With vaudeville stages banning German acts and resounding with anti-German sentiment, he may have had to let him go, although by one report Kukol was recalled for service in the Prussian army.

As nothing else had done, American entry into the fighting took Houdini's mind off the dead at Machpelah Cemetery. He immersed himself in the national cause. "My heart is in this work," he said, "for it is not a question of 'Will we win' or 'Will we lose.' WE MUST WIN, and that is all there is to it." One day after the congressional declaration of war, he mobilized the SAM to pledge its loyalty to President Wilson and, at Teale's suggestion, to offer to entertain at army camps. Later he persuaded the organization to invest a thousand dollars of its surplus funds in Liberty Bonds. Scheduled in the fall to begin a Keith tour, he canceled it so that he could devote himself to the home front. He performed before thousands of troops at Fort Slocum, Fort Dix, and other army camps, paying the salaries of three assistants himself, and did numerous Red Cross benefits, once making his entrance escorted by a company of marines, to thunderous applause. The fundraisers cut across customary theatrical lines. He found himself working with vaudevillians Sophie Tucker and Eva Tanguay; Metropolitan Opera contralto Louise Homer and the violinist Albert Spalding; boxers Jim Corbett and Benny Leonard; film stars such as Tom Mix and Fatty Arbuckle.

Houdini himself conceived and mounted a spectacular benefit for the families of troops who had been killed in the sinking of the transport *Antilles*—the first American dead of the Great War. With his instinct for theatrical knockouts, he secured for the event the immense, turreted New York Hippodrome, seating five thousand spectators and occupying almost an entire block on Sixth Avenue. With help from the SAM membership he planned to fill it with a Hippodrome-size Carnival of Magic, "the biggest

magical feat recorded in the history of magic and magicians." And to appear
in the show, he lured from decade-long retirement in California the greatest
and best-respected of his living predecessors, Harry Kellar (1849–1922).

Born Heinrich Keller in Erie, Pennsylvania, the son of German immigrants, Kellar had made himself a place in the pantheon of magic. Although
magicians had appeared in America since the colonial period, the leading
performers until the third quarter of the nineteenth century were visiting
Europeans. Kellar was the first native-born American magician to become
internationally known, the founder of a self-confidently American tradition
of magic. Houdini had met him in Atlantic City in 1908, but did not get to
know him well until the fall of 1916, when he invited Kellar to Flatbush to
see his magic library. Kellar was impressed, calling it "the finest Collection
of the kind in the world," and confessing himself "quite bewildered" by
card effects Houdini showed him. Houdini, as they grew closer, was no less
impressed: "I never knew how really clever he was," he said, "as I only
knew him years ago at a distance." Kellar was the only magician Houdini
ever acknowledged as his superior—as, that is to say, "the greatest magician the world ever saw."

Tall, strongly-built, and serious-looking, bald now but for a fringe,
Kellar in his early days had toured with the Davenport Brothers, as their
assistant and manager. He knew the secret of the Davenport Rope Tie and
had invented a hardly less baffling method of his own, still called the Kellar
Rope Tie, whose correct handling he taught to Houdini. In 1875 he created
a full-evening illusion show that he took all over the world. Stylistically
Houdini considered him "the last of the Grand Masters of the magic of the
past," meaning that Kellar worked not in the rapidfire manner of modern
vaudeville magicians, but with a sphinxlike dignity and perfection of detail
aimed not so much at entertaining as at utterly mystifying. His trademark
Levitation of Princess Karnac, one spectator said, left "no doubt in
anyone's mind but that the girl actually did float in mid-air." In a storybook
moment of magic history, at Ford's Opera House in Baltimore on May 9,
1908, Kellar had formally retired from the stage and passed on his show. As
the orchestra played "Auld Lang Syne," he ceremonially presented his wand
to forty-year-old Howard Thurston, who thereafter billed himself as
"Kellar's Successor."

During this apostolic laying-on-of-hands, spectators recalled, Kellar
wept. But not many knew that he had exacted from Thurston a down pay-

ment and royalty contract by which he received a percentage of his successor's earnings over the next ten years. A shrewd businessman, he retired on his savings, bonds, and real estate to a palmy mission-type mansion in Los Angeles, complete with ice-plant. He occupied himself improving his French with recordings, reading around in religion and philosophy, and hooking yellowtail marlin on light tackle: "it is some sport," he told Houdini, "believe me."

Staged on November 11, 1917, Houdini's Antilles benefit raised nearly ten thousand dollars and turned out to be a combined Kellar love-feast and patriotic magic-circus. As official patrons Houdini lined up the high-society Harriman, Whitney, and Vanderbilt families. He publicized the show in advance by a straitjacket escape on Broadway and Forty-sixth Street, hanging sixty feet from a derrick being used in constructing the Times Square subway. Bess and other SAM wives worked the crowd, selling tickets for the benefit as well as Liberty Bonds. The two-part program offered a roster of opera and musical comedy performers and a bulging cast of SAM magicians. The gala opened with Louise Homer singing "The Star-Spangled Banner" as a detachment of French sailors paraded French and American flags. Some advertised musical stars failed to appear, but Houdini himself cmceed, introducing a drill exhibition by Junior Naval Scouts, and then a razzle-dazzle simultaneous performance by seven prominent magicians. Strung out across the two-hundred-foot-wide Hippodrome stage, they began silently producing silks, flowers, and animals until the stage looked, by one account, "as if a huge department store had emptied its contents." As a climax they unfurled from nowhere a thirty-six-foot blood-red banner emblazoned in gold, SOCIETY OF AMERICAN MAGICIANS.

Houdini performed the Water Torture Cell, but not even that could compete with Kellar's return-to-the-stage, his first public appearance in ten years. Beaming at the audience of five thousand or more, he floated a small table in the air at his fingertips. Then, with a dramatic instinct rivaling Houdini's, he did a close facsimile of the historic Davenport spirit cabinet, producing manifestations although tied up inside. When he finished, Houdini in homage presented him with a large bouquet of roses, and announced that he would not be allowed to walk off. A sedan chair was brought, and while some performers toted Kellar about the stage, the audience stood up to sing "Auld Lang Syne"—a reprise of the Thurston succession ceremony. Others crowding around showered him with a wagonload of yellow chrysanthemums (paid for by Houdini). Touched, Kellar thanked Houdini for the imperial tribute as "a glory and honor such as come to the lot of few men." It could have been engineered, he added, by "none but the master-mind of our greatest showman."

Houdini had another "big surprise" ready for the Hippodrome: "my debut in America as Illusionist." As ever, that was inaccurate: he had walked through a brick wall in Boston three years earlier. But the new illusion did uniquely suit the mammoth Hippodrome, whose stage-apron alone could accommodate two circus rings, and whose pillars and niches were ornamented throughout with elephants—a living specimen of which he now intended to vanish.

Houdini had bought worldwide rights to the vanishing elephant from its British inventor, Charles Morritt (1860–1936), "whom I consider the world's greatest illusionist." The "creature"—borrowed from Powers' Elephants, a popular animal act—was said to be a daughter of Jumbo, P. T. Barnum's seven-ton, twelve-foot mealticket, once the largest elephant of its type in captivity, killed by a runaway freight train. Houdini reported his beast's weight to the press as "over ten thousand pounds"—in keeping with her supposed ancestry—but gave Kellar a figure some six thousand pounds lower. Two tons or five, Jenny, as Houdini called her, entitled him to brag that she represented "the biggest vanish the world has ever seen."

Houdini introduced Jenny about six weeks after the *Antilles* benefit, on New Year's Day, 1918. She lumbered onstage with a babyblue ribbon around her neck, a large wristwatch strapped to her left hind leg. "She is all dressed up like a bride," Houdini said. Asking for a kiss, he fed her a block of sugar as she lifted her trunk, pattering to the wartime audience that she was the cause of the sugar shortage. Twelve men then wheeled onstage a cabinet about eight feet square, a sort of super ghost house. Houdini showed all its sides, opening the back doors and raising the front curtains. As Jenny shambled in, spectators got a last look at the wristwatch, and in "two seconds," by Houdini's count, he reopened the doors and curtain, allowing the audience to see through the cabinet, from which the elephant had evaporated.

The eight-minute illusion quickly became not just "the talk of the town," Houdini said, but "the talk of the show world." He turned down offers to bring it to Canada and England, and to theaters and parks all over the United States, but accepted the Hippodrome's prolongation of his contract from six weeks to nineteen—the longest run of his career. Yet in both Houdini's and later versions, the excitement had more to do with the delightful conceit of vanishing an elephant than with anything the audience experienced. The huge Hippodrome stage not only accommodated Jenny, some magicians felt, but swallowed her up. And when Houdini opened the cabinet, only those sitting directly in front could look inside and see that she had disappeared. The rest of the audience had to take his word for it.

Whatever its real impact, the illusion remains talked about, and it showed Houdini something: "A creature weiging [*sic*] over 4000 pounds vanishes in full glare of the light," he wrote Kellar. "So I am still in the ring."

TEN

1918—1919

CHEER UP; CHARMIAN LONDON

THE FIRST SIX MONTHS of 1918 must have been the most hectic of Houdini's life. Like almost everything else about him, the jumbled pace itself made news: "Houdini, in his spare time," *Billboard* observed, "while not perfecting his new sensation for the Hippodrome, is attending to his film development factory in Hoboken, or else digging up new magical data, or else posing for his picture film, or else entertaining soldiers and sailors, or else working on the plans for a new flying machine." The list lacked one particular: he was also involved in a love affair with Charmian London, Jack's widow.

The one-man circus revolved around the Hippodrome, where Houdini starred twice a day in a patriotic extravaganza called *Cheer Up*. Its stageful of cyclists, tumblers, diving horses, and whatnot offered the wartime audience pageants such as "The Land of Liberty," bringing George Washington, Miss Liberty, and other inspirational figures to life in scenes from American history, with music by John Philip Sousa. Houdini, billed as "The World's Most Famous Dare-Devil," did the Vanishing Elephant and an indoor version of his Underwater Box Escape, made possible by hydraulic plungers that shifted the Hipp stage to reveal an eighty-four-foot elliptical water tank.

Houdini's forays in and out of the theater, all over the New York region, made for a tight schedule. Between shows he sometimes ran off to preside over an SAM meeting, keeping a taxi waiting to rush him back for his second turn. The hourlong sessions left him plenty more to do, down to looking after unpaid dues and supplying menu illustrations for the annual dinner (featuring escapes from miniature cuffs by his frisky new dog, Bobby Houdini, "the Only Handcuff King Dog in the World"). Heading across the river, to West Hoboken, he supervised the installation of new machinery in the three-story lab of his Film Development Corporation. The doubled capacity enabled the FDC to process a million feet of film a week, but also put him in debt: "private investments etc taking up my real time, and hope they will turn out okay." And he found a showless Tuesday in February to move from Hardeen's Flatbush house back to his uptown New York brownstone, requiring two vans to transport his magic collection and four more for his books and manuscripts.

Before and after performances of *Cheer Up*, Houdini also sped off to entertain at military compounds or join Harry Lauder and Will Rogers in a thirty-six-hour Liberty Loan drive. Hustling hard to raise money for the war, he reportedly sold, by May, a million dollars' worth of bonds. In honor of his father he organized the Rabbis' Sons' Theatrical Benevolent Association, which gave benefits and put up a "Jewish Welfare Building," seemingly a recreation center, for troops at a Long Island camp. The group elected Houdini president (again), to serve alongside two other sons of rabbis: Second Vice President Irving Berlin, and First Vice President Al Jolson, a performer Houdini admired as "the only man I know that can hold up a show on broadway [sic], all by himself."

Houdini found work for himself to do even during intermissions. With some fifty thousand doughboys and leathernecks now shipping for France each week, he wrote to Secretary of War Newton D. Baker, offering to teach them methods of escaping from torpedoed vessels—techniques for staying alive underwater, disentangling cables and broken pipes, forcing locked hatches. A room was fitted up at the Hippodrome to which, by telephoning in advance, officers could bring their men for tutoring during intermission. According to *Billboard*, the crash course was "daily besieged by hosts of boys in khaki." Houdini taught them how to escape German handcuffs, too, should they become prisoners of war. As combat training the instruction seems of dubious value. But it probably represented the only time in his life when Houdini willingly shared with laymen, or with anyone else, some of his select, authentic secrets. "I don't have to pick locks for stage purposes any more," he remarked, "for my performance has outgrown those original and small proportions."

Houdini did not stay idle in his dressing-room, either, where he kept a typewriter. Despite the daily scramble he got out his newsy column for *M-U-M* ("Mainly About Magicians"), published several articles ("Confessions of a Jail-Breaker"), pushed along in-progress books on the circus, on paper magic, and on fire eating. Much of the work was farmed out to researchers and ghosts, for instance the compilation of a history of magic in Boston since colonial times. He hired a man named H. J. Moulton to root in newspapers and theater programs for relevant items and type them up in chronological order, sending him sixty dollars every few months. Word by word there is no way of telling how much that appeared in print under Houdini's name was written by hirelings. But Oscar Teale did much editing and ghosting for Houdini, and later said that his boss's contribution was slight: "I have never known him to dictate more than *suggestive* thought, mere fragments, followed by instruction to '*Whip it into shape*' and the 'other fellow' invariably did the *real composition work*."

In the same few crowded months Houdini juggled a plan for erecting in New York a national theater and museum of magic, called the "Temple of Mystery." It would display and demonstrate the apparatus of famous magicians—much of it from his own collection—tracing the history of magic from pre-Christian times to the present. Customers would enter a high-tech version of an Egyptian temple, receive a ticket from a disembodied Oriental hand, pass through doors that opened by their own force, be led by a voice-from-nowhere to a seat that mysteriously lowered itself. (The voices would come from "talking machines" tripped as the patron stepped on concealed floor switches.) "No invention can be too freakish for us," Houdini was quoted as saying. "We want the latest things in science." He announced that he would present at the futuristic temple his long-elusive escape from inside a block of ice. He had Teale draw up some plans for the place, and gave it out that the opera impresario Oscar Hammerstein had offered to build it. But other experienced theater people advised him against starting out while the war raged, and he let the idea lapse.

Houdini knew no other dynamic than *crescendo*, and as if he did not have enough to do he undertook to produce at the Hippodrome, on April 21, a mammoth benefit for the mutual hospital fund of the SAM and the Showmen's League of America. That evening, he announced, he would attempt the most notorious effect in magic—catching a marked bullet fired at the performer from a gun. His hair-raising proffer was widely reported and dramatically timed. In London on March 24, his friend Chung Ling Soo had been killed performing the dangerous trick. He later learned from Soo's widow that some powder had trickled through a small crack of the double-barreled gun into the live barrel. Acting as a fuse, the powder sent a real bullet through Soo's chest, shattering a rib and penetrating his lung, heart, and liver before passing out his back, breaking another rib. When Kellar heard about Houdini's plans he dispatched an alarmed letter: "My *dear boy* this is advice from the heart. DONT TRY THE D——N *Bullet-Catching trick* no matter how sure you may feel of its success. There is *always* the biggest kind of risk that some dog will 'job' you." Out of respect and affection for Kellar, Houdini backed off, and substituted the Upside Down. Just the same, acting as chairman, emcee, and performer he raised several thousand dollars for the hospital fund. As auctioneer of Liberty Bonds during inter-mission, he brought in another fifty thousand dollars for the war effort.

It was amid this breathless scooting around that Houdini again encountered Charmian London. Widowed just over a year, she was spending a few months in New York City, at 125 Washington Place in Greenwich Village. At some time she and Houdini got in touch, and with his tickets she went to see him perform in *Cheer Up* on January 17. What happened between them over the next three months is known only through thirty or so telegraphically brief entries in her unpublished diaries, written before she returned to California at the end of April. More tantalizing still, she did write some longer entries about Houdini but in a stenographic code devised by her uncle, undecipherable except for the number "278," the address of Houdini's brownstone. The snippets offer little more than her impression of a few things he did and said. But, like bits of overheard con-versation, they convey a sense of subject and a mood.

London dressed alluringly for her reunion with Houdini, coming to the Hippodrome in a white serge outfit and white furs. He told her after the show that he did not recognize her because she looked "just like a young girl." The remark may have been calculated, since she was now past forty-six, some two and a half years older than he. On the other hand she remained sexy: dainty but with a Gibson-girl figure; tanned from an outdoor life of swimming and horseback riding; vivid, with twinkling eyes and an expansive radiant smile. She was not disappointed either, but found Houdini "charming as ever." He followed up the meeting much as he still wooed Bess, through bantering notes. During a "wonderful" phone conversation with her the next day, he said he had sent her "a letter within a letter," addressed to "the woman in white." The letter failed to arrive over the next few days, however, leaving her to think he had misaddressed it—and feeling disappointed. She returned to the Hippodrome to see him perform again on January 22, and wrote to him afterward.

However caught up in camp shows and his six-van move from Flatbush, Houdini responded with ardor. In calls to Charmian over the next few days he made a "declaration," she wrote, that "rather shakes me up." Evidently it was the prelude to an affair that began around February 13, after she had gone to see him again at the Hippodrome, sitting in the first row. At some time and some place—her diary does not say when or where—he touched her hand and remarked that she was "trembling all over." His visit to her in the Village one afternoon "stirred me to the deeps." Houdini was obviously wrought up too. "Now I know how kings have given kingdoms for a woman," he told her. "You are gorgeous—you are wonderful. I love you." For several nights she slept poorly, being "too swept still." The romance continued in this breaking-of-the-dam key into March, with more calls, notes, and occasionally, afternoon visits by Houdini to Washington Place. "I'm mad about you," he told her at one time. "I give *all* of myself to you." Or, at another tryst, "You don't seem human to me—I wonder if you have to *eat*"—a comment she thought "sweet."

Houdini and London made an unlikely couple. She had made it a guiding principle to "love dangerously." Her unconventional life with Jack had been filled with socialist friends and liberated sex, sealed by an atavistic sense of kinship that led them to call each other "Mate-Man" and "Mate-Woman." That was a far cry from Houdini's "Sweetie Wifie." It strains imagination to guess how London felt when, expecting a letter from him, she received instead one of his Cecilia-now-and-forever memorial cards with a full paragraph of Mother's Day prose. Or when he said to her, on another occasion, "I would have told her—my mother—about you." Yet she found in him not only a boyish charm but also, as in the wildly adventurous Jack, the appeal of at-the-brink danger. To watch him being chained and thrown into the Hippodrome pool, escaping in less than a minute, was "awfully exciting." She obviously did not at all want, however, a complicated liaison. While in New York she saw many other male friends. And she still grieved for "Mate," and felt homesick for their California ranch. So far as her feelings can be read from her jottings, a just-one-of-those-things affair with Houdini was the unsurprising outcome of knowing a vital, famous, handsome man of miraculous abilities. In her diaries she referred to him as "Magic," or "Magic Man," or "Magic Lover."

What Houdini wanted from Charmian can only be supposed, since none of his available papers mentions her. Her "gorgeous" looks excited him, as she recorded, and the world she came from glowed with the intellectual and artistic distinction he aspired to. For all the lovenotes and anniversary snapshots, too, his bond with Bess seems to have been held together by long, appreciative association and shared fun rather than passion, a commodity whose absence not a few long-married persons of middle age have been known to miss. He was certainly no skirtchaser. But no one of his magnetism and celebrity could have survived twenty-five years in show business without being presented the possibility at least of an attachment or a fling. Bess reportedly revealed that after his death she found a cache of love letters to him from several women, "one a widow whom she considered a very dear friend"—conceivably London herself. (And what did she make of the note from the living Houdini—clearly written under Charmian's spell—addressed to her as "Life Mate" and praising her "sweet woman consciousness"?)

Whatever his motives in the amour, the moralistic Houdini seems to have cringed at what he was doing. Some of his letters at the time refer obscurely to an unspecified inner turmoil. "Been having a hard time with my private affairs," he told one friend at the end of February. "It's been a bit cloudy of late for all of us," he wrote to Teale a few months later. Queasiness in Houdini may explain the several entries in London's diary, beginning in late March, concerning his failure to show up or call. "Expect HH, but no word," one says, and after that: "Still no word on phone from H. Can't understand it"; "HH was doing some benefit work and could not come." The last may have been true: in his all-but-unmanageable schedule he may simply have been unable to find time to phone or see her. More likely he could not stomach the infidelity.

London spent part of April in Boston, and by the middle of the month began planning her return to California. With her departure in mind Houdini began telephoning practically every day. "Am I never going to see you again?" he asked in one call. She interpreted his mood as despairing: "poor, sad, lonely thing," she wrote after another call. "He is *very* alone, & worse than he had feared." And after he rang her the next day, "HH calls up—so sorrowful." But her diary mentions no visits from Houdini.

Having taken a short plunge, Houdini seems to have been content, perhaps relieved, to maintain the pretense of an affair and to savor Charmian's presence by carbon vibrations. Backing out without backing down, he could Don Juan-ize on paper too. London no sooner returned, happily, to the Glen Ellen ranch than she received a letter from him beginning "Sweet-thought One," followed in the summer by a letter of which she quoted only the words "How I miss you,—the magic of memory." Occasional calls and letters, to look ahead, continued until the end of Houdini's life. But London does not seem to have misjudged Magic Lover when, having failed to receive his usual New Year message, she commented in her diary: "Cautious Soul."

THE MASTER MYSTERY; YOUNG ABE; MORE ON THE FDC

In July, Houdini began making his first motion picture. Through a businessman, Harry Grossman, he had been introduced to the film producer B. A. Rolfe; over lunch, the two men proposed that Houdini star in a serial. He considered Grossman a good salesman, and trusted Rolfe's experience, gained during three years in films and nine before that in vaudeville. The trust seems overeager. A rotund-faced Californian, Rolfe claimed descent from *John* Rolfe (and Pocahontas), and had played cornet in the Rolfonians, a novelty orchestra whose sidemen wore morning coats and silk hats. Houdini told Grossman and Rolfe that as he commanded a large salary in vaudeville, he expected substantial returns. He agreed to appear in the film for a weekly salary of fifteen hundred dollars, plus half the profits. The work meant not only a further turn away from stage performance, but also a further, major commitment. "With the Film developing Corp. I now have three businesses to attend to," he reflected, "hope I have not bitten off more than I can chew." Grossman and Rolfe took in a third partner, a leather manufacturer named Fischer, and organized as the Octagon Film Corporation.

Houdini was entering films at a turning point, marked by the multimillion-dollar success of D. W. Griffith's three-hour *The Birth of a Nation* in

1915. Replacing the earlier two-reelers, such ambitious features introduced a high standard of production that Rolfe made it known he would follow. The day of the "fight, fight, thrill" serials was over, he said; he would make a coherent feature film in which "the first consideration is story." Nevertheless, to write the scenario in collaboration with Houdini, he hired the team of Charles Logue and the mystery-writer Arthur B. Reeve, authors of the classic cliffhanger *The Perils of Pauline.* Rolfe used no better judgment in addressing the problem of how to photograph Houdini's "self-liberation stunts." The technology of motion pictures could make anyone *seem* to perform the same escapes. He said he would therefore shoot Houdini in "uninterrupted close-up," without a break and with no editing cuts. Useless, actually: filmed stage magic being indistinguishable from camera magic, the movie camera robbed magicians of their power to mystify. (As Houdini commented several years later, "*No* illusion is good in a film, as we simply resort to *camera* trix, and the deed is did.")

The serial was shot at a studio in Yonkers, one of many motion-picture services springing into existence around New York City. For Houdini it meant a twenty-eight-mile trip back and forth every day, although worth the effort. "I think the film profession is the greatest," he said in one of many press interviews, "and that the moving picture is the most wonderful thing in the world." Movies allowed him, he explained, to preserve his feats for posterity before he lost the strength to do them, and show them to people around the world. On the downside, Bess objected to his playing with younger actresses: "I guess the women folks do not like to see us around with others," he reflected, "but it just cant be helped."

In fifteen episodes *The Master Mystery* has the plot and atmosphere of an urban Gothic novel. Like many of its literary prototypes, it unveils the secret connections between the seemingly opposite spheres of aristocratic luxury and lower-class crime. Much of the action occurs at baronial Brentwood, a manor all circular driveways, blanket-size wall hangings, and medieval armor. These trappings, in actuality, conceal a sinister architecture of sliding panels and underground vaults. Similarly, the masters of Brentwood—a firm called International Patents, Inc.—appear to market the inventions of their clients but in reality suppress them, so that they can monopolize the market with inventions of their own. This state of affairs is uncovered by Quentin Locke (Houdini, lock). Working at Brentwood as a laboratory technician, he is in fact an undercover Justice Department trust-buster. The love interest involves his pursuit of the pretty brunette Eva Brent and avoidance of the superbly-named vamp, De Luxe Dora. Among too many subplots to count, the chief concerns his search through joss houses and opium dens for an antidote to Madagascar Madness, a horrible Oriental disease, induced by poisoned candle, that turns its victims into permanent imbeciles, forever laughing.

Focusing on the supposed culture of inventions and patents, the film features Automaton, a heavily-advertised "scientific villain" with metal body and human brain, capable of emitting lethal electric rays through its fingertips. Looking back toward the automata of Robert-Houdin and ahead to big-screen cyborgs, it probably represents the first robot character in films. Houdini took credit for having created in Automaton a "figure controlled by the Solinoid system, which is similar to the aerial torpedoes." Claptrap, naturally: anyone can see that underneath Automaton's ping-pongball glare and arms-out zombiesque stalk is a human operator, cheaply gotten up in what look like stovepipe-tube limbs, biscuit-tin feet, and a paintbucket head.

What fascinates in *The Master Mystery* is not its unfollowable plot or gimcrackery, but Houdini. In full-length shots he seems the Houdini neither of the stage nor of the street. His too-tight pinstriped suits and too-white makeup and heavy lipstick make him look like a musclebound mime. His 'acting' consists of three expressions: pucker-lipped flirtatiousness, open-eyed surprise, and brow-knitted distress. But closeups, many of them in profile, flatter his handsomeness, the large head and fine, medallionlike features described by his admirer Edmund Wilson: "Wide-browed and aquiline-nosed, with a cleanness and fitness almost military, he suggests one of those enlarged and idealized busts of Roman consuls or generals." His unusual hands appear in closeup as well, part concert pianist's, part homerun king's—the fingers bony and long, joints ridged with veins; the wrists beefy, broad as the hands themselves.

Each episode of the serial allows Houdini to escape some life-threatening peril: entombed alive in a collapsed cave; garroted Inquisition-style to a wall; wreathed in barbed wire, lying defenseless beside an approaching stream of frothing nitric acid. Two predicaments are of special interest in recording skills he had not allowed his stage (and perhaps his police) audiences to see. In one he picks a lock using an umbrella rib and piece of string. The other shows the odd dexterity of his toes, his ability to work them as if they were fingers. Shackled to a wall, he slips off his shoes and stockings, fishes a ring of keys from the pocket of an unconscious thug, sorts them to select one, and opens the door facing him. All this—snatching the ring, selecting a key, unlocking the door—he does with his toes alone.

The Master Mystery was released in January 1919, to capacity houses. Reviewers merely okayed Houdini's acting ("isn't half bad") but rhapsodized over his stunts and the novel robot: "this cracker-jack production," *Billboard* predicted, "will thunder down the ages to perpetuate the fame of this remarkable genius whose uparalleled achievements have reached from Aroostook, Me., to Singapore, China, from Zululand to Behring Straits." About the geography they were correct. Quentin Locke's exploits flickered on movie screens over much of the planet. The serial was shown in France under Pathé sponsorship—the publicity identifying Houdini as "*L'homme le plus populaire du monde entier*"—and was booked in the United Kingdom, the Scandinavian countries, South America, the Philippines, and Australia. Export & Import Film Company exhibited it in India, China, and Japan as well, giving Houdini for the first time an audience in Asia.

The global distribution brought Houdini a unique load of fan mail, from Japan especially. "I am one of the most admirers of you," wrote a Y. Hasegawa from Tokyo. "Charmed by your excellent art with a lovely face." Masao Fuyushiba of Yokohoma pleaded for Houdini's picture and autograph: "I beg you acknowledge me forever I have well-known your glorious name because I have often heard 'Houdini Houdini' among our movie-fun." The editors of a Japanese film magazine, *Cinema*, notified him that they planned to produce a special Houdini issue, to please his "many many admirers who belong mostly to the upper classes." Lots of fan letters and requests for souvenirs came from children, including the unfortunate Francis Sams of Leeds, England, who wrote: "Have you a lucky mascot? You could give it to me please because I have had nothing but bad luck."

Through part of the filming of *The Master Mystery*, in the fall of 1918, Houdini had continued to appear at the Hippodrome, in a lavish new revue, *Everything*. With songs and music by John Philip Sousa and Irving Berlin, it offered fifteen sketches or 'things'—among them "Country Circus" (with thirty-six female clowns) and "On the Beach"—Houdini's turn being featured as a separate 'thing.' He planned to do a "buried-alive" escape, but had to abandon it after seriously fracturing his wrist during filming.

Broken in three places, the wrist had to be set in a plaster cast, and remained weak and painful when the cast was removed. Adhesions developed in the joint, which had to be rebroken by a physician, then subjected to a "new baking electrical treatment." After six months the wrist seemed to him stronger than before, "as a ring has grown around the break," but still had not regained flexibility.

Defying the pain as usual, Houdini twice a day performed an indoor suspended straitjacket escape, twisting-twirling upside down from a wire high over the Hippodrome stage. For the other effect in his nine-minute act, he presented the patriotic "Whirlwind of Colors," using an American eagle. Bought for two hundred dollars from a New York bird importer and dubbed "Young Abe" (Lincoln), the eagle gave him some trouble when it developed "rheumatics." But it made a slambang opening for his act. Thrusting his bared arm into a large bowl of colored water, he pulled out a washlineful of large flags that stretched across the stage, from the center of which—an American flag—he produced the great flapping bird.

Houdini's work on *The Master Mystery* introduced him to some vagaries of the movie business. A few weeks after filming was completed, one of the partners, Harry Grossman, resigned as general manager of Octagon Film Corporation, ignoring Houdini's warning that he was "walking away from a fortune." But Houdini found the fortune walking away from himself. By his arithmetic the picture grossed $225,000, with a net of $80,000, to half of which his contract entitled him, atop his salary. When the money failed to come, he decided the partners had squandered it and were "trying to cheat me out of my 50% profit." He was forced to sue Octagon for some $43,000. As depositions and affidavits stacked up, the remaining partners sued one another over the sale of territorial rights, Rolfe returned to vaudeville, and the company, having produced one picture, went bankrupt. The legal mess gave Houdini some insight into other worlds of commerce: "I believe magicians are much, much too honest to succeed away from our own business," he wrote Will Goldston. "We are so busy with 'illusionary material' that the businessman in a legal way out trades us." ("[T]his is not a jest," he added, quite aware that of all the virtues magicians grant one another, honesty may be the last.) After four years in the courts, Houdini finally won a jury verdict of some $33,000.

Houdini's Film Development Corporation was becoming costly and aggravating too, returning no profit for the thousands he kept investing in it. To help run the large company he persuaded Hardeen to manage it full-time. The brokering illustrates the power he had over his younger brother. To Hardeen the move meant giving up a successful twenty-year stage career. He later explained, not very convincingly, that when the vaudeville circuit Houdini worked for (Keith-Orpheum) absorbed his own circuit (Klaw-Erlanger), he and his brother had to end their pseudo-rivalry, so he "went out of the escape business." A friend was probably nearer the truth when he said that Houdini "prevailed" on Dash to leave show business, and that Dash was "big-hearted" enough to agree. But even under Hardeen's management, the FDC's troubles mounted. Houdini's inventor-partner, Gustav Dietz, borrowed money from the company, which in its chancy condition was also sued by Houdini's friend Arnold DeBiere (1876–1934), a Polish-Jewish sleight-of-hand artist he had induced to buy FDC stock. "De Biere *double crossed* me!" Houdini yiped. "We are no longer friends."

Worse, Houdini had to worry about safeguarding the substantial investment of Harry Kellar. Sometimes exchanging letters with Houdini twice a week or more from California, Kellar had become a father-counselor to him, addressing him as "Dear Tyke" and confiding that he "loves you as his own son." As Houdini would tolerate no one else doing, Kellar could reduce him to "Harry" and treat him to finger-wagging: "Harry dont worry about your dear Mother . . . you must remember that she had lived to a ripe old age and had to go the way we all must go." Kellar also lectured him about pipedreams of processing miles of film every week: "I warn you not to go too deep into it as you have worked too hard for your money to throw it away."

Concerned about the company's solvency, Kellar wanted to sell off his 125 shares. But he promised Houdini that if the FDC went under he would take the loss without kicking, "as I went into the concern of my own free will & I am not a piker." He feared, however, that in case of a bankruptcy he might be held personally responsible, as a stockholder, for the company's debts, as happened under California law. When Houdini assured him that New York State law made him liable only for the face value of his stock, he agreed to hold on to his shares, and gave him a power of attorney so that he could vote them in battles with other stockholders: "you will *always* find me on your side." But Kellar continued to fret over his possible legal obligations. As the FDC began looking bound for doom, he advised

Houdini to sell out and save what he could, "for your time is too valuable to waste on a dead horse."

LOS ANGELES; *THE GRIM GAME*; MARTINKA'S; *TERROR ISLAND*

By October 1918, as the U.S. First Army inched German troops back through the gloomy Argonne Forest, at a cost of more than one hundred thousand casualties, the war was ending. The signing of the Armistice, on November 11, did not halt Houdini's momentum. In January he entertained wounded troops returned from the front, and in the early spring of the new year he headed for Hollywood. "Movie Fans are 'clambering' for another Houdini serial, and . . . that is much easier than my Self created hazardous work."

This time Houdini signed with Famous Players-Lasky Corporation. This was no one-shot Octagon Films, but a fast-growing motion picture empire whose productions starred Mary Pickford, John Barrymore, and Rudolph Valentino. With forty million Americans going to the movies each week by 1920, FPL contributed much to the public adoration of movie stars, the mushrooming of fan magazines, and not least the conversion of more and more vaudeville theaters into movie houses. Houdini and Bess left in mid-April 1919 for Los Angeles. He had last played there three and a half years before, when he got mighty Jess Willard hooted from the Orpheum. Meanwhile the place had grown phenomenally. Drawn by the warm sunny climate and fantasies of glamour, droves of new residents from 1910 to 1920 jumped the population 720 percent. They moved around on a network of electric railways and trolleys or in automobiles that by the late twenties already numbered one for every 2.25 persons, to the peril of pedestrians: one wit called Los Angeles "the city of the quick and the dead." Moviemakers, especially, had come to Southern California, which provided year-round shooting conditions; settings for desert, jungle, or city alike; and a nonunion workforce that accepted half the East Coast payscale. And set between the palmy Pacific coastline and the mountains inland, Los Angeles was a gem. To Theodore Dreiser, who lived there in 1921, the city looked from above like "a huge valley of diamonds at night—twinkling orange diamonds."

FPL's standard impressed Houdini. The company owned a two-block complex, with a wooden office building at the corner of Vine Street and telephone-pole-lined Sunset Boulevard. The company reportedly paid him a weekly salary of $2,500, plus an interest in his new picture, *The Grim Game*. FPL also hired two screenwriters, Arthur B. Reeve and John W. Grey, and built a big prison set. The deal was not entirely sweet. Houdini claimed that he wrote practically the whole scenario himself, but allowed Reeve and Grey to take credit because "I didn't have temerity to put 'Author' on same." And in escaping one of the prison cells, he again fractured his left wrist, not as badly as the year before but enough to have his arm wrapped and delay completion of the film by two weeks.

The Grim Game's murder-mystery plot allowed Houdini to defy death by the dozens. An advertising sheet told audiences what shockers they could expect:

> SEE him dive between the wheels of a speeding motor-truck and foil his pursuers!
>
> SEE him climb the side of a prison and crawl for a rope to the end of a flagpole swaying far from earth!
>
> SEE him on the brink of a gorge, fight a terrifying battle with his foes!
>
> SEE him leap from the roof of a skyscraper and release himself from a straight-jacket while hanging head downward on a rope!
>
> SEE him risk his life in a deadly bear-trap and set himself free!

In the film's heartstopper-of-heartstoppers, Houdini transfers himself in midair from one plane to another. The sequence begins when he jumps into the passenger seat of a biplane, which makes a vaulting takeoff toward a second, airborne biplane, in which the heroine has been abducted. As Houdini's pilot positions his craft above the kidnapper's, Houdini climbs over the cockpit onto the lower wing of the biplane, a hank of rope in hand. Seen now in a long shot, he sits down on the wing's edge, legs dangling in air some 2,200 feet above the grassy fields below, both planes wobbling on the currents. He ties the rope to a strut and begins climbing down to the other, moving plane.

Suddenly, just as Houdini lowers himself into the kidnapper's cockpit, the planes inexplicably come together. They seem to lock nose-to-nose like butting rams. In this machine-embrace, Houdini twirling helplessly from the end of the rope, the planes careen downward, sickeningly rotating top-like to earth. At the last moment they separate, glide, then crash. In closeup again, Houdini, shirt ripped off but for one sleeve, blood trickling down his bare chest, climbs with the rescued heroine from the smoking wreck.

The scene is still exciting to see, but Houdini played little more part in it than to take undeserved credit. The crash was unplanned and all-too-real. For the filming FPL rented a pair of Curtiss Canucks from its own director general, Cecil B. DeMille, who owned two of the three Los Angeles airports. As the machines rendezvoused high above Santa Monica beach, an upgust threw the top wing of the lower biplane into the landing gear of the other, from which it hung like a pendulum, the planes' propellers slicing each other's wings and fuselage as they dropped. From a third plane at higher altitude, the director, Irvin Willat, was photographing the scene, and he cranked away as the planes crazily spun down. The seemingly death-bound figure at the end of the rope was not Houdini but an ex–Air Service pilot named Robert E. Kennedy. Houdini had been willing to attempt the transfer despite his arm sling, but Willat refused to risk aborting his picture by losing his star. Houdini's climb from the cockpit to the wing was shot in closeup, on the ground; his midair descent was shot from afar, using Kennedy as a double. In the (fortunately) gliding crash-landings of the planes—wings chewed, propellers gone—Kennedy was slammed onto a newly plowed bean field and dragged to a stop, cut by stones but alive.

In talking about the sequence over the next few years, however, Houdini gradually Roosevelt-ized it, erasing Kennedy from the picture and putting himself in. At first he merely stressed to others that all the stunts had been "actually performed"—without mentioning by whom. He elaborated this technical truth during promotional appearances for the film, offering a (misleading) thousand-dollar reward "to any person who can prove that the airplane collision was not genuine." The fullblown Munchhausen was ready a year later, when he told an interviewer for *Picture Show* magazine: "I was dangling from the rope-end ready for the leap. Suddenly a strong wind turned the lower plane upwards, the two machines crashed together— nearly amputating my limbs," etc. etc. He even improved on the harrowing-enough details, including the altitude. Autographing an eight-by-ten publicity still that showed him clutching the biplane's wing struts—taken, however, on the ground—he wrote: "About 4000 feet in the air."

But in hooey and hype, Houdini easily found his match in Hollywood. FPL showered exhibitors and newspapers with lobby displays and glossy pressbooks advertising the filmed accident as the ultimate thrill in movie history. Their biographical sketch of Houdini even outboomed his drum-beating for himself:

> He was handcuffed, tied, and sewed in a canvas sack, and thrown from the Eiffel Tower, Paris. Half way down Houdini was out of the manacles and the sack and clinging to a parachute, on which he descended.
>
> He was thrown from the Brooklyn Bridge locked in a steel safe. He came up in one minute.

Most reviewers found *The Grim Game* "jammed full of thrills," an "avalanche" of "the most sensational feats which chill the marrow." On a motion by Howard Thurston, the SAM officially endorsed the film as "one of the most sensational boosts for magic that America probably has ever known." More soberly, but in this case with devastating truth, *Variety* remarked on the intractable problem in filming Houdini's feats: "no one is certain he is doing what he seems to do." Satisfied just the same, FPL signed Houdini to a new movie. Satisfied too, he described the picture as "the Greatest Melodram ever screened. (Am still as modest as usual)."

Houdini enjoyed working in Hollywood. He met Chaplin, got to know Gloria Swanson (another FPL star), had himself photographed surrounded by starlets or, as a gag, handcuffing DeMille. He was beginning to feel comfortable in motion pictures, but also challenged by them, intrigued by the difference between stage and screen acting. "The smallest movie star can make the biggest spoken stage star look like a nickle [sic] before the camera," he decided, "especially if they do not know the angle of the lens." His growing knowledge, he also felt, strengthened his claim to legitimacy in the larger world of the theater: "gradually I am of the dramatic profession even though I have to enter by strenous [sic] efforts." He had never shunned hard work, of course, but he had far to go before becoming King of Filmdom. Meanwhile he was willing to believe almost any sort of flattery about his potential. "They say," he reported, "I am the most sincere actor on the *screen*."

To Houdini's delight, living in Los Angeles allowed him to visit often with Kellar, who lived only a half dozen miles from the FPL studios, a large American flag flying in his front yard. Kellar had been robust-looking despite his age, but now Houdini found him just able to get about, the older man having suffered a stroke months after landing a 290-pound, tournament-size swordfish. Houdini paid a Los Angeles florist to deliver flowers to him every week for a full year. Kellar remained unhappy about his invest-ment in the Film Development Corporation, but he repaid Houdini's gen-erosity with interest. After much persuading he agreed to let Houdini write his biography, based largely on his letters to him (by Houdini's never-reliable count, more than a thousand of them). He also made Houdini the fabulous gift of his version of "Psycho"—an automaton in Oriental garb, on a see-through glass pedestal, that moved its head and arms and could tell the date of a coin held up by someone in the audience and give the day of the week of any date of any year in the century.

In June, Houdini and Bess celebrated their twenty-fifth wedding anniversary at the Hotel Alexandria in Los Angeles. They always made something playful and festive of their anniversaries, often returning to Coney Island to have their picture taken at some boardwalk studio with jokey honeymoon-cottage props. But for this silver anniversary Houdini got up one of his extravaganzas of hospitality. He invited two hundred guests to gather in the hotel's main dining room at one long table for a ten-course banquet, opening with Crab Supreme and gorging its way through Breast of Chicken "Virginienne" to Strawberry Parfait, champagne, cigars, and cigarettes.

Over the years Houdini had grown into the habit of expressing the importance to him of certain people and events by lavishing flowers on them. When his illusionist friend the Great Lafayette (Siegmund Neuburger [1872–1911]) died on a blazing stage during a famous Edinburgh theater fire, he paid to have Lafayette's funeral filmed, and sent for the gravesite a fabulous wreath composed of hundreds of pelargoniums and lilies of the valley, and thousands of forget-me-nots laboriously arranged as a floral replica of Lafayette's pet dog. For the regal anniversary dinner, he had the air scented with the fragrance of rosewater, given off by two brilliantly-lighted fountains. The guests' places were marked with tiny bouquets of orange blossoms, the vast dining table covered with sweet peas, roses, and orchids.

But Houdini's feelings that night were probably less unadulterated. While Bess was making up in their hotel room, he wrote a letter to give her after the dinner, when they were alone. It began with a double-whammy. "My Soul Mate Wife," he saluted her, in Charmian London-speak. And he continued: "if only my Sainted Mother were here, how she would nod her head with pride." He had not seen London since she left New York, but he did occasionally write. Her diaries over ten months in 1919–20 record at one time a "sweet letter" from him, at another "two love-notes." Still, however compromised by past and present attachments, the affection Houdini expressed in his letter for Bess, after twenty-five years, sounds heartfelt:

> We have starved, and starred together. We have had our little tiffs but your sunny smile, and my *good* (?) sense always smoothed out the bitterness. I love you—love you—and I know you love me. Your very touch, your care of me dearest and the laughter in my heart when you put your arms around me prove it. Think dear heart, twenty five years. . . . yours till the end of the world and ever after. Ehrich

A band played the Wedding March as Houdini and Bess entered the large dining room. She brushed off tears and apparently almost fainted, for he dashed for some wine to brace her, recalling, he said, "my old running days." Later, Will Rogers and others delivered toasts, Jesse Lasky of FPL presented the couple a ten-piece silver service, the guests danced until midnight.

Houdini made a quick trip to New York in July, partly to look after another new business venture. With three other investors, he bought historic Martinka & Co., the oldest magic shop in the country. As president and principal stockholder, he issued stocks, capitalized at fifteen thousand dollars, and leased an auditorium in the Bronx, opened to the public as Martinka's Magical Palace. At least for a few performances, at which a magician named Stefanik produced a large dog from a small foulard, he realized the idea he once had for a theater devoted to magic. But Martinka's turned out to be another of his get-in-and-get-out enthusiasms. He sold his interest by the end of the year and announced that he had withdrawn from the company.

Undisturbed to be "drifting away from vaudeville," and having "no plans re a return," Houdini started work in November on his new FPL film, *Terror Island*. Much of the shooting was done on rugged Catalina Island, off the coast, then being developed as a resort. He reached the place by seaplane from Los Angeles, ears ringing from the roar of the engine, excited to be flying at five thousand feet: "honestly I thought of my wife and the-

atrical collection." The film called on his swimming ability, but hardly prepared him for the real-life rescue attempt he made on November 28, which
nearly killed him. In sight of the guests at Catalina's St. Catherine Hotel, a
small FPL launch containing four men, its steering gear broken by a gale,
stood in danger of smashing on the rocks and sinking in the high seas.
Houdini seized a line, tied it around his waist, and, shielding his head with
a life preserver, tried to swim to the boat through the rough icy water. He
weakened, however, and two deep-sea divers had to be sent out to bring
him back, bleeding with cuts from the reef. (A motorboat that fought the
surf forty-five minutes finally towed the launch to shore.)

Nothing in *Terror Island* is quite so thrilling. The intertwined main
plots concern the trials of the inventor-philanthropist Harry Harper (HH)
in recovering a case of South African diamonds from a sunken ship and liberating the heroine's father from captivity by a savage tribe. He does this
largely by means of the submarine he has invented, equipped with an "electric periscope" for observation, and locks for leaving and entering the craft
underwater. The film's other novelty is the islandful of spear-waving, loinclothed natives, played by hundreds of black extras. In the finale they
threaten to exterminate a gang of white thugs in a veritable race war. Houdini gets to kiss and keep the heroine, but his professional skills are rarely
on display, except in an underwater swimming scene that records the
strong, froglike strokes he must have used in escaping submerged boxes.
Most reviewers found the slow-moving melodrama grossly improbable. In
one scene the heroine somehow survives after being stuffed by the natives
into a small safe and thrown from a high cliff into the deep sea. Such absur-
dities, *Billboard* reported, "caused the audience to laugh outright." *Variety*
dismissed *Terror Island* as "an excuse for bringing Houdini back to pictures." Houdini was more easily pleased by Houdini; in his diary he rated
the picture "Excellent."

When he returned from Los Angeles to New York, in December, it was
to prepare for his first trip abroad since 1914, more than five and a half
years before. This would not be a new tour. He planned to do no more than
fill contracts he had made before the war, then devote himself largely to the
movie business. A choice pleasure awaited him at the Harlem brownstone
when he arrived home. Over the last two or three years he had kept buying
books, playbills, manuscripts, and memorabilia on the drama, in pursuit of
the Boston collector Robert Gould Shaw. But in October, while he was in

Los Angeles, there occurred at the American Art Galleries in New York one of the great drama sales of the century, the dispersal of the collection of Shaw's friendly rival Evert Jansen Wendell. Proceeds went to the Harvard theater collection, to which Wendell had already donated part of his holdings. Houdini had corresponded with Wendell, mailing books and articles about himself as well as one of his photographs *à deux* with Roosevelt and an invitation to see his collection. Unable to attend the unique sale, he sent a knowledgeable buyer, with instructions to bid for whatever he thought Houdini *"ought to have."*

Houdini found the result when he returned to 278, before Christmas. His collection had been increased by thousands of items. He stayed up almost every night until 4 A.M. sifting through the bundles, the treasures—"Booth picture galors [*sic*] . . . Programmes by the thousands, and mezzotints until you hate to go on. Garrick I have a bunch." The sudden massive accession gave him, he could see, a new ranking. He now had "a young Harvard collection" and was on his way to having a "world famous" drama library. A joyous way to end the year, surely.

But a few days later, as Houdini boarded the Cunard liner *Mauretania*, sister ship of the *Lusitania*, more was ending than the year. He was on his way to a second, unforeseen, more miracle-filled career.

A MAGICIAN AMONG THE SPIRITS

A mouth that has no moisture and no breath
Breathless mouths may summon;
I hail the superhuman;
I call it death-in-life and life-in-death.

—W. B. YEATS, "BYZANTIUM"

Spiritualism is the Science, Philosophy and Religion of continuous life, based upon the demonstrated fact of communication, by means of mediumship, with those who live in the Spirit World.

—*Spiritualist Manual* OF THE NATIONAL SPIRITUALIST ASSOCIATION OF CHURCHES (15TH REVISION, 1991)

"It takes a flimflammer to catch a flimflammer."

—HOUDINI, INTERVIEW IN THE
Los Angeles Times, OCTOBER 28, 1924

ELEVEN

1920—1922

SIR ARTHUR CONAN DOYLE; SPIRITUALISM IN THE 1920S

THAT HOUDINI AND Sir Arthur Conan Doyle should have met and become close friends seems inevitable—as does their having parted, after three years, in mutual regret and scorn.

With his grizzled old-campaigner mustache, six-foot frame, and throaty voice, Doyle was to many the embodiment of ideal English manhood. To one friend he looked like a farmer, "a tall, big-chested, heavy-footed man, hard and muscular." Others likened him to a "great big, breezy athlete," or "two stolid policemen rolled into one." President of the National Sporting Club, he skied, hunted, and fished; played cricket, rugby, and golf; smoked pipes, cigars, and cigarettes. He had harpooned whales off Greenland, contracted typhoid fever in Africa, raced a twenty-horsepower Dietrich-Lorraine against a German team in a two-thousand-mile tour. He had taken a course in "muscular development" with Sandow. Especially he admired boxing and boxers. "Is not valour the basis of all character," he remarked, "and where shall we find greater valour than theirs." A "fair average amateur" himself, he had seen in action most masters of the ring since John L. Sullivan, and been invited to referee the 1910 Jeffries-Johnson championship. (He declined only because of the trek from London to Reno.) For all that, he was, with his gentle blue eyes, something of an overgrown boy. He consulted often and closely with his mother, "the Ma'am." The number of his surviving letters to her is around fifteen hundred.

Houdini's match in competitiveness and allegiance to the cult of virility, Doyle was also in reality the literary artist-intellectual Houdini fantasized becoming. Although trained as a physician and eye specialist, Doyle had become famous as a man of letters, the versatile author of stories, novels, plays, poems, histories, articles, and polemical writing. High-minded and generous, something of a world-saver, he often spoke out on social questions. He did so on the side, he said, of "freedom, tolerance, and progress," but within the limits of a gentlemanly etiquette of tradition, duty, and fair play. He remained best known as the creator, in Sherlock Holmes, of one of the most thoroughly-imagined, entertaining characters in world literature. But now, looking back on Holmes from his early sixties, Doyle saw him in a messianic light: "I was sent here for one purpose, to be the torch bearer of spiritualism," he told a reporter; "it was foreordained that I should create Sherlock Homes as one of the media to get recognition, perhaps friendship, at the firesides throughout the world."

It was Spiritualism that brought Houdini and Doyle together. At the time they met, Doyle's life and writing were absorbed in advancing the movement, which he regarded as literally a new Revelation. Raised a Catholic, he dated his conversion to 1887, when an elderly medium whom he had never seen before identified him as a physician and, in a trance, relayed the message that he should not read Leigh Hunt's *Comic Dramatists of the Restoration*—a book he had been debating with himself whether to buy. The personal message convinced him that "intelligence could exist apart from the body." In an outpouring of works such as *The New Revelation* (1918) and *The Vital Message* (1919) he proclaimed Spiritualism "absolutely the most important development in the whole history of the human race," a living faith worthy of replacing a Christianity deadened by "want of fact, want of reality." Spiritualists drew their knowledge not from remote prophets who lived three thousand years ago and spoke Hebrew, "but we get it direct ourselves either from our own loved ones who have just passed over, or from high teachers who give their credentials."

Characteristically Doyle also championed Spiritualism as a "more virile and manly doctrine" than Christianity. He chose for the epigraph to his *Wanderings of a Spiritualist* (1921) a quotation from Theodore Roosevelt: "*Aggressive fighting for the right is the noblest sport the world affords.*" He waged his campaign for Spiritualism in this bully spirit, a toe-to-toe evangelism. "It is when the sage and the saint build on the basis of the fighter," he wrote, "that you have the highest to which humanity can attain."

The Spiritualism to which Doyle gave himself differed dramatically from the movement that, in the 1880s, had incidentally given rise to theatrical escapes from handcuffs and chains. To recall briefly, as a (loosely) institutionalized religion, Spiritualism sprang into being in 1848, when the young Fox sisters in upstate New York first communicated with unseen agencies by raps. They quickly gained followers throughout the world. Over the next half century the movement rose and fell in popularity. But its phenomena grew more inexplicable and interested not just Doyle but many other distinguished writers. In Berlin, Thomas Mann attended a séance with a medium who made a typewriter click, untouched; Mann bore witness that "any mechanical deception or sleight-of-hand tricks were humanly impossible." In Italy the writer Gabriele D'Annunzio became a convert, although at one séance the medium's table was hurled at his head by the spirit of his rival, the recently dead poet Carducci, who declared that D'Annunzio's works were smoke. In New York, Theodore Dreiser sat working a Ouija board with H. L. Mencken (who afterward admitted pushing it), and when worried about his work asked his "psychic control" to show forth his future in a dream, which the control did.

Spiritualism intrigued scientists as well. Discoveries in electricity, radioactivity, and relativity theory suggested the existence of not-yet-understood laws and forces that lent respectability to beliefs in psychic intelligences. Many eminent scientists subjected mediums to controlled investigation. Some became convinced Spiritualists themselves, such as the English experimental chemist Sir William Crookes, a president of the Royal Society, and Camille Flammarion, a founder of the French Astronomical Society. Flammarion placed "bodiless spirit" in a cosmic zone comparable to Einsteinian space-time: "it lives in the fourth dimension, in hyperspace." Many scientists joined the British or American branches of the Society for Psychical Research, organized by prominent academics and intellectuals to systematically study mediumistic phenomena. Psychical research particularly attracted psychologists who were interested in the emerging concept of the unconscious. Some viewed trance-speaking, inspirational-writing, and the like as instances of the self operating apart from conscious awareness, as in cases of multiple personality. William James served a term as president of the American SPR; Freud contributed "A Note on the Unconscious in Psycho-Analysis" to the society's *Proceedings*.

During World War I and its aftermath, Spiritualism boomed. Its twin promises that the universe made moral sense and that the self survived death appealed to many whose faith had been threatened by the bloody murdering in the trenches. From the battlefields came reports of visions of Joan of Arc or Saint George, prophetic dreams of air raids; on the home front, Ouija boards spelled out "bayayonet [*sic*] still in me." Spiritualist fathers and mothers who had lost children to Moloch found comfort in their return from the spirit world: "*Only last night our beloved boy was again with us*," one wrote, "*and spoke for nearly two hours*, almost as freely as when present with us in the flesh." In the years after the war, newspapers and magazines of every quality reported on strange new psychic phenomena, and printed defenses or denials by an army of Spiritualists, ministers, scientists, psychologists, magicians, and laypersons.

It was a wartime tragedy that converted Sir Arthur Conan Doyle himself from believer to evangelist. His son by his first marriage, Kingsley, had been badly wounded at the Somme, and died in London of pneumonia just before the Armistice. About a year later, Doyle had a sitting in London with a medium named Evan Powell. The medium sat tied to a chair. Yet Kingsley came back. "His voice sounded, very intense and earnest, before me," Doyle recalled. Listening intently, Doyle heard Kingsley say, in a loud whisper, "Forgive!" He understood: Kingsley was alluding to the fact that while living he had opposed Spiritualism, "for certainly there was nothing else in his manly and beautiful life which could possibly have hurt me." Doyle assured him there was nothing to forgive, and asked whether he was happy. "He answered, 'I am happy *now*.'" Then Doyle felt a heavy hand upon his head and a kiss upon his brow. Since the sitting with Powell he had had several other communications from "my arisen son."

MEETING WITH DOYLE; EVA C.

Houdini began his relationship with Doyle on a false note of compliance that he would find impossible to keep up. While playing out his prewar contracts in England, he sent Doyle a copy of *The Unmasking of Robert-Houdin*. Doyle enjoyed the book, but a statement in it irked him. It was that one of the Davenport Brothers had reportedly confessed to trickery, saying that "all their work was skilful manipulation and not spiritualist manifestations." To Doyle the brothers were not the first escape-artists, as they were to Houdini, but vessels of the New Revelation, "probably the greatest mediums of their kind the world has ever seen." Like most Spiritualists Doyle swept aside admissions by mediums, including the infamous public demonstration in 1888 by Margaret Fox—the very founder of the movement—of how she had produced the first rappings, forty years earlier, by means of her large toe. "As to Spiritualist 'Confessions,' they are all nonsense," Doyle wrote Houdini. "Every medium is said to have 'confessed,' and it is an old trick of the opposition."

Anxious to open a correspondence with Doyle, Houdini did not press the point. "I can make the positive assertion," he replied, "that the Davenport Brothers never were exposed." He obviously meant that no one had proved that the brothers' manifestations depended, as he knew they did, on a devilishly clever rope-tie. But the remark was ambiguous enough to allow Doyle to take from it, as from everything else, nourishment for his Spiritualist beliefs. Doyle understood Houdini to mean not that the brothers "never were exposed," but that there was nothing *to expose.* He asked Houdini's permission to quote him to that effect: "our enemies continually allude to their 'exposure,' their 'confession,'" Doyle wrote him. "Unless I hear to the contrary, I will take it that I may use your authoritative statement as the occasion serves." Houdini said little to the contrary, for he desired Doyle's friendship, sensed that Doyle wanted his, and was willing to bend. He replied with some more fudging: "I am afraid that I cannot say that all their work was accomplished by the spirits."

Within two weeks of this first approach, Houdini and Doyle exchanged about ten letters. "Am only too delighted to correspond with you," Houdini wrote, "and if there is anything in my little Kingdom of Knowledge that you wish to know, will only be too pleased to give you any information that I may possess." Aware of Doyle's standing as the most admired spokesman for Spiritualism, he presented himself as a possible disciple: "I am seeking truth, and it is only by knowing that Analytical Minds are going in for it, that I am treating this matter seriously." The last was correct: he had always sought contact with "Analytical Minds" (and literary celebrities) such as Doyle. Concerning the productions of mediums, however, his vast knowledge of conjuring methods had shaped him to seek not The Truth but The Gimmick. Nor had he, over the years, had much contact with the Spiritualist movement. He had performed tent-show séances in the 1890s, but stopped when he found the locals taking his off-the-cuff predictions and spirit messages to heart: "When I noted the deep earnestness with which my utterances were received . . . I felt that the game had gone far enough, for I most certainly did not relish the idea of treading on the sacred feelings of my admirers." Otherwise he had been a casual, sometime observer of the Spiritualist scene.

Houdini portrayed himself to Doyle quite differently, however. Hoping for commerce between them, stirred by competition, and touchy as always about seeming a Johnny-come-lately, he presented himself as someone who had invested much of his career and thought in Spiritualism. "I have gone out of my way for years to unearth mediums," he wrote in one letter. "During my tour in Australia, I met a man who was supposed to have laid low Mrs. Piper; I was in Berlin, Germany, at the trial of Miss Rothe, the flower medium; I know the methods of the Bangs Sisters, the famous Chicago mediums; I was in court when Anna O'Delia Diss De Bar, who was mixed up with the lawyer Luther Marsh, was sentenced." He revealed (truthfully) that over the years he had made several compacts with friends that whoever died first would try to contact the other from the beyond. To further impress Doyle, he sent along books, clippings, and Houdiniesque not-to-be-outdones: "when you say there are ninety-six volumes on your desk, it may interest you to know that I travel with a book-case containing over one hundred volumes, and recently, in Leeds, I bought two libraries on Spiritualism."

On April 14 Houdini visited Doyle at Windlesham, his Sussex estate. A five-gabled house with red rooftiles, it sat in open country. Its decor included photographs of renowned boxers, a muddied cricket bat that enshrined Doyle's first century, and, on the walls of the huge billiard room, a frieze of Napoleonic weapons. Guests were greeted at the front door by a page in brass buttons. For some reason Bess could not attend, but Houdini lunched with both Sir Arthur and Lady Doyle, Jean Leckie. Doyle had sustained a platonic affair with her for ten years while tending his first wife through a long battle with tuberculosis. Although Doyle was in his early sixties, he and Lady Doyle had three young children.

Both parties enjoyed the visit. The Doyles were fascinated by the tricks Houdini performed, Houdini by the story that Doyle had spoken six times with his deceased son and the report that Lady Doyle did trance-writing.

Like everyone else who met Doyle, Houdini felt privileged and uplifted in his presence—"just as nice and sweet as any mortal I have ever been near." And while he felt skeptical, too, Houdini said nothing that could spoil the pleasant afternoon by starting an argument. "They believe implicitly in Spiritualism," he wrote in his diary afterward. "No possible chance for trickery."

Drawn more and more into Spiritualism by his eagerness to know Doyle, Houdini asked him to recommend some mediums with whom he might have a séance. For all Houdini's tact, Doyle understood that his polite silences represented serious doubt, and warned him at the outset that he must treat the séance receptively: "It wants to be approached not in the spirit of a detective approaching a suspect, but in that of a humble, religious soul, yearning for help and comfort." Frivolity and mere curiosity, he said, repel the forces beyond. "Something must come your way if you really persevere and get it out of your mind that you should follow it as a terrier follows a rat." This did not mean that Houdini should abandon his critical faculties: "Mental Harmony does not in the least abrogate common sense." Houdini assured Doyle that he would approach the sittings with an open mind, willing to believe. "I will put no obstruction of any nature whatsoever in the medium's way, and will assist in all ways in my power to obtain results."

Doyle sent Houdini to several highly-regarded mediums, including Mrs. Anna Brittain, whom he considered "the best." In a series of seventy-two clients he had sent her, she "got through" sixty times. She failed to impress Houdini, however. "Simply kept talking in general," he noted in his diary. She told him things about himself she could have learned anywhere: "this is ridiculous stuff," he decided. Doyle also arranged for Houdini to sit with the celebrated Mrs. Wriedt, who could summon the voices of lost ones. Houdini attended this séance in company with a Harley Street physician. After more than an hour nothing happened. "My belief—she was afraid of me," he noted. He was right, for the medium told Sir Arthur afterward that Houdini was "out to make trouble." Perhaps hoping to prove something to Houdini, Doyle, his wife, and a friend sat with Mrs. Wriedt only a few days later at Windlesham, with far better results. While the four of them sang together in the children's nursery, he reported to Houdini, he could clearly hear Mrs. Wriedt's voice on his right. Yet a fifth, "very beautiful" voice joined in powerfully. "Now, is not that quite final?" Doyle asked. "What possible loophole is there in that for deception?" Houdini offered no comment beyond calling Mrs. Wriedt mistaken about him. "I never look for trouble, and regret that she weighed me up in that light."

Houdini questioned Doyle closely about the French medium Eva Carriere, internationally known as Eva C., probably the most-discussed medium of the moment. Spiritualism had its fashions. Rappings dominated séances of the 1850s; in 1920 many newsworthy manifestations involved the glutinous material called ectoplasm. Doyle had sat with Eva C. and was enthusiastic about the four years of experiments conducted on her by the German physiologist Dr. A. Freiherrn von Schrenck-Notzing, who published the results in such works as *Materialisationsphänomene* (Phenomena of Materialization [1914]). Doyle considered these tests "the most notable of any investigation which has ever been recorded," an absolute proof of life after death. Eva C., after a thorough search, and in a room illuminated by strong red light, had been again and again able to exude gobbets and tentacles of ectoplasm from her mouth, ears, nose, and skin. At times the sticky stuff curdled into the shapes of human limbs and faces, which Doyle speculated might represent "thought forms from the brain of Eva taking visible form." When in full command of her powers, Eva C. could manifest a complete figure, molded to resemble someone deceased: "it moves and talks," Doyle wrote, "and expresses the emotions of the spirit within." He himself witnessed her producing an umbilical piece of ectoplasm six inches long. When he squeezed it, it seemed to thrill like living substance. "There was," he said, "no possibility of deception upon this occasion."

Houdini managed to obtain sittings with Eva C., but not easily. Her discoverer and companion, Madame Juliette Bisson, had brought her to England for investigation by the Society for Psychical Research. Bisson made it plain that she considered magicians biased against Spiritualism, and disliked them. "Our work is serious and real, and the gift of Mlle. Eva might disappear forever, if some awkward individual insists on thinking there is fraud involved." According to Houdini, he won over Bisson and Eva C. by luring them to a performance of the Water Torture, and sending follow-up tickets for a packing-case challenge. Bisson—the wife of a French playwright—was mystified by the escapes, and said to him afterward, "You are a magnificent actor, who cannot call himself a prestidigitator, a title beneath a man of your talent."

At Bisson's invitation Houdini attended at least six séances with Eva C., held in London at 20 Hanover Square, headquarters of the SPR. He documented the results in his diaries, and at greater length in letters to Doyle. The other sitters included Bisson; Dr. E. E. Fournier D'Albe, translator of Schrenck-Notzing's works; Everard Feilding, SPR secretary, a Cambridge graduate who had grown wealthy raising rubber in Malaysia; and the unpredictable Eric Dingwall, who would figure again later in Houdini's life—SPR research officer, amateur magician, curator of erotica at the British Museum, author of *Male Infibulation* and *The Girdle of Chastity: A Medico-Historical Study*, an illustrated history of chastity belts. ("Dingwall and I understand each other," Houdini noted, "not to let ourselves be hoodwinked.")

The séances took place on June evenings, in a darkened room. Each lasted three hours or more, and followed the same procedure. Eva C., a full-chested, heavyset, coarse-featured woman in her middle or late thirties, was first stripped and searched by female committee members in an adjoining room, although Houdini noted that the search did not include "the orifices of her body." After the search, she was dressed in tights, then placed by Madame Bisson into a "mesmeric sleep." Houdini found familiar roles being reversed. After a lifetime of inviting stage committees to examine his cuffs and chains to assure the audience that he was securely shackled, he himself was now the doubting audience, the wary committeeman. During several séances he occupied a "control" chair at Eva C.'s left, holding her left hand and wrist in both his hands, her left leg straddled by his legs. (Dingwall, on the other side, confined her right arm and leg.) He joined the other sitters in periodically intoning "*donnez*"—"give"—to induce her to bring forth ectoplasm.

Eva C. usually failed to do so. By Houdini's account most of the sittings were blanks or "nothing startling." To "help" her—as he put it, although clearly to lay a trap for her—at one séance he withdrew both his hands from her hand and wrist, breaking the control, "but she made no move whatever." The long unproductive sittings jangled nerves and made for friction, especially between Bisson and the SPR investigators. "She showed her peevishness to Feilding so plainly," Houdini recorded, "that I could scarcely conceal my smiles." She got angry at Dingwall too. After she told him and Houdini that Eva C. had once materialized the head of a blue-eyed American soldier that conversed in broken French, Dingwall asked how, in the dark, Eva C. could tell the color of his eyes.

But the sitting of June 22, lasting from 7:30 until after midnight, gave Houdini something to think about. As a special precaution to keep Eva C. from smuggling anything into her mouth, Dingwall sewed a black veil to her tights, enshrouding her head in a sort of bag or net. Yet this time Eva C. manifested. About five inches of a "froth-like substance," as Houdini described it, appeared inside the netting, perhaps discharged from her nose. More ectoplasm formed above her right eye, a "white plaster-looking affair." There also appeared a small face, about four inches in circumference, terra-cotta colored. At one point Eva C. asked permission to remove something from her mouth and, showing her hands empty, took out a "rubberish substance" that she displayed to the sitters by flashlight: "all saw it plainly," Houdini said, "when presto! it vanished."

In reporting this session to Doyle, Houdini again pulled his punches. "Well, we had success at the seance last night, but I am not prepared to say they were supernormal." That was a tame version of what he actually felt: "I was not in any way convinced by the demonstrations." The ectoplasmic froth, he believed, could easily have been lathered up from a scrap of soap concealed in Eva C.'s mouth, or regurgitated from her stomach. Houdini often told the story of how, in his circus days, a Japanese acrobat had taught him to swallow and bring up a billiard ball, developing his throat muscles by practicing with a small peeled potato on the end of a string. He said he found the skill useful when being searched for concealed keys and picks. He had met a regurgitator who could even disgorge a snake and a frog.

As Houdini also did not confide to Doyle, he spotted another familiar technique when Eva C. took out the "rubberish substance." She was doing, he saw, a mediumistic version of the needle swallowing trick: "She 'sleight-of-handed' it into her mouth. . . . I know positively that the move she made is almost identical with the manner in which I manipulate my experiment." He was not impressed by the terra-cotta face either, which resembled "a colored cartoon and seemed to have been unrolled." Moreover, he had concluded that Madame Bisson was not Eva C.'s patroness but her Jim Collins, "a subtle and gifted assistant" acting in confederacy with her to produce the manifestations.

Houdini's attempt to shield Doyle from his distrust was wasted. Like him, Doyle was immune to persuasion but offered little resistance to self-delusion. He considered spirit communication an established fact, and held that the real work of Spiritualism was to rouse humanity to a new moral earnestness. He therefore disdained merely physical manifestations such as Eva C.'s. "I am glad you got some results," he replied to Houdini. "It is certainly on the lowest and most mechanical plane of the spiritual world." Doyle found Houdini's report not only unimpressive but also faintly ridiculous. For he had become convinced that Houdini had mediumistic powers himself—a belief others had voiced before, but which became widespread during the postwar revival of Spiritualism. "I am amused by your investigating with the S. P. R.," Doyle wrote him. "Do they never think of investigating *you?* . . . why go around the world seeking a demonstration of the occult when you are giving one all the time?" He coupled Houdini with the Davenport Brothers in possessing a "dematerializing and reconstructing force" that could momentarily separate "the molecules of that solid object towards which it is directed," such as handcuffs. "My reason tells me that you have this wonderful power," he told Houdini, "for there is no alternative."

Houdini had one further brush with ectoplasm while in England. Doyle had received four photographs of the substance pouring from an Irish medium, Kathleen Goligher. "The stuff seems to come from the womb," he told Houdini. "Incredulity seems to me to be a sort of insanity under these circumstances." Houdini was not able to arrange a sitting with Goligher, but he did speak with her investigator, Dr. W. J. Crawford, a lecturer in engineering at the Belfast Technical Institute. In *The Reality of Psychic Phenomena* (1918), Crawford had described his experiments with the so-called Goligher Circle, involving glass U-tubes, dry cells, and compression balances to measure, for instance, the "Psychic Pressure" on a levitated table (.025 pounds per square inch). His use of such apparatus was not unique. In subjecting mediums to rigorous testing, many reputable scientists applied galvanometers and other tools of their trade, not to mention a Rube-Goldberg-heaven of contraptions specifically designed to detect auras, weigh the soul, or measure the will—Volometers and Sthenometers, Dynamascopes and Bioscopes, Kymographs and Dynamistographs, Howlers, Fluidic Motors, Pugh Tables.

On the basis of his calculations, Crawford advanced a "rod-projection theory" of physical mediumship that became popular in Spiritualist circles. It proposed that Kathleen Goligher especially, but also the other six members of her family, all mediums, levitated the séance table and thumped out the sound of trotting horses by issuing ectoplasm from their bodies in clammy, semi-flexible rods. Houdini was as disingenuous with Crawford as with Doyle. Having spoken with him for several hours and examined his photographs, he said the projected rods were "a wonderful affair and there is no telling how far all this may lead to." Privately he decided that Crawford was "mad." He may have been right. Crawford killed himself in Belfast the same year, leaving a note stating that his research into Spiritualism had nothing to do with his suicide.

Near the end of Houdini's stay in England, Sir Arthur told him about some photographs "far more precious" than those of the Golighers. The fortunate photographer had managed to snap four fairies in a Yorkshire wood, as well as a goblin—beautiful and luminous creatures, about eight inches high. "A fake! you will say. No, sir, I think not," he told Houdini, "it is a revelation." He said he was not allowed to send Houdini the pictures. But he published them not long after in *The Coming of the Fairies* (1922), with some other photographs of the wee folks and their world: a bearded gnome, diaphanous wood elves in a ring, and a cocoonlike "magnetic bath" woven by the fairies. The pictures were eventually exposed as cutouts from magazines, posed and photographed in the woods by some mischievous girls. They brought Doyle derision; H. L. Mencken, for one, speared him as "an almost fabulous ass."

It should be added that Doyle published the photographs as evidence of a "subhuman form of life," without bearing on the question of survival after death, and not as fully proven. Yet it is also true that he personally attested to phenomena no less worth seeing than magnetic fairy baths. He said that during a séance with an Australian apport medium—one able to bring objects (apports) from the other side—he witnessed the manifestation of a mossy bird's nest containing a small speckled egg, two young turtles swimming in a basin, and fifty-six Turkish pennies. And he approvingly repeated a list of apports that the medium—a "little, ginger-coloured man" named Bailey—had harvested from Beyond at other sittings, while stripped naked. It included eighty-seven ancient coins, eight live birds, eighteen precious stones, seven inscribed Babylonian tablets, an Egyptian scarab, an Arabic newspaper, a leopard skin, and a foot-and-a-half-long live shark tangled in wet seaweed that flopped about the séance table. "The results were far above all possible fraud," Doyle commented.

So far as is known, Houdini said nothing to Doyle about the fairy photographs. With whatever reservations, he admired Sir Arthur's country-squire refinement, good-natured sincerity, combative vitality, and high literary gift. He chronicled his meetings with him at unusual length in his diaries, recognizing that "Sir Arthur is a huge success in the literary world, and a great many things he says or does will be of interest at some future time." And as intimately as anyone else could, Houdini understood what it meant to live with insupportable grief over the death of a beloved family member. He looked forward to corresponding with Doyle after returning to America, and seeing him again soon. "I have had a wonderful lot of interesting sittings during my stay over here," he told Doyle, not at all untruthfully, "and thoroughly enjoyed them."

PERFORMANCES IN ENGLAND; *THE MAN FROM BEYOND*; THE WEEHAWKEN STREET CORPORATION; DEATH OF KELLAR

By his count, Houdini attended more than a hundred séances during his six months in Great Britain and week or two in Paris. Like most of his tallies, this one seems apported from the air, since his time abroad was filled with movie work and long-postponed appearances on the Moss circuit.

Reviving from the war, England was on a spending spree, Houdini discovered, the shops crowded with people seeking goods they had for years gone without. Yet he noticed many women dressed in black, and he had to carry a ration card for butter and sugar; prudently he had brought from the States a stock of tea, coffee, and cocoa. The Magicians' Club, of which he remained president, tendered him a banquet at the Savoy Hotel ballroom. The members gave him a heavy silver box, Harry Kellar sent a telegram: "I still think you are the greatest," it read, "though you say I am." Remaining something of an Anglophile, Houdini in his speech praised England as "the most wonderful country in the world for magicians." He had even more friends there than in the United States, he said.

Before going abroad, Houdini had reached a major decision. Instead of working for Famous Players—Lasky or another studio, he would produce his own motion pictures. He shot street scenes in London, Edinburgh, and Paris for a film about counterfeiting, tentatively called "The Dupe." But such large crowds pressed around him that he feared he would not be able to use the footage: "everybody wanted to put their face into the camera." With *The Master Mystery* playing in England for more than a year and creating a "terrific sensation," he found that people "think they know me personally." More than that, he had become a screen idol, to adolescents especially. *Boys' Cinema*, a British fanzine, painted him for its young readers as Superman, "with muscles of iron and a fine pair of eyes that have looked unflinchingly at death in a thousand guises." *Kinema Comic* puffed him as "the most daring cinema star in the world" and ran a fifty-week series entitled "The Amazing Exploits of HOUDINI." Through rotogravures, engravings, and prose tales it retold some of the desperate adventures enacted in his films, relocating them however to England, and supplying him with 'whilsts,' Savile Row suits, and a pipe.

As it affected his stage appearances, Houdini's film stardom was a mixed blessing. On the one hand his movie fans wanted to see him perform live. Despite his near six-year absence, he drew "bigger & better than ever," at double and triple his prewar salary. At the London Palladium he received $3,750 weekly, with extra money for matinee appearances—reportedly the highest salary ever paid a single performer at the theater. His dressing room became a "regular sallon [*sic*]" where he served tea every day for at least ten: "it is the spot of town and we have more visitors than any one who ever played the place."

While hospitable to the crush in London, Houdini rather took his provincial fans for granted. The half hour he gave them offered one or two tricks such as the Cut and Restored Turban and a familiar escape such as the Upside Down, but consisted mostly of smalltalk about his film career. It pleased him to think that "after all my hard work, I can draw the Public without killing myself." But as happened before when he tried to just get by, he sometimes got panned. The reviewer for a Nottingham newspaper, for one, apologized to readers for having "boomed" Houdini's appearance beforehand: "No one was more astounded than I was to see on Monday night Houdini's solitary feat, which of itself lasts only three minutes. . . . Why on earth should Houdini imagine that any audience would be entertained by hearing a long and uncalled-for account of what he has been doing during the past six years." Coasting or not, while performing the USD Houdini injured his ankle—the right one this time—and had to submit it to electrical heat treatments and keep it rubber-bandaged.

When Houdini returned to America, in mid-July 1920, his attention was fixed on film work. Over the next eighteen months, in fact, he gave not a single stage performance. As if to make it impossible for himself to turn back, before leaving England he unsentimentally destroyed $25,000 (his figure) worth of illusions he had bought—"never used even a thought." And when giving his customary shipboard performance for charity, he had himself billed as "the World Famous Cinema Star." A typhus scare briefly held the passengers at Ellis Island, and Houdini reached home too late in the day to visit Machpelah Cemetery. But after motoring there the next day with Hardeen, he went to the Hoboken laboratories of his Film Development Corporation.

Once reestablished in New York, Houdini began forming his production company, the Houdini Picture Corporation. With himself as (yet-again) president and Hardeen as secretary, the business was capitalized at a half million dollars, offering fifty thousand shares of common stock at ten dollars each. Houdini announced, ambitiously, that he intended to produce and star in four features a year. Although he had brought back street-scenes for a picture about counterfeiting, he also considered making a film version of *The Count of Monte Cristo* (one of his ten favorite books) or of some tales by Poe (whose grave in Baltimore he photographed). He dropped these plans, to write the scenario for a movie to be called *The Man From Beyond*. Filming began in the spring of 1921 and lasted eighteen weeks, taking Houdini to Lake Placid for the Arctic scenes and to Niagara Falls for a climactic river rescue. Now the boss-of-all-bosses, he nevertheless found himself often standing around waiting for something to happen, or doing nothing at all because of daylong rain, and once getting accidentally chopped on the arm by a hatchet.

Visibly influenced by Houdini's encounter with Doyle and Spiritualism, *The Man From Beyond* opens with a shot of a Bible, the text John 5:28 highlighted: "Marvel not at this: for the hour is coming, in the which all that are in the graves shall hear his voice." The plot unfolds around Howard Hillary, who is discovered inside a wall of Arctic ice. He has been frozen there a full century, since the shipwreck of his squarerigged sealing vessel in 1820. Hacked out and revivified, he is brought to the United States and the mansion of a scientist, Dr. Strange, arriving during the wedding ceremony of Strange's daughter, Felice. Recognizing in her the lineaments of his own fiancée of a hundred years before, also named Felice, Hillary breaks up the ceremony. For his outburst he is rushed off to a lunatic asylum. The rest of the action concerns his tussles with the usual cast of abductors and mad scientists, and his attempt to convince Felice that she harbors the soul of his long-dead love, as he does. The film ends with a superimposed image of the original Felice's spirit slipping into Felice Strange's body, and a shot of Hillary reading a statement in Sir Arthur Conan Doyle's *The Vital Message*: "The great teachers of the earth— Zoroaster down to Moses and Christ . . . have taught the immortality and progression of the soul."

Houdini masterminded his first independent production middling well. The icicle-hung sealer in the opening Arctic scenes looks authentic, and must have been expensive to build, and Nita Naldi, soon to appear with Valentino, makes a strikingly pretty vamp. Two action scenes generate suspense. In one, Houdini rassles a hoodlum on a treacherously sloping cliff, slipsliding down until he hangs over the void by his finger-ends. In the film's centerpiece, reportedly shot from different locations by eight cameras, he rescues Felice as her canoe rollercoasters down the raging Niagara River, the camera effectively cutting among the thundering falls, the helpless boat, and Hillary's head and arms thrashing through the whitewater foam. (As he swam, Houdini was attached to an unseen steel wire, fed from a reel on shore.) Otherwise, however, the film is torturously slow, a sanguaw of long-lingering camera shots of nothing in particular. Houdini performs only one brief escape, from a wet sheet, asking instead to be taken seriously as a romantic lead. But his Howard Hillary seems little more animated when alive than when frozen in the icewall.

The Spiritualist element in *The Man From Beyond* is puzzling. As a *Variety* reviewer pointed out, it ill-suits the action, straining to impose "high literary meaning" on bound-and-gagged adventure: "the net effect is pretty unsatisfactory. Serial melodrama and screen uplift won't mix." Aside from the formal problem, the credence the film gives to beliefs in Survival and reincarnation belies Houdini's experiences in England. Just two months after returning to the States, he published an article entitled "Why I Am A Skeptic," announcing that his "over 100" séances abroad had left him unconvinced, "further than ever from a belief in the genuineness of the manifestations." Yet his promotional booklet for *The Man From Beyond* promises that the film will console those who still grieve over the departed: "Audiences everywhere will welcome it as an evidence that loved ones gone to the great beyond are not lost to us forever." Houdini seems to have emphasized Spiritualist beliefs both because he remained open, half wishfully, to becoming convinced by them, and because, with their inherent mystery and contemporary appeal, they represented strong, commercial dramatic material.

Triply involved as author, star, and producer, Houdini worried more than usual over the film's success. "This is my first big venture," he said, "and I am very anxious to put things over properly." He launched his picture with all the publicity he could muster. In one come-on, he offered to sell distributors a boot with an incised heel that could be inked and walked around town, leaving the sidewalks imprinted "Houdini." He even hired a press agent, Jack Edwards, formerly associated with D. W. Griffith. "What earthly use the most publicized man in the world," *Billboard* observed, "wants with a press agent is beyond the conception of the theatrical world." For his film's premiere, on April 2, 1922, Houdini engaged the Times Square Theater, at Broadway and Forty-second Street, and after screening *The Man From Beyond* did a half-hour of magic and escapes, including the Vanishing Elephant—more effective in the small theater, some viewers felt, than at the Hippodrome.

By that time Houdini had been absent from the stage fully two years (except a nine-week Keith tour, "probably my last engagement in vaudeville," undertaken perhaps because he needed the $25,000). Nevertheless, to get his picture talked about he made personal appearances with it for about three weeks. He returned to performing straitjacket escapes a hundred feet up, sometimes offering a cash prize for the best photo taken of him. He also created four touring companies, hoping to gain a national audience for *The Man From Beyond* by presenting it in connection with "The Houdini Wonder Show of 1922." One or two well-known magicians or escape artists headed each unit, notably Frederick Eugene Powell (1856–1938), an old-timer whose magic equipment had been wiped out in the San Antonio flood of 1921. Houdini appeared at the opening show of each unit, and made it clear that these were *his* shows, combined with *his* movie. "Houdini was so greatly afraid someone would get a little advertising, in addition to himself," Powell complained, "that my name was not mentioned many times."

Houdini's publicity campaign had more at stake than his ego. His Film Development Corporation was losing, he said, "a lot of money"—how much is unknown, but he was forced to discount about $10,000 worth of notes for the company. In trying to keep FDC going, he formed a real estate holding company known as the Weehawken Street Corporation, with himself as president, Bess as vice president, and Hardeen as secretary-treasurer. Through the corporation he bought FDC's West Hoboken laboratory buildings, taking out a $35,000 bank mortgage. He then rented the laboratories to FDC for $541 a month, in effect hiring the laboratories from himself.

Houdini was out of his depth in this financial wheeling-dealing. For all his worry about ending up impoverished, like his father, he had never learned to handle his wealth but still fretted over the expense of clothes-pressing while splurging price-no-object on his collections. After two years his maneuvering through the Weehawken Street Corporation had saved him nothing and even put him out of pocket. And meanwhile the Film Development Corporation got hit with a costly lawsuit. In the fall of 1921, another company, Powers Film Products, sued FDC for some $3,000. Hoping to ruin FDC's reputation, Houdini believed, Powers obtained a warrant of attachment by charging, falsely, that FDC was a foreign corporation. The charge became news and led another film company to refuse to pay $8,000 that it owed FDC. Soon other debtors also withheld payment, and several ongoing FDC business deals collapsed, driving Houdini to file a $25,000 countersuit against Powers for damage to his company's credit and reputation. Two dissatisfied stockholders asked the courts to appoint a receiver to take control of FDC. They charged Houdini and Hardeen with manipulating the company's affairs to their own benefit and incurring losses that cut its capital by half, from about $121,000 to about $58,000.

The human cost of his development company concerned Houdini too. His brother had given up a stage career to run FDC, and worked "very hard," Houdini observed, "giving all his time to the laboratory." Not all: Hardeen was also burdened with a large, fictitious business correspondence as secretary-treasurer of the new Weehawken Street Corporation, writing long letters—mere legal formalities—to Houdini as president of FDC. The load aggravated his stomach problems, and he now needed surgery for ulcers. Houdini still could not put Kellar at ease either about his possible liability for the company's losses. "I am not worried about losing my money in the FDC," he wrote Kellar, "but would certainly worry about losing your friendship." Altogether, while digging himself deeper and deeper in, he wanted more and more to get out: "It will be a Godsend for all of us if we get away from it in a legitimate manner."

Kellar was given no more time to worry. Treated a while with quack "Electric Vibrations" for his inoperable stomach cancer, he died on March 10, 1922. The night before, he threw up blood that half filled a washbasin.

He seemed to rally, but in the morning had a bloody coughing fit. His niece described the event for Houdini: Before turning over on his side to die, Kellar called out, "Oh my God, what an awful pain, Oh, my God." Houdini could not get to the funeral, in Los Angeles, but he arranged to have it filmed, and made up a special cabinet to preserve Kellar's hundreds of letters to him, for use in writing his biography. During a train trip from Pittsburgh to New York, he also wrote a stilted eulogy, praising Kellar's hardfought struggle for success, his underlying good nature, and his ceaseless invention of tricks and illusions that seemed "actual witchcraft"—his endless pursuit of new magic.

278; ALFRED BECKS; SAWING THROUGH A WOMAN

As Houdini now neared fifty, crowsfeet showed around his eyes. Years of strenuous performance, he lamented, had made him look "ten years older than I really am." His little-giant physique was softening. When he appears on screen loinclothed in one scene of *The Man From Beyond*, his belly seems a bit flabby, his thighs slack. Where reporters once compared him to Sandow, one now described him as a "stocky little man"; another noted his "thickset frame a little inclined to stoutness." For all that, he would no more give in to age than to anything else. Attending the 1921 heavyweight championship between sledgehammering Jack Dempsey and the French military hero Georges Carpentier, he raptly watched Dempsey "sagging, ageing" in the second round, then revive and overwhelm Carpentier to win. "Such," he drew the moral, "is life." He collected newspaper items about others who triumphed over waning vitality: "Men and Women Need Not Fear Middle Age," "World's Greatest Workers/At Their Best Between/55 and 65 Years of Age," GREATEST SHOOTERS OF ALL AGES/HAVE BEEN MEN OF MATURE YEARS.

No longer on tour, Houdini for the first time had a chance to settle into the townhouse he had bought in 1904, rented out after his mother's death, but never fully occupied. In addition to its dozen or so rooms it offered such amenities as tiled baths, birch and maple paneling, a laundry, a basement gym, and fourteen closets. The place was shared by Bess's seventy-two-year-old mother, Balbena Rahner; Houdini's sister Gladys lived nearby, on Morningside Drive, across the park. In trying to "get back to home life," Houdini said, he got the house "all fix't up," and entertained often and largely—dinner parties for sixteen or more, Christmas dinner for twenty-five, a guest or two every few days, mostly well-known or rising magicians such as Nate Leipzig (1873–1939) and Silent Mora (Louis McCord [1884–1972]). "The refreshments," one magician wrote, "were such only as Mrs. Houdini is capable of in her best cuisine mode."

Visitors entered 278 through a long room crowded with tapestry-covered gilt-edged furniture—dark despite a chandelier—a little stuffy, the shouts of children playing street-games audible from outside. Houdini made the room a museum of his career. On a massive table stood the jeweled cup given him by Grand Duke Sergei of Russia, the coin-studded bowl presented by the Essen Coliseum management, the ebony-and-gold wand from the king of Belgium. In a tall bookcase were an assortment of wands wielded by John Henry Anderson, Alexander and Adelaide Herrmann, Kellar, and other famous magicians, and in a lower case the bronze statuette of Sarah Bernhardt. On a pedestal was a lifelike bronze bust of Houdini himself, commissioned in England, meant to someday be set over his grave. It was, one visitor said, "a veritable fairy-tale sort of a room."

Houdini worked in a top-floor nook, so crammed with cartons, shelves, pasteboard files, and piles of papers as to leave little space for his desk and swivel chair. This hole-in-the-wall opened into a larger, barefloored workroom containing a huge table, heaped with papers, a microscope, a pair of balances, and a typewriter for Houdini's secretary or stenographer. His collections flooded the upper floors of the house. Playbills, engravings, and photographs papered the walls, overmantels, and even door-frames. Books stacked or boxed were wedged into almost-impassable back rooms, overflowing into the front rooms and the cellar. "They seemed to be imprisoned there as in a dungeon," a visitor wrote of the volumes. "They lined the walls on all sides, pressing against one another for elbow-room and well-nigh touching the ceiling."

To control the chaos, Houdini brought in a full-time librarian. On the recommendation of Robert Gould Shaw he hired a seventy-five-year-old Englishman named Alfred Becks. For ten years Becks had been in charge of the Harvard theater library, arranging Shaw's collection. Houdini valued not only Becks's experience as a cataloguer and buyer, but also his theatrical pedigree. Like Evanion, Frikell, and other relics, Becks represented a "direct link," as Houdini called it, to a memorable past that he considered his own prehistory. Becks had been secretary to the Anglo-Irish dramatist Dion Boucicault, who had written plays for Madame Vestris; had known the leading nineteenth-century character actor C. W. Couldock, who had often seen Kean and Macready perform; had managed the millionaire singer-dancer Lotta Crabtree (but quit after she asked him, ingloriously, to take her wash to the laundry; he said he didn't take his own). Houdini saw Becks as the inheritor of a theatrical tradition stretching back to Garrick himself. He owed to Becks, he said, "what little knowledge I possess re history of drama." This "well-bred, courteous gentleman," as Houdini described him, took over a small bedroom at 278 in July 1920, eating and sleeping at the house for the next eighteen months. He showed up for work at nine each morning in a suit of Houdini's old clothes, then toiled among the books and papers, indexing and cataloging until nine each evening.

Becks thought Houdini's collection impressive but exasperating. At first glance he rated the thousands of playbills and magicians' portraits "very good," and two of the Booth letters as the "finest" he had ever seen. He gave a "fine" to the unrivaled library of magic books, but added that by rubber-stamping his name on the title pages Houdini had "'killed' them all." Even Becks the skilled bibliographer felt overwhelmed by the mountain of material. It would take more than a year, he told Houdini, to classify and arrange the books alone, some written in Dutch, Hungarian, Latin, Portuguese, Swedish, Chinese. But Houdini set Becks to work also cutting up and sorting old theatrical newspapers, and arranging his five to ten thousand autographs. And then there were the programs and prints. "Oh! what a task and time I have had on this collection," Becks wrote Shaw. "It beats anything I have ever manipulated in my career, and I shall be most happy when I have finished the work."

Houdini's top-floor office was also the focus of his literary ambitions. In 1921 Dutton published his most charming book, *Miracle Mongers and Their Methods*, an outgrowth of a work he had planned on fire-eaters. About half the book is devoted to divulging their methods—how to bite off chunks of red-hot iron, eat live coals, and drink burning oil. The rest exposes the techniques of poison-eaters, venomous-reptile-defiers, human ostriches, and the like. The book has an elegiac cast, looking back to a now-withering world of curio halls, "forms of entertainment over which oblivion threatens to stretch her darkening wings." Although based on Houdini's firsthand experience and his collections, *Miracle Mongers* was clearly ghostwritten, beginning with the opening references to Chaucer and to Samuel Johnson. Just the same Houdini dedicated the book to Bess as "My

Life's Helpmate," and sent an inscribed copy and photograph to Charmian
London (followed by a letter the next month, unfortunately now lost).

With little time to spare for magic and escapes, Houdini tried to avoid
being dragged into the famous controversy that erupted over the invention
of the best-known of all stage illusions. Sawing a Woman in Half became
the sensation of the 1921 vaudeville season, after being performed in England late in 1920 by the British magician P. T. Selbit. Selbit was challenged
by Houdini's old friend Horace Goldin, "the Royal Illusionist," who
appeared before crowned heads throughout the world (including the king of
Siam, who built a theater just for him in Bangkok). Goldin performed the
illusion himself, alleging that he had invented it in 1906 as "Vivisection"
and had submitted an improved version to John Ringling's circus in 1919 as
"Sawing a Woman in Two." Actually the two versions differed entirely in
appearance and method. Selbit's box rested on a very thin platform,
Goldin's on a suspiciously thick one; Selbit concealed the woman in the
box, Goldin allowed her head, hands, and feet to stick out.

War came when the Keith circuit hired Goldin and also put together six
touring companies to perform the illusion throughout the United States.
Keith's reaped more than a million dollars. That brought Selbit to America
to establish his sole right to Sawing a Woman and present his apparatus for
the rival Shubert circuit. Goldin piled up restraining orders and sued
everyone in sight. Within a year so many magicians were doing some version of the lucrative trick—and being sued by Goldin—that the theatrical
press declared it all but dead as a vaudeville attraction. A magician in
Cincinnati even performed it over the radio. Home listeners could hear the
sawing but had to visualize everything else.

Houdini got drawn into the fray sideways. He had no strong reason to
back Goldin, liking him personally but not admiring his magic: "nice and
clean," he called it. "Nothing startling." Selbit, however, opened a second
front against S. E. Josolyne, the British magician who had sold Houdini the
secret and rights to Walking Through a Wall. Selbit charged that Josolyne
too had pilfered his Sawing a Woman and was now performing in England—claiming to have licensed it from its real-and-true one-and-only
inventor, Houdini! Selbit charged also that Josolyne had had no right to sell
Walking Through a Wall to Houdini, since that illusion too was his own
invention.

Houdini had neither time nor appetite for this mess, an out-of-control case of chronic squabbling among magicians over priority. "Selbit seems to be seeking a lot of worry over here," he said. "I don't see any reason why he should attack me, but will try and keep out of the controversy if I possibly can." From the sidelines he had Hardeen write a formal letter for publication in *Billboard*, insisting that his brother had rightfully bought Walking Through a Wall from Josolyne, its inventor. Obviously on Houdini's advice and information, Hardeen pointed out too that the sawing concept was not new. Robert-Houdin's *Memoirs*, he showed, mention that the early-nineteenth-century Italian magician Torrini had described cutting in half a large woman and one of his twin sons. The irony of Houdini's resort to the discredited Robert-Houdin for support contains the finer irony that "Torrini" never existed. In ransacking old playbills and programs to unmask his predecessor, Houdini failed to notice that Robert-Houdin had dreamed "Torrini" up.

Although Houdini stayed mostly above the battle, it stimulated him. In his notes he worked out his own version of the illusion, wittier and more bloodcurdling than the originals. A woman or man would be placed in the box, which would be cloven by a log cutter or electric buzz saw. The halves would be rejoined, the fronts opened. Out would pop not the assistant but, in dress identical to hers or his, two small women or two dwarfs. He added a caution: "Great care must be exercised so that both woman and the small ones will not be endangered from saw."

TWELVE

SPRING 1922–SPRING 1923

DOYLE'S CARNEGIE HALL LECTURES; SPIRIT PHOTOGRAPHY; THE ATLANTIC CITY SÉANCE

YOU WILL LEAVE your mark for ever upon America." Thus the message that reached Sir Arthur Conan Doyle in his home circle, from spirit friends. It was reassuring, for as he prepared to bring his New Revelation to the United States, in the spring of 1922, he doubted that its truth would be well received. Americans were a practical people with a keen sense of humor, he reasoned, while he brought them a vision that could easily be made to seem ludicrous.

Doyle's messengers did not exactly deceive him, nor exactly did his reason. Americans gave him the most tumultuous welcome they had afforded a visiting literary light since Oscar Wilde in 1882. Headline-hunting reporters besieged him to ask, on behalf of their Prohibition-burdened readers, whether spirits in heaven had access to sex, cigars, and liquor. So many people came to hear his four scheduled lectures in New York, at Carnegie Hall, that he arranged to give three more in the city. Introduced at the first lecture by his friend Hamlin Garland, a dedicated Spiritualist who once had a communication from Walt Whitman, he began by describing the overwhelming scientific evidence for Survival, then related some poignant personal experiences, "how I had clearly seen my mother beyond any doubt or question." He explained that everyone has an "etheric body," identical to the physical self in each hair and pore; after painless passage into the afterlife it rejoins those it has longed to see. He depicted heaven minutely as being much like earth, with mansions, places of amusement, pets. His son had beheld Christ there—"Once," Kingsley had told him, "and I can never, never forget it."

Doyle's downright manner gave his relation of these wonders conviction and authority. "I have no eloquence and make profession of none," he said of himself, "but I am audible and I say no more than I mean and can prove." The columnist Heywood Broun, present at Carnegie Hall, was struck by how Doyle's very bulk lent force to his contrasting gospel of the Etheric Body:

> Sir Arthur is distinctly of our own world of matter. He is of the flesh to the extent of 200 pounds or more. His utterance is without distinction. His figures of speech are generally commonplace. Some of his reasoning is trivial and much of it illogical. Neither eloquence, grace nor poetry is in his message, and yet it seemed to us extraordinarily convincing.

Doyle most deeply moved his audiences, and got the most publicity, by his exhibition of spirit photographs. The first such pictures had been taken in Boston in the 1860s by W. H. Mumler. In photographing himself he captured on the same plate a so-called 'extra,' the ghostly semblance of a dead cousin. Like the production of ectoplasm, spirit photography was a specialty of some mediums, and after the war comforted grieving families with proof that their lost ones hovered nearby. Doyle projected several spirit photos on the Carnegie Hall screen by stereopticon. One revealed an extra looming beside him as he sat—Kingsley at about the age of sixteen. "It is not a very good likeness," Doyle remarked, "but you may realize how consoling it was to me, in any circumstances, to see my son again." He also displayed what he called the greatest spirit photograph ever taken. It showed an Armistice Day crowd at the London Cenotaph during two minutes of silent prayer for Britain's war dead. In the sky above could be seen a cloud of discarnate entities, the shoulderless, neckless heads of many men killed in battle, their faces fixed and stern. "When it was flashed upon the screen," the *New York Times* reported, "there was a moment of silence and then gasps rose and spread over the room, and the voices and sobs of women could be heard."

Houdini attended at least one of Doyle's Carnegie Hall lectures, but did not spend time with him for another three weeks. He had invited Doyle and his family to stay at 278. Doyle looked forward to seeing him again— "your normal self, not in a tank or hanging by one toe from a sky-scraper"—but declined, explaining that he had to remain "semi-public" for the sake of his mission. Meanwhile Houdini saved and briskly underlined the many news accounts of Doyle's lectures.

Having learned something about film development the hard way, Houdini had begun to explore spirit photography on his own. He was compiling information on the subject for a new book, tentatively titled "So This is Spiritualism." He experimented with taking pictures in the dark, and tried to learn about the most-discussed spirit photographers of the moment, two mediums in Crewe, England. The Crewe Circle, as they were called, allowed patrons to bring their own photographic plates, to eliminate the possibility of fraud. The leader, William Hope, could even register 'ghost-faces' without a camera, the plates simply being held between the sitter's hands. In this way he had produced for Doyle a picture that Doyle said closely resembled his elder sister, dead thirty years. Houdini hired a "special emissary at Crewe," the Glasgow illusionist (and fireworks maker) DeVega (Alexander Stewart [1891–1971]), whom he considered not easily fooled. He paid the expenses of DeVega and an assistant to go to Crewe, carefully observe the sittings, report back to him, and if possible "dope out some way" of duplicating the phenomena.

Houdini apparently did not say so to Doyle, but he deeply distrusted spirit photos. As he knew, the Society for Psychical Research had tested the Crewe Circle by secretly marking plates with a twenty-second exposure to X ray. The investigators found that the developed negatives contained 'ghost-faces' but lacked the X-ray tracings, confirming that the plates had been switched. Doyle—vice president of the Society for the Study of Supernormal Pictures (SSSP)—denounced the SPR's investigation to Houdini as "a stunt." But spirit photographs had a long history of becoming dis-spirited. Mumler's originary picture of his dead cousin was quickly revealed a fake created by double exposure. Doyle's sob-producing Cenotaph picture stood up no better. Some of the extras were soon shown to be the faces of quite-alive professional football players and the also still-earth-bound African boxer Battling Siki.

Before visiting with Houdini, Doyle had a remarkable experience in Washington, D.C. While lecturing there he met the Dane Julius Zancig (Julius Jörgenson [1857–1929]) and his second wife, Ada (active in performance 1920–29). With Ada as with his first wife, Zancig gave baffling demonstrations of mindreading. As she sat blindfolded on the stage, acting as a medium, he circulated through the audience. Spectators handed him notes or unusual objects—a dress sample, dog license, mummy's hand. In each case the only word he put to his wife was "This?" Yet she succeeded in repeating the contents of every note and identifying every object. The SPR arranged to test the Zancigs. The press, especially in England, devoted many columns to debate over whether they used a code—signaling by body movements, perhaps, or flashing Morse with their eyelids.

In Washington the Zancigs gave a private demonstration for the Doyles. Mrs. Zancig stood at the far end of the room from her husband, the side of her face to him. Doyle later reported to Houdini that although no word passed between the couple, Mrs. Zancig repeated names and duplicated drawings of a ship and other objects that he and his wife made and showed to Zancig. Doyle was impressed, the more so when Mrs. Zancig mentioned that in Cambridge, England, she had been unable to get her husband's message because her mind was full of the letter *T*—and it turned out that some students had united, for fun, in trying to send *T*s. "This surely is proof positive of telepathy," Doyle said, "for there was no reason for her to tell me this story." Doyle viewed telepathy as a simpler, lesser thing than mediumship, but speculated that the Zancigs' thought-transference might involve higher gifts, such as clairvoyance. Mrs. Zancig told him that when her husband transmitted a name, it often appeared to her as printed in the air. That seemed to Doyle similar to the inner experience of mediums. "Possibly," he wrote Houdini, "it is a real ectoplasmic formation like the figures of Eva."

Houdini again kept his counsel, at least for a while. But he could have said a lot. Zancig belonged to the Society of American Magicians. Among colleagues there he freely admitted that he and his wife were no mindreaders. In fact, Houdini noted, after the first Mrs. Zancig died, Zancig broke in a Philadelphia streetcar conductor to work the act. Houdini had often performed with Zancig on the same vaudeville bills, too, and had had "ample opportunity," he said, to "watch his system and codes" and admire them as "swift, sure and silent." Perhaps not so sure: the London *Daily*

Chronicle studied the Zancigs' performances and published a system close enough to theirs to enable audience members to call out the objects as soon as Mrs. Zancig did. Doyle knew of the exposé but tendered his usual hypothesis: mediums being no less flawed than other human beings, and becoming no less tired or anxious, they sometimes go through the motions. So the Zancigs, he granted, "may use codes when their powers are low."

Much remained unsaid when the Doyles came to 278 for lunch, on May 10. Houdini gathered up rare tracts from around the house and showed off his library, especially works he had acquired on Spiritualism. Doyle praised the many "good" books but pointed out that Houdini lacked classic works of the "great pioneers" and owned a surplus of "opposing" books—"which are really all worthless," he said, "since everyone knows now that phenomena do occur." Doyle may or may not have thumbed through any of the "good" volumes and seen the heckling horselaughs Houdini jotted down in the margins: "*Sheer Bosh!* . . . Ha! ha! ha! . . . does not know of what he is talking. . . . haha HoH—all Rot." Still, Houdini took Doyle's critique seriously. He decided to have Alfred Becks card-index his Spiritualist library, so he could see just what he had, and to assign an entire floor of the house to expanding it.

During the Doyles' visit Houdini discussed with Sir Arthur the phenomenon of 'spirit hands.' It dated back to 'paraffin séances' in the early days of Spiritualism. Sitters gathered around a pail of hot water topped with several inches of melted paraffin; on this surface an entity would leave the impress of its hand. The more recent manifestations were more powerful. Doyle was enthusiastic for a Polish medium named Kluski, at whose séances appeared not a mere impress but entire hands made of paraffin, supposedly created by ectoplasmic shapes dipping themselves in the molten wax. Doyle observed that no living being could have made them. The wrist openings were so small that no human hand could have been withdrawn from the mold without breaking it. "It could only have been done by dematerialisation—no other way is possible."

But Houdini explained to Doyle that a rubber glove could be blown up with air, then dipped in paraffin. When the paraffin cooled, the glove could be deflated and withdrawn, leaving a spirit hand. Doyle utterly rejected the explanation. (By experiment Houdini devised an improved method as well. He lubricated his hand with Vaseline before dipping it into the wax. That way he could pull his hand from the coating while the wax was warm and rework the still-pliable wrist opening, making it too narrow for any human hand to enter. Soon he was able to make in ten or fifteen minutes a perfect spirit hand "à la Kluski.")

Socially the afternoon was a success. According to Houdini, Lady Doyle commented that 278 was "the most home-like home that she had ever seen." He pleased Sir Arthur with the gift of a pamphlet that had been given to him by Ira Davenport, receiving in turn an inscribed copy of Doyle's *Wanderings of a Spiritualist*. But Doyle said that what interested him most was the trick Houdini showed him in a taxi as he took the Doyles back to their hotel. Houdini apparently removed the first joint of his thumb, showed it separated from the rest, then replaced it. Lady Doyle "nearly fainted," Houdini remarked. "You certainly have very wonderful powers," Sir Arthur wrote him later, "whether inborn or acquired." Doyle's response may have flattered Houdini, but cannot have increased his respect for Doyle's fraud-meter. The detached thumb-joint is kindergarten-level magic that can be done by a five-year-old. "Never having been taught the artifices of conjuring," Houdini noted in a memorandum, "it was the simplest thing in the world for anyone to gain his confidence to hoodwink him."

Before their soggier meeting the next month, Doyle continued his lecture tour into New England and the Midwest. He had visited the United States once before, in 1894. Unlike such earlier British literary visitors as Mrs. Frances Trollope, he had found little in the country to dislike beyond the sensationalistic press, hot-dog signs, and gum-chewing, "which does much to disfigure American life." Otherwise he considered America "the coming Power" and enthused over cafeterias, the willingness of people to lend him their cars, equal education, and baseball, "a splendid game which calls for a fine eye, activity, bodily fitness, and judgment in the highest degree"—as he knew from watching the Giants play the Dodgers on opening day. Especially, of course, he revered the United States as the home of Spiritualism. Boston was to him the place where, on "the historic day in 1861," Mumler "received the first extra upon a plate." When he passed Rochester, New York, near the home of the Fox sisters, it occurred to him to start an international subscription for erecting an obelisk. It would mark the sisters' first reception of spirit rappings, on March 31, 1848, "in truth the greatest date in human history since the great revelation of two thousand years ago."

While on the road Doyle looked up many mediums, and wrote to Houdini about some of the sittings. Generally he thought American mediums undistinguished. But he went out of his way for a séance in Toledo with an unnervingly calm, dark young woman named Ada Besinnet (or Bessinet). She did not disappoint him. The hour-and-a-half session was guided by two spirits, a guttural-sounding Native American named Black Cloud and the girlish, squeaky-voiced Pansy. Under their direction brilliant light curvetted about the room; an American soldier killed in the Philippines sang two songs; faces glimmered up out of the darkness, including that of the Arctic explorer Sir Ernest Shackleton. Doyle saw his mother and talked with his beloved son, who left a letter for him, written in the dark, saying "Oscar and Uncle Willy are both here with you." "Miss Bessinet is a truly wonderful medium," Doyle decided, "and so fine a character that the work produced carries weight."

Houdini was eager to sit with Besinnet. But Doyle reported to him that he was gaining a reputation among Spiritualists of being prejudiced against them. "I know that this is not so," Doyle added. "She is safe in your hands." He asked Besinnet the favor of including Houdini in a séance and wrote a formal letter of introduction recommending him as a "patient and sympathetic observer." But Doyle estimated Houdini's state of mind no more keenly than his detached thumb. Later in the year Houdini discussed Besinnet with Fulton Oursler (1893–1952), a magic buff and managing editor of McFadden Publications, who after speaking with Doyle had a séance with her. For his ten dollars, Oursler came away convinced that the glowing faces were masks lit by flashlights, that the spirit hand that touched his cheek was Besinnet's breast ("and a pretty hefty one at that"), and that the gramophone recordings were played to muffle the sound as she sneaked away from her chair. He put out a foot during the seance, he told Houdini, and Besinnet tripped on it as she stole about in the darkness. Over the next two years Houdini wrote to Besinnet four or five times offering to come from New York for a sitting. She did not reply.

When the Doyles returned to New York, in June, Houdini invited them as guests of honor to the annual SAM banquet and show, held in the grand ballroom on the twenty-fourth floor of the McAlpin Hotel. Ever the showman, he made it a celebrity bash. The guest list amounted to a Who's Who of magic, including Howard Thurston and Horace Goldin. Houdini also invited prominent non-magicians he counted as friends, among them the postmaster of New York, the director of the New York Public Library, department-store mogul Bernard Gimbel, Professor Brander Matthews of

Columbia, welfare-worker and journalist Sophie Loeb, and Adolph Ochs, publisher of the *Times*.

Houdini's feints and dodges had kept his friendship with Doyle on the edge of a misstep, and he now made one. He contrived for Doyle's "special benefit," as he told him, an after-dinner show featuring Spiritualist-like magic effects. Understandably, Doyle was incensed at being invited to see his passionate beliefs treated as entertainment, and at the crass misunderstanding of him that it represented. "I fear that the bogus spiritual phenomena must prevent me from attending the banquet, which you have so graciously proffered," he wrote Houdini. "I look upon this subject as sacred, and I think that God's gift to man has been intercepted and delayed by the constant pretence that all phenomena are really tricks, which I know they are not." There was no mistaking the anger in Doyle's stiff politeness. Houdini answered lengthily, assuring him "as a gentleman" of his goodwill, promising that no "indignity" would be offered, and mentioning that Thurston himself was "a firm believer in spiritualism." Doyle cooled off quickly and replied with his usual perky cheer: "My dear Houdini: Of course we will come. All thanks."

But at the dinner Doyle himself stumbled. As his contribution to the after-dinner entertainment, he set up a projector. Surprisingly he began showing moving pictures of prehistoric animals—dinosaurs, triceratopses, and giant reptiles clawing and fondling in the primeval slime. The banqueters were unaware that the animations had been created for use in a movie version of Doyle's novel *The Lost World*, then in production. But knowing the seriousness of Doyle's belief in spirit photographs, many were uncertain whether to respond to the film as High Mystery or a gag. Doyle spoke of it, one reporter said, "very guardedly," as though hoping it would be taken for a "psychic picture." The awkward fizzle left Doyle explaining after the event that he had thought it would be "very amusing" if he could get the audience of mystifiers "utterly mystified"—which he did. For the magic show Houdini dusted off Metamorphosis and climbed into the trunk wearing, or rather swimming in, Doyle's oversize coat; tiny Bess, when she emerged from inside after the switch, looked even more lost in it than he. "Mr. Chairman," Doyle wrote to him the next day, "I want to know how you got out of that trunk."

A few weeks later, a hearty invitation ushered in deeper misunderstanding between Houdini and Doyle. "Why not come down—both of you?" Doyle wrote from Atlantic City. "The children would teach you to swim!" One of the country's most popular family resorts, home of the Miss America Pageant, Atlantic City drew large crowds in summer. Its broad boardwalk of snackstands and curio shops flowed with promenaders and rolling chairs, and its boulevard-size piers offered vaudeville and music playing through the warm nights. Doyle thought that radio, then becoming popular, might prove useful in communicating with the spirit world. He had gone to Atlantic City in part to examine a huge amplifier newly installed there, which could pick up messages broadcast from Pittsburgh, some three hundred miles away.

Houdini and Bess went down for the weekend of June 17–18, taking a room next to the Doyles' suite in the Ambassador Hotel. The two men spent the later part of Saturday afternoon in the hotel swimming pool. They made a Mutt-and-Jeff pair, Houdini's ears coming up to Doyle's shoulders. Houdini taught the Doyle children how to dive and float, and showed off his underwater endurance, Doyle watching carefully as he inhaled and exhaled before submerging himself. Afterward they dressed and joined Lady Doyle on the beach. Stretched out in deck chairs looking toward the blue Atlantic, they discussed spirit photography. Doyle showed Houdini a picture of a coffin covered in white roses, attended each end by an extra. The shrubbery behind the excarnate spirits could be seen through them. Houdini was struck anew by Doyle's intelligence and sweet nature—Lady Doyle said he had "never spoken a cross word in his life"—but also by the fanatic intensity of his belief.

Nearby, Doyle's children played beachball. For worse and better, as Houdini saw it, they had taken on their parents' teachings and personal qualities. Death meant no more to them than life on a higher plane. Nor was any dear one, for them, ever lost: "even if they are dead," he noted, "they still live, and hold conversation." But the children had their father's tenderness, too. It touched him to see one of the boys turn from his play and approach Lady Doyle, saying he was so lonesome he came over to give her a kiss. "He kissed her caressingly on the mouth," Houdini observed, transfixed by the sight, "picked up her hand and kissed each finger in as courtly a manner as any prince kissing his queen's hand."

The next day, Sunday, Houdini's charged vision of mother-son love was replayed as grim parody when he joined the Doyles in their suite for an intimate séance. He and Doyle wrote several accounts of the episode over the next year, each more accusatory than the one before. In Houdini's earliest version, apparently written the same Sunday, he and Bess had been sitting on the beach taking the sun. Sir Arthur walked over. He told them that Lady Doyle had proposed an automatic-writing séance, "to see whether it was possible for her to give me some indication from the spirit world." Doyle apologized to Bess for not inviting her also. But two people of the same mind, he explained, "either positive or negative," might hinder his wife's contact with her spirit controls. A snapshot taken of the two men as they returned to the Ambassador shows them wearing straw hats under the bright ocean sun, burly Doyle in a neat dark suit, Houdini a crumpled white one.

Writing pads and pencils were placed on the table. The curtains were drawn. Sir Arthur, head bowed, began with a prayer, calling on the Almighty to grant a sign from friends in the beyond. Lady Doyle, Houdini noted, seemed "very charming." Fourteen years younger than her husband, but now dour-looking and no longer beautiful, she had been at the time of their marriage an expert horsewoman with a cultivated singing voice and dark gold hair. Doyle laid his hands on hers to bolster her power. Houdini closed his eyes and tried to rid his mind of all but religious thoughts: "I willed and concentrated like I would in the dark listening to sound." Lady Doyle picked up a pencil. The forces, she said, were taking hold of her more energetically than they had ever done.

In rough jerks Lady Doyle began striking the table. Then the pencil started to move. A spirit had come. "Do you believe in God?" she asked the visitant. Her hand beat the table three times, signifying Yes. "Then I will make the sign of the cross," she responded, marking the edge of her writing pad. While she spasmodically wrote, Doyle soothed her, as though cautioning the spirit not to use her forcibly. The couple spoke, Houdini observed, "as if there was someone in reality standing alongside of us."

Lady Doyle asked whether the spirit present was Houdini's mother. Her hand struck the table three times. *Yes.*

Houdini took the jolting moment seriously and increased his effort to concentrate. "If I had ever had an astral body or a soul," he wrote later, "that soul was out of my body as far as it was possible and still live." With whatever mixture of skeptical curiosity, sensation-seeking, and professional pride he approached Spiritualism, he believed in a future life. So had his father, who had spoken to him about it, he said, "for hours." What he questioned, rather, were claims that the dead wished to reach out to the living, or could. He doubted that those who had passed on were "in any way interested, physically or mentally, in the welfare of mortal man." He believed, anyway, that they existed "on a plane so different from ours that they cannot possibly communicate with those on earth." Yet according to Bess he often woke in the night and raised his head, asking, "Mama, are you here?" In whatever dream-recess of being he remained a prince who had kissed a queen's hand, he also retained there a hope-against-all-hope. So at the striking of the table three times he forced himself to be receptive, "waiting for a sign or vibrations, feeling for the presence of my dearly beloved Mother."

Lady Doyle's hand flew over the paper sheets as she tried to keep up with the rapidly incoming message from Cecilia Weiss. Opposite his wife Sir Arthur tore sheet after sheet from the pad as it filled with her tall-lettered, disconnected scribble, tossing each one across to Houdini. The first sheet began: "Oh, my darling, thank God, thank God, at last I'm through.—I've tried, oh so often—now I am happy. Why, of course, I want to talk to my boy—my own beloved boy. . . ."

Guiding Lady Doyle's hand, the spirit told how much she prized her son, urged him not to grieve, described her joyful life on the other side, able to view him on earth. At one point Doyle asked Houdini whether he would like to ask the spirit a question, such as, "Can my mother read my mind." Just when Houdini focused on the question, however, Lady Doyle began scrawling:

> I *always* read my beloved son's mind—his dear mind—there is so much I want to say to him—but—I am almost overwhelmed by this joy of talking to him once more . . . thank you, thank you, thank you, friend, with all my heart for what you have done for me this day—God bless you, too, Sir Arthur, for what you are doing for us—for us over here. . . .

By the time the séance ended, Lady Doyle had filled some fifteen sheets with automatic writing.

Before leaving the Doyles' suite, Houdini delivered a jolt of his own. In her long message Cecilia had asked him to try contacting her by automatic writing at home. He wanted to ask the Doyles about the technique, and idly, as if trying it out, he wrote the name Powell. Doyle looked shocked. He had just learned of the death of a close friend, Ellis Powell, editor of the London *Financial News*. Certain that Powell's spirit was seeking to come to him through Houdini, he exclaimed: "Saul is among the prophets! You are a medium."

In Doyle's account Houdini left the séance "deeply moved," and when they met in New York two days later remarked: "I have been walking on air ever since." In fact Houdini was deeply annoyed. As he listed his many misgivings now and over the next few months, they began with the sign Lady Doyle had set down on her pad: a cross. His mother—the wife, after all of a rabbi—would never have communicated a cross. In trying hard to imagine Cecilia beside him, too, he had brought to mind trivial, familiar things they had often discussed. Had she really been present, she would have alluded to them. Mostly, the statements that flowed through Lady Doyle ("I am almost overwhelmed by this joy") did not sound like his mother (*"Ehrich, vielleicht bin ich nicht da wenn du zuruck kommst"*). There was the fact, hard to get around, that Cecilia Weiss did not use English. Having for the first time seen Doyle in the act of confronting the spirit world, Houdini decided that he represented a case not merely of naive trust or self-deception, but of "religious mania."

At the time, Houdini spared Sir Arthur his disappointment—"I did not have the nerve to tell him," he said later. But he did protest Doyle's casting him as a medium. When writing the name Powell, he had had in mind not Doyle's deceased editor-friend, of whom he knew nothing, but the magician Frederick Eugene Powell—head of one of the *Man From Beyond* units. This Powell carried a drainage tube in his stomach as a result of drastic surgery, and had recently written to him. A few days after the séance, Houdini sent Powell's letter to Doyle, to prove that his supposed bit of automatic writing was "just one of those coincidences." Doyle remained certain, however, that his own friend *Ellis* Powell had momentarily used Houdini as a medium. "No," he answered Houdini, "the Powell explanation won't do." Doyle even thought that Ellis Powell's spirit had helped him bring into the open the psychic powers, long hidden from others, that enabled Houdini to perform his feats. "It is probable that at that moment," he wrote later, "[I] surprised the master secret of his life—a secret which even those who were nearest to him had never quite understood."

Sometime before returning to England, Doyle sent word to Houdini that a Brooklyn medium he knew, Mrs. Metcalfe, had received a further message from Cecilia Weiss: "My son has now told his wife that he is mentally convinced of the truth of this revelation, but he does not see his way and it is dark in front of him. He is now seated in his room thinking it over." Beside this Houdini wrote: "?Wrong as I did not have to think it over."

Houdini saw the Doyles and their children off when they sailed for home, on June 24. New York newspapers headlined the family's departure, noting that they intended to return next year. Doyle would then extend his lecture tour into the Far West, which was calling for instruction in Spiritualism. "Everybody has been lovely to us," Lady Doyle was quoted as saying, "and I dearly love the American public." The newspaper reports played up the hijinks of the Doyles' lively children, who were taking back with them a gift from the "snakeologist" of the Bronx Zoo—a five-foot king snake that the boys allowed to coil about their necks and bodies as they prowled the ship. Houdini, camera ever ready, snapped pictures of Sir Arthur and Lady Doyle as they stood by the steamer railing—"beaming with joy!" he said.

THE TALKING TEA KETTLE; THURSTON AND BLACKSTONE; *HALDANE OF THE SECRET SERVICE*

Whatever their religious meaning to thousands of sincere believers, the ectoplasm and paraffin hands of the 1920s, like the handcuffs and rope-ties of the 1880s, also made good theater. Many magicians tried to duplicate such manifestations onstage. Magic dealers of the period offered such effects as the "Mysterious Dr. Q 'Dark Trumpet Séance'" or the "O. K. Spirit Pictures." Houdini felt that the renewal of Spiritualism after the war gave his profession a fresh impulse and unusual public notice: "with this extraordinary wave of Spiritualism, Ectoplasm and Spirit Photography, Magic has been pulled into the limelight."

Since the earliest days of the Spiritualist movement, too, it had been recognized that fraudulent mediums were in effect magicians gone bad. It followed that magicians were uniquely qualified to expose their methods. In the 1880s Kellar in his own show explained table-tipping, spirit-materialization, and similar phenomena. Since the methods of the séance room and the magic show were sometimes identical, however, such exposés came perilously near violating the cardinal rule of magic: Don't Expose. The SAM tried to suppress a series of newspaper articles exposing fake mediums because it would necessarily, the society said, "have to explain certain fundamental principles of magic." The organization also set guidelines for distinguishing exposure from exposé. Basically it proposed that Spiritualist manifestations used by magicians should be considered magic tricks, and not exposed; Spiritualist manifestations produced in darkness that could not be reproduced in the light, might be exposed without penalty.

To his embarrassment as president of SAM, Houdini failed to mind such distinctions. In October 1922 he published an article in *Popular Radio* magazine, "Ghosts that Talk—by Radio." All the Spiritualist manifestations he had seen, he said, were "merely phenomena that are well known to the average magician." To illustrate, he described a talking teakettle that he said he had bought at the auction of some medium's property. It could answer questions put to it, in a ghostly whisper. The article and an accompanying drawing revealed that the ordinary-looking cookware concealed a wireless radio receiver, operated by a confederate in an adjoining room. Whether or not Spiritualist mediums used the talking kettle (very unlikely), several magicians presented it in their acts—as Houdini well knew, for in reality he had bought his from a New York magic dealer.

Houdini's teapot created a small tempest among magicians and in the theatrical press. Its inventor, David P. Abbott, accused Houdini of writing a "fake expose" for the sake of publicity. The Omaha Assembly of SAM, to which Abbott belonged, voted to express disapproval of their national president. One magician wrote to the editor of *The Sphinx* recalling that years before Houdini had forced a founding member of SAM to resign for having exposed the Milk-Can Escape, implying that Houdini should now call for his own resignation.

In the new hypersensitivity toward exposure Houdini soon found himself condemned again. In June 1924—to look ahead a year or two—the fourteen hundred members of SAM once more reelected him president. That fall the *New York World* began publishing a weekly Sunday supplement for young readers, under his name as editor. Called *Red Magic*, it consisted of eight pages of tricks, puzzles, brainteasers, jokes, and optical illusions. By his account Houdini arranged to have the material approved before publication by the SAM's Exposé Committee, newly formed in reaction to the Talking Kettle affair and other such rows. Even so, some magicians objected to the series. The journal *Magical Monthly* reported that Houdini was "getting into hot water by . . . exposing more or less valuable secrets. Considering that Houdini is the President of one of the biggest of magical societies, this will want a bit of explaining."

Only in the finger-pointing atmosphere of the moment could the party stunts in the *World's* kiddie-pages be considered exposures. But a yearlong ruckus followed. Houdini blamed the SAM for having failed to weed out offensive material. The Exposé Committee denied having approved his agreement with the *World.* Meanwhile he drew more fire by publishing an article on Spiritualism in *Popular Science Monthly* that included an explanation of the Thumb-Tie. In this penetration effect the magician—or medium—can pass solid hoops onto one arm although his or her thumbs remain tightly tied to each other. This was a real exposure: by one of many different methods the Thumb-Tie is still performed and can be mystifying. The article also contained an explanation of the Torn and Restored Cigarette Paper. "Houdini's reason apparently is to expose spirit mediums," an irate correspondent wrote to *The Sphinx,* "but who ever heard of a medium doing the torn and restored cigarette paper?"

In the end Houdini submitted to SAM a full report on his dealings with the *World,* including copies of correspondence. He probably did so reluctantly, hoping simply to end criticism of him. The documents proved that not he but the newspaper's editors had failed to submit the *Red Magic* articles beforehand to the Exposé Committee, as they had agreed to do. On the other hand the same documents made it embarrassingly clear that the editors and not he had written the articles. *The Sphinx* ran a long letter of explanation from Houdini to the magic community on its front page. He admitted that his exposure of the Thumb-Tie was an "error in my judgment," and announced the discontinuance of *Red Magic.* ("I do not mind telling you," he confessed to a friend, "I am heartily glad of same.") No one to take a bum rap, however, he admitted little more. He insisted that the children's series had revealed nothing "worth-while" and cutely said he intended "to stop all exposing in every way, that would have a tendency, according to the SAM, to injure the craft."

Not all magicians opposed Spiritualism, especially not Howard Thurston, the inheritor of Kellar's show and now Houdini's chief rival. Thurston's neat, bland appearance masked a secretive, turbulent inner life. Five times married, stepson of a fortune-teller, he had experienced a religious conversion in his teens and undergone three years of training at a Bible school, hoping to become a medical missionary. He also had put in time in hobo jungles, racetrack stables, and two-fisted western mining towns with names like Diamondville—picking pockets, burgling, operating a cheap-jewelry scam, hustling as a cane-waving checked-coat barker with the DeKreko Brothers Congress of Eastern Nations, a traveling hootchy-kootchy show. In some form his early religious education survived his training in hard knocks. His mother had passed away when he was seventeen, and he liked to feel, he said, that she "is my Guardian Angel and that she is aware of my actions." Experimenting with a radio set, he found that a glass of water nearby seemed to attract sounds resembling distant human voices. He attributed them to "very definite supernatural influence"—communications from the afterworld or, if not, from other planets. He had several sittings with Ada Besinnet, the medium who manifested Sir Ernest Shackleton for Doyle but spurned Houdini. Doyle considered Thurston the only American magician who had "real accurate knowledge of psychic matters."

Houdini, in contrast, considered Thurston "narrow minded" and clashed with him over Spiritualism and the exposure issue. They gave opposing speeches on Spiritualism at an SAM banquet in October 1922. At a meeting of the society, Houdini joined an attack on Thurston for such violations as enclosing pocket tricks in the "Thurston Box of Candy" he hawked at his shows: "wants me to keep my mouth shut on his exposes," Houdini noted afterward. But their real rivalry arose from comparable ambitions. Thurston was the only magician of the era who achieved anything like Houdini's stature. He had his own movie production company, Howard Thurston Pictures, and he toured the world with trainloads of stage-filling classic illusions, presenting what a fellow magician called "the old pistol-shooting, march-playing, slap-bang, jumping-in-and-out-of-boxes, old-time magic show that was thrilling and exhilarating." He had earned his reputation by his artist's obsession with craft. He got up at 5 A.M. for several hours of repetitive practice before full-length triple mirrors—so he could observe his card sleights from every angle—ritually bathing his hands each night in urine to keep them soft. ("Houdini has been King of Cards"—Houdini swaggered—"LONG before Thurston ever thought of doing a card act.")

Through their many differences, Thurston and Houdini stayed guardedly cordial to each other. Thurston started an SAM fund for a testimonial dinner honoring Houdini's service to magic, kicking in the first fifty dollars himself. Houdini went to see Thurston's grand show, though it meant enduring the other man's "posing," as he put it, "as the greatest in the world."

It deserves adding that Houdini now had another, peskier rival in Harry Blackstone (Harry Boughton [1885–1965]). Featuring such uncanny effects as the Dancing Handkerchief and Floating Lightbulb, Blackstone would emerge as the leading American illusionist in the years after Houdini and Thurston—the fourth and last master of a Golden Age of American Magic inaugurated by Kellar. "Look out for Blackstone," a friend warned Houdini. "Don't ever get in a lawsuit with him because he would spend thousands to get just one crack at you." Houdini did look out. When Blackstone visited at 278, Houdini had him promise "faithfully" never to perform any of his effects. But he soon learned that Blackstone was doing an underwater box escape at Atlantic City, and lodged a complaint with the National Vaudeville Artists' Association. The bad blood ran both ways. Blackstone announced that he, not Houdini, had invented the escape, and challenged Houdini to get out of the same box he used. He claimed credit for inventing the Vanishing Elephant as well, which Houdini, he said, "got away with" presenting as original.

Despite continuing legal and financial grief over his Film Development Corporation, Houdini invested in a projector that could show motion pictures at home—a novelty at the time—and decided to produce a new movie of his own. At a U.S. Customs Service auction of unclaimed films, he bought an Italian-made feature, *Il Mistero Di Osiris* (The Mystery of Osiris). The Roman company that produced it, Vera Film, had also published a lengthy scenario of the action, which Houdini had closely translated into English. He published this as a pamphlet, *The Mystery of the Jewel*, with his name on the cover. Giving no indication of the Italian original, he allowed it to pass as a scenario or short story by himself. He perhaps justified to himself this and his other ripoffs by mulling over the articles on plagiarism he collected. He wrote reminders on them, as if the literary thefts of admired writers such as Wilkie Collins licensed him to steal too: "Very Important. The Crime of R.L. Stevenson *Stealing other stories*"; "Shows where most writers obtain their plots"; "A. Dumas obtained *entire* story of Monte-Christo [*sic*]."

Il Mistero gave Houdini the notion of making a roughly similar film based on Eyptian ideas of reincarnation, to be shot partly at the Grand Hotel in Cairo. To finance it he organized late in 1921 a new company, Mystery Pictures Corporation, again headed by himself and Hardeen. He commissioned a photoplay, bought some stock footage of Egypt (the Nile, the

Sphinx, a flotilla of crocodiles), and put the film into production as "The Ashes of Passion," using FDC as a developing lab. The picture was retitled "Reincarnation," but however much of it he completed, if any, has disappeared.

Although Houdini now directed four linked motion picture organizations, his interest in film production was waning as his involvement in Spiritualism grew. He can have found no second wind either in the failure of his latest, and last, production, *Haldane of the Secret Service*, released in 1923. He stars as a U.S. Secret Service agent, Heath Haldane, grandson of Harry Harper in *Terror Island* by way of Howard Hillary in *The Man From Beyond*. Haldane tracks a gang of international counterfeiters and dope smugglers, headed by a mysterious Dr. Yu. Consciously, it seems, Houdini tried to out-Holmes Sir Arthur. His newspaper-size publicity book touted Haldane as a "super-detective" and promised that the plot was "handled with a skill and surety suggestive of Poe . . . and Doyle."

Houdini may have equaled Sir Arthur in cocksureness and passed him in telling ectoplasm from lather, but he was no Conan Doyle. The plot amounts to no more than the Yellow Peril intrigue worked to death in action melodramas of the period, helped out by the tying of Haldane, splayed, to a giant mill-wheel revolving under cascading water—Houdini's one escape in the film. Visually *Haldane* is a record-setting bungle. The outdoor scenes in London, Glasgow, and Paris are tinted sepia, while the sometimes dimly-lit interior scenes are tinted blue; as Haldane descends from the Eiffel Tower into a subterranean apache café he seems to be waltzing in and out of two different movies. Noting the thin crowd on hand for the film's premiere, *Variety* gave Houdini arguably his worst-ever zinging: "Perhaps the renown of Houdini is fading, or more probably the Broadway managers were wise to how bad a film this one is. . . . With all due respect to his famed ability for escapes, the only asset he has in the acting line is his ability to look alert."

DOYLE-HOUDINI CORRESPONDENCE; BERT REESE; DOYLE'S WESTERN TOUR

Even before Sir Arthur Conan Doyle returned to America for his second lecture tour, in April 1923, his friendship with Houdini had soured. The spoilage was done by mail. For nine months after the Atlantic City séance, Houdini and Doyle wrote to each other every few weeks. The ocean between them made it easier than before to create misunderstanding, and harder to patch wounds.

The correspondence got off cordially enough. When Doyle read about the death in New York of the well-known "Human Fly," in a ten-story fall from a ledge of the Hotel Martinique, he pleaded with Houdini, "For goodness' sake take care of those dangerous stunts of yours. You have done enough of them." Mostly the two men discussed Spiritualism. Doyle, busy completing a monograph on spirit photography, had joined in experiments to disprove the alleged exposé of the Crewe Circle. The Society for Psychical Research (to recall) had marked plates by X ray, whose absence in the developed negatives convinced investigators that the plates had been switched. Doyle informed Houdini that his own group had "knocked the bottom" out of the SPR's case by discovering that the X-ray tracings simply disappeared: "The evidence for that power is quite final." Houdini replied that his paid investigator at Crewe, DeVega, had detected and revealed to him the circle's "method of manipulation," an interesting one. "It is too bad you were so rushed when you were in America; otherwise, I could have shown you the report."

Houdini and Doyle also disagreed long-distance, a little less genially, over the branch of mediumistic performance known as pellet or billet reading. Doyle was interested in a Jewish billet-reader named Bert Reese (Berthold Riess [1841–1928]), in part because Reese had convinced Thomas Edison of his powers. (Not difficult: Edison was reportedly experimenting with a device to reach the other side, the Spiritograph.) Potbellied, popeyed, short, and bald, Reese could pass, a reporter said, "for a highly reputable dealer in delicatessen." But his preternatural psychic feats, much discussed in Europe and America, had also convinced the French neurologist Charcot (Freud's teacher), as well as Paderewski and Mussolini. He would ask his sitter to write five or six personal questions on as many small slips of paper, while he was out of the room, and to fold the slips. The billets were then mixed, and retained unopened in the sitter's hand or pocket. Yet Reese was able to divine the sitter's questions, and to answer them. The Nobel laureate and Spiritualist investigator Charles Richet, a senior member of the Department of Physiology at the Sorbonne, classified Reese's gift as "pragmatic cryptesthesia."

"I have no hesitancy in telling you," Houdini wrote to Doyle, "that I set a snare at the séance I had with Reese, and caught him." He beat Reese by outfoxing him. Even with Reese out of the room, he made sure that the billet-reader could gain no carbonpaper impression of what he wrote, and that no one was watching through a keyhole or peephole. Even so, he covered his pencil with his hand and body so that its movements could not be detected. In taking the further precaution of folding his billets in peculiar shapes, he nailed Reese. "When he came back he started to mix up the questions on the table," Houdini continued. "As I watched him keenly I noticed that one of my shapes straightened out, which meant that he had switched it so adroitly that I had not seen the substitution but like a piece of magic the crooked paper lost its shape and became flattened." With Thurston-caliber manipulative skill, crafty misdirection, and a wonderful memory—and after years of practice—Reese was able while making a few comments to exchange and open the billets, glimpse their content, and memorize the sitter's questions. Shrewd at reading character and fishing for information, he could also return satisfying answers. "I caught him red-handed," Houdini told Doyle, "and he acknowledged it was the first time in his life that anyone had ever 'recognized his Powers.' And I'll put it in writing he was the slickest I have ever seen."

The first real rift came in the wake of an article Houdini published in the *New York Sun* in October, "Spirit Compacts Unfilled." Speaking from his now considerable experience with Spiritualism, he in effect panned the whole movement. In the many séances he had attended, he wrote, "I have never seen or heard anything that could convince me that there is a possibility of communication with the loved ones who have gone beyond." Someone sent a copy of his article to Sir Arthur, to whom it came as a surprise punch. In Atlantic City, after all, he and Lady Doyle had provided Houdini fifteen entire pages from Cecilia Weiss, and had caught him receiving the name Powell. "[W]hen you say that you have had no evidence of survival," he wrote Houdini, "you say what I cannot reconcile with what I saw with my own eyes. . . . I saw what you got and what the effect was upon you at the time." Doyle balked at publishing a rebuttal—"I have no fancy for sparring with a friend in public"—but he admitted feeling "rather sore." He told Houdini that, having been given his proof of spirit contact, the responsibility now rested with him to accept or reject it. For himself he would say no more on the subject, but confine his letters to what they could agree on in "friendly converse."

Houdini would not let the subject go so easily. He had been making his views on Spiritualism known in public, and resented what he saw as

Doyle's attempt to censor him. "You write that you are very 'sore,'" he replied. "I trust that it is not with me, because you, having been truthful and manly all your life, naturally must admire the same traits in other human beings." With this backhand compliment to Doyle's "manly" ability to tell the truth and to take it, Houdini let him have it. For the first time he revealed that the Atlantic City séance had been for him not an epiphany but a washout. He found it incredible that Cecilia Weiss would send the sign of the cross and communicate in English—"my sainted mother could not read, write or speak the English language." In a sincere effort to sense his mother's presence, he explained, he had put off considering these matters, and had said nothing about them at the time. After rehashing the Powell-Powell "coincidence" too, he made clear to Doyle where he stood. "I know you treat this as a religion, but personally I cannot do so, for up to the present time, and with all my experiences, I have never seen or heard anything that could really convert me."

Doyle had vowed to stick to "friendly converse." But he would or could not let the now-disputed séance alone. He answered Houdini point by point. As for the cross, his wife put the symbol above the first page of everything she transmitted, to "guard against lower influences." As for Cecilia Weiss's English, there was "nothing in that." Lady Doyle was not a trance medium but an inspirational medium, with a gift for automatic writing: "any trance or half-trance medium might get the Hebrew through." (Cecilia Weiss spoke German.) In automatic writing, he explained, what gets through is not language but content; the message comes as a "rush of thought, which is translated in coming." And if the Powell transmission was coincidental, it transcended spirit communication itself, being "more marvellous than the very simple explanation that love can bridge the grave and show that it can."

To Houdini, Doyle seemed less eager to explain than to explain away. He decided to put his view of the séance "on record," beyond being distorted in case of his death. As if taking an oath from one of his assistants, he typed up and had notarized a legal-looking deposition headed THE TRUTH REGARDING SPIRITUALISTIC SEANCE GIVEN TO HOUDINI BY LADY DOYLE.

Neither Houdini nor Doyle was publicity-shy. They soon made their private quarrel a public rumble. The new phase opened in March 1923, with a sharp exchange of letters to the *New York Times*. It was touched off by a published interview in which Houdini boasted that he could duplicate the feats of any medium by conjuring methods, and was quoted—probably misquoted—as saying that he had attended ten thousand séances. Doyle wrote the paper to scold Houdini publicly for "talking wildly." Were he disposed to take up Houdini's challenge, he said, he would ask him to duplicate three manifestations he had witnessed himself, in the presence of others. Houdini must provide him "an intimate talk with my 'dead' son"; show him his mother, three feet away; and enable him to discuss family matters with his "dead" brother. "How absurd it is to assert that such results could be got by conjuring," he added. Regarding the ten thousand sittings, he said he knew of only two mediums Houdini had consulted, Eva C. and Mrs. Wriedt. To have attended ten thousand séances, he calculated, Houdini would have to have gone to one every day for thirty years, Sundays included.

Some three weeks later, the *Times* published Houdini's also-stinging rejoinder. He said he could not conjure up the three effects Sir Arthur proposed, "neither do I believe any one else can." He notified *Times* readers that several mediums who had produced the spirits of Doyle's relatives had been exposed, fined, and/or arrested as frauds. For good measure he brought up the Zancigs, the husband-wife mindreading team Doyle had endorsed as genuine telepathists. "It is with regret," he said, "I speak of how Sir Arthur Conan Doyle was convinced of the genuineness of Zancig, yet Zancig in my presence and of many witnesses, denied any supernatural or telepathic powers."

Doyle shrank from going another round, sorry for the mutual injury already done. But his convictions were at stake, and he felt caught up in the open combat over them. "Our relations are certainly curious," he wrote privately to Houdini, "and likely to become more so, for so long as you attack what I know from experience to be true, I have no alternative but to attack you in turn. How long a private friendship can survive such an ordeal I do not know but at least I did not create the situation."

By the time Doyle and his family reached New York to begin their Far West lecture tour, the press had wakened to the possibility of a championship fight and saw a good story in it. A headline in the *New York Mail* announced: "Sir Arthur Coming To Answer Houdini." As if providentially, Doyle's arrival the first week in April coincided with the death of Lord Carnarvon, the British Egyptologist who only months before had discovered the tomb of Tutankhamen. A cable from Cairo attributed Carnarvon's death to blood poisoning after an insect bite. Speculation spread world-wide, however, that he had died under a curse imposed by the pharaoh's guardian spirit. "There are many malevolent spirits," Doyle told the *Times* a few days after arriving. "I think it is possible that some occult influence caused his death."

Having agreed to a brief Orpheum tour, mostly for "the *Cash*," Houdini was then in California. When a reporter for the *Los Angeles Examiner* asked him for comment, he took a new shot at Doyle, coast-to-coast: "If, as Sir Arthur says, an avenging spirit . . . probably was the cause of the explorer's death, why is it that other Egyptologists never likewise have been slain?" Perhaps (Likely?) with Houdini's prompting, the SAM rubbed it in. The snickering exploitation of Spiritualism by magicians had goaded Doyle into making many condescending remarks about them, for publication. Magicians were "harmless and ingenious amusers of society," prone to putting on "airs of superior intelligence." Stiffing him back, the New York Assembly of SAM invited Sir Arthur to a benefit Carnival of Magic, promising that members would show how to make spirit photos and wax spirit hands. Doyle did not reply, but the invitation made a new headline: COLLEAGUES OF HOUDINI AROUSED BY CONAN DOYLE.

Even without the baiting by Houdini and the SAM, Doyle's second tour got off to a bad start. Although still ruddy-cheeked and hearty, he seemed to at least one observer subtly changed from the year before, more remote and visionary. During his opening, sold-out lectures in Carnegie Hall, he projected a spirit photo of a fire in Chicago, taken by an American medium. Within the smoke could be seen fifteen extras. Doyle said they had been identified by relatives as spirit heads of firemen and others killed in the blaze. A week later he acknowledged that he had been tricked; he declared the picture a fake and asked his audience to put it out of mind.

Dogged everywhere by controversy and the press, Doyle and his family headed for the West Coast by way of Chicago, planning to return to New York through Salt Lake City and lower Canada. While giving some one hundred lectures in forty days, he sampled the new craze of marathon dancing; had another séance with Ada Besinnet (whose control, Black Cloud, left her tied hand and foot); and met Douglas Fairbanks ("Save for Houdini, I know no one who has performed such reckless, dare-devil acts"). When Doyle left New York, Houdini was still in Los Angeles. But around

May 7 their circuits crossed in Denver, where both families had registered at the Brown Palace Hotel.

By this time, the newspaper duels and touchy correspondence had left both Houdini and Doyle much to forget or swallow before they could meet again amicably. The strain was not eased by a screaming headline in the local *Express*: DOYLE IN DENVER DEFIES HOUDINI. The newspaper reported that Doyle had challenged Houdini to attend a séance with him, vouching that he would there produce the spirit of "the Ma'am," his mother—each man to back up his belief with a wager of five thousand dollars. Doyle apologized to Houdini profusely for the published statement and denounced it to the newspaper's editor as "blasphemous and absurd," a mangled and sensationalized version of an innocent remark. Doyle explained that when the *Express* reporter had told him Houdini was offering to duplicate any feat of any medium, on a bet of five thousand dollars, he had replied, "To do that he would have to show me my mother." Houdini reassured Doyle that he had not seen the article and would not have been affected if he had, since "frequently the papers misquote people."

But the editor of the *Express* wrote Houdini that the reporter insisted on the accuracy of his story. Given the put-your-money-where-your-mouth-is tone of Doyle's alleged challenge, this seems extremely unlikely. Doyle was by instinct and breeding an uncommonly decent man who abhorred any suggestion of mixing Spiritualism with Mammon. Houdini was now ready to listen to ill of him, however, if not quite to think it. In a later retelling of the episode, Houdini said that he went to see the editor, who called over the reporter, Sam Jackson. Jackson stuck by what he wrote: "Sir Arthur distinctly made his statement in terms positive, that he was willing to challenge Houdini for $5,000." The reporter, Houdini recalled, brought out a colleague who had overheard the conversation. "I thought it was a very interesting incident so I paid particular attention," she said. "I am surprised that Sir Arthur now denies having made it." The editor offered to print a follow-up supporting the original story, but Houdini held back: "No, just let it go, we will let it pass."

Houdini's willingness to consider (invent?) the journalists' version came from more than accumulated distrust of Doyle. It also took in the rivalry with Doyle he had always dimly felt. While in Denver he said ruefully to Bess, "Doyle is a historical character and his word goes far, in fact much further than mine." In fancying that he might take Doyle on in a contest of words, Houdini was playing a losing game. But more realistically, if no more helpfully for their friendship, he saw Doyle as a competitor at the box office. He attended at least one of Doyle's talks in Denver and counted the house: "The Theatre was comfortably filled," he wrote afterward, "but I do not think it was a 'turn away.'" Here all the savvy was on his side, and he could comfortably regard Doyle as the minor-leaguer: "In my estimation, if this man was circussed he would be turning away thousands."

Doyle and Houdini got together several times in Denver, going out for a ride, lunching at the Brown Palace, sitting in the park. The meetings did nothing to repair the damage. During a chat in Houdini's dressing room Doyle remarked that he could detect trickery at séances, which Houdini denied. "He looked amazed at me," Houdini recorded, "and I said, 'Why, Sir Arthur, I have been trained in mystery all my life and every once in a while I see something I cannot account for.'" On Doyle's recommendation Houdini twice visited a commercial high-school-graduation photographer, Alexander Martin, whom Sir Arthur considered the outstanding spirit photographer in America. A pioneer who had made his way to Colorado during a gold boom, Martin had been capturing extras since 1879, when one of his routine baby pictures revealed spirit babies. Houdini had Martin photograph him alone and with Jim Collins. When printed, both pictures showed psychic extras. But Houdini felt certain they were double exposures, perhaps made by the wet-plate method: expose the plate, develop it, wash off the emulsion, refinish the plate with a new emulsion. All told, his new meetings with Doyle only renewed his earlier misgivings about him: "It is almost incredible that he has been so thoroughly convinced, and nothing can shake his faith."

An incident that had nothing to do with Spiritualism, at least superficially, set going the small but unretraceable step from misgiving to disenchantment. Houdini was unable to see Doyle off to Salt Lake City, where he would lecture to an audience of more than five thousand at the Mormon Tabernacle. But he wrote immediately, thanking Doyle for his promise to send, once he reached England, the manuscript of *Our American Adventure*, his recently published account of his first American lecture tour. "I will be pleased," Houdini said, "to put it among my prized possessions in my Library." Doyle's reply, sent only two days later from Utah, came as a you-must-be-kidding shock. Doyle had promised no more than to send him a copy of the *book*: "I think that you surely confused the book with the

MSS." He intended the manuscript to remain in his family for his descendants, he said, "for if this mission of mine has any appreciable effect in altering the religious opinion of the world then the time will come when the account of my travels may be very interesting and even valuable to those who follow me."

Now doubting Doyle's reliability altogether, Houdini answered at once, from Los Angeles. He repeated for Doyle the conversation they had had while sitting together in the dining room of the Brown Palace. He had asked Doyle for the manuscript; Doyle had protested that it was just an assortment of worksheets, much-corrected. That would be exactly the "charm" of having the manuscript, Houdini had said—at which Doyle vowed to send it as soon as he got home. "I am perfectly willing to release you from your promise," Houdini wrote, "but I want you to feel assured that you had promised to send it to me. . . . perhaps it escaped your mind but I assure you the conversation transpired as I explained."

The wrangle merely replayed on different ground the two men's disagreements over Eva C., the Crewe Circle, the Atlantic City séance, the Denver newspaper article. In again leaving unsettled who said what and what happened, it swelled a long list of issues that now hopelessly divided them, each unanswerable question the focus of an unrelievable resentment. "He is very forgetful and thoughtless, or both," Houdini decided. "There is nothing that Sir Arthur will believe that surprises me." Doyle was reaching his own disillusioned estimate of Houdini as a being of "strange contrasts," masterly in his profession and physically daring—"the bravest man in our generation"—but biased and childishly vain, preoccupied with publicity. Atop their quarrel over his manuscript came a "long screed," as Doyle called it, attributed to Houdini in a Los Angeles newspaper. It was Houdini, this time, who insisted he had been misquoted, but Doyle demanded that he retract. "I am very sorry this breach has come, as we have felt very friendly towards Mrs. Houdini and yourself, but 'friendly is as friendly does,' and this is not friendly."

Doyle would remain a large figure in the landscape for Houdini, both threat and target. But they exchanged letters apparently only once more, after Doyle returned to England, and they never saw each other again.

THIRTEEN

JANUARY 1923–SPRING 1924

HOUDINI'S SPIRITUALISM LECTURE; ARGAMASILLA; THE LIPPMANN READING

FROM BEING A part-time student of Spiritualism, Houdini rapidly became an internationally-recognized authority and aggressive investigator. In February 1924 he signed with the Coit-Alber lecture bureau to take on tour a lecture about fraudulent mediums. "Houdini, the magician," *Billboard* noted, "has become Houdini, the educator!" He had tried out the talk during his brief Orpheum tour, speaking at the University of Illinois, St. Louis University, the University of Wisconsin, and other schools, sometimes on the invitation of departments of psychology. He dealt with such weighty-sounding subjects as "Spiritualist Phenomena and the Psychology of Deception Among Fraudulent Mediums" and "Psychology of Mal-Observation of Audiences and Spiritualistic Seances."

The work gratified Houdini several ways. "Wait till Sir A.C. Doyle hears of my lectures!" he wrote in his diary. "Whew!!!" Aside from outdoing Doyle he especially enjoyed, he said, "meeting the intelligentsa [*sic*]." One way or another his Spiritualist interests were bringing him into contact with thoughtful people besides the creator of Sherlock Holmes. He exchanged letters with Thomas Edison, Upton Sinclair, and Rudyard Kipling, had a visit from Edmund Wilson, played golf with Carl Sandburg.

Rabbi Weiss's son felt proud to be taken, at last, for one of their company. He clipped from the *New York Herald Tribune* a review of one of his talks, which complimented him as "an amazing man . . . one of the most intelligent, I believe, of his time." Atop the item he wrote: "One of the best notices I ever had."

The Coit-Alber tour confirmed Houdini's new role. The bureau also managed such middlebrow intellectuals as the naturalist Roy Chapman Andrews, who discovered some of the world's great fossil fields, and the critic Carl Van Doren, literary editor of *The Nation*. Becoming respectable had its down side too, Houdini found. The bureau did not go in for circus-y advertising: "Am being properly mishandeled [*sic*]," he telegraphed the owners from Cleveland, "never no advance man no protection no billing. . . . How can I do business when there is no attention paid to exploitation." His twenty-four lectures, too, taking him through larger cities in the Midwest and as far south as Florida, were all one-night stands—a "hard grind."

Houdini presented himself to his audiences as a seeker after truth, a foe of fraudulent mediums but not of Spiritualism. Its followers he portrayed as sincere in their beliefs but often misled into reporting "what they *think they see*." His lecture usually ran about an hour and a half, although occasionally grew to two hours or more. Most often he divided the time into half-hour segments, beginning with a chatty preamble about his personal experience. The transcript of one of his lectures in 1925 gives a sense of his breezy platform manner:

> About thirty years ago in Garnett, Kansas, I was traveling with a small company—the man was a philanthropist—long beard and long hair, and he stood on the street corner and told the people that he would sell them a bottle of medicine worth a hundred dollars for a dollar. And I was the man that sold it for him. Then Wednesday morning at the hotel he said, "Houdini, things are a little quiet in the show business. Can't you do something on a Sunday night of a religious nature so we can get a house?" I said, "There is one thing I can do of a religious nature and that is make a collection." (Laughter) He said, "You will have to make one for me if business doesn't hurry up. . . . Why don't you do a couple or more tricks and I will advertise it as a spiritualistic seance." I says, "All right, go

ahead." He says, "I have got to square the chief of police." That was very easy, thirty years ago, to square the chief of police even in Garnett, Kansas. And he was a very fine chap, really, he was very fine. (Laughter) That Saturday—they had a weekly paper there—that Saturday the paper had great big headlines. "Houdini the World Famous Medium, who only gives seances in the largest cities in the world"—and I had just come from Appleton, Wisconsin, (laughter)—"has been prevailed upon by popular request of the public"—that was Dr. Hill—"to give a seance. Pianos will float over the heads of the audience, tables will be levitated by unseen hands, messages will appear." . . . I was good in that newspaper. I still have it in my scrapbook.

Well that Sunday night, ladies and gentlemen, I gave what I believe was the most sensational spiritualistic performance that ever took place in Garnett, Kansas. And I tell you why I was qualified to give that marvellous entertainment. That Sunday morning, accompanied by the sexton and the oldest inhabitant of the town, we walked out to the village cemetery, and I had a notebook, and what was not carved on the slabs of marble or granite tombstones—any information that was lacking, the sexton would tell me the missing data, and the old Uncle Rufus would give me the scandals of everyone sleeping in God's acre. (Laughter) And can you imagine going out there . . . and retailing that terrible stuff. Their eyes stuck out. I know one man named Obermeyer—I had brought back his grandfather, and I said "Obermeyer, you are not doing right by the grandson." He got up and said, "Tell my grandfather I will take care of him in the morning." (Laughter)

The introduction was followed by slides illustrating the history of Spiritualism, then by demonstrations of paraffin hands and other séance frauds, often with a few magic tricks thrown in. Houdini had the fifty-or-so slides made up from photographs, engravings, documents, and handbills: pictures of the Fox sisters and Davenport Brothers; of ectoplasm, levitating scissors, and materializing hands; of himself with Doyle and with Roosevelt.

Well-received in Pittsburgh, Birmingham, Daytona Beach, and other cities, Houdini's lecture was only a beginning. The Coit-Alber bureau engaged him for an additional eight-week tour later in the year. He accepted many additional invitations to speak: at Episcopal and other churches (which generally saw Spiritualism as a rival to Christianity and opposed it); over the radio, answering questions sent in by listeners; at banquets and conventions; and in open debate. His lecturing brought him a whole new reputation. He had been interviewed thousands of times as an escape artist and magician. But newspapers now sought him out as the "psychic Diogenes," asking not how he first became interested in locks, but about his knowledge of ectoplasm or his Atlantic City séance ("the joke was on Sir Arthur," he told a Springfield reporter).

Houdini's talks gained him a different class of fans. "Spirits tell me things by signs because i am Stone Deaf," he heard from a Robert McGill in Albany, New York. "When you escaped from the convict Ship, i was right in the corner near you"—earning from him the marginal comment, "*Nut.*" A Mr. Stuckel appeared at 278 with a Bible, saying he had just come from a conference with Bismarck and Jesus. "Ben Abor—you make me sad—I knew you in Egypt 6000 years ago," a ticket-buyer wrote. "You are known to us as a Yoggi of the third grade—and three Yoggi sons of Hind are your invisible helpers. Why do you not acknowledge them?"

Houdini did more than talk. He established himself as a leading investigator of psychic phenomena. In one much-publicized encounter he tested a nineteen-year-old Spanish psychic named Argamasilla. This boy-wonder had come to America with a testimonial from Richet, the French Nobel laureate, certifying his ability to see through metals. Houdini attended a private demonstration of his power on April 22, in the presence of a priest and the young man's manager-interpreter, a Brazilian known as Mr. Davis. Houdini took a liking to Argamasilla, a tall, smiling, egg-shaped fellow with a bulging midsection, a friendly Spiritualist giant in suit and vest. To Houdini he seemed both older than his advertised nineteen years, and wickedly clever, a "phenomenal mystifier."

Argamasilla allowed the company to freely examine his test device—a thick silver box large enough to contain a hairbrush. (He sometimes used an iron box with a zinc top.) The bottom of the lid had a ledge that fit snugly into the box, making it apparently impossible to see anything inside. As a double safeguard, the lid was fastened to the outside of the box by two hasps and staples, one pair secured by a small padlock. To safeguard the safeguards, Argamasilla's eyes were padded with cotton and bandaged with a white cloth. For one test a printed name was cut out of a business card, and the snippet laid in the box print-side up. Argamasilla went to a window and allowed light to fall on the padlocked box, which he held at various distances before his bandaged eyes. In Spanish he spelled out the name Mr. Vallace A. Smits. The name on the card proved to be Mr. Wallace E. Smith. In another test Houdini's hunting-case watch was reset and snapped shut. Using the same technique, Argamasilla announced the time on the dial to be seventeen minutes of two; it proved to be seventeen of one.

By the time Argamasilla gave his first public demonstration, on May 6, Houdini had easily figured out his quite-straightforward method. The blindfold was no problem. Magicians have devised scores of techniques for seeing not simply through cotton and cloth placed over the eyes, but also through half-dollar pieces, balls of dough, even a metal mask. Rather, Houdini fastened on Argamasilla's use of the window, and the fact that with two hasps on the box, the Spaniard padlocked only one. So: holding the box (or watch) between his hands and turning it round and about, Argamasilla was able, using one thumb, to slightly spring the lid on the unpadlocked side— enough to glimpse the contents, illuminated through the slit by sunlight coming over his shoulder. It was the work, Houdini pleasurably decided, of a "very clever manipulator."

Argamasilla gave his public demonstration before a group of scientists and a corps of reporters at the Hotel Pennsylvania. Sitting on a windowsill, he again read names placed inside the box, again with small errors, for instance omitting an *e* from the name of an ancient Japanese swordmaker. Houdini knew something about boxes. He came to the event ready to show up Argamasilla and create a scene for the press. Loaded for bear, he brought with him a tin box sealed with two strands of copper wire, soldered to the bottom and twisted on top—thus with no flexibility in the lid—and a round metal box soldered and bolted shut. He challenged Argamasilla to read through them. As the *New York Times* reported, he offered twenty-five-to-five odds that he could duplicate each of Argamasilla's feats. Davis, the Brazilian, protested that Houdini was acting "maliciously," and walked out with his prodigy. After the pair left, Houdini made good on his bet anyway. He read the time on his reset, closed hunting-case watch—blindfolded, and with five men holding their hands over his eyes. He called the time as ten minutes to one, missing by an hour as Argamasilla had, and probably just as deliberately—"a wonderful trick in the hands of a conjurer," he noted later.

Still unsatisfied, Houdini confronted Argamasilla a few days later at a second public demonstration, which included a two-hour shouting match among the young man's associates. This time Houdini accepted Argamasilla's own terms. With several reporters acting as judges, he placed a printed slip of paper inside one of Argamasilla's metal boxes. The Spaniard failed to make out a single word of it. Greatly to his disadvantage, the day happened to be cloudy. But that counted for less than Houdini's nifty dirty-work. He put in the box a real estate ad from a newspaper, in such squinty minuscule print that it could be read only close-up. As *Billboard* correctly summarized the test, "Battling Houdini went up against the Spanish kid . . . and knocked the X out of the latter's X-ray eye."

In his own home Houdini showed his ability to match mediums in telepathic power. He offered to reproduce some reportedly successful experiments in thought transference recently made in London by the noted classicist Gilbert Murray, a member of the British SPR. While Murray was out of the room a subject was decided on and announced aloud by some friends. All were considered beyond suspicion, like Murray himself. Yet when he returned he impressively managed to pick up the key words and images—Gladstone, the sinking of the *Titanic*, and so on.

For his rival demonstration at 278, Houdini invited a no-less trusty group of friends. The elite party included the eminent financier Bernard Baruch; Joseph Pulitzer Jr., publisher of the New York *World*, and his wife, Peggy Lynch; Herbert Bayard Swope, executive editor of the *World;* and Walter Lippmann, essayist, recently assistant secretary of war, and now as a *World* editor perhaps the best-respected journalist of the time. With his genius for publicity, Houdini had always stayed chummy with reporters. By now he had befriended owners and editors of many of the giant-circulation newspapers, people who could overnight turn nonentities into deities. He cultivated Lippmann's friendship especially, sending him reports of his Spiritualist investigations and tickets to SAM galas, receiving in turn a lunch invitation and flatteries in Lippmann's editorials. Lippmann told Houdini he felt grateful to him, "for the work you are doing, resisting superstition and credulity."

Houdini asked his guests to lock him in his third-floor office, with a guard outside the door. In the parlor downstairs, each guest wrote out some thought on a piece of paper and whispered it to Hardeen (who attended with his wife, Elsie). Lippmann thought of Lord Curzon in the British Foreign Office; Baruch wrote the slogan "Don't give up the ship"; another guest chose a monument to Buffalo Bill in Wyoming. Recalled downstairs, Houdini brought out the information bit by bit, as if it came to him with slowly increasing clarity. "I see a large plain," he began. "I see a great herd of black oxen. They appear to be stampeding. I see a man who is very hungry, and he is seated on a racing horse. He is chasing these oxen—no, they are not oxen, they are buffaloes; they have their heads down and are going like a whirlwind. He is shooting at them"—and so forth, until he had identified the Buffalo Bill statue. In the same way he saw a large body of water and soon arrived at the slogan, but he failed to 'get' Lord Curzon.

Houdini's second 'experiment' out-Murrayed Murray. He returned to his office with Lippmann and Pulitzer and stripped naked to show that he had nothing concealed. The two journalists locked him in a wooden box stretched across two chairs. As they stood watch over him, the guests downstairs concentrated on a single thought, a portrait of Mrs. John Barrymore. Wrapped in a blanket, Houdini descended three floors to the parlor, and began again, seeing a home at Stratford-on-Avon, then a large audience, then a famous theatrical family, and finally, John Barrymore. Close enough.

Whatever Murray's method, Houdini worked his swindle electrically. He had 278 wired with a "dictograph," a primitive bugging device with a buttonlike transmitter. Hardeen took the part of a long-distance Talking Teakettle operator, repeating downstairs the words or images chosen by the guests, loudly enough to be picked up by the receiver hidden in Houdini's locked box—"the last word in mysticism," Houdini said.

Houdini met the mediums on the ground of teleportation too, although as a gargantuan joke. The stunt involved "Doc" Wilson, erstwhile Methodist minister, druggist, secretary of the Railroad YMCA, and dean of the Kansas City University of Medicine and Surgery, who for twenty-eight years edited *The Sphinx*. He and Houdini had scrapped bitterly in 1906, stayed enemies for nearly a decade, then reconciled. Wilson was now nearly seventy, a hunched man with scanty white hair, drooping white mustache, and rimless spectacles. Houdini planned to use him at the annual SAM banquet for what he called "the finest piece of surprise magic in the history of the magic world."

Houdini enjoyed throwing parties on the scale of his success. He turned down a two-week Hippodrome engagement just to work on the

SAM dinner, a benefit for widows and orphans of slain policemen, attended by the commissioner of police. Through *M-U-M* he informed members of the society that Wilson would come from Kansas City as an honored guest. If unable to make the trip, he added, Wilson would address the banqueters by hookup from his local radio station, a special receiver having being installed in the New York dining room by the Radio Corporation of America. He built an authentic-looking radio cabinet, large enough to house Wilson comfortably; placed loudspeakers around the sumptuous dining room; and hired electricians in coveralls to pretend to be wiring the feed from Kansas City. For secrecy, on the day of the banquet he whisked Wilson by cab from Grand Central Terminal to 278, where he kept him on ice before sneaking him, disguised, into the McAlpin Hotel for the event.

Houdini announced to the diners that Wilson, unable to attend, would as promised address them from Kansas City. Suddenly the loudspeakers brought Wilson's voice into the room, realistically broken by static. Wilson thanked Houdini for his charitable work, then discoursed on the marvels of the decade. He prophesied that someday pictures would be sent by telephone and that, ultimately, human beings would be radioed from place to place. He said he would try the experiment himself, right now. To loudly crackling static, Wilson toppled out of the radio cabinet, eyes blinking, coat mussed, hair disheveled—a geriatric apport. Houdini, almost losing his balance, reached over the table to shake Wilson's hand, having produced what in mediumistic terms would be a full teleportation, "the first time in the history of the world," he said, when "a human being has been transported twelve or fifteen hundred miles through space."

A MAGICIAN AMONG THE SPIRITS; H. P. LOVECRAFT; THE BURGESS AFFAIR

Spiritualism gave Houdini a new arena for his literary ambitions. He approached it as a contender, publishing in the spring of 1924 his richest volume since *The Unmasking*—*A Magician Among the Spirits*. A dozen or so book-length exposés of fraudulent mediums had appeared since the first days of Spiritualism, such as *Spirit-Rapping Made Easy, or How to Come out as a Medium* (1860). The subject lent itself to lurid treatment, but Houdini aimed at writing something sober and cogent, on the order of Frank Podmore's scholarly two-volume *Modern Spiritualism* (1902). He tried to sketch the development of modern Spiritualism through chapter-length studies of a half-dozen celebrated mediums, followed by a miscellany on ectoplasm, spirit photos, magicians as detectors of fraud, and the like. He believed that the book would lose him money and make him enemies. But he considered the writing of it a duty, "an obligation and that is all there is to it."

The composition of *A Magician Among the Spirits* demanded at once patience and energy, reserves of both stick-to-it and get-up-and-go. Chapters had to be rewritten as methods that Houdini hoped to expose for the first time were revealed in the press—"somewhat of a blow to me," he said, "but I cannot stop the progress of the world, and I am pleased to see these frauds being exposed, whether I do it or someone else." Concerned about the legal implications, he meticulously acquired formal permissions for quoted material from publishers in the United States and England. He took pains to get dependable biographical information about mediums past and present, even trying to run down the correct birthdate of the famous medium D. D. Home by hiring DeVega, his man in Crewe, to obtain a copy of Home's birth certificate in Edinburgh.

At the same time, in gathering the inside secrets of the séance room, Houdini energetically exchanged hundreds of letters with informants at home and abroad. A Los Angeles man, for instance, sent him the method of a medium who produced manifestations under ingeniously difficult test conditions. Houdini wrote up the details: the medium was thoroughly searched before entering her cabinet, where she was left standing in a bowl of flour; she could not step out without leaving telltale tracks. "This is the way she works," Houdini recorded:

> She has two tubes made, one for her rectum and one for her vagin [sic]. In one she places about 7 to 10 yards of [blank] skin and in her vagin she conceals a pair of silk stockings.
>
> When the cabinet is closed as it is impossible to go out of the flour without leaving footprints she reaches and gets out the silk stockings, puts them on her feet, steps out of the bowl of flour, gets her second lot and is able to leave the cabinet without besmearing the floor or leaving foot prints. After the materializations she goes back to the cabinet, conceals her loads, takes off her stockings and steps back into the bowl of flour.

Houdini also learned of a male medium named Peck who similarly produced spirits although his trouser legs were sewn to the carpet. Peck was forced out of business, he noted, after a light was turned on during one of his séances, revealing him going about the room in his underwear.

In treating illustrious mediums Houdini doubled his efforts, as with Dr. Henry Slade, the most famous slate writer in the history of Spiritualism. Slade's appearance was dramatic: short iron-gray hair; brightly colored cheeks; haunted-looking, dark-circled eyes; and large hands, with the nail on the second finger of his right hand longer than the others. Under test conditions and in a trance state—from which he awoke with a cracking of muscles in his neck and jaw—he produced on blank school-slates spirit messages in English, French, German, Dutch, Greek, and Chinese, as well as the impression of a foot.

Many of Slade's prodigies had been reported in *Transcendental Physics* (English translation, 1901), by Johann Zöllner, a professor of physical astronomy in Leipzig. Zöllner experimented with Slade in the 1870s and concluded that his phenomena were explicable if one posited the existence of a four-dimensional space, not including, in Einstein's sense, time. Slade left a less metaphysical impression on the Seybert Commission, formed in the 1880s at the University of Pennsylvania to investigate mediumistic powers. It concluded that Slade used his body-shaking trance spasms as cover to gain access to a pencil, and his long fingernail to scratch the frame of the slate, imitating the sound of a pencil writing. Kellar testified before the commission and in broad daylight produced penciled slate-messages in a half dozen languages including Japanese and Gujarati. (The German spirit sent *"Ich bin ein Geist, und liebe mein Lagerbier"*—I am a ghost, and love my lager beer.) As was true of many other fraudulent mediums, exposures of Slade did little or nothing to stem his flow of clients.

Although Slade was no longer alive to be tested directly, Houdini outdid earlier investigators in picking him apart. From an elderly man who had roomed opposite the medium on Fourteenth Street in New York City, he learned that Slade drank hard, wore fake diamonds, and rouged his cheeks. "The wimen did not Like him," the informant wrote, "for they said he was half man only." A titled Englishman, Sir Horatio Donkin, told Houdini how, by pretending to be gullible, he had lulled Slade into becoming careless, then yanked the supposedly blank slate out of his hands; its underside was filled with prewritten messages. He sued Slade for defrauding His

Majesty's subjects. Houdini's best-placed source was a self-proclaimed
alchemist known as Remigius Albus, in reality a retired Philadelphian
named Remigius Weiss. No relation to Houdini, this Weiss had been even
more determined than he to discover Slade's secret. He drilled holes in the
doors and ceiling of a room so that observers could watch Slade's arms and
legs operate above and below the séance table. In Philadelphia he caught
Slade executing a so-called turnover move. Showing the slate blank on one
side, Slade reached for a sponge to wipe the other side. Under cover of the
gesture, he flipped the slate and then brazenly showed the first side again
as if it were the second, sponging it off. With this and other proofs, Albus
coerced Slade into signing a confession, under threat of exposure to the
police, admitting that his "pretended Spiritualistic manifestations" were
"deceptions, performed through tricks." Albus gave or sold the damning
document to Houdini for inclusion in his book.

Houdini interviewed in person Anna Eva Fay, whom he considered
"one of the cleverest mediums of history." Although he treated her in *A
Magician Among the Spirits*, he did not arrange the visit until a few
months after the book's publication, as if to confirm what he had written.
Taking along a movie cameraman, he located her in a woodsy suburb of
Boston, inhabiting a "regular showplace," surrounded by valuable rugs
and paintings. She had been giving séances since at least the early 1880s,
and had even performed in Appleton during Houdini's childhood there.
Delicate now, she weighed no more than ninety pounds and walked with a
crutch. Yet her "straw diamond white" hair and penetrating eyes, Houdini
observed, from which "great big streaks of intelligence would flash in and
out," still gave her a strong presence: "it is small wonder that with her personality she could have mystified the great mental giants of the ages,—not
our age, but of the ages."

Houdini spoke with Fay for five hours. Like the Davenport Brothers,
she had been in effect an early, superlative escape artist, another of his Spiritualist ancestors. Inside the cabinet, her wrists would be tied with cotton
bandages (the knots sewn through), her neck secured to a stanchion behind
her, her feet trussed, the rope ends carried outside the cabinet to be held by
committee members. Yet seemingly by spiritual agency, a full glass of water
placed inside the cabinet would later be found empty, a sheet of paper cut
into paper dolls, a nail driven into a board. Fay had been endorsed by Sir
William Crookes. To make sure that she could not slip her bonds, he tested

A Middle Eastern stop en route to Australia. Brassac appears at the left. *(Patrick Culliton Collection)*

Im looking for you Joe to give you a ride in my bi-plane. H. Houdini

At the wheel of the Voisin. *(Patrick Culliton Collection)*

(Sidney H. Radner Collection, Houdini Historical Center, Appleton, Wisconsin)

ABOVE AND BELOW: On the ground and aloft in Australia.

(Patrick Culliton Collection)

With Glenn Curtiss. *(Library of Congress)*

Notes for a trick. *(David Copperfield Collection)*

One of Houdini's underwater escape boxes.
(Robert Lund Collection)

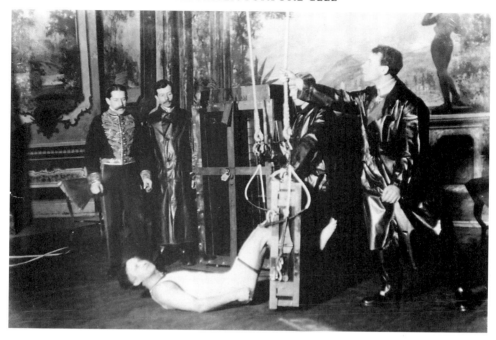

The assistant at far left is Franz Kukol. *(Sidney H. Radner Collection, Houdini Historical Center, Appleton, Wisconsin)*

(Morris Young Collection)

(Sidney H. Radner Collection, Houdini Historical Center, Appleton, Wisconsin)

Lithographic poster for the Water Torture Cell. *(Morris Young Collection)*

Poster for a Water Torture Cell copyist. *(Morris Young Collection)*

July 1.1910

With his mother and brother Leo at the grave of Mayer Samuel Weiss
in Machpelah Cemetery, 1910. *(Jacob Hyman Collection, Houdini Historical Center, Appleton, Wisconsin)*

With Ira Davenport, July 1910. *(Author's collection)*

An English floral tribute for his thirty-seventh birthday, Huddersfield, 1911.
(Patrick Culliton Collection)

The Weiss brothers in 1911. *From left to right:* Leo, Hardeen, Harry, Bill, Nat. *(Library of Congress)*

Houdini's replica of Robert-Houdin's Crystal Casket. *(Ken Klosterman Collection)*

Assistants Kukol, Vickery, and Collins at Keith's Philadelphia, 1912. *(Patrick Culliton Collection)*

Building the exedra. *(Sidney H. Radner Collection, Houdini Historical Center, Appleton, Wisconsin)*

Spectators gather to watch a suspended
straitjacket escape. *(Sidney H. Radner Collection,
Houdini Historical Center, Appleton, Wisconsin)*

Harry and Bess with Jack and
Charmian London. *(David Copperfield Collection)*

On Snark's lifeboat
Pennduffryn
1908

and Harry Houdini's
dear wife, with the
hope that we may
all gather in the
Valley of the moon
some nor far distant
day.
With delightful
memories.
Yours for adventure.
Charmian London
Glen Ellen, Cal.,
November 30, 1915.

Charmian London's inscription in *The Log of the Snark*.
(Author's collection)

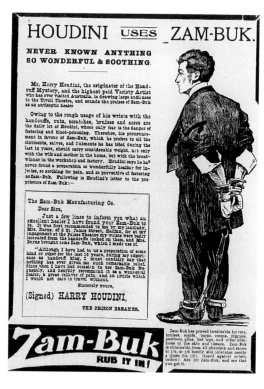

A Houdini endorsement. *(State Library of Victoria)*

A musical tribute. *(Morris Young Collection)*

With Harry Kellar. *(Billy Rose Theatre Collection, New York Public Library for the Performing Arts)*

HOUDINI'S VANISHING ELEPHANT

The vanishing elephant. *(Billy Rose Theatre Collection,
New York Public Library for the Performing Arts)*

Hippodrome display window during one of Houdini's engagements.
(Theatre Arts Collection, Harry Ransom Humanities Research Center, University of Texas at Austin)

With Charlie Chaplin in Los Angeles. *(Stanley Palm Collection)*

With unidentified starlets.
(John Gaughan Collection)

In makeup for *Haldane of the Secret Service*, with Bess and an unidentified actress.
(Marie Blood Collection)

Harry and Bess visiting on a set with Fatty Arbuckle *(lower left)* and Buster Keaton *(top left)*.
(John Gaughan Collection)

(Sidney H. Radner Collection, Houdini Historical Center, Appleton, Wisconsin)

(Theatre Arts Collection, Harry Ransom Humanities
Research Center, University of Texas at Austin)

(Museum of the City of New York)

Haldane of the Secret Service. (Theatre Arts Collection, Harry Ransom Humanities Research Center, University of Texas at Austin)

Mixing it up with heavyweight champ Jack Dempsey *(left)* and lightweight champ Benny Leonard. *(Bettmann Archive)*

In the library of 278. *(Sidney H. Radner Collection, Houdini Historical Center, Appleton, Wisconsin)*

In his office at 278. *(UPI/Bettmann)*

One of Houdini's letterheads. *(Library of Congress)*

With Argamasilla. *(UPI/Bettmann)*

The Doyle family in New York.
(Library of Congress)

"Margery." *(Library of Congress)*

With Margery and O. D. Munn,
J. Malcolm Bird in the rear. *(Author's collection)*

That evening I was in charge of her left hand which rested lightly on the palm of my right. With my index finger I could feel her pulse. In fact I used the secret system of the "touch and tactics" of the mind or muscle performer, (I had given performances or tests in this field of mystery) who is guided by the slightest muscular indication in finding a hidden article. *I was able to detect almost every time she made a move. Frequently she stretched out her arms to rest them and once I caught her using this motion as a subterfuge, leaving only her elbow on the chair while she pushed the table with her head (Fig. 5).*

FIG. 4.

"Walter," her guide and aide, is very autocratic, seldom asking anything but usually directing, and this evening he ordered everyone to move back from the table around which we were sitting so that he might

FIG. 5.

gather force. This was simply another ruse on the medium's part, for when all the rest moved back she moved back also and this gave her room enough to bend her head and push the table up and over. *I caught her doing this twice.*

Page nine

Houdini in the Margery cabinet, the bell-box before him. *(Library of Congress)*

Page from Houdini's pamphlet on Margery, illustrating how she overturned the table. *(Author's collection)*

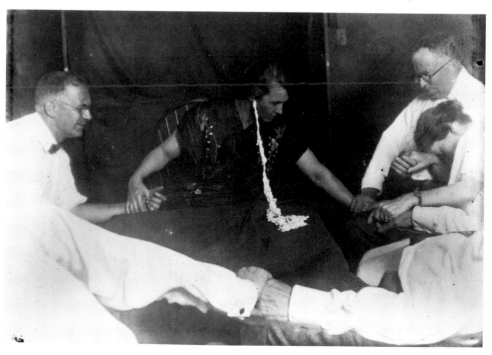

Margery exuding ectoplasm from her ear. *(Library of Congress)*

In disguise, to trap fraudulent mediums. *(Sidney H. Radner Collection, Houdini Historical Center, Appleton, Wisconsin)*

Examining the collapsible spirit trumpet of Mrs. Cook. *(UPI/Bettmann)*

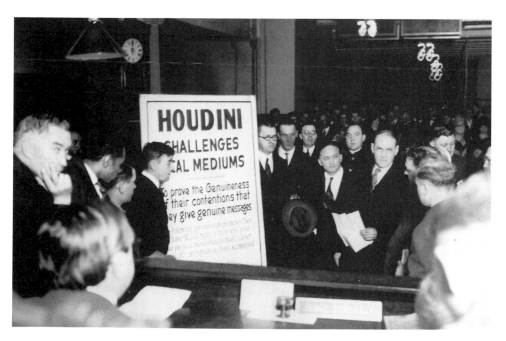

The anti-Spiritualist crusade in Chicago. *(Chicago Historical Society)*

Staging a full materialization. *(Chicago Historical Society)*

(*Museum of the City of New York*)

ABOVE AND BELOW: Two portraits in 1926.

(*Author's collection*)

Dorothy Young and Julia Sawyer with Houdini,
probably in "Welcome Summer."
(Arthur E. Moses Collection)

Oak coffin for
challenge escape
in Boston, 1907.
*(Kevin Connolly
Collection)*

Female assistants for *HOUDINI (left to right)*: Dorothy Young,
Tessie Vittorelli, Julia Sawyer, Julie Karcher, Bess. *(Kevin Connolly Collection)*

BUTLER
CHICAGO

25

Mrl Karchen   *Houdini*   *Julia Sawyer*

A real magician. *(Kevin Connolly Collection)*

Poster for Houdini's last performances. *(Morris Young Collection)*

Preparing to submerge at the Shelton swimming pool. *(UPI/Bettmann)*

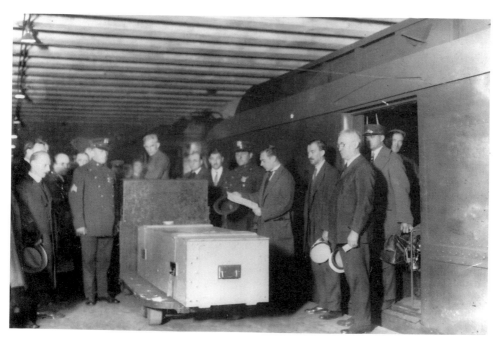

The bronze casket arrives in New York from Detroit. *(UPI/Bettmann)*

Houdini's funeral, the casket being borne across West Forty-third Street. *(UPI/Bettmann)*

her in his own laboratory with an electrical instrument. After tying her, he had her clench both handles of a battery, so constructed as to interrupt the current if she let go either handle, and send the meter to 0. Fay produced her manifestations even though the contact remained unbroken.

"She spoke freely of all her methods," Houdini noted after the interview. "Never at any time did she pretend to believe in spiritualism." Fay revealed that she had gulled Crookes by the simple expedient of gripping one handle of the battery beneath her knee joint, keeping the circuit unbroken but leaving one hand free to do as it wished. She spoke of her two years with the Russian occultist Madame Blavatsky, founder of the Theosophical Society, a woman driven by greed: "Her method was to marry rich old men," as Houdini recorded what Fay said, "and then divorce them, saying she wanted children and her husband was impotent." Touchingly Fay confided to Houdini that every day she visited the grave of her son John, a suicide, but was unable to find for herself the wish-fulfilling comfort she had brought to others: "I . . . don't want messages or sentences," she said, "one word from John would be enough. If I only got one word I would proclaim it to the world. I would walk bareheaded and unshod through the streets. . . . Even Christ could not be more sincere than I. I would say I know."

Given his unique and roving research, Houdini considered *A Magician Among the Spirits* a new claim on immortality, "part of my *monument*." The book was reviewed widely and favorably, and its peeks inside the medium's cabinet remain entertaining. But only Houdini's vanity could have mistaken them for a monumental investigation or historical sketch of Spiritualism. The coverage is skewed by his rancorous assault on Sir Arthur Conan Doyle, which includes three pages of excerpts from Doyle's personal letters to him. And he chose to treat only physical mediums, those able to lift tables or manifest lumps of coal. He ignored the less spectacular psychical mediums, on whom much of the most respectable scientific investigation focused. He did not mention (and knew little about) the most acclaimed of all psychical mediums, Mrs. Leonora Piper, or her famous investigator, William James, who worked with her some twenty-five years. Piper's ability to disclose confidential details of her sitters' private lives, including his own, led James to conclude that she possessed "supernormal receptivity of some kind"—although, it needs saying, he may not have known that a maid in his household was friendly with a maid in Mrs. Piper's.

Others more knowledgeable than Houdini were quick to point out the book's numerous factual errors and misquotations. He misattributed a statement to the popular novelist Margaret Deland, a member of the SPR, who pressured him into making a retraction in the *New York Times*. He blamed many of the mistakes on his publisher, Harper & Brothers, who by his estimate cut one hundred thousand words from the manuscript and "mutilated" the book. He gave in to the butchering because he felt ominously oppressed: "I had a slight premonition that perhaps I would not live to see the book in print if I waited much longer, so I allowed them to rush it, against my judgment." Maybe, but the far longer Ur-version he submitted was unpublishable—typed-up scraps from books, newspapers, Spiritualist journals, letters from friends, cut-and-pasted into an incoherent collage. He may not have put together much of the hodgepodge anyway. His elderly factotum, Oscar Teale, later claimed to have "originally written . . . the damnable work."

Authorship is beyond question in the three Spiritualist-inspired stories Houdini published at this time in the classic pulp magazine *Weird Tales*: "The Hoax of the Spirit Lover," "The Spirit Fakers of Hermannstadt," and "Imprisoned with the Pharaohs." The first two relate his clashes with sham mediums. They purport to recount events that actually occurred, even though the second involves the deaf-mute caretaker of a Gothic dungeon in Transylvania. The interest of the third tale lies in the fact that its creation is fully documented in the correspondence of its gifted ghostwriter—H. P. Lovecraft, on his way to becoming an admired writer of science fiction. Houdini first told the story to the publisher of *Weird Tales*, who retold it to Lovecraft for transformation into a short story "by Houdini and H. P. Lovecraft." It stunned Lovecraft to think that Houdini intended to pass off the corny plot for a real-life adventure. Stopping in Cairo en route to Australia, it went, Houdini was kidnapped by two Bedouins and left inside a deep-buried pharaonic crypt; he escaped only after suffering a "hideous experience" he hesitated to disclose.

"I don't know how far I can go," Lovecraft yelped. "It seems this boob was (as he relates) thrown into an antient subterraneous temple at Gizeh . . . all bound and gagged as on the Keith circuit." To see whether Houdini's caper could have happened, he checked out some of the Egyptian detail in a library. No sunken temple at Gizeh. "Houdini's story is *all* a fake," he concluded. "He's supremely egotistical, as one can see at a glance." Chalking Houdini up as a "bimbo," Lovecraft wrestled with how to make supposedly actual events take place in an actually nonexistent temple. "BOY, that Houdini job!" he griped again a few weeks later. "It strained me to the limit." He tried to solve the problem by treating the Cairo kidnapping realistically, then letting all imaginative hell break loose. For the macabre crypt scene he invented what he called "the most nameless, slithering, unmentionable HORROR that ever stalked cloven-hooved through the tenebrous and necrophagous abysses of elder night." This included Houdini's lacerated crawl up a staircase of porphyry blocks to witness a sacrificial offering of "unmentionable food." Lovecraft's solution cost him some self-contempt. But Houdini, he found, "took to it marvellously." Not only that. Houdini soon turned over to him voluminous notes for a major new book tracing in anthropological and psychological terms the rise of superstition.

Houdini's literary presumptions, as cheeky and devious in their way as his escapes, brought him a new scandal among magicians. Late in 1923 appeared a three-hundred-page volume entitled *Elliott's Last Legacy*. Cardworkers had awaited it eagerly, for Dr. James Elliott (1874–1920), recently deceased from diabetes, was for them a revered figure, strong claimant to the invention of the back palm. His religion was card sleights. He would rent an unfurnished room, his legend had it, and with nothing but a table and chair practice card moves up to ten hours at a stretch. *Elliott's Last Legacy*, advertised as containing private material from the master's notebooks, appeared with Houdini's name in large type on the cover, spine, and title page as editor. Nor did he conceal himself in the text, which contained a blurb for his stories in *Weird Tales*, a photo of him as president of SAM, and gross self-praise of his early card-king days: "Elliott and I were unsurpassed in that particular line of manipulative skill."

Houdini's right to identify himself as editor was disputed by the magician Clinton Burgess (1880–1932), who insisted that he had edited the heralded *Legacy* himself. He claimed that Elliott had asked him to collaborate on the book, as he did until Elliott's death, after which he continued the labor alone for eighteen months. Because he could not afford to publish the completed manuscript, he said, he approached Houdini, who offered to bring it out and gave it to Oscar Teale for minor revisions. But the published *Legacy* acknowledged Burgess as no more than its nondescript 'compiler,' and in type so small, he howled, "as to almost require the use of a magnifying glass to read it, whereas HOUDINI'S name was plastered all over the book."

Houdini denied all that. He said that Burgess had approached him with a hard-luck story. A descendant of Governor DeWitt Clinton who billed himself as "New York's leading Society Entertainer," Burgess had been reduced to gumshoeing for a detective agency. Houdini said he gave Burgess $25, and more handouts after that. When he learned that Burgess had been threatened with arrest for milking $150 from subscribers to the Elliott book—which Burgess had no way of delivering—he agreed to publish it himself. But the manuscript was in an "impossible publishing state," Houdini said. He therefore hired Teale and a salaried secretary, and worked with them to pull together the jumble, at a personal cost of more than $2,500.

Typically Houdini left unclear how much of the rewriting was done by himself and how much by Teale. But for the rest he may not much have exaggerated. Burgess's contributions to *The Sphinx* are ungrammatical, clumsy, and repetitious, leaving little doubt that the manuscript must have needed major editorial bloodletting. And Elliott's own father deposed that Burgess had touched him for $25 for a lithograph that cost $20 and $75 for a typewriter he never bought.

Burgess's squawk set off two years of apoplectic roughhousing between him and Houdini. The affidavits, depositions, and catcalling make too redundant (and trivial) a story to recount fully. Burgess in essence denounced Houdini around the American magic community. In a letter published in the French journal *Le Prestidigitateur*, he blasted him for conniving to "enrich himself financially and in his reputation at the cost of others." Houdini took revenge by getting Burgess kicked out of SAM, for "conduct unbecoming a member." He could not however repair the damage Burgess did him among French magicians, who had never forgiven *The Unmasking*. He appealed to *Le Prestidigitateur*, but got back a huff of Gallic astonishment: "If you consider yourself insulted by Mr. Clinton Burgess's letter, what must we say, we French citizens . . . of the outrage you have offered to our respected master and great French conjurer, Robert-Houdin." The president of the Association Syndicale et Internationale des Artistes Prestidigitateurs coolly advised Houdini to settle his vendetta against Burgess by himself: "As you should know, there are duels for people of courage and courts of justice for those who are lacking in it."

The irony in the affair is that if Houdini's itch to publish did not again seduce him into taking credit for another man's literary work, it at least led him to stamp his name all over a book of no importance. The *Legacy* barely mentions Elliott and passes on few of his card secrets, offering instead minor magic and designs for apparatus, few if any of which have made their way into the magic repertoire. Card experts who bought the book expecting to be bowled over felt gypped.

THE *SCIENTIFIC AMERICAN* COMMITTEE; CARRINGTON, BIRD, PRINCE; THE VALENTINE AND PECORARO SÉANCES

Houdini's most intrigue-ridden and controversial engagement with Spiritualism began in January 1924, when he was asked to serve on a new investigating committee sponsored by *Scientific American*. Founded in 1845, the monthly magazine often published news of psychical research alongside profusely-illustrated articles on progress across the whole range of modern science and technology—steel manufacture, entomology, ballistics, anesthesia, relativity theory, commercial invention ("Pen and Pencil in One"). Houdini had known the magazine's owners, the Munn family, for at least five years, having filed for patents through their law office, and was known to its readers as the author (?) of such articles as "Handcuff Releases Under Difficulties." The editors justified their inclusion of a magician on the panel on the ground that Houdini had made himself an experienced psychical researcher. He would serve, they said, "as a guarantee to the public that none of the tricks of his trade have been practiced upon the committee."

The magazine launched its investigation in the form of a contest for cash. It offered two prizes of $2,500 each to the first person who could, under test conditions, produce a "psychic photograph" or an "objective psychic manifestation of physical character." The contest rules were elaborate, requiring among other things that mediums state in advance the phenomena they designed to bring about. The editors stressed their intention of subjecting the mediums to a search and of using such recording instruments as microphones and galvanometers, as well as their reluctance to sit in absolute darkness for the tests. Awards would be made on the basis of a unanimous vote of the five investigators, or a four-to-one split in the medium's favor.

All levels of the American press found in the contest a steady source of news for the next two years. In New York the proceedings were closely followed by the *World*, the *Tribune*, and the *Times*. Their owners and chief editors had of course often been guests at Houdini's home and at SAM banquets, and he had not befriended them for nothing. "Mr. Houdini ought to be the best judge in the world of such matters," Pulitzer's *World* editorialized. "If he is not satisfied, it is probable that all is not as it seems." Some editorial writers regretted the committee's decision not to test psychical as well as physical mediums. But most depicted the test séances as a chance to separate, by scientific means, mediumistic fraud from genuine phenomena of potentially great human significance. The scores of articles, editorials, and letters to the press that accompanied the investigation moved Houdini's name out of the theatrical news and into the context of social, religious, and scientific concerns.

The intense public interest in the contest made Houdini wary of staking his reputation on the judgments of a committee, much less a committee of laymen. In magic as in fake mediumship, much depends on actions so innocent-seeming that no untrained person notices or thinks of mentioning them, such as Slade's reaching for a sponge to wipe his slate. It worried Houdini that others on the committee would be looking in the wrong places. "Men easily deceived might be selected," he told the *Tribune*, "and if a medium's work should be accepted by them, I would be the laughing stock of the public." For that reason, as the price of his service he insisted on the right to reject appointments to the committee.

Houdini was also wary of staking too much on his own insight. He had no illusion that his magisterial knowledge of magic and escapes prevented him from being fooled in the séance room. "It is manifestly impossible," he wrote, "to detect and duplicate all the feats of fraudulent mediums, who do not scruple at outraging propriety and even decency to gain their ends. Again, many of the effects produced by them are impulsive, done on the spur of the moment, inspired or prompted by attending circumstances, and could not be duplicated by themselves." In recognizing these and other limits of magicians as investigators, Houdini took a failsafe position comparable to that of many Spiritualists. They argued that because a performer could duplicate some manifestation by conjuring methods, did not mean the medium used those methods. Houdini wanted the public to keep in mind that his or any one else's failure to detect fraud should not be taken as proof that it did not exist. "Were I at a seance and not able to explain what transpired," he wrote, "it would not necessarily be acknowledgment that I believe it to be the genuine Spiritualism."

Houdini's place on the committee brought him into alliance, and conflict, with an accomplished and in some cases distinguished new cast of characters. Individually, the members were too complex and quirky to be easily characterized. Overall they made a group of serious, rather conservative academics. These "Learned professors," as Houdini often referred to them, were: Dr. William McDougall, chairman of the department of psychology at Harvard, and president of the American SPR; Dr. Daniel F. Comstock, an industrial engineer, formerly in the physics department of MIT; Hereward Carrington, a prolific writer on psychical research; Dr. Walter Franklin Prince, of the American SPR; and J. Malcolm Bird, associate editor of *Scientific American*, formerly a member of the Columbia University department of mathematics. With the first two members Houdini had slight contact; his far closer involvement with Carrington and Prince came later and appears in the next chapter. With J. Malcolm Bird, however, he crashed head-on from the beginning.

As secretary to the committee Bird had no vote, but he was responsible for corresponding with applicants, arranging sittings, and writing up the results for *Scientific American*. A science journalist and editor of a collection of semipopular essays entitled *Einstein's Theories of Relativity and Gravitation* (1921), he styled himself a Regular Guy, someone of wit and feeling—"really a human being," as he put it, "and not a scientific iceberg." To prepare for the SA contest, he went abroad to sit with British and continental mediums and sample overseas techniques of investigation. A Berlin medium brought him apports of a stone and a sprig of leaves. Sir Arthur Conan Doyle entertained him in London, arranged sittings with the Crewe Circle, and counted him an ally. Bird had even been privileged to sit with the Doyles in Toledo as the selective Ada Besinnet levitated the entire heavy séance table. Indeed, with his cloth cap and thin, beak-nosed face, Bird resembled not only his own name but also Sherlock Holmes. He became Houdini's Enemy Number One on the committee.

Like Houdini himself, mediums may have been made cautious by the intense publicity, and certainly were by the committee's minefield of rules. For about three months, none but second-rate candidates, screened and quickly rejected, applied for the cash prizes. At last in May the committee accepted for testing a medium named George Valentine, of Wilkes-Barre, Pennsylvania. He was no ideal prospect, since he specialized in old-fashioned manifestations that had often been exposed. The *Tribune* called the committee's efforts with him a "[w]aste of Science," an investigation of "stale magic" that was already "old stuff in the General Grant era." Nevertheless the committee set up stringent controls. According to secretary Bird, it took days to install the lablike array of instruments: induction coils, electroscopes, sound-and-heat detectors developed during the war; a scale with spring balance, its movements registered by a stylus on a drum; a device to sense whether the medium discharged electricity. Melted paraffin was also provided to invite a spirit hand. The committee gave Valentine some preliminary sittings, without control, to allow him to adjust to its presence and to the physical conditions. "If these conditions are such as to make him mentally or physically uncomfortable," Bird explained, "one cannot expect the same results, either from fraud or from genuine psychic power, as might be obtained if he were comfortable."

The first official test took place on May 24, at the *Scientific American* office in the fifty-six-story Woolworth Building. Ignoring the rest of the committee, the *Times* headline read HOUDINI ATTENDS/AN EVENING SEANCE. The sitting was conducted in total darkness, the windows hung with black draperies. Committee members, plus a few reporters and other spectators, sat in a circle around Valentine and his associate (named Worrall)—in shirtsleeves because of the warmth of the room. As an extra control a strip of paper was attached from Valentine's chair to the floor; it would break if the chair moved much. Luminous disks were fastened to his hands, although the committee agreed to cover the markers until he actively produced manifestations. In front of him stood two spirit trumpets, long metallic horns about five inches wide at the mouth, banded with luminous paint to be distinguishable in the darkness.

The séance began with prayers and the singing of hymns, but for about an hour nothing happened. The voice of a Dr. Barnett, an excarnate chemist, asked for patience. Then in the pitch darkness some committee members felt their knees being touched. A few said they perceived spirit lights—lustrous, varicolored wisps drifting through the darkness. A faint voice whispered to Bird, "Hello, Malcolm," and identified itself as "Harry"—bringing some chuckles. "Friends," Valentine's associate protested, "I must really ask that you treat this seriously. After all, this is a religion to many persons." One phosphorized trumpet waved overhead about the room, coming to rest between the legs of Walter Franklin Prince. As a Native American spirit-control named Kokum called out, the other trumpet whacked Houdini on the head—an "awful clout," he said.

Valentine was scheduled for another test séance the following night. But he announced that he had to go back to Wilkes-Barre and might not be able to return for some time. Probably he was just getting out of town fast. In a call to the *Times*, Houdini disclosed that the committee had caught Valentine flatfooted in an "outright fake." More accurately, the committee had snookered him. It had visibly heaped the séance room with coils and balances, but kept the crucial detectors altogether hidden. Under the rug beneath Valentine's chair, Houdini revealed, an electrical expert from *Scientific American* had placed strips of wood bound together with canvas, on which were copper contacts. With Valentine seated, his chair closed a circuit that lit a lightbulb in an adjoining room. There sat two stenographers with headsets. One recorded the exact times when the bulb went off, indicating that Valentine had left his chair, whose weight alone was insufficient to maintain the circuit. The other stenographer, able to listen-in to the séance room through a dictograph, recorded the time and point of origin of the various manifestations. Comparing the two stenographers' time-sheets showed that whenever a trumpet had thumped or spirit tapped a committee member, Valentine had left his seat—in all, fifteen times during the séance.

The *Times* published Houdini's exposé as a front-page story. But it got him no thanks. As secretary of the committee, J. Malcolm Bird denounced him for having violated the members' agreement to keep test-results secret until a unified report could be written, and released with the blessing of *Scientific American*. Bird made headlines himself by announcing that Houdini had been ousted from the committee for betraying its trust. Houdini may well have acted in bad faith. But professionally he had always abided by no other lawgiver than Houdini, and he was not about to take orders from a committee, much less be put down by really-a-human-being Bird. Through the press he denied having pledged himself to secrecy, and pronounced Bird an "amateur" who could be "fooled by any high class magician." He also explained that he had spoken out because he could not let his friends think he had been taken in. They had taunted him as a "simpleton" for getting involved with the committee, which, he said, had agreed to act like "a lot of boobs."

The New York papers generally rated Houdini the committee member best qualified to detect fraud, and Bird the worst because of his trust in Spiritualist phenomena. Yet they all disapproved Houdini's exposé, less for jumping the gun on the other committee members than for running into them. Even the friendly *Times* predicted that, knowing about the trap set for Valentine, other mediums would be scared off. "This is a regrettable consequence of Mr. Houdini's hurry to convince his jeering friends that he was not such a 'simpleton.'. . . Except for that, probably half a dozen Valentines could have been exposed, and the impressiveness of the disclosures would have been greater." Houdini evidently soon had second thoughts himself, since he smoothed things over with Bird. Through the *Tribune* he also promised that other mediums applying for the prize had nothing to fear. "They're sure to get a square deal," he said, straight-faced. "Valentine got the squarest deal he ever got in his whole life."

Houdini's encouragement went for nothing. Wary of being ambushed, no acceptable medium came forward to be tested for another six months. Houdini, busy meanwhile with his lecture tour on Spiritualism, kept a hand in the committee's affairs by screening some possible candidates. Apparently for this reason he visited a Philadelphia medium, Sarah M. Mourer. A commercial artist, she seemed to be about fifty, with bobbed white hair. Around her kitchen were spread, Houdini estimated, about 150 of her hand-colored greeting cards. He had a hard time keeping up with her rambling talk. Among other subjects it concerned her ability to predict to coworkers the success of their fishing trips ("you're going to catch three fish and one is a flounder"). It also dealt with the penetration into her bedroom, as she slept, of a table leaf. The leaf woke her up but obeyed her command to depart and reentered the furniture. "There is something gone wrong with the lady," Houdini put down in his notebook, "she is just a bit 'broke off.'"

In demonstrating her powers to Houdini, Mourer offered to cure him of his nearsightedness. In reality he only feigned the impairment to account for the eyeglasses he wore—ordinary-looking but fitted with magnifying lenses for viewing manifestations close-up. Smacking her hands together, she commanded him to close his eyes. Then she put one hand on his head and the other on the back of his neck, saying "Do you feel anything?"

I replied, "Yes, I feel your hands." She asked, "Don't you feel anything else?" And I said, "Yes, your hands are cold." "But you must feel something," she replied. So to pacify her I said "Yes, I feel something like a very slight shock of electric running through one of her [sic] hands to the other." She told me, "That's it. You're cured."

She made him promise to write about the shock in his report to the *Scientific American* committee, and before he left disclosed that she had foreknown his visit.

In December the committee entertained a candidate of real promise, a twenty-four-year-old Neapolitan named Nino Pecoraro. Able to speak only a few words of English, he was accompanied by a Dr. Anselme Vecchio, his interpreter and patron. One feature of Pecoraro's mediumship gave it unusual interest. His spirit control was the greatest female physical medium in the history of Spiritualism, Eusapia Palladino. This thickset illiterate peasant, her dark hair gashed by a snow-white patch, had been rigorously tested by noted physicists and medical men all over Europe and America. She had survived many exposés. Her very frankness about her cheating induced many investigators to consider it only occasional. One called her "the *crux*, the pivot upon which the whole case for the physical phenomena turns."

Houdini had followed Palladino's career long before he became engrossed in Spiritualism. For in evoking wonderment she equaled or outdid the great magicians of the period. Her séances were raucous, erotic, exhausting. While examiners held her hands and feet, disembodied spirits felt, tickled, and kissed the sitters, pinched their ears, pulled their hair. Tables fell over, curtains bulged and shook, sparkles and human silhouettes appeared, Palladino all the time shouting in Italian, groaning, yawning, panting, weeping—and afterward occasionally vomiting. Doyle, during his first lecture tour in the United States, had experienced her presence at a séance with the new *SA* candidate. With Pecoraro in a deathly-pale trance, she spoke whisperingly through him to Sir Arthur, now and again with mysterious snoring, rattling, scratching, and nerve-jangling screams. An unaccountable breeze said to blow from the region of Palladino's forehead, seeming to issue from a scar under her hair, especially intrigued Houdini. He had known a dime-museum performer who could inflate balloons through his eyes, and had heard of a boy who could blow through a never-healed fracture in the back of his head. Perhaps correctly, he believed that a similar "freak make-up" enabled Palladino to work some of her airspouting amazements.

Touring again with his Spiritualism lecture, Houdini did not attend the first two official committee sittings with Pecoraro, perhaps because, as he implied later, Bird did not let him know they were being held. Tested in the

SA law library before the rest of the committee, Pecoraro submitted to an almost Houdini-grade tying-up. Heavy mittens were sewn to his coat sleeves. His forearms were crossed and placed together straitjacket-style, as if he were hugging himself. Each hand was inserted into the glove at the opposite elbow. Then the ensemble was wound end to end in picture wire. Just the same, Pecoraro produced. Hands clapped, a trumpet tooted, a bell came flying, spirit voices conversed in English. He did not fail to honor his fabulous spirit control either. He apported dollar bills—money owed by Palladino, who spoke through him in a Neapolitan dialect. Bird reported being "nearly asphyxiated by the garlic on Pecoraro's breath," and wondered, in all seriousness, whether it represented "celestial garlic on Palladino's breath."

Houdini did learn about the third test séance, on December 18. He broke his lecture schedule to come in for it, though that meant a trip from Little Rock, Arkansas. After all, Pecoraro had produced his manifestations under seemingly foolproof conditions, raising the possibility of actual spirit agency and making him a serious candidate for the *SA* prize. On meeting the young man, Houdini sized him up as one escape artist might another— "a powerfully built fellow," he noticed, with "great curved shoulders and an enormous amount of endurance." In fact he felt that Pecoraro had better physical equipment for escapes than himself. On the other hand Pecoraro had never been hog-tied by the proprietor of "W. H. Hodgson's School of Physical Culture," lashed to a skyscraper girder, or coiled in Weed tire-chain grips. Houdini did up Pecoraro not so much as one escape artist might another, but as no other creature had ever been tied.

Pecoraro's hands were first sewn into gloves strung to his underwear, then thrust into the sleeves of his reversed coat, the gloves sewn to the sleeves as well. The sleeves were in turn sewn to the coat and the coat to his trousers. Houdini then put Pecoraro in a chair and roped him. In several books and articles Houdini had pointed out that it was virtually impossible to bind someone in a long rope without introducing slack: the longer the rope, the easier the escape. So in securing Pecoraro he used dozens of small pieces of rope, linked by intricate loops and knots. The job took almost an hour and forty-five minutes. To finish it off he put Pecoraro into a cubby-hole formed by hanging some black curtains in a corner of the room and screwing the curtains into the floor through metal bands. He commented, by one account, that he "wouldn't guarantee that Nino couldn't get loose, but he would guarantee that he would never get back."

Pecoraro spent eighty-one minutes sewn up in the web of ropelets. No handclapping this time, no flying bells, no blaring trumpet, no apports. He eked out only a few rappings à la the Fox sisters ("by striking his foot on the side of the cabinet," Houdini proposed). And he piped through to the sitters the voice of Eusapia Palladino repeatedly complaining that Houdini had made Pecoraro very uncomfortable.

Pecoraro's patron, Dr. Vecchio, blamed the failure of the séance on Houdini's manhandling. But Houdini denied that he had bound Pecoraro in a way to produce discomfort, "aside from the fact that he could not move." Bird, resembling his mentor Doyle in being eager to excuse, reported that a neurologist who examined Pecoraro afterward declared at least his trance to have been genuine; if Pecoraro had practiced any deception (and this time Bird, too, had doubts), it was not deliberate but "subconscious." Houdini agreed only to the extent of believing that Pecoraro was insane and really thought that spirits aided him. Sane or not, the strong-shouldered young Italian had been no real match for him. *That* he found in a young American, a woman far worthier of being mentioned in the same breath with the great, earthy Palladino.

FOURTEEN

SUMMER 1924

THE CRANDONS; THE JULY SITTINGS

IN MID-JULY Houdini had the first of his five sittings with the most formidable candidate for the *Scientific American* prize. She little resembled the others personally or socially. A blue-eyed woman in her early thirties with light-brown hair, reportedly an accomplished cellist, she took no money for her séances. She also shunned publicity, even taking the *nom de séance* "Margery" in place of her own name, Mina Crandon. She lived in Boston on historic Beacon Hill with her husband, Dr. L. G. Crandon, a prominent surgeon nearly twenty years older than she. Slender, graceful, well-read, he boasted descent from passengers on the *Mayflower* and taught at the Harvard Medical School. He had operated on Margery in 1917, months before U.S. entry into the war. They had met once again and married during the war, while she was serving as a volunteer ambulance driver at the New London Naval Hospital, where he was a lieutenant commander. To their friends and acquaintances they seemed an urbane, charming society couple.

After her marriage to Crandon, however, Margery had discovered a psychic gift in herself. Small groups of Harvard friends were invited to witness her abilities, at the Crandons' four-story brick house at 10 Lime Street, a warren-like place of shaftways, back stairs, and dumbwaiters. Any suspicion the intricate interior may have aroused was quickly disarmed. From the moment when guests were ushered in by the Japanese butler, the evenings had more the atmosphere of a soirée than a séance. On his visit Hamlin Garland found Margery gowned for the occasion, Crandon in dinner dress, and his fellow guests anything but devious or seedy: "They impressed me as a group of cultivated people who were seriously pursuing an investigation of occult forces, while remaining quite normal in their social relationships." Margery led the company into a tasteful dining room, for good food, wine, and tabletalk. "Her vivacity," another guest recalled, "with the doctor's poise and dignity, made them a delightful pair for an enjoyable dinner. Both had a very diverting sense of humor and the conversation would never lag." Afterward guests socialized in the clubby library, all books and comfortable chairs. Then they adjourned to the top floor for the private demonstration of mediumship.

The séance room, eight by seventeen feet, looked out on Beacon Hill, but was bare except for two sofas and two bookcases. Like Palladino and many other mediums, Margery sat at a plain table, within an alcove that theoretically acted as a gathering place for psychic energies. Her storehouse was little more than a three-panel screen some six feet high, the top covered by a curtain that hung down in front to below her face. Dr. Crandon arranged the sitters in a circle around his wife, hands linked. The Victrola was started—to soothe and calm the group—and the lights were turned out. Darkness, music, the human chain—these were traditional elements of the séance. The amenities of Lime Street made unthinkable the purposes they often served: to prevent accurate observation, drown out telltale sounds, and keep too-curious sitters from getting up.

Where most mediums specialized in producing one or two phenomena, either psychical or physical, Margery commanded many of both. Those invited to Lime Street witnessed how, in a trance, she conveyed messages from beyond in Swedish, classical Greek, anglicized Chinese. As she slightly groaned and faintly moaned, now and then jerking her head and limbs, yellow rosebuds appeared on the tabletop. And there were raps, levitations, psychic lights, catlike brushings of the sitters' legs. But what gave Margery's seances their distinctive, rowdy vigor, were the uncouth antics of her spirit-control, Walter.

Walter was Margery's deceased brother, a fireman on the New Haven Railroad who in 1911 had been crushed to death between a derailed train car and an engine tender. He usually made known his presence by a whistle, then began speaking in a hoarse whisper, referring to his sister as "the kid." His voice was "independent," that is, able to speak not only through Margery in trance but also by itself, even while Margery spoke. Hamlin Garland described it as the voice of a "humorous, rough-and-ready man of twenty-five or thirty, with such intonation as a Canadian youth . . . would use." But to some other auditors it sounded like Margery, herself a native of Ontario. At the least Walter shared his sister's vivacity. An incurable wiseguy, he set loose his tame psychic bat, Susie, to swish about the séance room. With what one guest called "his peculiar Japanese chuckle," he cussed and sassed the sitters, reeled off limericks and snappy repartee: "Shall we gather at the river?/Shall we eat a pound of liver." At the end of one séance he announced, "Continuous performance, good as Keith's." A ghost vaudevillian, on the Summerland circuit.

Before being tested by *Scientific American*, Margery had given successful séances abroad, incidentally proving that her ability did not depend on the Lime Street house. She had sat for Richet in Paris, for the spirit photographers in Crewe (who captured Walter hovering near her), and for the Doyles in London. With Sir Arthur gripping her feet in his lap, as a control, she induced Walter to whistle in his ear. "That Margery is a very powerful medium," Doyle concluded, "is beyond all question." In the first half of 1924, she had also sat more than thirty times with J. Malcolm Bird and various *SA* subcommittees, although not with the full official committee. During the séances, a psychic clock struck as from a distance, furniture moved, a pigeon passed through solid matter. Bird pronounced her mediumship to be "of unquestionable genuineness and extreme importance."

Houdini attended none of the thirty *SA* sessions, and in fact knew nothing about them until they were over, in mid-June. The failure to keep him posted was variously explained, and in this resembles everything else about the Margery investigation. In trying to judge the nature of so many mysterious phenomena, the committee members came to quarrel among themselves and to take sides for or against the Crandons, who likewise came to quarrel with them and with each other. As a result no description of what happened or what was said went unchallenged in some letter, phone call, article, or newspaper interview, leaving a half-dozen sides to every story. The official séances are difficult to reconstruct because they are known only through the aggrieved, conflicting accounts of the participants, who saw them in terms of their private dramas of intrigue and betrayal, finding portentous significance in trifles and leery of an ever-growing enemies-list of other participants. Begun as a scientific investigation, the Margery case quickly fell apart into a paranoid free-for-all.

So too for the long delay in telling Houdini about the investigation. Bird, who arranged and joined in the preliminary séances, claimed that Houdini had not been notified because he was on tour. The investigators saw no need to "bother" him, Bird said, unless they suspected a type of fraud they could not penetrate, or the prospect arose of declaring Margery a genuine medium. Houdini, however, believed that Bird simply wanted to keep him from interfering. More than that, he thought that Bird had befriended the Crandons and fallen for Margery, and wanted to award her the *SA* prize. Bird admitted that he had been the Crandons' houseguest for three weeks—allowing him, his justification went, to move freely about the place, on the lookout for concealed gimmickry. But Houdini attended a meeting at the *Scientific American* offices in July, at which Bird spoke of the problem of bestowing the prize on Margery while keeping her identity hidden, as she wished—implying that the award was imminent. Alarmed, Houdini warned the president of the Scientific American Publishing Company, Orson D. Munn, that handing over his cash to Margery would "make a laughing stock of his paper." He offered to forfeit a thousand dollars if he failed to "detect her in fraud." A series of sittings with Margery was arranged for him and some other committee members, to begin on July 23.

Having arrived in Boston, Houdini dined with the always-hospitable Crandons but stayed at the Copley Plaza Hotel. "It is not possible to stop at one's house [*sic*]," he explained, "break bread with *him* frequently, then investigate *him* and render an impartial verdict." Unlike Bird, who remained a houseguest at 10 Lime Street, Houdini would not in any case have been welcome, and not only because of his growing reputation as a fraud-buster. At a séance two weeks earlier, the irrepressible Walter had broken out a bit of singsong jewbaiting: "Harry Houdini, he sure is a Sheeny." Walter's hate was privately shared by Dr. Crandon, who in a letter to Sir Arthur Conan Doyle expressed regret that "this low-minded Jew has any claim on the word American." Crandon's literate, well-bred air in fact masked a seething defensiveness toward most of his wife's investigators. He had them hand over signed copies of their notes after each sitting, in effect depositions he could use to impeach public announcements they might make later. "I have the material to crucify them," he told Doyle, "and they know I shall not hesitate to treat them surgically if necessary." Welcome or not, Houdini was fairly impressed with 10 Lime Street, and with his hostess: "Very nice home, neat taste," he noted in his diary. "Mrs. Crandon is an attractive woman, which explains Bird's reports."

For the first sitting, in the top-floor séance room, Houdini was joined by Dr. Crandon, Bird, Munn, and an assistant of Dr. Comstock's named Conant. For various reasons, the other SA committee members did not or could not attend, so the session was not considered official. Houdini studied the seating and handholding arrangements, mindful of a crafty technique used by Palladino. Under cover of darkness, she would maneuver into one of her hands the fingers of sitters on either side of her. That led the sitters to feel and believe they each held one of her hands, but in fact left a hand free.

With Margery seated at a table just within her screen-cabinet, Houdini sat at her left, holding her left hand with his right. He also positioned his right foot against her left foot, pressing her ankle. Dr. Crandon sat at her right, across from Houdini, holding her right hand. The committee members distrusted Crandon's very presence at the sittings. But Bird, typically, argued that the phenomena were stronger with Crandon present and speculated that he might be a "co-medium." He proposed that in order to preserve Crandon's psychic force while eliminating the possibility of confederacy, he would sit at the edge of the group, enclosing in one of his hands the fingers of both Margery and her husband. Houdini apparently consented, although he thought the arrangement fishy, since it left one of Bird's own hands free.

In the darkness, with Houdini and the other sitters joined hand-to-hand in a circle, Walter signaled his coming by a whistle, then began whispering. Several times the spirit of Margery's brother nudged Houdini's right leg. Eerily it rang the so-called bell-box, a quasi-scientific apparatus that had been introduced into the earlier Margery séances by Dr. Comstock, the former MIT engineer. Sort of a wooden shoebox, it had a clapper-like, jointed lid held up by a spring; pressing the lid rang an electric bell inside. Bird considered the bell-box proof-positive, "the climax of the mediumship, so far as sheer inescapable demonstration of validity is concerned." At that evening's session the box was set on the floor between Houdini's legs, his right foot posted between it and Margery's left foot. Just the same the bell within the box rang.

Two other strong manifestations occurred when Bird momentarily left the dark room to retrieve a plaque for a later test. Walter suddenly called for control. Margery gave Houdini her right hand and pointed out that he now held both her hands. Yet suddenly, violently, the screen in back of her was overthrown and came crashing down. Apparently only moments later, Walter called attention to a megaphone that had been placed in the room. "The megaphone is in the air," his spirit-voice said. "Have Houdini tell me where to throw it." As Margery now also placed both her feet near his, Houdini asked Walter to throw the megaphone toward him. It instantly fell at his feet. It fell there even though he had both of Margery's' hands and feet secure, so that there was no possibility of her using them. The ringing bell-box, toppling screen, and spirit-flung megaphone dominated the evening, but the lesser effects included the illuminated plaque levitating itself and standing afloat at a sixty-degree angle, and a self-starting, self-stopping Victrola.

After this initial séance Bird drove Houdini and Munn back to the Copley Plaza Hotel, but first parked on Beacon Street so they could discuss what they had witnessed. "I've got her," Houdini said as they sat in the car. "All fraud."

Houdini had seen no reason in the Crandons' civility to drop his guard, and he had come to Lime Street with a secret sensitometer. Knowing that the bell-box would be tested, he had kept his right leg below the knee firmly wound all day in a rubber bandage. By the time of the séance the leg was swollen and tender, hypersensitive to any movement of Margery's leg as it pressed his. In the darkness he also rolled up his trouser-leg so that her silk stocking contacted his bared sore skin. During the bell-box experiment he could feel her ankle slowly sliding against him as she gained space to raise her foot off the floor and push the clapper. When the bell finally rang, as he later wrote, "I *positively felt* the tendons of her leg flex and tighten as she repeatedly touched the ringing apparatus. . . . Then, when the ringing was over, I plainly *felt her leg slide back* into its original position." As for the screen, Houdini decided that as Bird left the pitchdark room to get the plaque, momentarily breaking control, Margery tilted a corner of the screen enough to get her free foot underneath. She capsized it as the tests began again, merely by raising her foot. "I distinctly felt her body give and sway," Houdini reported, "as though she had made a vigorous lunge."

The megaphone was something else, "the '*slickest*' ruse I have ever detected," Houdini called it. Margery had, after all, somehow managed to throw the megaphone in his direction while he held her hands and feet. How? By using a confederate, he thought at first. But he recalled having heard or read about an Austrian medium who in a recent test with Schrenck-Notzing had apported a stone. The medium hid the stone under his chair but in the darkness transferred it to the top of his head, from where he could drop it on the table at any time, even with his hands and feet secured. In Bird's brief absence Margery had not only slipped her foot beneath the screen but had also lifted the megaphone from the floor and set it on her head, duncecap-style. When the séance resumed, Houdini decided, "she simply jerked her head, causing the megaphone to fall at my feet."

Houdini's explanations convinced Munn. But not Bird: "Either he is as dum [sic] as I think he is," Houdini wrote Bess, "or the good time he is having causes him to mislead the public." Whatever Bird's brainpower or pleasant mooching at Lime Street, he resented Houdini's easy assumption of superiority, his air of having after one sitting seen through deceptions that had fooled other committee members for thirty. Houdini came on, Bird wrote, as "the one member whose abilities were of any moment." In truth Houdini was too long accustomed to headlining every bill and being president of every crowd to be a team player. His private account of his work with his colleagues lived up to Bird's description. "I caught her red-handed after she had given forty-eight [sic] seances and was pronounced genuine by them. I was not called in until they had Failed." It needs adding on Houdini's behalf that however smug and garbled, this was basically true. But Bird could stomach neither his conceit nor his keenness. Some time later Bird reminded him that the stopping and starting of the Victrola remained unexplained. Houdini looked at him, he said, with a "very foxy leer" and claimed he knew how that was done too: "somebody," Houdini said, "got up and stopped it."

Before a follow-up séance the next evening, Bird confirmed Houdini's worst suspicions about his closeness with the Crandons. At some time during the day Houdini spoke with Margery. She said she felt offended by his comments to the committee, especially his saying that he had caught her foot tapping the bell-box. Houdini's report had been meant for the members only, of course, and he tried to learn how she had found out about it: "she positively admitted Bird having told her," he wrote, "but asked me not to say anything to Bird about it." He half-obeyed her. That evening, in Bird's presence, he told Munn that Bird had broken the committee's rule of confidentiality. Bird denied it, leaving Houdini stuck for proof, as he had promised Margery to say nothing to Bird about her disclosure. But he was not willing to let Bird get off. Without going into details, he explained that Margery had mentioned his claim to have detected her, that he had seen Bird speaking privately with her, and that he put two and two together. He left hanging the accusation that Bird was a snitch.

Maybe because of Houdini's report to the committee, test conditions that night were tightened. The session was moved from Lime Street to Comstock's rooms, in an apartment hotel on Beacon Street. Margery was searched beforehand, disrobing and taking down her hair to be examined by Comstock's female secretary. The seating and handholding arrangements remained the same, but this time Houdini planned to investigate aggressively. One of his great advantages, he felt, was that having for years worked inside trunks and packing cases he had learned to maneuver without light. He forewarned Munn, seated to his left, that he might let go of his hand in the darkness—freeing his own hand to explore.

The séance began about nine, Walter touching Houdini's knee and chortling, "Ha, ha, Houdini." Margery's screen shivered, the megaphone slid around the floor, the Victrola stopped. But the bell-box failed to ring. Houdini himself was puzzled. He had again rolled up his trouser-leg and again felt Margery's leg muscles working against him, but nothing happened. Margery said:

"You have garters on, haven't you?"
"Yes," I replied.
"Well, the buckle hurts me."

Reaching down to undo his garter, Houdini discovered why the bell had stayed silent: his garter-buckle had snagged Margery's stocking. Once he took the garter off, the ringing began: "She made so bold a sliding movement with her ankle to reach the box that I think she was under the impression that I was badly fooled or was going to help her like others."

If Margery counted on Houdini's going along, as she may have, she was badly mistaken. Forty-five minutes into the séance, Walter ordered the sitters to move back from the table—so that he could gather force—then move in again. The table was no more than a card table, with the bell-box now resting on it. Although the controls made it impossible for Margery to move her hands or feet, the table began rocking and tilting, the bell-box sliding off. Its spooky movements are described in an "Ediphone" record dictated by Dr. Crandon during the seance:

> Pause, 9:50. Houdini says the table is falling over on him. At present it is leaned up against him, that is it is on two legs. . . .
> Pause, 9:52½. There was a fairly loud sound of the table. Houdini says the table has dropped back again on four legs. . . .

A few minutes later, startlingly, the table completely overturned:

> Pause, 9:55. Table is being upset. Mr. Munn says. Box dropped off the table onto the floor. This was at 9:56. At the instant when the table went over Houdini, Bird and Conant all report that all of their controls were perfect. . . .

Crandon made his dictation in order to have a basis for challenging accounts of the séance made by the committee members. But he failed to record and did not notice that, as the table began to move, Houdini dropped Munn's hand, as forewarned, and groped underneath.

What Houdini sensed there was Margery's head. When the sitters pushed back their chairs at Walter's instruction, Margery had enough room to bend forward, get her head under the table, and lever it up and over with the back of her skull. To make sure of what he thought he sensed, Houdini groped again: "*she ran her head directly against my outstretched fingers,*" he wrote, "I do not think she was more surprised than I."

Trying to cover up, Margery said something about dropping hairpins, and cagily appeared after the séance with her hair loosened. But Houdini met with the committee members in another room, told them what he had found, and demanded that she be exposed as soon as possible. Bird objected, but Houdini pointed out that the committee had rapidly exposed other mediums who tried to fleece them. As Bird saw the situation, Houdini was fired up to grab headlines by descending on New York with "a flaming newspaper expose." What cooled him down, Bird said, was a pledge of sittings with Margery before the full committee next month, followed by the issuance of an official report. For whatever reason, Houdini agreed for the moment to keep quiet.

Houdini suspected, however, that Bird had tipped off Margery about his latest discoveries too. He entered some memos in his diary, on the midnight train back to New York: "Bird is a *traitor*.. . . He must have helped her at seances. He is very intimate with her." However disgusted with Bird, Houdini felt pleased with himself. Margery was "a slick performer," and he had found her out. By about six in the morning he was back at 278— "elated," he noted, "and very tired."

WALTER FRANKLIN PRINCE; THE AUGUST SITTINGS

The official sittings with Margery were arranged for late August. Over the monthlong break Houdini tried to restrain Bird. By his account he got Bird to admit to publisher Munn that Margery had "wormed things out of him by cross-examining him." He persuaded Munn to curb Bird's future work for the committee, requiring Bird to show the members his reports before he sent them to New York, and forbidding him to discuss the séances publicly until the series ended. At considerable expense to Munn, Houdini also had him withdraw from the September *Scientific American*, already in press, an article by Bird praising Margery's mediumship.

Actually Bird had grown even closer to the Crandons than Houdini sensed. When in Boston, Bird often stayed overnight at Lime Street, and accompanied the Crandons to the theater. A steady stream of letters passed between them. Dr. Crandon addressed the committee secretary as "Birdie" and virtually dictated his announcements and activities on Margery's behalf. Bird in turn confided to Crandon his gleeful scorn for Houdini, "the sardonic enjoyment I get out of maneuvering him into difficult positions from which it is very hard for him to escape." He evidently shared Crandon's prejudices too: "Houdini is a Jew," he wrote later, as if that said enough, "his paternal name being Weiss."

While keeping Bird leashed, Houdini sought an ally for the new sittings in Walter Franklin Prince, one of the original committee members. Slope-shouldered, paunchy, and hard-of-hearing, Prince had a doctorate in psychology from Yale, and was the chief research officer of the American Society for Psychical Research, as well as the only American, except William James, ever elected president of the British SPR. He considered himself, and was, a cautious, hardheaded empiricist, "a kind of scrutinizing, analyzing and rationalizing monster," he wrote, "quite unpleasant to the tender-minded." Bird thought him a cantankerous pain, "one of those people in whom rugged intellectual honesty sticks out all over, like spines on a cactus." The feeling was mutual. Like Houdini, Prince thought Bird's views "half-baked," and questioned both the lights-out groundrule of the Margery séances and Crandon's handholding presence at his wife's side, "no matter how distinguished a surgeon he may be." He had had little to do with the committee since the early sittings. Their journalistic atmosphere, he felt, compromised his scientific integrity. He had become "disgusted beyond the point of endurance" and was ready to resign.

Yet Prince enjoyed magic, and liked and respected Houdini, up to a point. Like many others, he found Houdini imperious, unable to brook rivalry or even cooperation: "he could hardly credit any sagacity on the part of other persons than himself." Largely because Prince argued by evidence and strong logic, however, he could frankly point out Houdini's limitations to him without turning him gaga with rage—an ability no one else could claim. And he believed that Houdini was willing to acknowledge Margery's psychic power if she could demonstrate it. Perhaps for that reason and out of personal affection he agreed to work with Houdini during the new sittings. To Bird they seemed an unholy alliance, leagued up to take over the committee: "They got together," he said, "agreed on a program, and jammed it through as far as they were able."

With Prince's approval Houdini did try to ordain the place, time, and conditions of the official sittings. He encountered not much resistance because, of the three other committee members, Professor McDougall could not be located, and Hereward Carrington, the psychical researcher (and amateur magician), stood ready to endorse Margery as genuine, and felt no need to attend. Houdini proposed holding the séances in New York or at Harvard, to "neutralize the tests." Dr. Crandon settled on again using Comstock's Boston apartment. Houdini insisted, however, that the series not be scheduled during his appearances, on a new Orpheum tour, at the Boston Keith's. He wanted to devote all his time to the séances, he said, and especially to avoid any appearance of publicity-seeking.

The committee also imposed stiff new controls on Margery. In consultation Houdini, Munn, Prince, and Comstock decided to devise a restraint that would leave her comfortable but secure her independently of the sitters. Houdini came up with the idea of a roomy wooden box, made of inch-thick boards. It resembled a health-club steam-cabinet, except for side ports through which Margery could extend her arms. The bell-box would be placed on a table in front of the cabinet. Margery would be challenged to evoke a ring while she sat inside, her agile feet entirely enclosed. Houdini, no slouch at designing boxes, volunteered to supply the apparatus. He realized that once Margery saw the cabinet she might refuse to enter. If so, he said, "we will simply have another point against her." He sketched what he wanted, and turned over the cabinetmaking to his assistant Jim Collins. In case alterations were needed, he brought Collins along with the bulky box when he went to Boston for the first sitting on August 25, a Monday.

Bird did not attend. Publisher Munn apparently had gone beyond Houdini's demands and, according to Houdini's understanding, arranged to keep Bird away from the new series altogether. The séance began with a battle of wits anyway. On seeing Houdini's cabinet for the first time, Margery rejected part of his design—a six-inch-wide wooden frame, covered with fine wire screening. One of the front boards of the cabinet could be removed and replaced by the screen. Houdini explained, plausibly enough, that the screen would allow Margery to pass ectoplasm through the cabinet, should she project an ectoplasmic rod to ring the bell-box. But clearly the screen could be used for another purpose as well: for suddenly shining a flashlight through the cabinet to see what she was doing inside. But Margery was just as tricky as Houdini. She refused to sit behind the screen, on the also-plausible ground that the committee might charge her with extending wires through the mesh. Her round.

Round two was a draw. The Crandons insisted that Margery be permitted to try out the cabinet before the session began. She had to be sure it was comfortable, they contended, and to get Walter's consent to its use. Houdini partly countered by insisting that he must remain in the room until she had seated herself in the cabinet, and the apparatus was sealed by fastening the top—two flaps, as in a sweat-box, with semicircles that met around her neck. He won the point. But after Margery was locked in, the committee withdrew to another room, allowing the Crandons to hold their private trial, with some séance-friends. The circle sat for half an hour, during which Walter reportedly whistled, talked, and OKd the box for the official test.

The séance began at 9:45, and with a bang. Arms through the portholes, Margery sat in her cabinet, the bell-box on a table that nearly touched its front. Houdini held her left hand, his own left hand holding Munn, who held Crandon, who completed the circle by holding Margery's right hand. Prince took over the exiled Bird's spot, sitting at the edge of the circle grasping the hands of both Margery and her husband. After seven or eight minutes, as the committee waited to hear whether the bell-box would ring, there was a violent clatter. Houdini realized at once what it represented: the collarlike top of the sweatbox was being broken open. Thinking fast, he decided that the Crandons would say Walter had done the mischief—a victory for them. Beating them to it, he immediately announced that anyone sitting inside the cabinet could shoulder open the flaps, which were held together by nothing more than "two thin brass strips."

Houdini's suspicions went beyond Walter, though. He believed that Margery had been trying to raise herself up inside the cabinet, stretch her neck, and depress the bell-box with her head, rather as she earlier had managed to tilt and overturn the card table. When he said as much, Crandon demanded to know how his wife could carry off such a primitive fraud when Houdini and the others had constructed, as they said they had, a fraud-proof restraint. Houdini observed that he and Prince could defeat Margery if, instead of sitting in the circle, each held one of her hands as she sat in the cabinet, making it impossible for her to rise inside. The exchanges became so sharp that it was decided to take a fifteen-minute break before continuing the séance.

The sitters resumed their places at 10:35, in an oh-no-you-don't air of heightened distrust. With Margery again cooped up, they waited for the bell, but nothing happened. Eight minutes later Walter needled Houdini for inventing vaudeville dates at jacked-up salaries and, more important, blamed him for sabotaging the proceedings:

> WALTER: Houdini . . . You think you're smart, don't you? How much are they paying you for stopping phenomena here?
> HOUDINI: I don't know what you're talking about; it's costing me $2,500 a week to be here.
> WALTER: Where did you turn down a $2,500 contract in August?
> HOUDINI: In Buffalo.
> WALTER: You had no work for all this week. How much are you getting for stopping these phenomena?

Walter instructed Comstock to take the bell-box out of the séance room and examine it in the light, which Comstock did. Wedged into the angle of the clapper, near the hinge, he found a pencil-top rubber eraser. It did not prevent the lid from closing and completing the circuit. But Comstock estimated that with the stub jammed in place, it took about four times more force than before to ring the bell.

This time no one barked accusations. But Houdini believed that the Crandons had planted the eraser to cast suspicion on the committee, and keenly felt that he was the leading suspect. He volunteered that he did not know of the eraser and had not placed it there. Surely with some spite, he asked whether Walter thought he had—"to which," he wrote later, "Walter did not reply." The discovery of the eraser left the séance floundering, and the members adjourned for the night.

Not to be caught off guard again, Houdini prepared for the next day's session cautiously. In the morning he and Collins modified the cabinet, adding hasps and staples so that the top could be padlocked. Dr. Crandon had required that the half-moon cutouts for Margery's neck be enlarged for her comfort. Whether Houdini gave in is unknown, but he believed the Crandons were scheming. After the séance he had observed them from another room; backs toward him, they had stood near the cabinet measuring the neck opening. Trying to keep a step ahead of them, Houdini tested his taunt that if he and Prince held Margery's hands, she would be unable to ring the bell-box. This turned out to be a bad mistake. By having Collins and Conant grasp his own hands as he sat in the cabinet, Houdini found that, using the seat as a foothold, he could stretch his body and reach the bell-box, twenty-two inches in front of him, with his forehead. On the chance that the Crandons might try to exploit his too-hasty dare, he typed up and signed a statement retracting it.

For all his looking-out, Houdini failed to anticipate one surprise. When he arrived for the séance that evening, there was J. Malcolm Bird. Bird wanted to know why he had been shut out, and what the objections were to his being there. Houdini bluntly told him that he had "betrayed the Committee" and hindered its work. When Bird denied it, Houdini reminded him of his admission that Margery had "wormed things" out of him. "Well," Bird humphed, "then I will resign as Secretary." According to Houdini the committee then and there accepted his resignation and elected Prince in his place. Bird told the story differently: because of Houdini's ability to cow the committee, he said, he decided to "refuse to attend further sittings with him," leaving the tests to the two "self-constituted dictators." Whatever the case, Bird walked out of the room. "When do you leave for New York?" Houdini asked. "You go to hell," Bird said.

The session was further stalled by jockeying for position. While Houdini had been trying to outguess the Crandons, they had been trying to outguess him. Dr. Crandon pressed for a change in seating arrangements. Probably having heard from Bird that, in an earlier sitting, Munn had freed Houdini's hand to rove, he demanded that Comstock, not Munn, hold Houdini's left hand and pledge not to let go at any time. More than that: while clasping Houdini's hand, Munn must hold it to Houdini's head, resting his elbow on Houdini's shoulder. Houdini was sure that the weird control aimed at pinning him down, "so that in case she used any instrument of any nature, I could not discover it in the dark." The committee gained a tactical advantage for itself in having Prince moved from outside the circle to inside, replacing Crandon in holding Margery's right hand.

Nothing else in the many séances sponsored by *Scientific American* set off such to-the-bitter-end controversy as did the first test of the evening. Seated again in the cabinet with the bell-box on the table, Margery was to take up Houdini's dare, producing rings while he and Prince controlled her hands. Houdini may have been playing a chancy game, counting on her to fail but ready with his signed disclaimer if she succeeded. In any case, Margery was searched beforehand, although the nature of the search itself became hotly contested. According to Crandon and his faction, Houdini rejected an offer to subject Margery to a full anatomical examination by a physician of the committee's choosing, or even to examine her himself— rejected it because the last thing he wanted, they said, was proof of her honesty. Houdini's account mentions no such offer, noting only that Margery was taken to an adjoining room and gone over by a female stenographer. But once Margery entered the cabinet, at about 9:15, he reached a hand inside, presumably through a porthole, and affirmed that he found nothing there but her. The padlocks were inspected, the bell-box was tested, the lights were extinguished, and the session at last began.

Within ten minutes it became a hanging party—with the difference that it was uncertain who should be hanged. As Margery was being padlocked into the box, Houdini noticed that she was "pulling down on her neck," as if reaching for something. Once the séance started, he again and again told Prince not to release her right hand, as he sat on the other side of the box holding her left. In the darkness he also called out to the stenographer to record each one of his instructions. He repeated them so often that Prince, not knowing what he had in mind, resented it, he said, "thinking that I thought he might not understand." Margery herself questioned Houdini:

> "Why do you keep saying, 'don't let go'? What do you mean by, 'don't let go until the release, until the box is opened'?" These are not her exact words, but I remember distinctly saying—"Do you really want to know," and she answered, "Yes."
> I replied,—"Well, I will tell you. In case you have anything smuggled in the cabinet-box, you could not now conceal it."

At least according to his own account, Houdini had allowed Margery to convict herself. As he saw her "pulling down on her neck," he decided she might have taken an instrument into her enclosure, something he had done countless times himself. He kept quiet for the moment, letting her do what she wanted. Then, with Prince's help, he so clutched her hands that she was helpless to conceal the evidence of fraud, whatever it was, now locked up with her inside the cabinet—a fruit of guilt begging to be pounced on, plucked.

But Margery kept her wits. At 9:23, a familiar low whistle heralded the visitation of Walter. He began speaking in a loud, clear voice, damning his sister's predicament as a setup. In Houdini's record

> Walter says:— "Houdini, you are very clever indeed but it won't work."
> Walter says:—"I suppose it was an accident those things were left in the cabinet?"
> Houdini asks:—"What was left in the cabinet?"
> Walter says:—"Pure accident, was it?"
> Walter says:—"You were not here Houdini but Collins was."

A carpenter's folding-ruler, Walter went on, would be found in the cabinet, under a pillow at his sister's feet. He strongly implied that Houdini or Collins had planted it there to convict Margery. "Houdini, you God damned son of a bitch," he shouted, "get the Hell out of here and never come back." Walter's foulmouthing was no surprise to Margery's sitters, but his vehemence came as a shock. Houdini took the cursing-out with a philosophical pleasure, however, at least in writing up the episode: "it just expressed Mrs. Crandon's feelings to me," he decided, "as she knew I had her trapped."

A folding-ruler: Houdini well knew the reaching-rods often used by fraudulent mediums. In the dark, push-up poles or collapsible fishing rods could be opened out even to six or eight feet, to knock over a distant glass or make a luminous handkerchief dance near the ceiling. Houdini himself owned a pencil, made of thin steel, that could be extended to four feet. He believed that Margery intended to keep the tool hidden until the second test, when her arms were to be withdrawn into the cabinet and the portholes boarded up. To ring the bell-box in front of her, she could easily open the folding-ruler its full length, slip it extended through the neckhole, and manipulate it to depress the clapper.

With the obvious necessity of searching the cabinet hanging over the séance, and threatening to condemn either Houdini or Margery, the sitters drifted for fifteen minutes or so, figuring out how to proceed. Comstock came up with a possible facesaver for both sides. He suggested that during construction of the cabinet, a ruler or other instrument might have been left inside accidentally. The company agreed to turn on a red light, suspending but not ending the session, and in the semi-darkness to summon Jim Collins from another room. Wary of being entrapped himself, Houdini asked that someone explain the circumstances to Collins before he did, to eliminate any possibility of collusion. Munn went off and briefed Collins, who said that his folding-ruler could not be in the cabinet because at the moment it was in his hip pocket. When Collins entered the séance room to speak to the full committee, Houdini had him take (and later write out and sign) an oath, avowing the truth of his statement "by the life of his mother."

With nothing settled and the cabinet still locked, the séance continued at 9:45. Walter reappeared and apologized for having cursed Houdini. The company would understand why he spoke so, he said, being "a brother of the kid," but he asked to have his "nasty words" stricken from the record (they stayed in). The red light was turned on and off, the bell-box retested, and the séance went on for an hour, but with no manifestations. All the participants obviously wanted to avoid dealing with the cabinet that stood before them, no less a steam-box than a time-bomb. Comstock later described the atmosphere as "volcanic. . . . All of us were on edge."

At last, at 10:53, Houdini suggested opening the cabinet. As he and Prince tightly grasped Margery's hands, to the last moment, the padlocks were undone, the flaps lifted. On the floor of the cabinet lay a narrow sectional ruler, folded into six inches but two-feet long when extended—more than long enough to reach the bell-box from inside.

Houdini's or Margery's? With a second test scheduled for the same night, and a final official séance for the next day, neither side made charges. Anyway Houdini and Prince had agreed on a policy of non-interference, letting Margery go "as far as she liked in her 'stunts,'" Houdini wrote, and making no attempt to stop her "until everything was over." According to Crandon, however—and to no one else—Houdini told her, "I am willing to forget this, if you are." Collins was called in once more, this time to look at the actual ruler. He said it did not belong to him. Houdini turned the ruler over to the stenographer, asking her to mark and hold it as "an exhibit."

An effort was made to test Margery inside the boarded-up cabinet. She sweltered there until nearly midnight, without activating the bell-box or producing anything else phenomenal. At the end she said, "I do not believe any medium could manifest under these conditions." It was the wrong thing to tell Houdini, one-time prince of jail escapes, who offered to be stripped to the skin, searched by surgeon Crandon, and boxed without portholes, and still ring the bell: "*I'll do it right now!*" Comstock remarked that it would prove nothing. "Oh, yes it would," Houdini said. "It would prove that these things could be accomplished by trickery."

Houdini stayed chin-out the next day, in the wake of the unresolved ruler episode, but Margery felt combative too. Before the last sitting, they dined together with Prince, Munn, and Dr. Crandon outside Boston. According to Houdini, Margery said that she had heard he planned to expose her during a performance at the Boston Keith's—Bird again, he suspected. She protested that she did not want her twelve-year-old son to read that his mother was a fraud. "Then don't be a fraud," Houdini told her. She came back with a threat:

> "If you misrepresent me from the stage at Keith's some of my friends will come up and give you a good beating."
>
> "I am not going to misrepresent you," I replied, "they are not coming on the stage and I am not going to get a beating."

Still chippy that evening, Houdini arrived for the séance with an "athletic suit" (presumably gym shorts and top), offering to be stripsearched and to wear the scanty outfit during the sitting, "lest anything should turn up and suspicion should be directed towards me." Crandon said he was willing for Houdini to sit in his street clothes.

The sour generosity on both sides was unnecessary: the séance failed. With Houdini and Prince again holding Margery's hands, the cabinet was replaced by a new control-apparatus devised by Comstock—a knee-high compartment into which Margery and an investigator opposite her placed their legs, the bell-box set to her left. The bell-box did not ring. Nor were there any other manifestations, except a warning from Walter. At one point Margery said it would be wonderful if Houdini himself went into a trance state. "If Houdini were seized in a trance," her husband added, "I would give $10,000 to charity." Houdini dryly replied, "It may happen—but I doubt it." The dismal session was called to an end after an hour, another total blank.

Houdini thought about the blank séances when he returned to the Copley Plaza Hotel that night. For him Margery's' failure to perform clinched the fact that he had caught her out. In writing his final report to the committee, he directly accused her of sneaking the folding-ruler into the cabinet. Generalizing about the five sittings he attended, he pulled no other punches either: "I charge Mrs. Crandon with practising daily her feats like a professional conjurer," he concluded. "She is not simple and guileless, but a shrewd, cunning woman."

But Houdini's mood was not just accusatory. On leaving the hotel next morning, he ran into his old vaudeville crony W. C. Fields, in trademark straw hat. Houdini had Collins snap a picture of them together, which he later sent on to Fields, who said he had been glad to see "Friend Harry" again, "and to find you looking so well and happy."

FIFTEEN

AUGUST 1924—FEBRUARY 1925

THE COMMITTEE DELIBERATIONS

Although shrouded in the darkness or red light of the séance room, the Margery tests became glaringly public events, covered by newspapers throughout the United States and abroad. Houdini relished the publicity, different from the sort he won for jumping off bridges. Reporting the blank August sittings, the *New York Times* commented: "Sir Arthur Conan Doyle is a detective after [the spirits'] heart, but a gentleman who knows everything about legerdemain makes them very uncomfortable." "A most remarkable compliment," Houdini wrote on his clipping of this. "Three of the great newspapers of the world The New York Times, New York World and New York Tribune, use Houdini materials and in Editorial. I certainly feel complimented."

Having exposed Margery as a charlatan, he believed, Houdini was anxious for the *Scientific American* committee to issue its report denying her the prize. In part he wanted her methods revealed, and at least equally to let the world know it was he who had seen through them. But like many other prize juries, the *SA* committee reached a decision only after bickering, posturing, and delay, vexed by almost as much behind-the-scenes intrigue as the séances themselves. The original five members had never sat together at the same time with Margery, and disagreed on what they had seen and what it meant. Approaches also differed: some took a scientific attitude—detached observation, empirical proof; Houdini took a Handcuff King attitude—surprise the hell out of everybody, be carried back to your hotel by the crowd. After the August tests Prince, now the committee's secretary, estimated that agreeing on a report would take a few weeks. It took nearly six months. In that time the public awaited the decision as expectantly as they might the jury verdict in a celebrity murder trial. And Houdini's impatience with his fellow committee members rose through stages of woundedness and outrage until he took them all on in a public brawl.

To double his frustration, as Prince tried to work out an agreement Houdini was forced to watch from afar and while gagged. Early in September he began a three-week Keith's tour (needles, straitjacket, subtrunk), followed by an eight-week lecture tour of the West, on the topic "Can the Dead Speak?" Until he returned to New York in December, he got no closer to the deliberations than letters back and forth to Prince from one-night stands in places as far off as Pocatello, San Francisco, and Chapel Hill ("College boys. Great audience. Gave me the college yell"). Worse, committee members had been sworn to reveal nothing about the sittings until they could agree on a single report. Yet Dr. Crandon and the ousted Bird were under no such burden, and both gave the press descriptions of the séances that Houdini considered black lies. Crandon, for instance, told some Boston newspapers that Houdini had refused to allow anyone to examine the cabinet; in fact, according to Houdini, everyone in the committee had gone inside it. In not replying, so as to honor his committee vow, Houdini acted for once with restraint, but not without pain. "I honestly want to keep my obligation to keep silent," he moaned to Prince, "but you must allow me to defend myself, please." Meanwhile Crandon spread insinuations that Houdini had spiked the bell-box with the eraser and loaded the folding-ruler, the case against him being, Crandon wrote, "circumstantial and deductive, the sort of thing which convicts most murderers."

While honoring his vow to say nothing, however, Houdini refused to *do* nothing. Probably to get the deliberations unstuck, he proposed to Prince that the committee kick out its most convinced defender of Margery, Hereward Carrington (Hubert Lavington [1880–1958]). A well-versed amateur magician and a prolific writer on psychical research, Carrington had known Houdini for fifteen years or more, visited him at 278, and published such works as *Handcuff Tricks and Escapes* (1913) and *Magic For Every*

One (1920). He had sat with many of the foremost mediums in America and abroad. His knowledge of magic and his skepticism made him no easy mark for séance fraud. But he believed that consciousness survives the dissolution of the organism. He reportedly intended to photograph the "astral body" of a cat by forcing it from the animal's unconscious physical body into water vapor—before trying a similar experiment on a human.

Carrington had not joined Houdini for the tests because earlier sittings with Margery had already convinced him of her genuineness. But Houdini had a different explanation, which he offered to Prince as a reason for ousting Carrington. He believed that Carrington—like Bird, a frequent houseguest of the Crandons—had helped Margery fake her manifestations and feared being found out. Whether Prince credited this or not, he had no power to act, since the committee had been appointed by *Scientific American*. Houdini took his suit to the publishers and let it be known through the press that Carrington was "not qualified to sit or pass judgment on any spiritualistic investigation." Carrington at first replied mildly, characterizing Houdini, during a church lecture, as "clever and sincere" although not "entirely fair." But before long Houdini was proclaiming that Carrington had purchased a phony Ph.D. degree for seventy-five dollars in Oskaloosa, and Carrington was clobbering him, in the *New York Times*, as a "pure publicist." Despite Houdini's fulminating, Carrington remained on the committee, joining Bird in Houdini's mind as a single hated entity, always thenceforth mentioned together, a Carrington-and-Bird.

Some small relief for Houdini's mounting irritation, and the growing public curiosity, came in mid-October, when *Scientific American* and the *Times* published a preliminary committee report. It did no more than acknowledge that the group was divided, and briefly give the views of each member. Prince stated that the experiments had not proved to him "scientifically and conclusively" the exercise of "supernormal powers." Comstock agreed that Margery had furnished no "rigid proof" but added that "the case at present is interesting and should be investigated further." The hard-to-locate McDougall, who had been unavailable for the séances, could not be reached for an opinion either. Beside these equivocations-or-less, Carrington and Houdini spoke in relative thunder. Carrington enthused: "genuine supernormal (physical) phenomena frequently occur at her seances." Houdini sneered: "everything which took place at the seances which I attended was a deliberate and conscious fraud." The *Times* gave

Dr. Crandon space to comment on the report, but he chose mainly to answer Houdini. He said it had been apparent from the beginning that Houdini would charge fraud, and he warned that it might become necessary to let the public know the truth about him, "as a man, as a psychic investigator and as a member of the Scientific American committee. We hope not."

The publication of the committee report, however inconclusive, released the members from their vow of confidentiality, at last freeing Houdini to speak out. Early in November he published an illustrated forty-page pamphlet entitled *Houdini Exposes the tricks used by the Boston Medium "Margery."* Hungry for his overdue recognition as the unmasker of Margery's secrets, he issued it at his own cost and spent some $2,500 on advertising. The cover photo showed him inside the cabinet, the bell-box on the table before him, his upper torso thrust forward so he could depress the clapper with his head. The pamphlet explained how Margery threw the megaphone, tipped the screen, and so on, illustrating her maneuvers in convincing photographs and drawings. It openly indicted Dr. Crandon as her confederate, and implicated Carrington-and-Bird in their flummoxing. On his lecture tour Houdini also began demonstrating some of Margery's methods from the stage, well aware that her supporters would challenge him. "Am looking forward with great interest," he wrote a friend, "as to the alibi the folks interested will make."

With the national press eager to cover a possibly scandalous set-to involving Houdini, Margery's backers raised a small army in her defense. In December the sixty-five churches of the Illinois State Spiritualists' Association staged a mass protest in Chicago's Orchestra Hall. The city's newspapers reported that the speakers praised the honesty of Bird and Carrington, while putting down Houdini's demonstrations as "a few silly tricks" and dismissing him as ignorant, an "itinerant paid magician"—a slight he would not forget. Eastern newspapers carried unnerving headlines with some variant of DEATH PLOT AIMED AT HOUDINI. The stories related that several Boston mediums had forecast Houdini's death within a year as punishment for impugning Margery. The *Boston American* depicted him as "exceptionally put out" over such mysticalized threats. In several interviews he laughed them off as preposterous. But he added that if he now became the victim of a lethal accident, Margery's champions could make it seem his doom. "Can you imagine what these worthy Boston witch-doctors will claim," he told one reporter, "if by chance, [I start] to cross Fifth Avenue . . . and don't get to the other side."

Houdini's sympathizers spoke out as well. They included Margery's ex-husband, a shopman named Rand, from whom the Crandons still bought their groceries. Calling Margery's mediumship bunk, he revealed in several newspaper interviews that when married to him she had displayed no psychical gift, but had quite ordinarily served as secretary of the Union Congregational Church and performed in amateur theatricals. He gave out unsavory personal details about the Crandons' relationship. Among other tidbits, he disclosed that when Margery and Dr. Crandon met, both were married, Crandon to his second wife. In a messy divorce proceeding, Crandon accused the woman of riding at midnight to a mountaintop with a party of men, "live ones," and not returning until four in the morning. Rand also disclosed that in a recent sitting Walter predicted that Houdini had only one more year to live.

The preliminary report that freed Houdini to speak out about the séances, freed other committee members too, and usually not in his favor. As scientists, Comstock and McDougall bristled at being told by a magician that they had been deceived. The Boston press relayed their views at length, as coming from prominent local academics. Although Comstock remained undecided about Margery, he complained to reporters that Houdini had prejudged her:

> Houdini appeared to be convinced in advance that the phenomena were fraudulent, and always reasoned from that basis. For instance, in discussing a certain test he said to me, "She did that with her hair." "Hold on, Houdini," I interrupted, "how do you know that." "Well, I've been thinking it over," he answered, "and that's the only way it could have happened." You see, he argues in a circle. . . .

McDougall had never sat with Houdini on the committee, but griped to the press about him anyway, for implying that he, Houdini, had saved the members from their own folly: "It makes him seem to have a monopoly of intelligence and of caution. I do not require Houdini to teach me something about which I probably know more than he does." McDougall also let it be known that the magician originally proposed for a place on the committee had been not Houdini, but Howard Thurston.

Coming from respected Cambridge-Boston university men, such stabbing comments cut into the complex resentment that underlay Houdini's respect for intellectuals. From the beginning he had felt that the genteel circumstances of the academic committee members disabled them for spotting sharks. "How can a man trained to deal only with facts and whose mind runs along channels of rectitude," he asked, "hope to cope with an individual whose whole stock in trade is a bag of tricks." Yet when included in *Who's Who*, he protested against being identified as "magician," and asked to be listed instead as an "actor, inventor and author." His distrust of people like Comstock and McDougall and pride in his own intelligence were enough to make remarks like theirs rankle. But on top of that he still felt belittled by his lack of education. When jolted by remarks about the "ignorance of the itinerant paid magician," the sensitive mix of distrust, rivalry, and shame exploded.

"Men like Professor McDougall . . . and Conan Doyle are menaces to mankind," Houdini bellowed in one interview, "because laymen believe them to be as intellectual in all fields as they are in their own particular one." Insulted by McDougall's claim to "probably know more" about psychical research than he, Houdini ripped him for having sat with Margery fifty times without noticing that she cheated: "as an investigator of spiritualism, he may be a great psychologist." To prove that McDougall's academic learning was no substitute for escapological knowhow, he publicly offered a bet, for a stake of the professor's "annual salary at Harvard University." The bet was safe enough: "his knowledge of psychology will be useless to him if he lets me nail him into a heavily weighted packing case and throw him into the Charles River, or, after being stripped nude and searched, he permits me to lock him into one of the numerous cells in Boston." Not content with splattering an egghead, Houdini also wished it known that by heritage he was one himself: "Although I have been called an 'itinerant magician,'" he added, "I come from a family of scholars and generations of culture. . . . Professor McDougall need not hesitate to accept my challenge."

THE SYMPHONY HALL EXPOSÉ

Through his escalating war with the Crandons, Carrington-and-Bird, and now McDougall, Houdini kept pressing for the release of a final committee report that would vindicate him by denying Margery the prize. In mid-

December he wrote to the chief editor of *Scientific American*, E. E. Free, calling on him to act. "We owe it to the public to decide one way or the other," he said. "Either Mrs. Crandon is a genuine medium or she is not, and I respectfully ask that a final decision be rendered." To try to end the impasse, Prince as secretary scheduled new sittings, hoping they might produce decisive results either way.

Houdini, lecturing in the West, could not attend. But he bombarded Prince with pointers on how to manage the test round, certain that "after the cursing she gave me," Margery would "stop at nothing to pull the wool over your eyes." Be sure no one can enter or leave the room in the dark, he warned Prince repeatedly—advice so obvious that Prince stiffened at receiving it, "something," he told Houdini, "like telling a person he should go in when it rains." Prince more willingly accepted Houdini's help in remodeling the bell-box. During the new séances, in December, Margery made the box ring when Prince was controlling her. But the sound seemed to him slightly muffled, and he suspected she had rung a second bell, concealed somewhere on her, that in the dark could pass for the original. By correspondence he and Houdini designed a new box with a small red bulb that would dimly light when the clapper was depressed, indicating that the rings actually came from within.

But after the new sittings, the "scientists(?)," as Houdini privately called his colleagues, still failed to reach a verdict. Exasperated and disillusioned, he decided to break the deadlock himself. Or rather get around it, by in effect writing off the *SA* prize contest and sponsoring one of his own. In a fedora and heavy winter coat, he traveled to Boston's City Hall on December 30, bearing ten thousand dollars in bonds, which he spread in a fan for news photographers before posting with the city collector. He offered half the amount to Margery and the rest in her name to charity, if she appeared with him at Symphony Hall on January 2 or 3 before a select jury, and produced any manifestation that he could not show to be fraudulent. "If Professor McDougall believes in Mrs. Crandon's psychic power," he added, "why does he not urge her to accept my $5,000 challenge, the tests to take place . . . before his class at Harvard University?" He promised that if Margery did not turn up at Symphony Hall for the eight-thirty challenge, he would fill the evening by giving the audience a complete exposé of her séances. In this way, he said, the controversy would once and for all be put to rest: "We can't both be right."

The first evening, Symphony Hall was packed by 7:45. The audience included Boston's rascally Mayor James Curley, flush with graft and kick-backs, and Houdini's medium friend Anna Eva Fay. An overflow of a hundred flanked the stage, together with Houdini's private committee of rabbis, priests, journalists, and magicians. Uncertainty over whether Margery would show up made for suspense, heightened by published reports that, because of threats and dire prophecies from the spirit world, guards had been posted to protect Houdini. It turned out that Margery did not come to either evening; she explained to the press that a magician and a Spiritualist had nothing in common.

In Margery's absence Houdini reenacted all the crises in his séances with her. He draped hoods over the heads of three volunteers to give them the illusion of sitting in the darkened séance room. At the same time he took Margery's place in the circle and worked her deceptions in full stage light for the audience to see. With the back of his head he lifted the table and from the top of it tossed the megaphone, much to the merriment of the crowd and mystification of the hooded sitters. He had Collins bring out the sweat-box—the "Margie Box," he had come to call it. "This is the first time this has been seen outside of the seance room," he announced, "because I was bound to secrecy by the Scientific American." He explained how Margery had forced the top and smuggled in a tool. "I did not know it was a ruler at the time, but I am here to tell you that she called me a vile name. She told me my father was never married to my mother. . . . Culture!"

With this snort at Brahmin Boston, Houdini offered his own variants of Margery's feats. He was locked into the cabinet, a tambourine, a hand-bell, and the bell-box resting before it. A black cloth with slits for his protruding head and hands was thrown over the box, hiding the articles in front. With Houdini locked inside, his head showing and his hands clearly held by the committeemen, the bells rang and the tambourine jumped about beneath the cloth. One-upping Margery again, he invited a volunteer to sit across the table from him, holding his hands and stepping firmly on his feet, beside which rested another bell and tambourine. Despite the seemingly perfect control, the instruments beneath the table began tinkling and jangling. What "convulsed the spectators," as one reporter put it, was what they could see and the dumbfounded sitter across from Houdini could not—Houdini withdrawing his foot from his shoe. Reinforced with a steel toecap, the shoe remained held down by the volunteer's own shoe, giving no sign of movement even while Houdini grabbed the bell handle and tambourine rim with his toes, which stuck out through toeless socks.

Houdini turned his two hours on the stage into a mocking tribunal. He passed sentence not only on Margery but also on Carrington-and-Bird as her confederates, and Spiritualism in general. In his jokey platform style, he got laughs by reading aloud credulous passages from the works of Richet, intoning the magic words "Fizzy, fizzy," and wisecracking: "Sir Arthur states I am a medium. That is not so. I am well done." Ridiculing his ex-friend as a "great big boy," he told the audience that when he informed Doyle, after the Atlantic City séance, that his mother could neither read nor write English, Doyle replied: "when your mother died she went to college and now she is educated." From somewhere in the audience came a tart response that touched Houdini in the wrong place, turning him vicious:

A VOICE: I will tell you one thing, you can't fill a house like Conan Doyle did twice.

MR. HOUDINI: Well, all right, if ever I am such a plagiarist as Conan Doyle, who pinched Edgar Allan Poe's plumes, I will fill all houses. . . .

THE VOICE: Do you call him a thief?

MR. HOUDINI: No, but I say that his story Scandal in Bohemia is only the brilliant letter [*sic*] by Poe. . . . I walked into his room at the Ambassador Hotel [in Atlantic City] and I saw twenty books, French, English and German, a paragraph marked out of each one of the detective stories. I don't say he used them. . . .

Houdini spared McDougall, announcing that he had received an eight-page letter of apology from him that reconciled their differences. (An eight-page apology? Baloney, surely, but they at least had a long talk over dinner at the Harvard Club.) He said that he now considered McDougall a "gentleman and a scholar," and reminded his audience that it takes one to call one: "when they shout the words 'itinerant magician' I want you to come to my home in New York and look at my library."

With this lively public exposé, Houdini might contentedly have rested his case against Margery. But he still felt burned up over the committee's continuing failure to accept his judgment of her as final. A letter and a statement published in the *New York Times* four days after the Symphony

Hall lecture raised his indignation to hopping-hot. The letter questioned his oft-repeated charges of collusion against Bird and Carrington:

> . . . no proof of the culpable conduct so described on the part of the named gentlemen has come to our knowledge directly or through Mr. Houdini. He has indeed made general assertions, but no intelligible specifications, much less proved them in a manner which would be admissible in a court of justice.

To Houdini's sore astonishment, the letter was signed by Prince, the only committee member with whom he had not yet violently quarreled, and by McDougall, to whom he had just given his public blessing as a "gentleman and a scholar."

The *Times* also published, as if it were linked to the letter, an accusation by J. Malcolm Bird. Bird charged that the cabinet and the bell-box Houdini used at Symphony Hall were "entirely different" from the apparatus used to test Margery. He was probably right about the cabinet. Collins had put together more than one, and Houdini's technique of covering the Symphony Hall "Margie box" with a cloth strongly suggests that it was a gaffed replica. Bird was certainly right about the bell-box. At the lecture Houdini was able to make it ring not only by foreheading the clapper, but also from a distance, while the box was moved around the stage—a very different thing. He confided to a friend that, quite as Bird realized, "I was carrying a trick box which rang at command."

Houdini brazened out Bird's statement by calling it "beneath notice" and not answering. But the published letter from Prince and McDougall left him feeling doublecrossed. "There evidently is a mistake," he wrote Prince. "I am really surprised at your action." He pointed out that for months he had petitioned Prince to have Carrington unseated, only to be told that he must address his appeal to *Scientific American.* Yet here was Prince, he said, taking his criticism of Houdini and defense of Carrington not to the magazine or even the committee, but to the *New York Times.* Prince saw no analogy between the situations, and scolded Houdini for being oversensitive about a "plain colorless statement," especially considering how he had thrashed their colleagues: "you have been banging everybody connected with the case all over the country. If you will reconsider all that has occurred I think that you will find it a little

amusing that you resent a little pat at the same time that you are wal-
loping right and left."

But Houdini was not amused. On the contrary, he felt so betrayed and
frustrated that he now began a tangled, unrelenting exchange of pages-long
letters with Prince. He rehashed every controversial detail of the Margery
investigation, arguing each trivial fine-point with such how-can-you-do-
this-to-me intensity, and returning to it so often, as to exhaust the patience
of anyone who did not share his obsessive overinvolvement in the case.
Prince certainly did not. He wanted to keep their pleasant personal bond,
but not be drawn into what he rightly called an "interminable debate." (In
some handwritten remarks about Houdini in relation to a "test," he slipped
and wrote "pest.") He had also come to find Houdini hotheaded and illog-
ical, unappreciative of the efforts of trained academics to deal in specifics
and stay fair. Houdini had not, after all, in any scientific sense 'proved' that
Margery faked. Perhaps simply to stop having to tell him for the nth time
why the committee could not dump Carrington, and to end the barrage of
complaint, he at one point read Houdini the riot act:

> I object to—that is to say I do not like—your making attacks on
> Drs. McDougall and Comstock while you are still their colleague;
> you are exploiting the Margery case for commercial ends while the
> case is still pending, and becoming a public prosecutor while you
> are still technically a judge; you are issuing challenges which no
> man of dignity could notice on grounds not integrally relevant
> (unless you have been misreported); to your general belligerent and
> defiant attitude not consistent with the true spirit of investigation.

As had happened to Houdini's valued friendship with Sir Arthur Conan
Doyle, his also-valued friendship with Prince was blowing up in his face.

Doyle was not far off. Having sat with Margery in London, endorsed
her, and introduced her to the *Scientific American* committee, he had followed the investigation closely and corresponded with Dr. Crandon about
it: "a really bad incident," he said, "and needs showing up." With Houdini
lampooning him in lectures, newspaper interviews, and the Symphony Hall
exposé, he published a long, copyrighted newspaper article on the case,
meant to discredit Houdini completely. "It should be the last of him as a
Psychic Researcher," Doyle said, "if he could ever have been called one."

He portrayed the Crandons as a cultivated, self-sacrificing couple, victims of a "very deadly plot" engineered against them by Houdini in his thirst for "world-wide advertisement." Assessing, Holmes-like, the discovery of the pencil-eraser in the bell-box, he asked, "Who placed it there? . . . It took some deftness to fasten that rubber into the right place. Who was there present who might have had that cleverness of touch?" In his retelling of the ruler episode, Walter's "son of a bitch" became "you unspeakable cad!" and Houdini exclaimed upon the revelation of the tool, "Oh, this is terrible! I don't know anything about any ruler," then became befuddled by guilt, "with his head in his hands in a state of prostration. . . . 'I am not well, I am not myself!' he cried."

This and the rest of Doyle's detailed narrative reveal little more than his readiness to be taken. He based his article unquestioningly on séance records sent him by Dr. Crandon, in which the outbursts of Walter and Houdini appear as he quoted them. "Is not the whole transaction as clear as noontide," he nevertheless asked. He ended by appealing for justice to Margery. He had always thought Houdini vaguely "foreign,"'—"as Oriental," he once wrote, "as our own Disraeli"—and his call for the committee to punish him carried just a whiff, way off, of anti-Semitism: "knowing her complete innocence, as they must do, these American gentlemen allowed a man with entirely different standards to make this outrageous attack. . . . Surely they cannot leave the matter where it stands."

Far from being squelched by Doyle's article, Houdini announced that he would sue Sir Arthur for slander. "There is not a word of truth in his charges against me," he told a reporter. He attributed the harshness of Doyle's attack to his being "a bit senile," therefore "easily bamboozled," and to a desire for revenge: he had once told Sir Arthur that Lady Doyle was "not a valid medium." Houdini's suit got no further than the headline-making threat of it—HOUDINI STIRRED BY ARTICLE—and did nothing to deter Doyle. Sir Arthur diagnosed for the press an "abnormal frame of mind" that he called "Houdinitis," one of whose symptoms was the belief "that manual dexterity bears some relation to brain capacity."

Having taken on the Crandons, Carrington-and-Bird, McDougall, Prince, and now Doyle, Houdini needed no more opponents. But, then, he *was* Houdini: "old fighter," his friend Chung Ling Soo once told him, "I believe you would rather scrap than eat." Already blasting away on a half dozen fronts, Houdini managed to also antagonize Orson Munn, the dapper, pipesmoking publisher of *Scientific American*. Munn felt that Houdini had all but ruined his magazine's investigation by creating a widespread but false impression that it concerned Spiritualism rather than psychic phenomena, and by turning it from a scientific study into a three-ring circus starring himself. He had also had enough of Houdini's war-unto-the-death with his managing editor, J. Malcolm Bird. Houdini kept telling reporters and lecture audiences that *Scientific American* had stopped press in order to throw out an article by Bird favorable to Margery. Recently he added that Bird had been forced to resign his editorial post for supporting her. To Houdini's horror, Munn denied both stories in an interview with the *New York World*, making him a liar for all to see.

Houdini backed off his charge that Bird had been forced to resign, which was untrue. Bird resigned in order to make a bureau-sponsored college tour, à la Houdini, lecturing on "My Psychic Investigations." Houdini did not withdraw his other charge, however, concerning the supposedly suppressed article. He sent photostats of the page proofs to Hardeen, as "evidence," with instructions to safeguard them "in case anything should happen to me." Then he put Munn on trial. He defiantly posted a copy of the article in front of the Keith theater where he was playing, "to allow the public, as judge and jurors," he said, "to use their own judgment as to the true state of affairs." The sideshow disgusted Prince. "Houdini is out of this case," he wrote Munn, "from this time on."

Prying Houdini loose would take more than Prince's say-so. But Prince and Munn were now allied with the Crandons and Doyle in criticizing him for treating the investigation as show business. They were not wrong, of course, but what else, from a crackerjack showman, did they expect? Shortly after the Symphony Hall demonstration, Houdini began a six-week stint at the New York Hippodrome, glitteringly billed as the "World-Famous Author, Lecturer, and Acknowledged Head of Mystifiers." His forty-minute turn included a new escape from a wooden box, all sides of which were pierced by iron rods, welded together—"which will give the spiritualists," the program noted, "more cause than ever to claim that he can actually materialize and dematerialize." He also offered a dramatic skit set in the séance room of Zanetti, a character purportedly based on several high-living fraud mediums. At one performance Zanetti-Houdini produced on blank slates the message that Balto, a famous malamute then leading a dog team to Nome, Alaska, with antitoxin, was not dead, as had been reported; and that two large ships, the *Empress of Scotland* and the *Scotts-burgh*, had collided.

This intelligence from the spirit world was astounding, for neither piece of news had yet appeared in the press, and both turned out to be true. Houdini's method, however, was characteristically simple and nervy. He had arranged with his journalist pals a direct wire from the editorial rooms of the *World*, which sent the breaking news to Houdini's assistant back-stage, who wrote it on the slate he secretly handed to Zanetti. Houdini's show, *Variety* wrote, "surpasses anything he has ever attempted before on account of the world-wide interest in spiritualism." The Spiritualist pro-gram proved so popular that during his last two weeks at the Hipp, Hou-dini repeated it in an earlier performance at the Albee Theater in Brooklyn. Each night he negotiated the five or six miles of city traffic with the help of a motorcycle police escort specially assigned to him.

While Houdini was turning Spiritualist exposé into theater, the Cran-dons were preparing to fight him with his own theatrical methods. In replying to his public exposé at Symphony Hall, they hired Boston's thousand-seat Jordan Hall and announced through the city's press that Margery would prove her powers by offering there, for the first time, a public séance. Houdini greeted the tit-for-tat announcement with scorn, as if it were indecent: "A woman who will drag her dead brother from the grave and exploit him before the public as a means of gaining social prominence, would do anything." Just the same he sent off lengthy telegrams to friends in Boston urgently trying to learn what she planned. Prince, who seems to have known, refused to tell him. "Can you beat this?" Houdini grumbled. "They not only have been unable to detect the medium, but they even put stumbling blocks in my way."

As it happened, the Crandons thought better of trading blows with Houdini, and announced a major program-change. Margery would not demonstrate her feats live; instead, they would be illustrated and discussed in a slide-lecture. Hardly the same things, as Houdini exulted: "They said they were going to show me up and denounce me by having the medium present her manifestations in front of an audience, and all it turned out to be was a lecture." The new program offered enough to provoke him, though. The chairman for the evening was to be the sometime-gentleman-and-scholar, Professor McDougall. And the scheduled speaker was Eric Dingwall—the SPR research officer, amateur magician, and historian of chastity belts with whom, five years earlier in London, Houdini had shared control of the ectoplasm medium Eva C. Over the years Houdini had counted Dingwall a fellow-magician and friend. Yet Dingwall had turned up at Symphony Hall, demanding from the audience to examine the bell-box. Like Bird, he had detected Houdini's substitution of a trick box for the original. For one magician to challenge another this way was a sin almost unheard-of. Since then Houdini had been denouncing Dingwall too in the press as "honest but stupid," a down-and-out hired flack for the Crandons who could not afford to pay his SAM dues.

However modified, the Jordan Hall lecture gave sensational evidence of Margery's latest, and changed, manifestations. Tickets were not sold to the public but went instead to the faculties of MIT and of the Harvard and Tufts medical school. With good reason, for Dingwall's lantern slides might have come from textbooks on pathology. Taken by red light during recent sittings with Margery, in the presence of McDougall and an Episcopal minister, they showed her pouring ectoplasm from the orifices of her head. The effusions covered her face and crown or spilled over onto the séance table, resembling by turns swaths of luminous cheesecloth, blobs of dough, piles of white noodles, dark, disgusting turds, mounds of decayed liver—most of the repellent masses being connected by a twisted cord to her nose, mouth, or ear. By Dingwall's account, the clammy "teleplasm" had also slowly oozed itself outward to ring bells and flip over papers. Much of his remaining lecture he devoted to razzing Houdini as someone "whose knowledge of the art of self-liberation is as profound as his ignorance of the methods of scientific investigation." The description, according to one Boston newspaper, "was greeted with prolonged applause from the audience." In concluding, Dingwall granted that he had not been able to subject Margery to rigorous scientific study, since the necessary laboratory equipment could be obtained only in London—where he was advising her to go for further testing.

On getting reports of the lecture, Houdini saw clearly enough where things were headed. Speaking with the *New York World* two days later, he mocked Dingwall's claim that Margery could not be satisfactorily investigated in the United States but must take herself to Britain: "it strikes me," he said, "she is just trying to get away from Houdini."

THE MARGERY VERDICT

The committee at last issued its verdict on February 11, 1925, six long-drawn-out months after Houdini's sittings with Margery. The verdict was

made possible not by any shift in the members' positions but by the Crandons' unwillingness to any longer suffer Houdini. Prince had proposed
still another round of new sittings. Dr. Crandon refused, unless *Scientific
American* removed Houdini from the committee. Publisher Munn refused.
The investigation was over.

By four to one the members voted to deny Margery the prize, Carrington
alone supporting her. The final opinions were published in *Scientific American* and summarized under banner headlines: COMMITTEE DECIDES
"MARGERY" HAS FAILED. *SA* emphasized that Margery was "the most
famous of mediums since Palladino," of a different class from the run of "fee-
taking spiritualists." But for all that, she had not convinced the committee:

> We have observed phenomena, the method of production of
> which we cannot in every case claim to have discovered. But we
> have observed no phenomena of which we can assert that they
> could not have been produced by normal means.

Prince and McDougall released separate statements as well. "No sitting
at which I was present," Prince told the *Times*, "was to me convincing,
and I am still profoundly unconvinced." McDougall said about the same,
and "humbly" apologized for having chaired the Jordan Hall lecture.
Anxious to protect his scientific credentials, he explained that he had
expected Dingwall to speak noncommittally about Margery's ectoplasm
séances; he was dismayed to hear him speak instead in her favor, and
hoped that "no harm was done."

The committee's published verdict infuriated Houdini. Its polite
double negative—they had observed no phenomena that could not have
been produced by normal means—gave no hint of the reality, which was
that he had found her hornswoggling by head, shoulders, and foot, forced
her into giving blank séances, caught her red-handed in a deliberate con-
game. He protested the verdict to Prince, vehemently and without letup:
"This is a very important thing in all of our lives, and I contend that she is
fraudulent in all of the manifestations that I have witnessed." Hardly less
tenacious than Houdini himself, Prince fended off his complaints with the
reminder that Houdini had publicized his discovery of Margery's methods
in his pamphlet, at Symphony Hall, and in his lectures: "You have given
your testimony and it speaks for itself."

For himself Prince had become so fed up with the vaudeville surrounding the investigations that he resigned as chief research officer of the American SPR. His departure left the society under the leadership of its already dominant pro-Margery faction. In his place they installed J. Malcolm Bird. The exaltation of this "traitor and fool" was too much for Houdini, who resigned from the society as well. "This does not mean anything," he said privately, "as any one can join for $10 a year."

Nor did the pale verdict mean anything to Houdini, for he had no thought of letting Margery beat him. While continuing to flog the Crandons from the stage, he probably wrote or had written a scurrilous anonymous leaflet about them entitled *How a Tricky Young Lady Trapped Stupid "Scientists."* It identified the couple as a "spirit-fakir . . . happily wedded to a man with a title and a large bank account," and depicted them bribing Carrington-and-Bird at Lime Street with "downy beds . . . ice cream and hooch": "We can easily see Hereward and Birdy, with napkins stuck into their collars, pushing custard pie into their faces with their knives, and wondering how they managed to strike such easy graft. Is it any wonder that they decided in favor of the lady?"

Driven about equally by sneaking admiration and vindictiveness— "She *sure* was *resourceful*! & *unscrupulous*," he noted in his diary—Houdini kept watch on Margery's latest doings. The announcement that a new investigator had dared her to undergo laboratory testing made him suspect a ruse by the Crandons to cover their defeat. He had seen the game played in Germany, when a fighter was challenged by a superior opponent. The fighter would sometimes pay an inferior opponent to challenge him and kick up some dust, drawing attention away from the real challenge. "A woman that can pull the wool over the eyes of scientists and alleged scholars and investigators for two years," Houdini warned, "would be crafty enough to resort to German wrestlers tactics."

The Crandons, too, denounced the committee's verdict. Dr. Crandon explained to the press that he and his wife had been willing to continue the tests, but not until the committee disowned Houdini, as it refused to do: "We have done the dismissing, not they." Now the study of his wife's powers could proceed, he said, "unhampered by a handcuff king and his allies."

Apparently the verdict satisfied no one but Walter, Margery's flamboyant spirit brother. When some sitters chatted about Houdini's being blackballed, he commented, "Rather say black-bald." He explained that he referred to Houdini's balding head, and to a fringe of his hair that was dyed black. About ten days after the verdict, he composed a song to the tune of "It Ain't Gonna Rain No More," and sang it in real Keith's style:

> *Oh Houdini wont talk no more, no more,*
> *He aint goin to talk no more.*
> *What in hell will the newspapers do,*
> *When Houdini wont talk no more?*
>
> *Houdini wont write no more, no more,*
> *Houdini wont write no more,*
> *He writ so much that his arm got sore,*
> *Houdini wont write no more.*

Houdini of course was not present for the sitting, and missed a treat. The records indicate that Walter beat time to the tune by banging Margery's séance table with her megaphone.

SIXTEEN

FALL 1924–SPRING 1926

THE ANTI-SPIRITUALIST CRUSADE; ROSE MACKENBERG

THE "MARGERY" CASE turned Houdini from a part-time investigator of Spiritualism into a full-time crusader against it. His shift coincided with national antifraud campaigns in the United States and Britain, led by government agencies, Christian churches, and Spiritualists themselves, who said they wanted to purge their ranks of tricksters who brought the religion into disrepute. The prosecutorial mood echoes in the wariness of T. S. Eliot's "famous clairvoyante," Madame Sosostris:

> .... *If you see dear Mrs. Equitone,*
> *Tell her I bring the horoscope myself:*
> *One must be so careful these days.*
>> THE WASTE LAND (1922)

Earlier Houdini had been satisfied to expose reaching rods and discourage credulity. Now he tried bringing to light the movement's seamy underbelly and disastrous social effects—and getting Madame Sosostris convicted. "I am waging war," he said, "on the fraud mediums in this country."

The twin themes of Houdini's crusade, onstage and off, were Exploitation and Misery. Money taken for contacting spirits, he said, was "the dirtiest money ever earned on this earth." Those victimized were sometimes prominent and well-off, such as Mrs. Sarah Winchester, widow of the arms magnate, whose monstrous residence he visited in San Jose. Told by her spirit guide that as long as she kept building the place she would live, she built and built for thirty-six years, squandering five million dollars to produce a home-from-outer-space of 160 rooms, 47 fireplaces, and 10,000 windows. More often, fraud mediums preyed on Mr. and Mrs. John Q. Citizen, "the good, sound, solid people of the small towns and farms and suburbs and city uptown streets who do the world's work," as Sinclair Lewis described them, "upright, industrious—but because of their very closeness to drudgery, they are not hard to deceive, if you come with an appearance of having divine mysteries." Like Lewis and others, Houdini counted the effects of Spiritualism in numbers of average folk stuck with forged checks or bilked of savings and insurance money, their families broken up by separation and divorce. The more susceptible lost their minds, committed suicide: "the neurotic believer in spiritualism is surely on the way to the insane asylum," Houdini wrote, "without a return ticket."

Houdini's view was not new or extreme. Nineteenth-century medical psychologists had associated the convulsive trances of the early mediums with hysteria. In the 1920s the *Times* and other leading newspapers often ran stories of Spiritualists who at the behest of spirits had amputated an arm, killed their own children, or drunk Lysol hoping to join loved ones Across the Barrier. Houdini collected similar testimony by continuing to poke around insane asylums, in part from recurring fears that he was not immune to mental illness himself. A physician at a midwestern asylum told him that the Ouija board craze was a "direct cause of sending folks crazy." After visiting ten asylums Houdini recorded that he had "found mediums in each one," and concluded that Spiritualism had the same effect as "dope, or immoral acts or drink." (Like many, he conceived insanity as including epilepsy, drug addiction, and sexual perversion.) He had experienced the minor of what the patients suffered: if he stayed up late at night browsing Spiritualist books, he noticed, "when I look up I see forms go by and hear voices."

Houdini waged his crusade against séance fraud inventively, on many fronts. He telegrammed judges calling for "drastic legislation" against it; spoke at Rotary Clubs, often reading out the names and addresses of local fakes; tried to interest Henry Ford in the cause; petitioned President

Coolidge for a government investigation. He enlisted the help of newspapers: "If you have been robbed by a medium, write to Houdini, care of The GRAPHIC, 25 City Hall Place, giving complete details and the medium's name, and he will help you obtain redress." For three months he taught at the New York Police Academy, lecturing a class of 150 detectives and rookies on séance deceptions. These he sometimes went overboard to illustrate. For instance, in returning miraculously apt answers to sealed questions from a Hippodrome audience, he had his assistants rifle the pockets of coats that ticketholders had checked in the theater's cloakroom, looking for letters and other telltale documents. The *Times*, usually his champion, criticized him for violating personal property. But he had appointed himself the Hammer of Spiritualism, sworn to protect the gullible and weak. He fired back in a letter to the editor: "May I please inform you that I am exposing fraudulent mediums' methods and enlightening the public as to how mediums get inside information? . . . May I please point out that any persons who have had their letters read will never be duped by a fraudulent medium?"

In educating the public Houdini ended his lectures and demonstrations with a question-and-answer session, his "Open Forum." To be ready for whatever came he carried extensive files of information. He kept American and British clipping services busy sending him hundreds of articles about Spiritualism, especially in relation to crime: "The Vanishing Nun," "Spiritualism in Child Murder Mystery," SPIRIT WOMAN/LURES FATHER/OF FIFTEEN. He read and annotated them voraciously, filing what he needed under such topics as "Seances" and "Messages." He also acquired scrapbooks dealing with the earlier Spiritualist movement— filled with mediums' business cards and ads for séances—and complete runs of the leading Spiritualist journals, such as *Light* and *Banner of Light*. He even bought the business records of the defunct Banner of Light Publishing Company of Boston—boxloads of minutes of board meetings, tax records, bankbooks. His portable files did not stay idle. If challenged from the audience about some assertion, he called offstage for the supporting evidence, which a secretary dug out and brought to him. "And maybe Houdini didn't love those moments!" a reporter recalled: "his bitter wit flowed free, he hurled back challenges, and it took a castiron clairvoyant to get out of the house undamaged in mind and soul." As time for the "Open Forum" was limited, he invited the audience to write to him for information about séance crime, enclosing a stamped, self-addressed envelope.

One of Houdini's most dramatic weapons was his ten-thousand-dollar challenge, first thrown down to Margery and now to any and all mediums who could present a manifestation he could not duplicate. Mediums flocked to his shows and lectures, and he often invited them by name to come onstage and try for his money. There were few takers. Many had been scared off by the Margery case, and put down Houdini's prize as old news: "he is still in the stage-coach era of the spiritualistic idea," one said, "placing all importance on the physical demonstrations which spiritualists have ceased to consider of importance the last 75 years." Others objected to performing on a stage, without the supportive conditions of the séance room. "Sure they must have their conditions," Houdini smirked, "but when I was escaping from handcuffs, I did not say, I must have conditions—I challenged the world to produce any handcuff that would lock and unlock and I would get out of it, anywhere, or any time or any place, even at the bottom of the sea."

Accepted or not, Houdini's challenges from the stage made for raucous theater, a two-in-one cockfight and witchhunt. In Denver he called out to a local medium, the Reverend Josie K. Folsom Stewart—a small, nervous woman seated in the audience with her husband, Charles, a gaunt man with a pronounced limp. Mrs. Stewart had been exposed several times, once for spirit photos whose extras turned out to be ad illustrations for "Syrup of Figs." Houdini offered the Stewarts all the house receipts if they delivered "one message from the beyond." They declined, challenging him to "fight it out" at a séance the following night. Houdini said he had to move on to Laramie, and again urged them to the stage. "Do it now!" someone shouted. The audience took up the cry as a chant. "I paid to come and hear you, not to help you put on your program," Mrs. Stewart said, as the *Denver Post* quoted her. "It's only fair that you come and hear me—and expose me if you can." With the Stewarts standing at their seats, and people all over the house shouting and gesticulating, Houdini read out records of a St. Louis court case involving the Stewarts, his voice trembling: "You stand convicted and I know it." The theater, the *Post* said, "became a bedlam." "She cannot come to the platform now," the elderly Stewart told the jeering crowd. "Her health is impaired." Afterward the audience filed out slowly, many lingering for a closer look at the couple, who left under the eyes of the police, unmolested but pale.

Houdini did not merely wait for mediums to come to his stage and be exposed. He went out hunting them. Much as he once went after Kleppinis and other would-be Houdinis who claimed to be miracle-workers, he tracked them down, hounded them, shamed them, and if possible hauled them to court. His zeal was personal, but molded by the decade's moonshine busts and Red-scare roundups of communists. Rather as the U.S. attorney general's department had created a General Intelligence Division (soon to be called the Federal Bureau of Investigation), he organized what he called "my own secret service department."

Houdini's private FBI had informants and paid undercover agents all over the country. The brassiest and most knowing of them was a Toledo magician, Robert Gysel (1880–1938). Considering himself a sort of Houdini Midwest, he ridiculed Doyle as "the nickle plated dumbell of Spiritualism," performed his own Margery exposé, and boasted that he could explain the methods of any medium "from Kansas City to New York City." At the least he had exquisite taste in bamboozlements. He sent Houdini his pamphlets on "Psychic Fakery," which set out such niceties as the best fabric to use for materializing spirit-forms (French veiling boiled in olive oil and water, then dipped in phosphorus, and fireproofed in a bath of alum). The mimeographed sheets also divulged a gorgeous technique for writing on slates while one was sealed in a large cloth bag, fingers taped, hands in baseball mitts sewn to your sleeves (by holding a sharp slate pencil in your mouth and writing through the bag). Gysel had much to say too about mediumship on the wild side. He thought all mediums "oversexed," and knew about a so-called "developing class" in Chicago, where, for a fee, females could develop their psychic gifts: "The stunt was that the male medium would ask the girl or woman to take the mediums penis and place it in her mouth and to draw the semen from it, the medium claiming that it is nothing but pure blood, mingled with said wonderful supernormal power. Can you beat this?"

Gysel despised Spiritualist frauds and tried to vex them. His standard method seems overstrenuous: harassing the medium until the medium prosecuted him. In Buffalo, for instance, he deliberately knocked down a medium with his nightbag, cursed him out, and jumped on a train back to Toledo. Next day police appeared with a warrant for his arrest—much to his satisfaction, for he then sued the medium for slander. Houdini often wrote to Gysel for the lowdown on midwestern mediums, and even collaborated with him in exposing a Toledo fraud, yet considered him dangerous—"crazy," in fact.

The most capably devious of Houdini's undercover agents was Rose Mackenberg, a dark-haired young Brooklynite with a large sloping nose. While employed by him she investigated, by her count, some three hundred mediums. Traveling several days ahead of his shows and lectures, she would attend séances in the city of his destination, disguised in frumpy clothes and eyeglasses as a smalltown widow, jealous wife, or neurotic schoolteacher. She sent him long, sometimes notarized reports on the local mediums. Her summaries paint a tired world of furnished rooms and back parlors, where for a dollar or two handed to some Reverend Odessa Champlain, the spirits of dead infants and faithless husbands relayed twenty minutes of clarification, advice, and solace: The baby died of throat trouble; Do not marry a Catholic; I am happy and with father. In their trances many male mediums grabbed her arm or brushed her knee, Mackenberg said, and she so often became the object of "sex attacks and obscene suggestions" that Houdini suggested she carry a gun (she refused).

A typical example of Houdini's hit squad in action is his campaign against the Indianapolis medium, Reverend Charles H. Gunsolas. Gunsolas purveyed "Spiritual Readings" from a rented room, as well as "scientific instruction" in piano, strings, and wind instruments at the "Gunsolas College of Music." He had made himself a target by writing to Houdini in the fall of 1925, presenting himself as "one of the leaders of spiritualism in America" and throwing down his own dare, a mean one: "It might be of . . . interest to you when I tell you that I know *how all of your tricks are performed*. While you are making an exposure of spiritualism, it might be interesting if we made an exposure of your tricks and published it in the papers. This would interest the public and other magicians, don't you think so?" Houdini replied by sending him Rose Mackenberg. Her baby had died a few months ago, her story went, and she wanted to know whether it was happy.

At his small, weatherbeaten house Gunsolas explained that he had a thousand-year-old Hindu guide and a spirit-wife named Ella. Enduring his "oily" manner, Mackenberg accepted his offer to "develop" her, for twenty-five dollars. Over several sittings he taught Mackenberg to gaze into a bowl of water—"don't stare, just gaze"—and discern the clouds, then the forms. Being Jewish, she asked whether she would have Jewish spirit-guides. "I see you are going to have three guides: a Jewish, German, and Italian," Gunsolas prophesied. "Does this meaning anything to you, Sholom Alecham?" He apparently had heard rumors of Houdini's spy network, for in one sitting he hinted that she might be a "Houdini operator." Houdini's method, he said, was to send a woman to get the medium to "make advances" to her, putting him in a state that might lead to "quite a frame up."

Frameup was right. Gunsolas was in the audience when Houdini opened in Indianapolis a few weeks later. By newspaper accounts Houdini "hurled charge after charge" at him, and spread out the evidence. He brought Mackenberg to the stage to testify that, although she had never been married, Gunsolas had given her spirit-counsel about her husband and children. He asked for a spotlight to be trained on various people in the audience, identifying them as members of his "large corps of detectives" who had also investigated Gunsolas and reported to him. They included a representative of the National Detective Agency who announced that he had turned over to Houdini a complete dossier on Gunsolas's past. Houdini invited Gunsolas to reply. Way outnumbered, the medium managed no more than to admit that he had given Mackenberg a reading and to side with Houdini in wishing to stamp out fraud, before bowing himself out of the theater.

Houdini often assured Spiritualists that he was not attacking their religion but only the crooks among them, and for this deserved their thanks. Yet he particularly used Mackenberg to disgrace the Spiritualist ministry and churches. "To be a real minister you have to spend eight to eighteen years," he pointed out in his lectures, "but to be a spiritualist minister you just have to say I hear voices." To prove what he said he dispatched Mackenberg to various cities to get herself formally ordained, over and over, as a Spiritualist pastor, with power to marry and bury. She usually obtained her papers by shelling out five dollars and undergoing a ten-minute rite. Although she worked under many aliases, as a minister she went by the names Florence B. Rush (B for "Bum's"), or Frances Raud (F. Raud, or "Fraud"). Among Houdini and his assistants she became known simply as "The Rev." Through her Houdini amassed "sheaves," he said, of bargain-basement ministerial licenses. He pasted them together in a roll, and during his performances unfurled and displayed them as one long long sheet.

Houdini used Mackenberg also to demonstrate that one could just as easily buy a whole Spiritualist church. As Mrs. Frances Raud she purchased for him the charter and incorporation papers to the Unity Spiritualist Church of Worcester, Massachusetts, for only $13.50. Its pastor for twenty-seven years, the Reverend Frederick A. Wiggin, should have known better, being the medium Gysel had clobbered with a nightbag, then sued. Mackenberg, a black veil obscuring her face, told her story to Houdini's audience at the Worcester theater. "I drove the fakers out of California," Houdini added, Christlike, "and I intend to drive them out of Massachusetts."

Cleansing the temple turned out to be rough work. The Reverend Wiggin, who claimed to receive direct communications from Jesus, charged that Mackenberg stole the charter, and he sued Houdini for defamation, for one hundred thousand dollars. The Massachusetts State Association of Spiritualists won a temporary injunction from a Boston court, preventing Houdini from disposing of the charter. "It's bought and paid for and it's mine—to do with as I please," Houdini told a reporter. "Of course they don't wish it to be known that it is so easy to get a church." He brought a retaliatory suit against the association, but a superior court ultimately made him return the charter to the Unity Church.

Houdini went undercover himself and brought several mediums to trial. He of course knew his way around police and other law enforcement agencies, and was able to enlist their help. In Cleveland, disguised by old clothes and thick glasses, he took along a county prosecutor to snare the highly-regarded George Renner, who had practiced trumpet mediumship for forty years. Trumpets floated about during the séance, conveying the spirit voices of, among others, an opera singer who favored the sitters with "Nearer My God to Thee." At a decisive moment Houdini suddenly turned a flashlight on the medium. It showed that Renner's hands and face were daubed with greasy soot. When the lights were switched on, Houdini explained that he had brought with him a can of lampblack, and managed to smear some on the trumpets. Renner now sat coated by the stuff, proving that he had held and blown the instruments himself. He was tried for obtaining money under false pretenses, facing a fine and a jail term of up to sixty days. Houdini gladly testified, well-stocked to deal under cross-examination with the issue of Spiritualism-as-a-religion: "I had ready in my pocket all the allusions in the Bible against witches, familiar spirits, and when the defendant's lawyer pulled a pro I replied with an anti." After one ballot the twelve-person jury found Renner guilty, but his lawyer seems to have won a new trial on appeal.

In trying to bag Mrs. Cecil Cook of New York, Houdini by chance gained a rare prize. She was the former editor of the Spiritualist journal *Communication*, and pastor of the city's W. T. Stead Memorial Center— one branch of an association with centers in Chicago and Los Angeles as well, named after a famed Spiritualist who had died on the *Titanic*. According to her brief autobiography, *How I Discovered My Medium- ship*, she first heard voices at the age of four, and as a "child medium" contacted spirits named Bright-Face, Snowdrop, and Pat (a one-hun- dred-year-old Irishman), whose voices she soon directed through a thirty-six-inch fiber trumpet. She also practiced spiritual healing and projection, taking "astral trips" to the Other World. Proud of having been arrested four times, she compared herself to the persecuted early Christians.

Houdini saw Mrs. Cook differently—as the dirtyhanded owner of a fat bank account, a country estate, and a ninety-thousand-dollar home in Manhattan: "in my estimation," he said, she "heads her profession." Putting her under surveillance by his operatives, he learned something about the source of her wealth: she gave not only private séances, all day, but also large group sessions for poorer people at a dollar a head. In July 1925 Houdini raided one such séance at the Stead Center, accompanied by a *Herald-Tribune* reporter and a policewoman. He got himself up as an old man, white-haired, cane-carrying, and, strategically, rather deaf. At the gathering he found some thirty men and women seated in a circle, about a quarter of them African-American. The heavy Mrs. Cook sat in the middle, before two trumpets and a basin of water. The spirit-voices began with some message for each sitter. When one of the black women asked whether she should have an operation, a spirit identifying itself as "Dr. Sten" said, "No, you don't have to take it." When Houdini, in his turn, was contacted by "Alfred," he played hard-of-hearing:

> The voice repeated, "Alfred." I said, "Alfred?" She said, "Yes, your son." The medium said, "Your son, Alfred." I said, "Is that Alfred, my son?" She said, "Yes." I said, "How are you?". . . . He said, "Is that you, dad?" I said, "Yes."

Like the other cutrate voices, Alfred's quickly passed. But it returned fifteen minutes later with a message for Houdini: "Dad, you have had a very very hard time but it is all over and I will take care of you and brighten up everything for you."

Houdini listened hard for a whistling sound. By faking deafness he had induced Mrs. Cook to produce for his sake a louder-than-usual spirit voice, amplifying too the slight breath-whistle that meant the trumpet was close to her lips. When he heard it he shined his flashlight on her: "there she sat with a trumpet in her mouth," he said, "just as pretty as though she was posing for a picture." By his account Mrs. Cook screamed "What is that? What is that?":

> And her aide-de-camp said, "Why, that is the old man." "WHAT is that; what is that?" I said, "Why, you have the trumpet in your mouth. I thought the spirits were speaking."... She rose immediately and said, "You rascal, you rascal." I said, "You are getting money under religious disguise. You spoke through the trumpet and there is a witness to bear it out."... She said, "I have been pastor of this church for a long time ... the spirits will get after you."

According to the reporter present, a male member of the center rushed at Houdini but was stopped, apparently by the policewoman. With the revelation of a police presence, some sitters headed for the door, only to be turned back by an inspector and two detectives. A half hour later, Mrs. Cook stood at the blotter of the West One-hundredth Street police station, charged, like Renner, with accepting money under false pretenses. She was locked in the Jefferson Market jail downtown to await arraignment the next morning.

Houdini testified at Cook's trial before a magistrate's court, during which she denied touching the trumpet or even being aware, in her trance state, of the confrontation. The transcript does not show the outcome, but Houdini's efforts brought him something he greatly desired, the "most sensational feature," he said, of his New York crusade: Mrs Cook's "sucker list." Such lists were secret money-machines, impossible to come by. They were compiled and exchanged, Houdini told his lecture audiences, within a well-organized league of fraud mediums, an "information bureau" that provided genealogical, financial, and other intimate data about possible clients culled from newspapers, municipal registries, and tombstones, even from the gossipy owners of local beauty salons and Turkish baths. The New York *Graphic* published a photograph showing Houdini looking over Mrs. Cook's long lists, which named sitters in every state, about two thousand of them in the East, including persons to whom she sold spirit messages by mail.

Houdini's fingering, badgering, and trapping of mediums inspired read-all-about-it headlines: SPIRITUALISTS BATTLING HOUDINI; UPROAR OVER HOUDINI; HOUDINI TALK STARTS NEAR RIOT. The big-city and national press solidly supported him. "It may be indeed that Houdini has appeared at a crucial moment in the history of spiritualism and that he is destined to play an important role," Edmund Wilson wrote in the *New Republic*. "It is difficult to understand how a credulous disposition toward mediums can long survive such public exposures." On the other hand Houdini's assaults angered or offended Spiritualists of every conviction, especially sincere believers. In an article entitled "Houdini Cornered," *Reason Quarterly* called on the faithful to unite, "band themselves together and assist in sending this mountebank back to his handcuff performances." Many Spiritualists tried to do that. One group distributed a booklet entitled *Houdini Unmasked*. A state convention featured a lecture on "Houdini and the Future of Spiritualism." "They are holding indignation meetings all over America," Houdini observed. He might have added Paris, too, where a speaker at an international Spiritualist congress assailed "a certain magician" for "persecuting" mediums, and appealed for strong action to protect them.

Houdini heard the chorus of reproach but shrugged it off. "They sure are panning H——— out of me," he said, "but consider it a compliment."

OFFSTAGE AND AT HOME

Houdini's crusade left him not much spare time, but he plugged every moment of it. "I am busier when I am not working," he said, "than when I am."

With his usual here-there-and-everywhere energy, Houdini found time to patent a Houdini windup toy. Stood upside down on its flat head, the doll struggled to escape its straitjacket. He and his ghostwriters turned out a romantic detective thriller, *The Zanetti Mystery*. Loosely based on his Hippodrome skit, it concerns the efforts of the mesmeric Zanetti (parchment complexion, shoulder-length black wig), to mulct a widowed octogenarian by promising to materialize his dead wife. Still serving as president of SAM, he joined Eddie Cantor and Irving Berlin in founding the Jewish Theatrical Association, and to his many memberships added the Masons. He threw himself into the affairs of the St. Cecile Lodge of New York—whose theater-heavy roster included D. W. Griffith—wrote for the organization's magazine, and zipped through the ranks, being raised after two years to the degree of Master Mason.

Among much other charity work, Houdini gave benefits and free shows for the United Jewish Campaign and for crippled children at hospitals. These days he did far fewer risky stunts than before, however, although in working for some Boy Scouts at a San Francisco amusement park, he had himself manacled to a stake surrounded by kerosene-soaked faggots, ready to be lighted. He estimated he could break out in ninety seconds, fast enough to be singed but not burned. But a breeze drove smoke and flames straight at him and, choking, he scrambled away from the stake on hands and knees, his clothing on fire: "the wildly applauding spectators," he wrote, "did not realize the torture I was suffering." Once again he performed on Christmas Night at Sing Sing, where he escaped a hangman's noose and forwarded a spirit-question from Benjamin Franklin ("Who stole the ham?"). On this trip he had a good friend inside—Charles Chapin, once the famed city editor of the *New York World*, now serving a life sentence as #69690. Chapin had owned fast horses and a yacht, sported neckties colored baby blue or flaming crimson, and speculated wildly to cover his extravagances. Overwhelmed by debt, he had shot his wife of thirty-nine years in the head as she slept to spare her a future of beggary. Houdini chatted with him half an hour and asked, Chapin said, "if I'd put him on my visiting list and let him come as often as his business engagements will permit."

The movie business also kept Houdini on the go, but now only as a litigant. Except a brief appearance in one installment of the *Pathé Review*, demonstrating card flourishes, and an effort to import a Swedish film, *The Witch*, presumably for American distribution, his career as a film star and producer was over. But in its wake came lawsuits involving several hundred thousand dollars. Shareholders in his Houdini Pictures Corporation were suing or preparing to sue him: "promises were made," as *Billboard* described their complaint, "regarding the wealth that was sure to accrue to holders of the motion picture stock." In other actions Houdini himself was the plaintiff. As a trustee of the bankrupt Octagon Films, producers of his first picture, he sued a film export company for some $35,000 owed to Octagon from foreign sales; the company countersued for $100,000. He brought a suit for nearly as much against the widow of one of the original Octagon partners, a leather manufacturer named Fischer, largely for stocks her husband had agreed to buy but had never paid for. The complex court case dragged on nearly three years in fancy lawyering and stacks of show-cause decrees. Houdini and Fischer's widow accused each other of having stolen the defunct company's business records, which otherwise had vanished.

Houdini spent his happiest off-moments on his collections. He toured the Huntington Library in California—"worth going miles to see," he said—and revisited the Harvard theater collection, where for some reason, perhaps pure joy, he began singing on the stoop. "I only work five months in a year," he told a friend. "The other seven I am in my library." Although he calculated its extent and value variously, in a letter of August 1925 he said that he then had more than fifty thousand books and pamphlets, not including playbills and programs. The same year he told a journalist that he had a quarter of a million manuscript pages, and had insured the library for $350,000—a vast sum for the time. Houdini's estimate of what was his always ran high, but however many books he owned, he felt less that he housed them than that they housed him. "I actually live in a library," he said. If his collections kept growing, he thought he would have to buy a separate library building in New York or move to a larger home outside the city.

The very completeness of his conjuring library stopped Houdini from buying much on magic. But his crusade gave urgency to his acquisitions in Spiritualism. Atop the scrapbooks and business papers, he bought "several thousand" letters of the pioneers of Spiritualism; more than a hundred by Robert Ingersoll, "the great agnostic"; and rare items by the reputedly atheistic Tom Paine. He also became seriously interested in material relating to Abraham Lincoln—in boyhood "my hero of heroes," but now a hero to Spiritualists as well. Sir Arthur Conan Doyle, for instance, wrote that Lincoln had been "a convinced Spiritualist," susceptible to Influences. "I don't think it would be fair," Houdini said, "to have the Great Abraham Lincoln known as a Spiritualist when such is not the case." He countered by sometimes rapping out spirit-messages from Lincoln in his lectures, and manufacturing a spirit photo of himself with Lincoln's shade. In educating himself about Lincoln's beliefs he came into correspondence with the president's son, Robert Todd Lincoln, and befriended Oliver Barrett, a Chicago lawyer and the preeminent collector of Lincolniana, who showed Houdini through his holdings.

Mostly Houdini swelled his drama library, by the carload. He bought the entire forty-six-year theatrical correspondence of a defunct opera house in Cedar Rapids—25,000 letters, he reckoned—and enough theatrical posters from the well-known Strobridge Lithograph Company, when it too went out of business, to fill a five-ton truck. At important sales he acquired "major, star portions" of the libraries of other noted collectors, including five hundred letters to the drama critic William Winter and seven packing cases filled with choice American theater programs, mostly from Philadelphia but including dozens of exceedingly rare programs from eighteenth-century South Carolina and Virginia. Among other fine miscellaneous items, he picked up letters of Sarah Siddons and Jenny Lind, and early-nineteenth-century playbills that listed among the cast members Edgar Allan Poe's father and mother, both actors.

In the standings of public and private drama libraries, Houdini now gave his own fifth place. Ahead of him were Robert Gould Shaw at Harvard; the British Museum; the financier Henry E. Huntington; and Henry C. Folger, board chairman of Standard Oil and renowned collector of Shakespeareana. ("His money is limitless," Houdini noted.) But he considered himself very much in the race: "if I am not running side by side with Harvard, I certainly am within hailing distance." He expected that in about five more years, he would have not the largest private drama collection in the world, but the largest period.

Houdini's ambitions, and his affections, suffered from the death in April 1925 of his eighty-year-old librarian, Alfred Becks. On and off the genteel old man had indexed and catalogued for him for more than a decade. "He knew everyone in the show business as well as in the newspaper game for sixty years," Houdini said. "When he died an invaluable fund of information was lost to the world." Houdini had been on the road when Becks fell ill with bronchitis and was taken to Roosevelt Hospital. Having returned to New York, he visited Becks on successive days but found him hardly able to speak, his mind wandering, asking to have his feet tied together so that he would not fall apart. Although Becks left a sizable estate of more than $25,000, Houdini was concerned that his relatives might give him an undistinguished burial. To ensure a display of homage without antagonizing the family, he sent three bunches of flowers to the funeral under three different names. But as he suspected, Becks was buried in his old working clothes, "as if he had directed a funeral himself." Houdini spoke briefly at the ceremony and when he returned home, according to his biographer Harold Kellock, he sat in a chair and wept.

Houdini bore another important death, within his own family. His older brother Bill died in Saranac Lake, New York, plagued by swollen legs, unable to swallow, after years of moving around the country to find a climate that might halt his advancing tuberculosis. Houdini had traveled to see him and had kept in touch by phone, but was stunned by the sight of his corpse and its here-not-here nullity: "Calm and in a silence that was loud and thunderous I gazed into his face." Bill was buried near Cecilia Weiss at Machpelah Cemetery. Houdini still visited her grave there, and had never stopped thinking of her. He saved the reproduction of a painting that showed President Coolidge beside his own mother's grave directly after he took the oath of office, cap pressed to his heart. At Bill's funeral the thought of his brother united with their mother brought with it a pang of what seems old rivalry. "Slowly his wooden home was lowered into Mother Earth's breast," Houdini wrote in his diary. "Asleep near his own mother, my mother. . . . Strange that I only think of Bill being . . . near mother as our father is right over there. But mother 'babied' Bill all her gentle life."

The thought of his own mortality also played on Houdini's mind. "My fifty-first birthday!!!!" he exclaimed in 1925. "Can't believe I am so old." The summer before, he had made out his will. It specified the manner in which he should be buried—one part of a labyrinthine document of many provisions and many confusing exceptions to them. Some of the intricacy arose from bitterness. Houdini tried to foresee and spell out any circumstances, and prevent any means, by which any of his estate might descend directly or indirectly to Sadie (Glantz) Weiss, the loathed sister-in-law who had divorced his businessman-brother, Nat, to marry his physician-brother, Leo. The bitterness also took in Leo, to whom Houdini expressly denied burial in the family plot. He left his magic library to the Library of Congress (where it remains), and his library on Spiritualism to the ASPR, although when he learned of J. Malcolm Bird's appointment as the society's chief research officer, he revoked the bequest. His huge drama library he left to Bess, together with all his personal and household effects and jewelry. The will also provided for a trust to be administered by a New York bank, reducing the rest of his estate to cash for investments, the profits to go biannually to Bess and to his surviving brothers and sister and their offspring. Among the minor bequests he left one thousand dollars to the SAM and five hundred dollars each to his three assistants and former assistants, James Vickery, Franz Kukol, and Jim Collins.

Like her husband, Bess fretted over advancing age: "Stop thinking that at 48 1/2 years You are old," he chided her. "Tush-tush—and a couple of *'fiddle-de-dees.'* We have our best mature years before us." For their thirtieth wedding anniversary, in June 1924, they posed for their usual gag photos, one showing them lashed together at the waist, kissing. "Me and mine roped together," Houdini wrote on it. Not a comfortable position, perhaps: for all the tush-tushing, Houdini's thoughts sometimes strayed to Charmian London, and hers often to him.

They met once again when Houdini played San Francisco, late in October 1924. Then as earlier, what (if anything) happened is known only through telegraphically brief entries in London's diaries. They reveal that Houdini and Bess asked her to dine with them, but she declined, feeling, she wrote, "like a fool!" She spent a wakeful night dreaming of him, however, "Too intense from Magic." He called the next day and arranged to meet her at her apartment for an hour. But her cryptic diary entry suggests that he either stood her up, as he had done in the past, or that she decided to run out before he arrived: "Meet planned & I wait alone in apt., & finally sorrowfully leave. . . . Feel queer—about Magic but sense of integrity." A few days later she sent him a wire that he failed to answer, making her wonder whether it brought on a row with Bess, "raised ructions." She did receive a letter or note from him a few weeks later, but otherwise the fleeting encounter left her with nothing more than a revived sense of loss: "Keep thinking of Magic," she wrote after his departure; or again, "I feel 'Magic' atmosphere."

Not everyone who knew Houdini found him so enchanting. With his anti-Spiritualist crusade adding a new fame to his old fame, many colleagues in magic found his ego twice as hard to take. "Every magacian [*sic*] in this country," an Ohio magician observed, "would like to see Houdini BEAT in the Scientific American Psychic prize." The outspoken British magician Harry Leat (1874–1929) called him "the best hated conjurer in America." To prove it, he quoted letters he had received from the States:

> One American conjurer writes:— "I do not speak to Houdini. I never get the chance. He does all the talking." Another says: "Provided you let Houdini talk about himself he will stay with you for hours." Another: "Houdini called on me, but I had little chance to speak to him, as he is a non-stop talker, about himself."
>
> Houdini thinks, Leat summed it up, "he is the God amongst conjurers."

Leat exaggerated only in suggesting that, for Houdini, there *were* any other conjurers. Asked to supply the entry on "Conjuring" for a supplement to the *Encyclopaedia Britannica*, Houdini lauded his escape act as the "most radical development in conjuring in the present century." In the glow of that he described and praised one by one his Water Torture Cell, Underwater Packing Box, Milk-Can Escape, Elephant Vanish, and Needle Swallowing. Incredibly, for an encyclopedia article on "Conjuring," he thought it sufficient to mention no other magician but himself, not even the idolized Harry Kellar.

Advancing age, probably, also made Houdini tetchier than ever, readier to act out his Champion fantasies in live dogfights. When a Los Angeles newspaper ran photographs of two minor performers but omitted one of him, he charged into its pressrooms and "raised hell": "All wrong on my part," he noted in his diary, "*but I could not help it*. I was so sore. I was so sore I had a headache all that afternoon." When he learned of a New York firm called the Houdina Company, he went haywire. Convinced they were exploiting his name to promote their product—a device to control an automobile by radio—he confronted the owners in their office. Surviving accounts of what happened differ, but according to the *New York Times* and the *Los Angeles Times* Houdini ripped a Houdina tag off a packing case. When he refused to give it back, four men tried to prevent him from leaving. He then took up an oak chair, smashed an electric chandelier with it, and began busting up the furniture.

As usual Houdini's own version was in Technicolor: "You know the 'Gorillas' here get a man on the floor and kick him insensible, cripple him and send him to the hospital. Two of the men started towards me and two were behind. . . . Had no idea I was smashing up chandeliers. All I thought was to save myself." It was not lost on Houdini that his antics recalled Heath Haldane or Harry Harper punching out yeggs or savages. "I picked up a chair," he said, "and acted in real life the scenes that I have portrayed before the camera."

Next evening Houdini was at the broadcast studio of New York station WOR, getting ready for a fifteen-minute talk over the airwaves on spiritualistic manifestations. The firm's secretary and two policemen entered and served him with a summons, issued by a city magistrate, to appear in court on a charge of disorderly conduct. The Houdina Company, it turned out, was owned by an electrical engineer named Francis P. Houdina. Instead of appearing in court or sending a representative, he dropped the charge. But Houdini understood why the firm had summonsed him. It had nothing to do with his having played Attila the Officewrecker. "Because," he said, "they failed to beat me up."

MARGERY AGAIN AND AT LAST

Incapable of giving up, Houdini still meant to justify his claim that Carrington-and-Bird had aided Margery, and to be credited with having exposed her methods. He was shut out from her ongoing séances. But he infiltrated a mole into them, Stewart Griscom, an admiring reporter for the *Boston Herald*. Griscom sent him diagrammed reports on the sittings, and patiently answered Houdini's questions: "did you feel the vibration of the bell as you held it? Think carefully whether the sound cannot have been made by a duplicate bell. . . . And were the lights turned out immediately after you placed the box on the table. How soon after that did the bell start ringing? It is by this sort of description that I can tell exactly what took place." After "getting a line" on the Crandons' latest attempts from Griscom, Houdini incorporated what he learned into his stage exposé, leaving his audience "greatly surprised," he said, "to think I knew of their progress." In a nice twist Dr. Crandon suspected that Houdini had a spy afoot in Boston, but wrongly targeted him as someone named Mansfield.

Other surprising twists brought Houdini near his hope of vindication. In the late spring of 1925, Margery had submitted to investigation by faculty members of the Harvard psychology department. Houdini protested to President Abbott Lowell of Harvard, calling it a shame to permit Margery to use that "wonderful institution" as a stage for her deceit. The sittings nevertheless went on, one aim being to test a tentacle-like ectoplasmic hand Margery had recently manifested. The results were reported in the November *Atlantic Monthly*, in a sensational article entitled "Science and the Medium: The Climax of a Famous Investigation," by Hudson Hoagland, a graduate student in psychology.

Hoagland disclosed that during one sitting Margery slipped a control—a luminous band that had been placed on her ankle to track its movements in the dark. Walter denied and tried to obscure the fact, but the band had fallen to the floor. When a luminous paper disk floated about the room, too, an investigator managed to make out that it was in the grip of a human right foot. Later examination of the disk confirmed his observation, revealing a crease on the periphery where Margery's toes had clamped it. From other substantial evidence, the Harvard group concluded that Margery had also used her right foot to ring the bell-box and pull the sitters' hair. Finishing herself off, Margery fell into the trap of accepting an offer from one experimenter to release her hand during a séance. When he did, she opened her robe and began removing objects from the region of her lap to manipulate on the séance table, one of them shaped like a baby's hand. The move gave some credence to gossip that Dr. Crandon had surgically enlarged her vagina to give her storage.

Hoagland's article succeeded where Houdini had failed, or felt he had, in convincing the public of Margery's fraudulence. People unwilling to accept the say-so of an 'itinerant magician,' onstage or in a self-published pamphlet, had no trouble believing Harvard scientists announcing the results of their experiments in the highbrow *Atlantic*. Throughout the Margery circle, the article generated upset, anxiety, and offense. Griscom reported to Houdini that Margery herself privately remarked, "Just think how Houdini will shout."

Houdini did more than shout. He cock-a-doodle-doo gloried. "Have you seen the Atlantic Monthly of November?" he wrote to Walter Lippmann. "A certain group of Professors after roundly abusing me, have accomplished in half a year what I did in one night. . . . This has been a wonderful vindication for me." In fact he felt twice vindicated. By making it known that Margery had accepted an offer of collusion, the article bolstered his charges against the SA committee's gruesome twosome. "I openly accused J. Malcolm Bird and Carrington as being her accomplices, and this proves my verdict." He sent similar victory proclamations to other friends, and apparently to other committee members, who now took his side: "the Professors who one time pronounced her genuine have repudiated her," he reported. "I have written apologies from the Harvard gentlemen."

No about-face meant more to Houdini than that of Walter Franklin Prince. Prince had the intelligence to see, and the decency to admit, that much of the time Houdini had been right. As if to make amends, following publication of the *Atlantic* article he told other investigators that reports of Houdini's misconduct were "greatly exaggerated," and rebuked "old lies" about him. He also condemned Bird as "crooked" and called the word of Dr. Crandon "worth absolutely nothing." "The evidence," he declared, "has accumulated so that for me there is no longer any question that the case is fraudulent." Resuming friendly correspondence with Houdini, Prince let him know that Harvard physiologists and zoologists had studied samples of Margery's ectoplasmic tentacle-hand. They found marks of trachea, proving that it had been fabricated out of some animal's lung tissue.

To increase Houdini's delight, the *Atlantic* exposé appeared only a few months after publication of *"Margery" The Medium*, a tome of more than four hundred pages by J. Malcolm Bird. Because of the article, Houdini gloated, the "two inch thick affair, now stands before the world as a monument of falsehoods." Bird devoted about half the book to defending Margery, using materials supplied by Dr. Crandon, and the rest to humiliating Houdini. As many Spiritualists did also, he attributed Houdini's interest in Margery to his running scared, desperately seeking publicity to boost his flagging career: "Houdini is past fifty years old," Bird wrote, "and he faces the necessity for building up something new to keep him among the headliners of his profession."

Buoyed by the *Atlantic* article, Houdini decided to take on Bird no-holds-barred in a climactic public showdown. On February 21, 1926, Bird was scheduled to address a meeting of the Universal Spiritualist Brotherhood Church in Philadelphia. Booked to appear that same Sunday evening in Reading, some sixty miles away, Houdini canceled his engagement for the sake of duking it out with Bird before an audience. He would take along his stenographer to record it all.

The evening at the packed Broad Street Theater began on a note of good citizenship. Mrs. Elizabeth Goetz, pastor of the Third Spiritualist Church of Philadelphia, welcomed the audience as "intelligent respectable

Americans." Dramatizing the point that Spiritualists belonged to the well-behaved mainstream of national life, all joined in singing "America," and then a Spiritualist hymn, "Only a Thin Veil Between Us."

The lean, bespectacled Bird, second speaker of the evening, began by minding his etiquette as well. With Houdini listening from an orchestra seat, he gave a sober overview of Margery's mediumship, classing her powers as both telekinetic and clairvoyant. When he came to Houdini's role in her history, however, he turned shrill. As he had done in his book, he plowed into Houdini's accounts of the séances. Houdini accused Margery of having shouldered open the cabinet, but in fact it had been sundered. The wood was cracked, the screws stripped, sawdust strewn around the floor—signs not of fraud but of a supernatural force. Houdini hinted in his performances "about relations between Margery and myself," but in fact when staying with the Crandons he had usually been accompanied by Mrs. Bird. Spewing rancor and sarcasm about the folding-ruler and the rest, he ridiculed Houdini's myth that he had been fired from *Scientific American*, when in fact he had resigned. "I suppose I might have hung on there for ten or fifteen years against my own desire, so as to rob Mr. Houdini of the opportunity of telling that particular lie about me, or something else."

When he finished, Bird invited Houdini to take the stage, with what the *Philadelphia Inquirer* reported as "a courteous gesture that bore its full burden of scorn." Seemingly to cool down the atmosphere, the decorous mistress of ceremonies, Pastor Goetz, remarked on her pleasure in Houdini's presence. "I do not believe that Mr. Houdini is half as bad as he tries to make himself appear to be," she said, "and I think if he could really reveal his real self we would like him real well."

With this Houdini vaulted to the stage, the *Inquirer* reported, like "a raging lion." Notes and manuscripts heaped under his arm, he began his response to Bird by laying out his own version of the Intelligent Respectable American, a personal testament of honesty, industry, scholarship, good faith, and I'm-not-taking-any-crap-from-you:

> Ladies and gentlemen. I have never been arrested. I have never had anything of any nature against me or mine. I've had to work very hard for everything I have obtained. I come from a race of students and I am not entirely illiterate, and I do read and study. I want you to know, ladies and gentlemen, and I hope you are going to believe

me, that I am sincere in my endeavors to search for the truth. I am making this statement because I am forced to call Bird a liar, and I am going to prove it.

That said, Houdini let loose. He damned Bird as "the only newspaperman I ever met that betrayed his employer." He railed that "I caught him with his hand free when he was supposed to be holding Margery." He jeered that if he had accepted Bird's invitation to "go to hell," he would have met better people there than Bird. Turning to Bird's book, he trounced its claim that he had not allowed the steam-cabinet to be examined. "He has a sneaky way out of every chapter he writes," Houdini said. "And in his book he lies." Houdini called to his assistant:

> Mr. Collins from the rear of the theater: Here I am.
> Mr. Houdini: Collins, how many days was that box lying exposed
>   in Dr. Comstock's room?
> Mr. Collins: Three days and two nights.
> Mr. Houdini: You liar, you contemptible liar. . . .

Through the storm of abuse and peals of "lies" and "liar," Bird sat uneasily in his chair onstage, saying not a word.

Houdini moved on to Bird's slurs on his character and background, evidently so angry he could barely speak:

> You lied in your book when you said my father was not married to
> my mother. Ladies and gentlemen, in his book he said Houdini had
> his hands soiled and said that that is his trouble—that my father
> was—now, do I look like a man like that? If a man would have said
> that to me, I would clean the floor up with him. . . .

The evening already well out of hand, the audience joined in with cheers and boos, through which Houdini thundered on:

> I haven't a quarrel with anyone, but when a man puts two inches of
> pages out in a book and calls me a liar and all kinds of names and I
> can prove him to be a contemptible liar, then I want my word.
> Here's a letter he wrote to the New York Tribune full of lies. In his

book every other page is filled with misstatements. . . . Read your book (addressing Mr. Bird).. . . he double-crossed a Jesuit priest, Father Heredia. Here is the photostat right here (indicating).

As the meeting neared the three-and-a-half-hour mark, the unfortunate Mrs. Goetz stepped in to announce that time was nearly up, "and we must leave the theater in order." According to the *Inquirer*, no order arrived until a policeman was called in to calm "the overheated emotions of the throng."

No doubt to savor the deliciousness of his onstage thrashing of Bird, Houdini bought up twenty-five or more copies of every newspaper that carried an account of it. But still sweeter revenge was in store. He learned from Prince that Margery had been exposed anew by J. B. Rhine, a young Ph.D. from Chicago, and later the founder of the noted ESP laboratory at Duke University. Rhine had detected Margery tipping the megaphone with her foot, clenching the edge of a basket in her teeth, and loosening the setscrew of a test balance with her fingernail. He pronounced Bird "a Crandon tool" and the séances "wholesale fraud."

Houdini also learned from Griscom, his man in Boston, that the "Harvard crowd" had developed a theory to explain the Margery séances. Dr. Crandon, it went, had a "double personality," believing in his wife's manifestations at the same time as he participated in her trickery—he had "amnesia," Griscom wrote, "is cuckoo, nuts, or what have you." In fact a full case study of the couple was emerging from Cambridge and Boston. Much of the gossip, speculation, and strong evidence that lay behind this new understanding came to Prince, who preserved it, unpublished, in a thick dossier of letters and notes. He identified his sources only by their initials, but several were clearly Harvard psychologists and psychical researchers. In their composite view, Margery's séances were a convoluted marital charade. Her actual audience was not Houdini or Doyle or the *Scientific American* committee but her husband, whom she helped to delude himself in order to save their collapsing marriage.

According to this analysis of the situation at Lime Street, the Crandons' marriage had been doomed from the start. Margery was fun-loving where her husband was overserious. The ex-wife of a grocer, she lagged intellectually and socially far behind him. On his side the twice-divorced Crandon had grown bored with his wife and wanted to get rid of her. (It was rumored that he had been expelled from a Boston hospital for "actions with nurses.") But Crandon was also vulnerable, plagued by a morbid fear of death. In trying to keep him, Margery hit on the idea of relieving his dread by manifesting spirits. It worked: Crandon found his fear of death put to rest by the discarnate return of Walter. With half a million Spiritualists in the country regarding Margery as a sort of Messiah, too, his passionate involvement in his wife's mediumship made him seem a martyr. He could liken himself to Galileo, enjoying the prestige to which he felt entitled because of his surgical skill. Crandon not only needed and encouraged Margery to produce her entities but also came to demand them. As Walter Prince's notes put it, he established an "emotional ascendancy of fear over the psychic, [and] used downright brutality in forcing her to continue the mediumship." Many of Prince's sources believed that Margery would give up her séances and confess to fraud, except for knowing that it would end her marriage.

Whether Prince divulged this profile to Houdini is unknown. But it would not have surprised Houdini to hear the Crandons described as "two oversexed people matched together with little else in common." From the beginning of the SA investigation he had been alive to the erotic elements of the séances. He told one Harvard investigator that Margery acted seductively, "making advances to every man in sight." (For himself, he said, he was immune: "her applesauce meant nothing to me.") He evidently also saw the photographs Dr. Crandon sometimes displayed of Margery nude or seminude, oozing teleplasm from her navel. Nor can he or anyone have missed the sexual charge in the dark séance room, the close-friends-for-the-weekend atmosphere, the disrobing, Margery's spread legs pressed against her controls, her dress hiked above her knees. In his diary Houdini recorded that during one séance he caught Bird "with his hand under Margery's dress . . . *grouping* [sic]." From prudishness, probably, he had refrained from exploiting what he knew or believed, although in his writings he had hinted at it. "Read between the lines," he told a friend, "and you will see I accused Margery of using 'sex charm' and it has been authenticated."

"Authenticated"? Possibly. Years later Carrington told an associate that he and Margery had carried on a several months' affair, with the understanding that it would not affect his committee report on the genuineness of her mediumship. Bird later fell out with the Crandons. When he did, he made it seem that Margery's séances had served him only as pretexts for traveling from New York to Boston—to keep going his own romance with her. If true or nearly true, that may explain his confederacy with Margery, about which Houdini had not been wrong. Houdini did not live to hear it, but in 1930 Bird admitted that he had seen Margery using her feet to tilt a séance table, yet had said nothing. He also admitted that during one of the sittings with Houdini, Margery had asked him to secretly ring the bell-box, or do something else that might pass for a manifestation by Walter. According to Bird, Carrington too had kept quiet after seeing Margery produce psychic lights by means of luminous paint daubed on the soles of her stockings.

About the only person not heard from in the rush of new revelations about Margery was Mina Crandon herself. A family member depicted her at the time as "frightfully nervous," exhausted by the continuing investigations and under great strain, "reaching her limit nervously." What depths her desperate séances had stirred in her can only be guessed at. But she was headed for chronic, and finally killing, alcoholism. In 1932, cocktail-soaked and reminiscing about her alleged lovers, she remarked to Walter Prince's secretary that Carrington "*was* good-looking" and that she had nicknamed him "Carrie." In hot-weather sittings the other SA investigators looked dilapidated, she recalled, but Carrington looked "like a million dollars." He had an upstairs room at Lime Street, where he would refresh his appearance. ("Why he's a pink one," her maid broke in. "He has rouge, cold cream, lipstick etc. in his room and uses it all the time!") Bird, however, she said she found "disgusting looking," the kind of man "you feel you want to sweep the house out after." In one of his trips to Boston, she said, Bird had picked up some woman, registered with her at a hotel, and sat drinking with her at the bar. "The girl sat on Bird's lap and wet all over him, that's the kind of girl she was."

How much if any of this Houdini heard about is uncertain. But he did get new information about Margery from his spy Griscom, who provided the strangest revelation of all. Griscom said that when he and Margery were alone, it was "tacitly admitted" between them that mediumship was all fraud. "Aren't people damn fools, such damn fools," she said with a grin. "The investigators most of all." She disclosed that she admired Houdini for not being taken in by her, and for not being afraid "to say where he stands." Not only that: like Houdini himself she felt out of place in Boston-Cambridge society. She found him a pleasant contrast, she said, to "certain men high in academic circles."

It was an odd case. More than Houdini had known or could ever have supposed, he and Margery in their intense encounter had been covert companions, challengers who were at heart semblances of each other, not rivals and enemies really but secret sharers, allies against a world of suckers and swank. "I respect Houdini more than any of the bunch," she told Griscom. "He has both feet on the ground all the time."

PALIGENESIA

Dann magst du mich in Fesseln schlagen,
Dann will ich gern zu Grunde gehn!

Then you're free to clap me in chains,
Then I'll gladly perish!

— GOETHE, *Faust*

escapemaster-in-chief from all sorts of houdingplaces
— JAMES JOYCE, *Finnegans Wake*

TOM: You know it don't take much intelligence to get
yourself into a nailed-up coffin, Laura. But who in hell
ever got himself out of one without removing one nail?
— TENNESSEE WILLIAMS, *The Glass Menagerie*

SEVENTEEN

JANUARY–AUGUST 1926

HOUDINI

DURING THE 1925 Christmas season, patrons of the legitimate theater in New York had an unusual choice of what to see. There was Shaw's *Arms and the Man*, with the much-applauded acting couple Alfred Lunt and Lynn Fontanne. There was Ibsen's *The Master Builder*, starring his outstanding American interpreter, Eva Le Gallienne. At the Shubert Brothers' Forty-fourth Street Theatre, the evening's entertainment was *HOUDINI*. "Pretty good," as he had once told his diary, "for Dime Museum Houdini."

Presented at a Broadway playhouse, in ticket-competition with top actors in major dramas, the show ended Houdini's career-long search for theatrical respectability. A Houdini carefully-combed and in jacket-and-tie gently smiled from the handsome souvenir program. The text touted his international standing, his versatility in aviation and films, his omnivorous reading and collecting: "He is recognized by scientists and mingles with Savants. . . . His home is a Mecca for theologians and writers . . . at one time he taught a Junior Class in his father's college." Booked to play legitimate theaters across the country, *HOUDINI* had opened its New York run late in December, heralded by a calliope piping up and down Broadway.

For the always-adventurous Houdini the new show meant not only a fulfillment but also, as he neared fifty-two, a headlong change of course. By contrast with his thirty-minute vaudeville turns, *HOUDINI* ran two and a half hours, usually divided into three acts with two ten-minute intermissions. Act 3, entitled "Do the Dead Come Back?" consisted of an hour's exposé and forum. Act 2, "Houdini Himself, in Person," featured three quintessential blockbusters, "Feats That Have Made Him Famous": Metamorphosis, Needle Swallowing, and the Water Torture Cell. But the surprise innovation was the sixty-minute first act, "Magic." Here Houdini performed some fifteen large-scale tricks and illusions. Except for the "Grand Magical Revue" he had briefly mounted in England in 1914, this was far more magic than he had ever presented at one time. It would not exaggerate the novelty of Houdini's 1925–26 show to say that, after a lifetime in magic, it marked his professional debut as a magician.

"Magic" began with two female assistants walking out from the wings on either side and parting the curtain. They disclosed a stage neatly-set with tables and magical apparatus, before a curved, vaguely Moorish backdrop. A clock struck mysteriously. Enter Houdini, in evening clothes and white tie, startlingly pulling off his sleeves. The gesture all but hollered Nothing Up There, and through at least some of the show he performed in an odd short-sleeved dress coat that revealed his bare arms. The costume underscored his (studied) informality. The cups-and-balls master Bartolomeo Bosco (1793–1863) had used the same bit of business for an additional reason as well. Bosco "had very handsome arms," Houdini noted, "and when he would take off his sleeves, (his coat or suit was so arranged,) every one admired his arms." After this attention-getter Houdini presented his opening effect, usually, as in his English revue, Robert-Houdin's Crystal Casket.

The salutes to Bosco and to Robert-Houdin were pure Houdini. Probably no other magician has worked with such a broad, felt awareness of the history of magic. The note of homage continued in "Paligenesia" (rebirth), a once-famous illusion invented by the plump popular Victorian magician Dr. Lynn. Houdini's theater program highlighted the effect as having "Startled and Pleased Your Grand and Great-Grand-Parents," and pointed out that he was "the only living performer legally authorized" to recreate it, using Lynn's IDENTICAL ORIGINAL apparatus. The magician ropes his assistant to an upright door, against an all-important dark backdrop. With a large, dangerous-looking knife, he hacks off the assistant's arm and leg, tosses them on a chair, severs the assistant's head, then restores the limbs and head to the body. (An amusing antique, "Paligenesia" would not chill or mystify an audience today, and is no longer performed.)

Constantly dropping or adding effects, Houdini at one time or another featured a half dozen other large illusions, most involving young female assistants. Keeping step with the Jazz Age, he outfitted them in shimmering silvery camisoles, exposing eyefuls of leg, arm, and chest. In "Radio of 1950," he displayed a large rectangular table, topped by a giant radio cabinet with outsize dials. Lowering its front and rear panels disclosed nothing inside but some tubes and wires. Yet when Houdini turned the dials, music blared from inside, the top popped open, and out stepped an assistant in flapper scanties, who swung into the Charleston. In "Wintertime" and "Summertime"—sometimes presented separately, sometimes together—three tables were set up pyramid-style, the top covered by a sheet. An assistant climbed under the sheet, which at the words "Good-bye, Winter" was whisked away: she had vanished. In the companion illusion, Houdini exhibited a tall slopesided box, a sort of truncated pyramid—empty. When he said "Welcome Summer," shooting off a blank pistol, the cover flew off and "Miss Summer" appeared, garlanded with flowers. He sometimes closed with the "Miracle of Mahatma"—still another empty cabinet, which in this case spilled out no fewer than six female assistants.

Memorable among Houdini's smaller effects were the ingeniously mechanical "Flight of Time" and "Magic Rose Bush." In the first, he threw a row of ringing alarm clocks one at a time into the air, where they vanished. They reappeared one by one hanging from watch-chains at the other side of the stage. As a topper he made the clocks expand to nearly the size of snare drums. In the other, a large barren bush visibly sprouted red roses—an automatonlike marvel of eighteenth-century ancestry that reportedly cost Houdini more than three thousand dollars to build. He also threw a jumbo deck of cards at a large metal star, inducing six cards selected by the audience to stick to its points ("Herr Doebler's Masterpiece"—another tribute); caught live goldfish at the end of a fishing rod, in midair ("Izaak Walton Eclipsed"); made a lamp disappear from one table and come back on another ("Conradi's Alladin's Lamp"); and produced from an empty bowl yards and yards of gaily-colored silk handkerchiefs, followed by the flags of all nations ("A Whirlwind of Colors"). Still other silks tied and untied themselves or jumped from one bottle to another; papers and cloth, burnt or cut, became whole again; from or into thin air came or went rabbits, doves, a rooster, stacks of fishbowls, birdcages (twelve at one time). The pace must have been brisk: Houdini said he "jammed one and a half hours performance into an hour."

HOUDINI cost no small care and expense. Handling dozens of tricks, illusions, escapes, and demonstrations called for smooth logistics and tight scheduling. Houdini prepared a timesheet charting the minutes and seconds allowed for individual tricks, the lighting cues, the bits of patter: when producing a bunny, "to prove that I am a magician"; swallowing the needles, "how do they taste—a little sharp." He kept notes on past mistakes, reminding himself to show some cylinder empty, freshen production-flowers, keep flags from trailing on the floor. He also commissioned a musical score, bought or rented animals, and paid the expenses of eight onstage assistants. These included three relatives: Bess (identified in the program as "Miss Beatrice Rahner," an homage to his own tent-show days); Bess's twenty-one-year-old niece, Julia Sawyer (nicely built for illusions, Houdini noted, "as she is a little girl"); and Sawyer's aunt Julia Karcher, who helped Bess sew costumes. After the show they dined with Houdini and reviewed the evening's performance.

Houdini engaged a large backstage staff as well. Besides a personal representative, company manager, and business manager, he hired an advance-man to whip up publicity, a secretary to deal with correspondence, and local attorneys to field lawsuits arising from the Spiritualism demonstration. To attend to props, costumes, and sets he also carried a full-time carpenter, electrician, and property master, supervised by Jim Collins as stage manager. Electrical equipment alone—spotlights, orchestra lights, feed cables, a switchboard—filled three crates and some fifteen boxes. The contents of as many as fifty crates and trunks had to be set up, knocked down, stored, and hauled in a sixty-foot railroad car. The movable stage-ware included a curtain that was lowered during intermissions, quilted with ribbons bestowed on Houdini by European theater managers, to signify, his program noted, record-breaking receipts—"a la Marathon winner."

Despite some thin houses, Houdini's extravaganza made money. It played Chicago for an unusually long run of eight weeks, sometimes grossing ten to twelve thousand dollars a week. "I have been told," he said, "this is the biggest hit ever made by any magician." The designation of himself was novel, for he had often said, accurately, "I am not a magician, but a mystifier." His peers differed in their opinions of his ability to do straight stage magic. *The Sphinx* editorialized that his hour equaled or sur-passed anything since Kellar. Editor A. M. Wilson privately told Houdini that it packed in "more magic . . . than Thurston has in his entire evening show." (Gratifying: a friend reported him saying, "We're going to shove Thurston right off of the boards!") On the other hand a *Sphinx* reviewer found the show "rather a disappointment"—too long, too unpolished, and too much The Great Houdini: "the word 'I' . . . is overworked all through."

Whatever others thought, Houdini himself was pleased. He considered his initial nine-month tour "the most successful, (financially and artisti-cally,) one that I have had," a career-peak. Among the minuses, a few weeks after opening in New York he slipped stepping out of a taxi and broke a bone in his left foot. Although hobbling on crutches he continued to per-form. For several weeks he skipped the Water Torture Cell, however, to avoid being winched up by his ankles. *Billboard* applauded him for "courage nothing short of Spartan," and recalled the woeful predictions during the Margery investigation that he would soon meet his death. "Hou-dini is very much alive," the magazine commented, "and the worst that hap-pened was a broken bone that couldn't even keep the magician off the stage. 'Margery's' crystal seems to be a bit misty."

CHICAGO RAIDS AND LAWSUITS; THE CONGRESSIONAL HEARINGS

At the same time that he mounted his show, and with help from it, Houdini brought his anti-Spiritualism crusade to a climax. During the eight-week Chicago run, he claimed, he and his investigators exposed in the city no fewer than seventy-nine fraud mediums. The *Chicago American* covered its front page with the story of how he cornered Mrs. Minnie Reichert during a basement séance with nineteen sitters, eight of them his operatives. The exposé included a dead-to-rights flash photo that showed her raising a spirit-trumpet to her lips with a handkerchief, to prevent fingerprints. In the pandemonium that followed, the camera had been passed hand-to-hand among Houdini's crew, five of whom climbed out the window, taking the camera with them. "I get letters from ardent believers in spiritualism," he told the *American*, "who prophesy I am going to meet a violent death soon as a fitting punishment for my nefarious work."

During the same Chicago run three mediums and a manager for sev-eral other mediums, Arthur McNally, filed a quarter-million-dollar lawsuit against Houdini and the theater for libel and slander. They alleged that from the stage Houdini had named the mediums individually, labeled them frauds, and called McNally a "dirty crook," and that in substance the theater's billboard and canopy repeated his remarks. With scores of Chicago mediums jamming courtroom and corridors, Houdini, a sign painter, and other defense witnesses convinced a judge that the theater advertising had not included the words "fraudulent mediums exposed." "Every one of the spiritualists who got on the stand committed perjury," Houdini said after the trial. Other allegations remained to be tried, however. Not without pride, Houdini estimated that he was the target of lawsuits totaling more than one million dollars.

Seeking for the first time a governmental forum, Houdini took his crusade to Washington. His chance to do so came when an anti-fortune-telling bill was proposed for the District of Columbia. Several states already had such bills and used them to prosecute séance swindles. The bill for the District was sponsored by Sol Bloom, a U.S. representative from New York who had been in the theatrical and music-publishing businesses.

Probably at Bloom's invitation, Houdini testified before Senate and House subcommittees during four days of hearings in February and May 1926. In essence the bill required that anyone "pretending to tell fortunes for reward or compensation" should be treated as "a disorderly person," subject to a fine of up to $250 and/or imprisonment up to six months. Some committee members considered the bill another infringement on personal liberty, along with Prohibition. Others thought it frivolous, aimed at abuses not worth noticing. Nearly all questioned its loose language, which in places seemed to violate constitutional guarantees of religious freedom. By including persons who sold "charms for protection," for instance, the bill could be construed as taking in the sale of St. Christopher medals among Catholics. The attempt to find precise language, moreover, was mired in disagreement about the validity of the Spiritualists' claims. As a Washington lawyer testified, "the whole field of psychic phenomena is still so far a mystery that not even those who pretend to understand it can be trusted to frame a single prohibition upon human conduct in that field which will stand the test of logical analysis." She advised the committee to give up.

The hearings were riotous. Witnesses and spectators talked and yelled over each other. Testimony was interrupted by laughter, whistles, gavel-banging, cries of "shut up" and "faker." Houdini estimated that "between

150 and 300" mediums and Spiritualists from the Washington area attended. Angry over recent arrest of mediums in Boston, Chicago, and other cities, they wanted to make sure that the bill clearly defined the difference between "fortune-telling" and Spiritualist prophesying. With all the chairs in the room occupied, some squatted on the floor, applauding, hissing, and otherwise keeping up a running fire against Houdini. He no sooner rose to speak than mediums and their allies began shouting, "Liar!" During the May 18 meeting an adjournment had to be called when the committee was unable to restore order. As witnesses and audience filed into the corridors, the uproar continued and threatened to erupt in fistfights, some members demanding that the police be called. The day after the final hearing Representative Bloom, the bill's sponsor, fainted in the House lobby.

Far from passing out, Houdini soared on the hullabaloo. During his own testimony he tagged mediums "mental degenerates," unspooled his fifty-foot scroll of fake pastoral licenses, manifested slate writings and trumpet voices, threw down on the meeting table a challenge-bundle of ten thousand dollars in cash, trotted out clippings about sexual assaults at séances, hooted the notion that Spiritualism was a religion: "How can you call it 'religion' when you get men and women in a room together and feel each other's hands and bodies?" Allowed to produce and interrogate witnesses himself, he hotly cross-examined mediums on the stand. When one denied selling charms, he warned her that "If you do I will catch you." "You will never catch me," she shot back. "No, sir. I am as slick as you are, thank you."

Knowing in advance the identities of two of the mediums slated to testify, Houdini sent his investigator Rose Mackenberg to them for a sitting a few days before. He instructed her to pay in marked bills and to pencil-mark the wallpaper to prove she had been in the séance room. Called to the stand, The Rev attested that for two dollars she learned from a Mrs. Coates, a member of the American Order of the White Cross Societas, that she would take a trip with a man with whom she had been "intimate." Mrs. Coates, who was present, shrilly denied that, as well as Mackenberg's testimony that she had said she liked Houdini:

MISS MACKENBERG. You said . . . you thought he was very nice; and, in fact, you felt he was misdirected.

> MRS. COATES. I said I thought Mr. Houdini was mentally deranged.
> MISS MACKENBERG. You said he was very nice, and you felt like
> putting your arms around him—
> MRS. COATES. Oh, no.

Coates protested that she had said she felt sorry for Houdini and wanted to protect him from his own fanaticism: "if he kept on exciting his mind to the state it was in it must of necessity snap and he would find himself in an insane asylum. . . . Mr. Houdini has placed so many people mentally in the asylum in these talks that his thought may return to him and place him there."

Houdini's trap for Mrs. Coates netted a bombshell. Mackenberg testified that the medium had told her Houdini was "up against a stone wall" because many senators practiced Spiritualism themselves. "I know for a fact," Coates allegedly said, "that there have been spiritual seances held at the White House with President Coolidge and his family." The outing of closet table-tippers on Pennsylvania Avenue provoked howls of "That's a lie" in the committee room and made headlines the next day; the White House issued a quick denial. *The New York Times* editorialized that the story could not be taken seriously, since the president's "cool New England mind is about the very last to have any patience with things of that sort." But Coates retracted only to the extent of saying she had had in mind not the Coolidge family but Mrs. Harding, who had openly visited mediums during her husband's administration. And Houdini told Walter Lippmann "in strict confidence" that he credited the story: "I have heard on rather good authority that they do hold seances in the White House and am looking for further proof regarding same."

Amid the screeching and browbeating, an elderly representative from North Carolina, William C. Hammer, provided an interlude of travesty. A former schoolteacher, he had never heard of Houdini. He asked the chairman's permission to inquire "who he is and if he is not an astrologist":

> MR. HAMMER. I didn't understand what your occupation is.
> MR. HOUDINI. I am a syndicate writer; I am an author, and I am a
> mystifier, which means I am an illusionist.
> MR. HAMMER. You don't claim to be able to do anything by divine
> power?

MR. HOUDINI. No, sir; I am human. But mediums are trying to say
I am psychic. That is not true. . . . But I do tricks nobody can
explain.

Some Spiritualists had informed Hammer that Houdini simply refused to
acknowledge being a powerful medium himself. Hammer bore in on
whether he might not in fact be gifted with powers of the East:

MR. HAMMER. The Original Houdini was a Hindu, was he not?
MR. HOUDINI. No.
MR. HAMMER. You are Houdini the second?
MR. HOUDINI. No.
MR. HAMMER. You are the original Houdini?
MR. HOUDINI. No; the original Houdini was a French clock maker.
MR. HAMMER. I thought he lived in Allahabab.
MR. HOUDINI. Are you joking?
MR. HAMMER. No; I am in earnest; . . .
MR. HAMMER. Have you ever been in Allahabab?
MR. HOUDINI. No, sir.
MR. HAMMER. You have read the Arabian Nights stories?
MR. HOUDINI. Yes, sir.
MR. HAMMER.. But you have never been there?
MR. HOUDINI. No, sir.

With many Americans worried about homegrown cabals of Reds and anar-
chists, Hammer's antennae twitched at information that Houdini headed
some society of magicians. He wanted to know whether it was a "secret
organization," and if so, whether it had foreign branches, for instance in
Russia. "Not in Russia," Houdini replied.

Spiritualists present at the hearings gave Houdini about as good as
they got. The head of the National Spiritualists' Association, from the witness stand, called him "a pronounced atheist and infidel." Madame Marcia
gibed that his crusade had actually helped her: "You have given me more
advertisement than I ever had before. I could be a freak at present and get
$10 to look at me. And my telephone ringing. So, thank you for the 'buggy
ride.' [Laughter and applause]." Like the Spiritualist controversy itself, the
hearings bared racial and ethnic tensions. With several African-American

mediums in the audience, Houdini condemned the excesses of a Pennsylvania medium, "a colored man, and he gets white women in there." Clearly referring to Houdini and Representative Bloom, a medium testified that "3,000 years ago, or 2,000, Judas betrayed Christ. He was a Jew, and I want to say that this bill is being put through by two—well, you can use your opinion; I am not making any assertion."

Houdini made his case with customary pep—too much so, he later felt, to make it effectively. He treated the hearings as one of his staged anti-Spiritualist lectures, speechmaking and trying to hold the spotlight, to the annoyance of some congressmen. "Are you going to run this?" one beefed. "You are so used to running your show, I know." Unable to resist clowning and gushing, either, Houdini at one point called Bess to the stand as a character witness for himself:

> MR. HOUDINI. . . . Step this way, Mrs. Houdini. One of the witnesses said I was a brute and that I was vile and I was crazy. Won't you step this way? I want the chairman to see you. . . . There are no medals and no ribbons on me, but when a girl will stick to a man for 32 years as she did and when she will starve with me and work with me through thick and thin, it is a pretty good recommendation. Outside of my great mother, Mrs. Houdini has been my greatest friend.
>
> Have I shown traces of being crazy, unless it was about you? [Laughter]
> MRS. HOUDINI. No.
> MR. HOUDINI. Am I brutal to you, or vile?
> MRS. HOUDINI. No. . . .
> MR. HOUDINI. Thank you, Mrs. Houdini. [Applause]

In the end what Houdini did did not matter. The subcommittee could find no way of treating Spiritualism under the bill without stepping on First Amendment guarantees, and did not recommend the bill for action.

Houdini, however, felt he had too much distracted the congressmen, and blamed the outcome on his all-too-entrancing showmanship. "I think they were more interested in my manifestations than they were in the mediums," he reflected. "I was sorry to see that as I really am sincere about the law."

THE SHELTON POOL MIRACLE

A different kind of fraud goaded Houdini into attempting an awesome feat of physical endurance.

About a week after the hearings ended, he went to look over a much-talked-about new performer, a handsome Egyptian fakir named Rahman Bey. Appearing at the Selwyn Theater in New York, Bey put on a gripping show. As the orchestra played Oriental music, a slowly rising curtain revealed him, dressed in flowing white raiment, standing atop a white stairway in an attitude of prayer. Attributing to himself a mysterious mastery of physiological functions, he hypnotized animals, demonstrated that he could control his pulse, forced steel hatpins through his cheek into his mouth and out his lips. Stretched full-length between two sharp swords supporting his neck and feet, he also allowed a flat stone to be placed on his body and pounded with a hammer, which cracked the stone. In his most impossible-seeming test, he entered a cataleptic trance and was placed in a coffin that was then nailed shut and buried under sand. He stayed inside for eight minutes or more.

Even apart from getting impressive reviews, Bey's show contained much to nettle Houdini. For one thing he had himself presented the buried-alive stunt years before. For another, sideshow fakirs for centuries maybe had turned themselves into pincushions or lain down on swords, by means Houdini had already explained in his *Miracle Mongers and Their Methods*. Mesmerizing chickens and rabbits was old hat too. "There is as much hypnotism in this," Houdini scoffed to Walter Lippmann, "as there is lack of liquor in America." The worst irritants in Bey's show, however, were first his solemnities about "cataleptic anathesia [sic]"—a "lot of bunk," Houdini called it, not much different from the phony trances of mediums. And the master of ceremonies for Bey's shenanigans was Hereward Carrington, of the rouged cheeks and seventy-five-dollar Oskaloosa Ph.D. Houdini had wanted to expose Bey on the spot. But Carrington noticed him in the audience and cagily declared that Bey operated by natural, not supernatural means. "That alone spiked my guns," Houdini said.

Over the next two months, while laying off for the summer, Houdini kept looking for Carrington or Bey to make some public claim of psychic ability that would justify lacing into them. But as he bided his time, they earned themselves more newspaper space. Early in July the *New York Times* headlined Bey's attempt to stay submerged in the Hudson River while sealed within a bronze casket, remaining there in "self-imposed catalepsy" for an entire hour. Four minutes into the hairy test, as the casket was being lowered into the water, an emergency bell inside began ringing urgently. Workmen jerked the casket back and tried to open it with chisels and shears; to slash through the lid took them about fifteen minutes. Although Bey had not stayed underwater the promised hour, he was able to boast that he had gone without air for some twenty minutes. As to the emergency bell, he had no recollection of having touched it. Carrington, emcee for the event, explained that Bey, in his rigid trance, had unawares rolled over on the mechanism, the weight of his body tripping it off.

Houdini had a simpler explanation of what had happened inside Bey's coffin: "he got 'yellow' and rang the emergency bell." The episode ended Houdini's moratorium: "now that [Bey] claims to be a super-normally gifted human being, a miracle man," he told Prince, "am compelled to go after him." To the press and to friends, he mocked Bey as "the Italian, who claims to be an Egyptian"; he insisted that Bey had been *sealed* in the coffin not twenty minutes but only four. Houdini's one-of-a-kind friend Robert Gysel joined in, offering Bey a thousand dollars to do as he could do, namely: "Pierce my arm with six rusty needles every hour of the day . . . burn my arm in six different places every hour of the day . . . and with blowtorch to melt lead, dropping it upon my tongue." As had to happen, Houdini also issued a challenge, and advertised it widely. "I guarantee," as he wrote the *Evening World*, "to remain in any coffin that the fakir does for the same length of time he does, without going into any cataleptic trance."

Houdini spoke too hastily. Bey followed up his failed attempt in the Hudson by trying again at a New York swimming school. At poolside he was soldered inside a zinc casket, in which he remained for thirty-six minutes. The casket was submerged in the pool, and with six men standing on top to keep it down, it stayed underwater another twenty-four minutes. At the fifty-ninth minute, an air-valve on the casket was opened, and workmen began cutting Bey out. Unbelievably, miraculously, he was still alive. FAKIR SEALED IN A CASKET ONE HOUR, *The Times* reported.

Houdini now had to make good on a public challenge that committed him to going without air for an hour or more. Beyond possibility as that seemed, he undertook three weeks of do-or-die training for it. No other mortal, of course, had ever spent so much time in airtight boxes, boilers, and cans. He had passed time in coffins too, where in tempting death he came upon his own melancholy horror of it. (After being measured for an escape-coffin in 1907, he noted, "I wonder how soon I'll be in one for real.") And before making his first manacled bridge jumps, he had submitted to a long, punishing regime of breath-holding and icebaths. But he was then nearly twenty years younger and twenty pounds lighter. Over the years he had thickened from 150 to 170. In his first breathing practices he found himself struggling to get his lungs "accustomed to battle without air."

During the war Houdini had put his underwater skills to patriotic use by offering troops instruction in escaping battered ships. Feeling that his breathing tests might be similarly helpful to miners trapped in collapsed shafts, he contacted a physiologist with the U.S. Bureau of Mines, Dr. W. J. McConnell, offering to report to him on his practice-runs "from a humanitarian viewpoint." Not only McConnell welcomed the information, it happened, but so did coal companies, ventilating engineers, and manufacturers of mine-safety equipment, who all requested his data.

Houdini conducted his first experiments secretly. He worked in a back room of the Boyertown Burial Casket Company, a large New York firm that had supplied a coffin for Bey, and now provided a trial-coffin for him too. He reported to McConnell that it held some 26,428 cubic inches of air. Admittedly anxious about the possibility of an accident, he had the box made with a glass top so that he could be closely watched, and simply stayed inside without being submerged. He kept a physician in attendance nearby, too, and at one point could hear him say, through the glass, "I would not do that for $500." After about forty-five minutes, scarcely moving, he started to perspire, and soon became soaked. Several times he shouted, "Get me a towel," but then had to gasp for breath. By the time the lid was taken off, the fresh air feeling icy cold, he had matched Bey's record and then some, having remained encoffined for an hour and ten minutes. But he distrusted the result. At no time had his body felt wracked—which made him suspect that some air must have seeped inside to help him.

For his next tryout, apparently a few days later, Houdini had the coffin made airtight—lined with galvanized iron and sealed with thirty-two bolts and screws. Once inside, he had himself submerged in a tank, under an inch and a half of water. By thermometers placed at his head and his feet, the interior temperature could be charted through the glass top at five-minute intervals, data he sent on to Dr. McConnell for the Bureau of Mines to consider. Houdini found the coffin very moist and a bit cold, and after about fifty minutes he began drawing slow, long breaths. But generally he felt comfortable. What stuck out was his irritability. "I was annoyed by movements, annoyed by one of my assistants swaying over my head, even twisting of the key," he informed McConnell. He thought it just a case of nerves, "simply temperament on my part." After an hour and ten minutes—about the same time as his first experiment—he signaled to be let out.

The morning of the actual challenge to Bey, August 5, 1926, Houdini ate a light breakfast of fruit salad and half a cup of coffee, having taken a physic the day before. While training he had tried to slim down. He lost thirteen pounds, bringing him to just a few pounds over his Handcuff King weight. Feeling somewhat nervous—from excitement, he said, not fear—he traveled from his brownstone on 113th Street to 49th and Lexington Avenue, site of the thirty-four-story Hotel Shelton. Recently built, the hotel advertised itself as having "one of the most magnificent and costly swimming pools in the country." Houdini had sent engraved invitations to Walter Lippmann, Adolph Ochs, and other friends, who now mingled amid potted palms with a hundred or so fellow spectators on the tiled mosaic path around the pool—strawhatted reporters with writing pads, tinsmiths and other workmen in bib overalls, assistants in tank suits, the government physiologist Dr. McConnell, and several physicians. Handsome though the pool area was, it troubled Houdini to find it also overly warm.

Boyertown Burial Casket had furnished Houdini a new coffin, which lay at a corner of the pool. It was an unembellished gray box of galvanized iron, six and a half feet long and about two feet wide and high. Larger than his practice coffins, it held 34,398 cubic inches of air—"close" air, however, filled with carbon dioxide. Some physicians estimated that a human being could survive on such air for only three to four minutes. The lid had two five-inch portholes—one at the head, one at the foot—covered with bronze discs. Left open while the lid was being fastened, the portholes allowed Houdini to breathe naturally until the last moment. And in an emergency, should the casket have to be yanked from the pool, they could be quickly unscrewed to give him fresh air. Two wires ran through the coffin. One, through the side, connected a pushbutton within the coffin to a signal bell outside. The other, a telephone wire through the lid, enabled Houdini to speak through a battery-operated phone to Jim Collins on the walkway.

Stripped to brown trunks and white shirt, and wearing a wristwatch with a radium dial, Houdini spent several minutes inhaling and exhaling to store up reserve oxygen. He lay down in the casket just before noon. The tinsmiths took eight minutes to solder down the heavy lid, its portholes open. Spectators crowded three-deep to watch, a few standing on chairs to see over other heads. The box was then lowered into the warm water— close by the wall of the pool, so as not to snap the telephone and bell wires. Although girded by a raftlike frame of weighted iron bars, to help sink it, the casket stayed only partially submerged until eight assistants in bathing suits slipped into the pool and sat on the lid to force it underwater and keep it there, with Houdini inside.

For the first half hour, Collins announced the time to Houdini by phone every five minutes. Because of the unexpected warmth, Houdini felt far less comfortable than during his practices, and his irritability was "pronounced." His assistants in the pool from time to time shook the coffin to stir the air inside, but in his testy mood he was tempted to tell them to stop. He controlled himself until, in one shaking, an assistant fell off the casket, which shot into the air, bounced, and almost turned over. The thud made Houdini fear the coffin might have split, forcing water in and drowning him. "What's the big idea?" he phoned through. "What struck me?" To save his breath he had said nothing until this moment. The effort left him gasping for air.

A half hour having passed, Collins began relaying the time to Houdini every minute. The invitations described the event as "HOUDINI'S experiment of attempting to remain submerged one hour in an airtight metal coffin." But after fifty minutes he found himself breathing heavily, and soon began panting. He was not sure he would be able to hold out for an hour. He recalled that in his practices, the thermometer at his feet had registered a few degrees less than the one at his head. He slid himself toward the foot-end of the coffin. Sometimes he pressed to his lips a damp handkerchief he had brought with him. It felt cool but had no air value. Houdini stayed still, silent, having in his mouth the taste of metal. The bell rang, indicating, at last, that an hour had elapsed. From some wetness around his shoulder, he realized that the coffin was in fact slightly leaking.

When Collins phoned to say that he had been inside an hour and twelve minutes, Houdini decided to try to hang on for three more minutes, to beat Bey's record by fifteen. In his trial-runs, the temperature inside the box had stayed constant at about eighty degrees. It was now above ninety-nine. But he had somehow grabbed a second wind. His lungs rising and falling accordionlike, he felt he could stand the strain even longer than another three minutes.

At one hour and twenty-eight minutes Houdini began seeing yellow lights. Drowsy, he forced his eyes wide open, monitoring himself intently to stay awake. To take weight off his lungs he moved onto the broad of his back and pressed his left buttock against the coffin so that he could wedge the telephone receiver to his ear without holding it. Sensing that he might nod off despite his efforts not to, he told Collins to haul him up at an hour and a half no matter what.

As the coffin came out of the water, Houdini experienced a combination of physical elation and his curious irritation. With the reduction of pressure on the box came, he said, "a relief all over my body." And when the lower porthole disc was unscrewed, the coffin itself seemed to expand. Swoonily he felt lifted off his back by the inrush of air. Yet it irked him that the upper disc had been left in place. It was no sooner removed than he thrust his arm through the porthole for Dr. McConnell to take his pulse: 142. Meanwhile, spectators crowding around, four tinsmiths literally tore open the casket, peeling back the lid like that of a sardine can. When Houdini climbed out, his thinning hair plastered down with sweat, McConnell measured his respiration-rate, temperature, and blood pressure. He reported them not drastically changed, the before-and-after temperatures being 98.6 and 99, the blood pressures 141/84 and 162/42. Whatever the readings, Houdini was running with perspiration and, by one account, "deathly white." That evening he felt weak-kneed and listless, and still had in his mouth and stomach the sensation of metal.

But he was alive. He had remained underwater, soldered in an airtight coffin, for one hour and thirty-one minutes.

HOUDINI WINS, the *Times* boomed. BEATS HINDOO'S RECORD. Aside from enjoying his triumph over Bey and Carrington, Houdini thought over its implications for miners, submariners, and others trapped in closed compartments. What killed them, he decided, were "fear and exertion." If they could be taught to feel confident of their safety, to breathe shallowly, and to make no unnecessary movements, they could survive just as he had. Impressed, Dr. McConnell talked up Houdini's ideas around and outside the Bureau of Mines. Some experts thought them worth pursuing, others considered them wrong, a few simply disliked having the bureau, one said, "connected up with a man like Houdini."

For different reasons, Houdini got a mixed reaction from magicians as well. Some suspected he must have had a hidden air supply; perhaps the telephone and bell lines actually piped in oxygen. He wrote to many friends insisting that he had survived without secret loads or gimmicks: "there is no invention to it, there is no trick, there is no fake; you simply lie down in a coffin and breathe quietly."

EIGHTEEN

AUGUST–NOVEMBER 1926

THE SUMMER OF 1926

EXCEPT THE Hotel Shelton marvel, Houdini tried to relax over the summer before taking his full-evening show on the road again in the fall: "I believe I deserve a rest," he said. But as ever, a "rest" meant a chance to throw himself into his other interests, and to plan the future.

Running *HOUDINI* in legitimate theaters had wakened a yen for supertheatrical enterprises, something on the scale of the defunct Houdini Picture Corporation. During his layoff Houdini conceived an entertainment megalith. Operating simultaneously as publisher, agent, producer, theater owner, and manager, it would buy and publish books, scenarios, dramatic works, and musical compositions; represent the creators; and produce or license plays, operas, films, and magic shows. He took out corporation papers for Houdini Attractions, Inc., with capital stock of $310,000.

Houdini also tried to make progress on his book about superstition. In studying the history of astrology and witchcraft he pored over the Bible and consulted biblical scholars, "up to my head," he said, "in lexicons, encyclopedias, and different translations of old Greek and Hebrew." For assistance he again hired H. P. Lovecraft to do some research and writing. Lovecraft had at first rated Houdini a "bimbo," and still found the work "beastly laborious." But in one area of study he had come to see in him genuine understanding and knowledge. Concerning the human capacity for self-delusion, he said, Houdini had "a tremendous amount of penetrative skill and workable erudition." And he now credited him with being "incredibly honest in his researches"—despite, he added, "his general lack of culture."

That lack still dismayed Houdini too, especially as it might affect the reception of his new book. "I have not a college grade nor possess degrees, and therefore it may not be taken as serious as I would like it to be." He had always judged himself by a double standard, of course, letting his raging ego romp on the stage but feeling humbled by the world of letters, his father's world. The difference had become more painful now because, as he had always hoped, people often treated him as an educator—"get scores of letters Doctor Houdini." He planned, when the new season ended, to enroll at Columbia University and take a freshman course in English.

Houdini even planned to found a Columbia of his own—"the first college of magic in the world." He had the Society of American Magicians appoint a committee to discuss the feasibility of granting degrees in magic, based on successfully-taken exams. Meanwhile he worked out and announced a tentative curriculum. It included surveys such as "History of Magic," theoretical courses on "Philosophy of Magic" and "Psychology of Magic," practical courses on advertising, showmanship, and presentation. In every phase of this learning, he would offer promising young magicians his knowledge and experience. By means of his school, he foresaw, "magic, as an art and as a science, will be elevated to a higher level."

Over the same summer Houdini readied an article on Masonry and occultism, spoke of writing his autobiography, considered a request from Clark University to address an all-star symposium on psychical research, celebrated with Bess their thirty-second anniversary. The rainy day prevented their ritual return to Coney Island; they saw two movies, then had a late supper. Houdini of course issued one of his notes, this time to "my sweet little Handsome Brownhaired white cowlick Bride." Without telling her, he prepared in August a codicil to his will. He put it in his safe deposit vault for her to find after his death. It accompanied a bundle of negatives that he bequeathed her as "the *only one* who has actually helped me in my work." The negatives have not survived and their nature is unknown. They must have been intimate, domestic, recording some humdrum self he had shielded from public view. For in telling her what to do with them he noted, "I am not important or interesting enough for the world in general." He instructed her to preserve them only if she decided to have a book written about him, or to write one herself: "but otherwise destroy all films," he said. "Burn them."

Houdini also prepared new effects for the fall version of his show. He had Boyertown make him a bronze casket, at a cost of $2,500, for use in his tour as a publicity stunt—"Buried Alive! Egyptian Fakirs Outdone." He expected, he said, "an extraordinary season."

ALBANY AND MONTREAL

After rehearsals and a few tryouts, *HOUDINI* reopened in New England in mid-September, launching a five-month tour coast-to-coast. In Worcester Houdini exhibited for the first time his done-over casket mystery, planning to ballyhoo it every two or three weeks. The original version, for his challenge to Bey, had been rather an anti-escape than an escape, a matter not of getting out but of staying in. In its new form, the coffin containing him was lowered into a vault with a glass front, so that it could be seen. Then nearly a ton of sand was poured into the vault, burying the coffin. He escaped in about two minutes.

From Providence, Rhode Island, Houdini headed for the Midwest, by way of Albany, Schenectady, Montreal, and Detroit—a route he had often traveled. But in Albany he suffered a serious onstage accident. Tiredness may have played a part, since for several days he had gone with little sleep. He had stayed up an entire night in Providence with Bess, who had become nauseated and developed a high fever from ptomaine poisoning. And the next day he had taken a midnight coach for a quick business trip to New York. After buying some apparatus for the show and discussing with his lawyer impending suits by several mediums, he took the milktrain to Albany, arriving at seven in the morning. He napped an hour or so, then talked with reporters and began setting up for his opening that evening.

As Houdini was being hoisted upside down from the stage into the Water Torture Cell, during act 2, the cables twisted or swayed. The lurch cracked the clamped footstock and fractured his left ankle. In one sense he was lucky. A physician later told him that if the stock had not broken it would have amputated his foot. He had just set out on tour, however, and only eight months earlier he had broken a bone in the same foot, putting him on crutches. Unable to stand on his left leg, he omitted the Upside Down but continued the show. The injured foot bandaged by a doctor backstage, he gave his act 3 anti-Spiritualist demonstration from a chair. With the aid of a splint and a leg brace he got through two more days of performances in Albany and three in Schenectady before opening in Montreal.

On his second afternoon in Montreal, October 19, Houdini lectured to students at McGill University, on an invitation from the head of the psychology department. Announced in the school newspaper, the talk drew an enthusiastic crowd to the union. But his appearance surprised at least one student, Samuel Smilovitz. He had expected to see someone awe-inspiring but instead found Houdini sickly-looking, limping to the slightly-raised platform with "drawn face and dark shadows under tired eyes." As Smilovitz recalled the talk, Houdini at some point cracked, "If I were to die tomorrow, the Spiritualists would declare an International holiday!" To illustrate his more recent lesson that one can control fear, he stuck a needle through his cheek, showing no pain. But there must somewhere have been pain, lots of it. "I spoke for an hour," Houdini recorded later, "my leg broken." It was his last entry in his diary.

The assault on Houdini in his dressing room three days later has been described often, mostly from secondhand sources, and much mythologized. The most reliable testimony, used here, comes from two eyewitness accounts: an unpublished narrative by Samuel Smilovitz, together with his sworn affidavit before a Montreal superior court; and a sworn affidavit by Houdini's niece and assistant, Julia Sawyer. Smilovitz had drawn a sketch of Houdini while attending his lecture. Some of his fraternity brothers took it to Houdini's evening performance at the Princess Theatre and showed it to Houdini afterward. He autographed the sketch—"Houdini/Born April 6—1874/Appleton, Wisc."—and asked them to tell Smilovitz to come to his dressing room the next morning to draw another portrait, for Houdini's own collection.

Smilovitz did that. At about eleven-fifteen he appeared at the theater with another student, Jacques Price. Houdini's dressing room, as he remembered it, was small, about eight feet by ten. Houdini invited the young men to sit on chairs and made himself comfortable. Collar open at the neck, shirtsleeves rolled up, he lay back on a small couch along the wall, his right side facing the seated students. Close up, he seemed to Smilovitz kind, affable, down-home, trying "to impress upon us that he was 'one of the boys.' " He apologized for reclining, remarking that he needed all the rest he could get. An accident had left him limping, but he had concealed the limp during his Montreal performances by "force of will." Despite Houdini's cordiality the close quarters confirmed to Smilovitz the impression he had had at the lecture of someone "much in need of a long, carefree vacation." Houdini's complexion was sallow, he observed, his skin tightly drawn, his eyes tense and darkly circled, the muscles of his temples and mouth nervously twitching.

After Houdini looked through some mail, bolstered by pillows, Smilovitz began sketching. Sitting at the foot of the couch, he could have leaned over and touched Houdini, who in the small room lay only two or three feet away. As Smilovitz sketched, Houdini discoursed. He said that he found film production "highly interesting" but would not return to it because the profit proved "rather meagre"; that in a year or two he would write a book containing many of his secrets, but would withhold publication for a long time; that he had endured his coffin ordeal by conquering his fear.

As Houdini rambled, someone knocked at the door. A secretary ushered in another young man. Smilovitz later identified him as Whitehead, a first-year student at McGill. Some biographers of Houdini have identified him further as a J. Gordon Whitehead, but the only freshman with that surname, according to the school's yearbook, was named Wallace (Wallie) Whitehead, a good-looking twenty-two-year-old with slicked-down hair, manager of the class hockey league. Whatever his actual first name, Whitehead struck Smilovitz as well-built but affected. Ruddy-complexioned, he stood about six-foot-one and 180 pounds, Smilovitz estimated; he appeared in the dressing room wearing a blue gabardine coat that seemed too small for him. For all Whitehead's physical bulk, however, Smilovitz thought him a "very genteel type," who spoke with "an exaggerated Oxford accent." He carried several books under his arm, one of which Houdini had loaned him, and which he had come to return. Houdini invited him to sit in a chair opposite his head.

To his annoyance Smilovitz discovered that Whitehead was talkative too. Whitehead barraged Houdini with questions, and to answer them Houdini turned to face the young man, breaking his pose. Just the same Smilovitz found some of the exchange interesting. Houdini commented that he had unraveled so many mysteries and read so much detective fiction he could piece together the plot of any detective story from hearing three or four scattered paragraphs of it. Whitehead happened to have a "mystery book" with him, and tried the experiment. After he read three or four excerpts, Houdini did give the gist of the story. After more questions and conversation, Whitehead asked Houdini his opinion of the miracles mentioned in the Bible, and looked taken aback when Houdini declined to comment on "matters of this nature." Then the inquisitive young man began asking about his physical strength: "Is it true, Mr. Houdini, that you can resist the hardest blows struck to the abdomen?"

The question surprised Smilovitz, coming he said "out of a clear sky." It was, in fact, a surprising question. Nowhere in the available record does Houdini claim to be able to absorb punches to the stomach, although such a story may have gotten around along with much other spurious Houdini lore. Houdini ignored the question and, Smilovitz sensed, tried to divert attention from his abdominal muscles by having the students feel his forearm and back muscles instead. His dodge did not satisfy Whitehead, however, who asked again if it was true that his stomach could withstand very hard blows. When Houdini again referred to the strength of his arms and back, Whitehead asked, "Would you mind if I delivered a few blows to your abdomen, Mr. Houdini?"

Houdini accepted the challenge, as he had so many others. "Houdini was reclining at the time with his right side nearest Whitehead," Smilovitz said in his affidavit, "and the latter was more or less bending over him." Hovering over Houdini, elbow bent, Whitehead began punching him in the stomach. The punches, Smilovitz said, were "terribly forcible, deliberate, well-directed." They apparently caught Houdini just as he began to rise off the pillows bolstering him. After the second punch, the other student, Jacques Price, cried out in protest. Smilovitz remembered his words as, "Hey there, you must be crazy. What are you doing?" Whitehead socked Houdini two or three more times. Smilovitz was certain that the blows landed low, to the right of Houdini's navel. Then Houdini "made an arresting gesture with his hand and mumbled almost inaudibly, 'That will do.'"

Houdini and the three students enough overcame the stunned atmosphere in the room to allow Smilovitz to finish his drawing, which he signed and dated. Smilovitz recalled that as he, Whitehead, and Price got ready to leave, at about one-fifteen, Houdini remarked, "You made me look a little tired in this picture. The truth is, I don't feel so well." He thanked Smilovitz anyway, and promised to write to him at McGill.

Houdini's niece Julia returned to his dressing room in midafternoon. She found him "in pain," according to her affidavit, and heard a different narrative of what had happened. He had told the students, Houdini explained, that because of his physical conditioning blows did not bother him. To prove it he would allow himself to be hit. He had intended to stand up and brace himself, but before he could do so, and while he was reading his mail, one student began punching him, "possibly because of a misunderstanding of his remarks."

Next day, Houdini planned to celebrate his last scheduled show in Montreal with a "champagne party," as Bess called it. He heralded the occasion in a note addressing her as "*Champagne* coquette." But during the evening's performance he retreated to his couch during intermissions, in a cold sweat. After the show he was unable to dress himself. Scheduled to open in Detroit the next evening, he, Bess, and their entourage got to the train late that night. Once on board he experienced such severe stomach pains that a wire was sent ahead asking for a physician to meet the train at the Detroit station in the morning.

GRACE HOSPITAL

Houdini arrived in Detroit with a temperature of 102. After examining him hurriedly, a physician found signs of appendicitis. Houdini nevertheless checked into the Statler Hotel, where for a half hour he shook with chills. He was determined to give his opening-night show, even though at curtain time his temperature had risen to 104. He handled the magic apparatus in act 1 clumsily, and by the time he reached the concluding "Whirlwind of Colors" felt so weak that he could not pull the yards and yards of silks out of the glass bowl. A magician in the audience noticed that he seemed to be rushing, and carrying on a whispered conversation with someone in the wings. A reporter for the *Detroit News* thought he appeared "a little hoarse and more than a little tired." When he left the stage after the first act he fell down and was taken to his dressing room. He revived, gave the rest of his show, and collapsed again.

When he returned to the Statler, Houdini was examined by the substitute house physician. The young doctor summoned Dr. Charles S. Kennedy, chief of surgery at Grace Hospital, who came to the hotel at three in the morning. After learning of the stomach punches, he speculated that Houdini had either a ruptured intestine or a clot in the large blood vessels feeding it. He urged him to enter Grace. Houdini refused to go without consulting by phone with his own physician in New York, who persuaded him. The hospital, a gabled stone-and-brick building, had no available bed but in a double room. Dr. Kennedy was impressed by Houdini's "considerate" response, which more likely reflected his lifelong habit of selective scrimping: "that will do for me."

Houdini was operated on at three that afternoon, October 25. His ruptured appendix was removed—"a great long affair," Dr. Kennedy said, "which started in the right lower pelvis where it normally should, extended across the midline and lay in his left pelvis." The rupture had produced peritonitis, an infection of the membrane lining the stomach and surrounding organs that produces intense pain and extreme weakness. The toxic material had spread uncontrollably through Houdini's body. Kennedy and three other physicians at Grace issued a statement indicating that he was near death.

Houdini had challenged death too often to give in so fast. In trying to check the peritonitis, physicians at the hospital dosed him with an experimental "serum," recently developed in a Detroit laboratory. They refused to discuss its nature, but whatever it was, it brought his temperature down to 101 and let him spend a fairly comfortable night, although his pulse and respiration rate remained high. The following day his temperature came down to near-normal. The doctors attributed the improvement to his unusual physical strength and his "mental attitude." Despite having in short order broken his ankle, been hammered in the stomach, developed massive infection, and undergone surgery, he remained not merely conscious but also keen and alert. It struck Dr. Kennedy that no attendant mopped his brow or gave him a sip of water without his looking up, smiling, and thanking them.

But Houdini's victory-only mentality may have worked against him as well. The ruptured appendix uncovered by surgery casts a backlight on the description, by Samuel Smilovitz, of his appearance as he lectured in Montreal—sallow, drawn, tense, "dark shadows under tired eyes." The signs of distress suggest that Houdini was already feeling symptoms of appendicitis but, as usual, trying to beat down his pain, in the process allowing the infection to grow in him.

Daily newspaper reports on Houdini's progress brought to the hospital hundreds of telegrams, letters, and bouquets from friends, magicians,

vaudevillians, and other admirers and well-wishers. "The magical fraternity is with you in your fight for health," a typical cable ran. "You are the
greatest of them all." "If you can squeeze out of boxes and other con-
trivances," another said, "you can certainly squeeze out of this job." Many
of the messages were addressed to Bess. Houdini's collapse, however, set
back her convalescence from ptomaine, so that she had to be carried to his
bedside for brief visits. Hardeen came to Detroit to be with his brother,
together with brother Nat and sister Gladys, but not the traitorously-married
Leo, whose presence might have been upsetting.

As Houdini battled peritonitis, *HOUDINI* lay unpacked at the Garrick
Theater and needed looking after. Jim Collins took charge of crating the
apparatus, sets, lighting equipment, and animals, and shipping them back
to New York, for storage by another of Houdini's assistants, Jack Arden.
Each day he wired Arden an inside medical report. In the wake of Houdini's
receiving the experimental serum he sent: HAS IMPROVED WONDERFULLY
DOCTORS PLEASED WITH RESULTS BUT STILL VERY GRAVE. . . . SATURDAY
DECIDES THE TURN.

The turn came sooner than that. On Friday, October 29, after spending
a restless night and day, Houdini was operated on again, this time to relieve
"paralysis of the bowels." With the virulent peritonitis overrunning his
system, he did not respond well. His temperature rose to 103, his heart
pounded, his pulse raced at 130, nearly twice the normal rate. In releasing a
prognosis to the public, hospital officials tried to make the worst sound like
the next-to-worst: "hopes of his recovery have not been entirely abandoned." According to Bess, when she saw Houdini on this day he held her
hand to his heart and told her to "be prepared, if anything happens." As she
interpreted the remark, he had in mind not only his death, but also the compact they had made, that if he died he would try to reach her from beyond
the grave.

Either the next day, Saturday, or Sunday morning, Houdini made a
final statement to Hardeen. As Hardeen recalled his words, he said "I can't
fight any more."

REACTION

Houdini died at Grace Hospital on Sunday, October 31, at 1:26 P.M. Dr.
Kennedy listed the cause as "Diffuse peritonitis (Streptococcic)." By a
weird happenstance, when *HOUDINI* was packed up and sent back to

New York, the bronze coffin Houdini had ordered for his buried-alive stunt was temporarily lost in a Detroit warehouse. Left behind, it was now used for his corpse. The coffin was loaded into a special Pullman car for shipment home. After reaching Grand Central Terminal on Monday morning, the coffin was taken to the West End Funeral Parlor on West Ninety-first Street. There it was blanketed with purple violets, garlands of southern smilax, and a scroll tracing in white violets the word "Husband." A heavy floral scent permeated the chapel.

Even as Houdini's funeral was being arranged, his death became a subject of controversy. Physicians at the hospital had told reporters that his appendicitis had resulted from punches to his abdomen in Montreal. But the manager of the Princess Theatre there claimed that Houdini had been ill when he arrived in the city (likely), and the psychology professor who had invited him to lecture, William D. Tait, claimed that Houdini had not met with any students (false). Some physicians with no professional connection to the case expressed doubt that a punch could set off an acute attack of appendicitis, which after all resulted from a bacterium. The sensationalistic *New York Evening Graphic* charged the Detroit hospital and staff with having caused Houdini's death themselves, by surgical "gouging" and by overtreatment. The physicians should have put nothing into his system, the paper observed; instead, they gave him food and injections that spread the sepsis. The *Graphic* called his death an "unpunished crime" and demanded an investigation.

All the major American dailies carried headline accounts of Houdini's death, and story-length obituaries. The news went out through the Associated Press as well, and was picked up in hundreds of smaller papers—the Madison, Iowa, *Evening Democrat*, the Elkhart, Indiana, *Truth*, the Honolulu, Hawaii, *Star Bulletin*. Magic journals and the theatrical press published long tributes and black-bordered farewells. Jewish publications such as the London *Jewish World*, Canada's *Jewish Daily Eagle*, and New York City's *Forward* praised Houdini's "strong Jewish feeling" and emphasized that he had been the son of a rabbi. Some accounts offered bizarre sidelights: reports of home circles having received the message, "Houdini is doomed, doomed, doomed!"; of Houdini muttering with his last breath the name of the agnostic Robert Ingersoll; of Houdini's "daughter" hovering at his deathbed.

Reporters sought out people close to Houdini for publishable comment. Howard Thurston compared him in "force of character" to Theodore Roosevelt. From London Sir Arthur Conan Doyle expressed fondness and shock: "I greatly admired him, and cannot understand how the end came for one so youthful," he said. "We were great friends. . . . We agreed upon everything excepting spiritualism." Margery joined Doyle in sorrow, calling Houdini a "verile [*sic*] personality of great determination." No reporters of course interviewed Charmian London at her California ranch, but she too marked his passing. "Stirred with regret," she wrote in her diary, "I scan his lovely profile picture with magnifying glass. Sad over my Magic Lover—dead."

In the flood of homage, three images of Houdini surfaced again and again, and help explain his lasting fame. First, as a writer in the *Times* commented, he "stepped out of the old tradition of gas footlights to face in broad daylight a public leaping to sophistication, if not to knowledge, in physics and chemistry." Dangling straitjacketed from a derrick or telephoning from his underwater coffin, Houdini, practitioner of the most ancient art, belonged to no other century than the twentieth. His career was an icon of modernity, inseparable from skyscrapers, headlines, biplanes, radio, automobile tires, submarines—not in their threatening, dark aspect but in their sleek power, which he fed on.

An obituary writer in *The New Yorker* captured the second image in calling Houdini "a profoundly individual person; the romantic master of a romantic trade." Houdini was a unique character in the history of entertainment—scholar, inventor, aviator, freak, bibliophile, publicity-mill, film-producer, psychic-investigator, handcuff-king. On fire to make his individuality count and last, to impress his color and energy on the void, he achieved afterlife as a fabulous archetypal being, compact of Romantic Hero, Confidence Man, American Success Story, and Eternal Magus.

One thing more. Houdini's greatest feats were modern miracles of near-biblical proportions. How did he do them? Many newspapers observed that his techniques were "locked in death" or had been "carried with him"—HOUDINI TAKES MAGIC SECRETS TO HIS GRAVE, as the *New York Sun* put it. That was not entirely true. Expecting that Hardeen would carry on after him, Houdini bequeathed his apparatus to his brother, with the condition that upon Hardeen's death it should all be "burnt and destroyed." Jim Collins and Bess too surely knew most of his methods; some are known today. Yet many did vanish with him. Jimmies and shims from Houdini's "burglar's kit" have survived. But not the knowledge of where he hid them, stripped nude at some jail or stationhouse. (Brass capsule? Bribe the police? Both possible.) The Mirror Cuffs still exist. But no one knows for certain how he opened their one-of-a-kind, nested Bramah locks. (Fantastic skill? Maybe. A stooge slipping him the key? Could be.)

How did he do it? The gnawing uncertainty has been the main preservative of Houdini's fame. Like great unsolved crimes, his escapes offend the wish to live without ambiguity. They itch for solution, and remaining unsolved perpetuate their mystery.

HOUDINI'S FUNERAL

After some talk of allowing Houdini's body to lie in state at the Hippodrome, his funeral was held instead on November 4 at the Elks Clubhouse on West Forty-third Street, in sight of Times Square. Some fifteen hundred to two thousand mourners crowded the large ballroom and its two balconies. Just as many packed the street outside. The profusion of flowers included a cover of amaranth for the casket, a large wreath at its foot inscribed "Mother Love," and a hundred floral offerings sent in sympathy. Bess reportedly received more than three thousand telegrams. She felt "crushed and broken," she said; "the world will never know what I have lost." Veiled, and supported by a nurse, she kept her composure until the massive bronze lid was screwed on the coffin, hermetically sealing it, when she half-fainted. Hardeen, Nat, and Gladys of course attended, and by at least one account, Leo did as well.

The services began just after ten-thirty. Prayers and eulogies were spoken in Hebrew and English by Rabbi B. A. Tintner, whose father had married Houdini and Bess, and by Rabbi Bernard Drachman. To help the Weiss family out of a pinch during their first days in New York, Drachman had bought a set of *The Codes of Maimonides* from Mayer Samuel Weiss's library, which Houdini later bought back from him. Heads of theatrical associations and prominent magicians offered memorial statements. Fellow masons of Houdini's from the St. Cecile Lodge laid a white lambskin on the bier and filed by, dropping bits of evergreen on it, emblems of immortality. The SAM devised a special rite for the occasion. An appointed member broke and laid on Houdini's casket a wooden wand, ancient symbol of the magician's power over nature.

Borne by Houdini's assistants, the heavy casket was then taken out to the street; the honorary pallbearers included Martin Beck, Brander

Matthews, Adolph Zukor, Bernard Gimbel, and Adolph Ochs. From here a procession of fifty automobiles was scheduled to wind through the theatrical district, pausing at the Forty-sixth Street clubhouse of the National Vaudeville Association—its American flag at half mast—before proceeding to Fifty-seventh Street and then to and across the Queensboro Bridge for the trip to Machpelah Cemetery.

In his will Houdini had set out the manner of his burial in meticulous detail. His corpse would go into the family plot he had purchased in 1904, already containing the remains of his father, mother, grandmother, brother Bill, and half-brother Armin. Disregarding Jewish funerary prohibitions against graven images, he directed that atop the monumental granite-and-marble exedra should be placed the bronze portrait-bust of himself he had commissioned in England. He wished his interment to follow as closely as possible that of Cecilia Weiss. He asked that his body be embalmed and enearthed "in the same manner in which my beloved mother was buried," and placed immediately alongside her grave. In a separate, typed statement, he directed that all her letters to him should be put in a black bag to serve as a pillow in his coffin: "My wife may read the letters if she desires," he added, "and then let her place them under my head." If the letters were not found until after his burial, he asked that they be burned. They were located and used to cradle his head.

Houdini had filmed the funeral of Harry Kellar, and surely would have been pleased to know that someone filmed part of his. Only a minute or so of the footage remains, fragments of the procession of cars and the burial. The action begins as the casket is borne from the Elks Club to the waiting hearse, many spectators on the street baring their heads. A brisk fall day, it seems—everyone wearing overcoats, a few men in formal mourning clothes, with silk tophats. The casket is piled high as a hedge with flowers. The scene jumps to somewhere in Queens, en route, a neighborhood of one-family houses. Through it slowly rolls the cortege of black automobiles, headlights shining. The scenes shift quickly. The cemetery entrance: gloved policemen at the gate salute. The exedra: its bench bedecked with ribboned wreaths. The graveside: ten-deep crowd pressed shoulder-to-shoulder. The two rabbis in black robes.

The last twenty seconds of the film are surprising, almost like a magic trick. As Houdini's casket is lowered into the grave, one of the mourners throws a flower after it. Hardeen tosses another. Suddenly the screen is filled with a rain of flowers. Hands raised above the heads of the crowd can be seen flinging buds and blooms, plucked perhaps from the exedra or the casket. From all sides the flowers arc, loop, plummet, making in the slightly-slow film a shower of blurry streaks through which it is impossible to see the faces of the mourners, much less read their expressions. Are they surprised? Uncomfortable? Maybe just tired? Or as they watch the flowers fly into the grave, could they be at the same time turning inward, ruminating on themselves—thinking, could it be, that they too will take their secrets with them.

APPENDIX AND
SOURCE GUIDE

APPENDIX

RECOLLECTIONS OF
HARRY AND BESS HOUDINI

Marie Hinson Blood

I WAS IN THE limousine with my grandmother and Aunt Bess. They had veils over their faces. I sat on the jump seat and when we rode down Broadway, I saw people on either side packed along the sidewalk. I did not understand why all the people were there. I excitedly said to Grandma and Aunt Bess, "Look, look at all the people, what are they looking at?" They never looked up. At the cemetery Hardeen helped Aunt Bess out of the car, but my grandmother and I stayed inside.

They were burying my Uncle Harry. My mother, Mae Rahner Hinson, was Bess Houdini's younger sister. When she married my father, John A. Hinson, in 1911, Houdini made them a present of their wedding reception, which included a horse-drawn carriage to take them to the reception and, after, to where they were to spend their wedding night. Houdini wanted to do it up big—so he made arrangements for a fireworks display. As the happy couple were leaving in their carriage, the horses shied at the noise of the fireworks and started running frantically down the street with everyone screaming, including my parents. It took several people to finally catch the horses and quiet them down. My father was a cabinet maker and could do all types of carpentry. He would often meet with Houdini and Jim Collins. Houdini would tell my father about a trick he wanted to do and my father would build it.

During summers when they were in town, Houdini or Aunt Bess would call my mother and ask if I could come for a visit. I would usually stay at their home on 113th Street about a week at a time; it was a large house and I loved it. Downstairs was a long hall, entrance foyer, large dining room and kitchen, and a fenced-in courtyard where I often played. It had small gardens and lots of flowers and a swing. In the huge kitchen there was an aviary about six feet square with all kinds of birds. There was also another, smaller cage with a black-and-gray parrot. Upstairs in the Houdinis' bedroom was a cage with another parrot, a green one called "Laura." You could say, "Laura, what did you do with your money?" She would make terrible tear-jerking sounds like crying and say "Poor, poor Laura, she lost all her money, oh my, oh my." The only other pet I remember there was a large old turtle called "Petie." I would try and coax him out into the back yard where I could chase him around the flower beds. Usually Petie preferred staying inside.

I don't remember anyone telling me where I could or could not go in the house. My room was on the fourth floor at the top of the stairs. Next to it was my grandmother's and Aunt Julie's room and then the bathroom. Aunt Julie was Julia Karcher, and she and Aunt Bess knew each other from school days. I always called Julie "aunt." She not only was the housekeeper but also Aunt Bess's companion abroad and on shopping expeditions, and one of Houdini's assistants in his show. She would bounce me up and down real wild like and sing funny ditties to me. My grandmother would watch us and laugh and once in a while would shake her head at Julie and say something in German. They all spoke German, and whenever they didn't want me to know what was said, they said it in German.

The rest of the fourth floor was a large room and a smaller one—Houdini's office. There were always lots of people in there and everyone was busy. I rarely went in; only when I was on an errand. The cellar, or basement, was also a place I never went. I heard years later that Houdini had a workshop there for creating tricks and illusions.

On the third floor was Houdini and Aunt Bess's room. In the morning I would run down the stairs and listen at their door. If it was quiet, I would go back to my room and wait a little while longer. When I heard voices, I would knock on the door and Houdini, knowing it was me, would say, "Come in, Marie," and in I'd go and jump in bed with him. They had twin beds, which later became my sister's and mine after Houdini died, including the rest of the bedroom set. I slept in Houdini's bed until I got married.

Houdini would throw me up and down and I'd holler, and Aunt Bess would watch us and enjoy every minute. Then Houdini and I would lay very quiet with our hands and arms on top of the covers; it was a game we played. I was about four or five years old. All of a sudden he would pinch my legs and I'd yell, "you're pinching me, you're pinching me." He'd say, "No I'm not, look, my hands are on top of the covers." I'd yell, "You're doing it with your toes," and we would all laugh.

I loved to watch Aunt Bess and Houdini in the morning. Breakfast was brought up by the dumbwaiter and was put on a table between the twin beds and everyone would eat. Houdini would have lots of pillows in back of him and have the daily newspapers all around and his coffee next to him. Bess would be getting dressed. She was a tiny person and had tiny feet— only a one-and-a-half shoe size. Her shoes fit me and I would try on different pairs and prance around showing off to Houdini and he would admire me. He and Aunt Bess would call back and forth about something he read in the paper and then the dumbwaiter bell would ring and I would pile all the dishes on it and send it down.

There was a gold-leaf curio cabinet in the bedroom, with a curved glass door. Inside were treasures—the gold Fabergé ladle Houdini received for his performance before royalty in Russia; the famous Mirror Handcuffs; silver engraved rice bowls from China; and a beautiful little ivory baby carriage with a tiny satin pillow and coverlet. I loved looking in the cabinet and all of a sudden one day Houdini was in back of me and he said, "You love all those things in there, don't you?" I said, "Oh, yes." He said, "Pick out anything you want in there and you can take it." He opened the glass door and of course I picked the small doll carriage, which I am sure he knew I would take.

Later in the day Aunt Bess would either call up the dumbwaiter or stand at the foot of the stairs and call, "Houdini, lunch." Though she had a strong voice, sometimes she would go up the stairs and then call. As soon as he heard the word "lunch," he would come down the stairs from his office, swing her around, then me, and then down we would go to the kitchen. He loved to eat and was always interested in what we were going to have.

Houdini loved to walk along the river in the early dusk or evening, a strange looking man wearing baggy pants, overcoat, and an old brim hat. He would be planning his next show; the river would give him the psyche he needed. Aunt Bess and I were at home alone. Aunt Bess said to me, "I told Houdini (she rarely called him Harry, it was either Houdini or a love pet name) that he was going to get a special dinner tonight. All his favorites—Hungarian chicken, spätzels, and custard bread pudding with bing cherries." Aunt Bess put a large bowl of cherries in front of me and a machine. I would put a cherry in and turn the handle and a pitted cherry would come out. Everything was ready. We waited and waited but no Houdini. Finally Aunt Bess gave me my dinner and eventually I went to bed. Next day Aunt Bess told me Houdini forgot about the dinner as he was walking and thinking and never thought about time. He did this so often, Aunt Bess was used to it. She no doubt didn't like it, but never would tell him. During the day a big bunch of red roses would come and she knew he was sorry to have missed the special dinner.

If we heard Aunt Bess call "*Mister* Houdini," everyone knew he was in trouble. That would be the only time she ever would use "Mister." He knew this and he would come fast. I only heard this once when I was there and it didn't worry me as I never saw them when they weren't loving and happy.

When the season opened and Houdini was playing in New York, he would call my mother and ask her to bring me to the theater. Mom would dress me in clothes with shoes to match that Houdini and Aunt Bess would send me from Europe, and I would sit on the left side in the middle of the theater. Then the lights would dim and the orchestra would start playing "Pomp and Circumstance." I would listen and watch all this and think, "That's my Uncle Harry." Houdini would come out on the stage and say, "I have a surprise for you—I have a little niece in the audience I want you to meet."

Meanwhile I would be excited and jump up and down. Mom would be smoothing my hair and dress. I knew what was coming and I would be ready. As soon as I would hear him call, "Marie, Marie," Mom would let go of me and I would race down the aisle, yelling, "Here I am, Uncle Harry," and I would jump into his arms. He danced me around and around the stage and he would say, "This is my little niece, Marie." I would throw kisses right and left.

I had a cousin who took dancing lessons and could dance on her toes. I tried this on my own and kept falling down. I practiced in front of a mirror and then waited for the next phone call. I did not tell anyone what I was going to do. When the call came, I was ready. Mom took me to the theater and when Houdini called me up and was dancing around with me, I whispered in his ear, "I can do a dance, do you want to see me do it?" Houdini stood still and said to the audience, "Now I'm surprised. Marie says she wants to do a dance for us." He put me down and I did my version of a shimmy—only a one-sided one. I shook my left arm and left leg as hard as I could. I guess my head shook with it. Well, Houdini and the audience loved it and applauded and cheered. He enjoyed it so much he had my mother bring me back many times in New York and then even go on the train as far as Chicago to show off my shimmy.

I will always remember the last time I saw Houdini alive. He was performing at the Forty-fourth Street Theater and I was in the audience. He called me to assist with a trick which involved a long black domino box. There were three sections. Houdini opened the box and showed it empty and gave it to me to hold. He inserted a large die in one section and said to me, "don't shake it." In my excitement, I did not hear the word "don't" and I shook the box from side to side. Houdini said, "Now wait, let's see if all that shaking moved the die." I knew then that I had done wrong and could have spoiled the trick for the person I loved so dearly. Tears welled up in my eyes and Houdini saw them. When the trick was over he picked me up, kissed me, and rubbed his cheek on mine. I don't remember just what he said but it was an endearment. He knew I was upset and kept me backstage for the rest of the show. Every chance he had he would either pat me or kiss me.

After Houdini died, Aunt Bess asked my mother and father if they would sell their house, in Maspeth, Long Island, and move with her to New York City, to a home she would buy. She did not want to stay at the brownstone house. My father agreed and started to help Aunt Bess look for a place. They found a beautiful two-family redbrick house in a wonderful section, on Payson Avenue in Inwood. Across the street was Inwood Hill Park and a block away was the Hudson River, with the Cloisters up the hill.

The house was everything anyone would want: two glass-enclosed rooms in the front with the park for a view. Aunt Bess was totally exhausted, though, and for a few weeks she went into a sanitarium. Then she moved upstairs with her mother, Julia Karcher, the housekeeper, and Julia Sawyer (Karcher's niece), who had been Houdini's secretary and stage assistant. Aunt Bess had my mother for a companion on shopping trips and as someone she could confide in. Houdini's sister, Gladys, was a frequent visitor to Payson Avenue and we loved her. She was a sweet-natured person. She also received money from a trust fund from Houdini; she was well taken care of. Hardeen and his wife, Elsie, were also frequent visitors.

A woman named Rose Bonnano, who had lived across the street from Houdini on 113th Street, bought Houdini's house from Aunt Bess after he died. She and her sister said Houdini came to them in a dream and told them he had buried a treasure in the cellar of the house. I think they spent the first year they lived in the house digging up the cellar.

Aunt Bess had brought a lot of costumes to the Payson Avenue house that they had used in the shows. During the month of May, there were children parades in the neighborhood and Mom would alter the costumes to fit us kids. I remember one of them that Aunt Bess called "Miss Midnight." She wore it in one of the shows. Houdini would show all sides of a cabinet and the empty interior—then open the one end and out would step three ladies. This is when Aunt Bess wore this gown. It was deep blue velvet and one side was held up with a large silver half moon and silver stars, all edged with silver sequins; a silver headdress finished it off. I wore this in one parade and held up my arm the way I was told. I won first prize.

Charles E. Chapin had been an editor of the *New York World* and was also a good friend of Houdini and Aunt Bess. He was put in prison for the mercy killing of his wife. He would write almost daily to Aunt Bess and she to him. Every few months my mother, sister, brother and I would accompany Aunt Bess in a taxi from Inwood to Ossining, New York, to Sing Sing prison. When Aunt Bess went in, we waited in the taxi. Charles Chapin was in charge of the prison gardens and had a sitting room and bedroom in the prison. One day I came home from school and there was a large prison van in front of our house. Trustees were carrying plants into the house— the two enclosed front porches were loaded with beautiful plants, all sizes. The trustees also landscaped our small backyard garden with flowers and small leaf plants on each side. I would invite my friends to come and admire it. I don't remember how I explained that we got them from Sing Sing Prison. I still have two of the plants, a pandanus and a dracena.

Aunt Bess had lots of magician friends and was ready to try her hand at business. In 1929 she rented a place on West Forty-ninth Street in New York and opened a tearoom. She bought lots of unpainted chairs and tables. My father, brother, and a couple of uncles spent all their spare time painting them (a burnt orange color). My mother, Julie, and several other friends helped with the menu. The tearoom opened, but not for long. Times were hard and every magician that was down on his luck heard about the tea room and Aunt Bess's good nature and got fed. The tearoom closed. The whole building was soon demolished to make room for Rockefeller Center. I never heard how much Aunt Bess lost on the venture but I know it was a lot.

Aunt Bess was still a young woman, only fifty-one, when Houdini died. I have read that some folks thought her black hair turned white after his death. This is untrue; her hair had been graying for several years and she had been dying it, but it really wasn't the way she wanted it. Jean Harlow was appearing in the movies and when Aunt Bess saw her beautiful platinum hair, she knew that's what she wanted, and it also made her look much younger. Aunt Bess's hair was very beautiful—thick and shiny.

Aunt Bess loved parties and went to many. Houdini never cared for dancing. Aunt Bess never really got her fill and still had this craving for it. One night while at a party she met a young man named Al. He was very handsome—a mixture of Rudolph Valentino and Ramon Navarro: very Spanish with olive complexion and jet black shiny hair. He always looked as though he was on show or posing for a picture and was well spoken and danced like a pro. He was a "gigolo." A cab would come to the house to take Aunt Bess and Al to a restaurant and then to the Roseland Ballroom, Arcadia Ballroom, or a nightclub. Aunt Bess could then dance as long as she wanted. I remember we kids would try and step on Al's black-and-white shoes and get the white part dirty. My grandmother would sprinkle holy water in the vestibule when he left. I don't remember Al being around too long, but I know now that he satisfied a need in Bess for dancing and gay nightclub life.

In 1930 Aunt Bess bought a summer house in Rye, New York, a block or so from the beach and Playland Amusement Park, and also a car and hired a young man, Carl, as chauffeur. This enabled her to go back and forth to New York City as she needed for business and pleasure. My family would move to the Rye Beach house for the whole summer season. We had a great time on the beach all day and then walked to Playland each evening for frozen custard. On weekends there would also be aerial acts, magicians, etc.

It was in the large enclosed pavilion building where some of the acts performed that Aunt Bess met Edward Saint. He was a mind reader and crystal gazer and a refined and soft-spoken gentleman. Aunt Bess could never pass a gypsy tent, or a palm or mind reader without going in for a reading. I think she always felt she might hear something from Houdini. Every year on the anniversary of his death she held a séance at Payson Avenue, attended by quite a few well-known magicians. The friendship with Edward Saint grew and he became Bess's adviser and companion. He was good for Bess as she still was vulnerable and many people were trying to get her to go into different business deals. Saint kept these folks at bay and of course was feathering his own nest. He had no income and was no longer working in Playland. He was always very well dressed and was being paid by Aunt Bess to manage her affairs, which he did quite well.

Aunt Bess moved from Payson Avenue to Florida in 1932 with Saint. My grandmother went to live in Brooklyn, New York, in her own apartment and the two Julies went to live with Julia Sawyer's mother and brother. Aunt Bess and Saint would come to Payson Avenue several times a year from Florida. In the basement of the house was a room used for storage and one whole wall had filing cabinets filled with papers, letters, pictures of Houdini, etc. Saint spent days at the files on each trip and took boxes of items away at a time. The items belonged to Aunt Bess and they were hers to do with as she wanted. I think they were sold to collectors and enabled Aunt Bess and Saint to live as well as they did. Aunt Bess was very happy. Everyone held her in the highest regard and this was important to her well being. She was "Mrs. Harry Houdini" and deserved recognition.

In 1934 tragedy struck my family. My oldest brother, Harry Houdini Hinson, then twenty-one years old, loved magic and was an amateur magician. Since he was twelve years old, Houdini started him with books and parlor magic. My brother enjoyed performing and was giving shows locally. In 1930, a New York newspaper, in an article about Bess, described him:

Nephew Learns Profession

As for the future of the Houdini family in the world of magic Mrs. Houdini has high hopes for her nephew, Harry Houdini, named after his uncle. Young Harry is attending Fordham Prep and has already been taught the rudiments of the profession. He knows the theories and needs more practice and has given shows at his school. Mrs. Houdini says he will inherit from her most of the Houdini trophies and accessories now in her possession.

My brother even performed Houdini's needle trick and got his picture in the *New York Times*. He also loved airplanes and studied flying. He would take my younger brother and sister and me to the airport to watch when he took his lesson. The mechanics of a plane were of great interest to him. He invented a part that would have improved the performance of a plane but after developing it and applying for a patent, he found that someone else had already applied with a similar idea.

During the early part of February 1934, there had been a heavy snowfall. Harry had remodeled his large sled with a joystick steering mechanism. He and another friend went into the woods across from our home to the top of a hill. Coming down the slope fast, he hit a tree and the joystick went into his abdomen, bursting his spleen. He partially walked and dragged himself with his friend's help to the hospital, which was just nearby. He was operated on, and just like his uncle, Houdini, they just closed him up again. There were no antibiotics at that time and peritonitis set in and several days later he died. During the night that my brother died, my father went down to the basement and chopped up all our sleds and in the morning, the broken sleds were all in a pile in front of the house for the rubbish man.

Several months later I met my future husband-to-be, Forrest Blood, and some of our fun times began again. Aunt Bess and Saint would come up from Florida and Saint would spend his time downstairs with the files. We began again our showing of Houdini's movies. The storage room downstairs had many shelves with round metal containers on them, the complete movie reels of all the films Houdini made. Every few weeks on a Saturday night neighbors and friends would be invited and my father would show one of the movies. It was wonderful. We thought Uncle Harry was the best actor in the whole world.

One day the fire inspector came on a routine inspection trip, and my father took him all over the house. When they got to the storage room, he asked my father what the metal cases contained. My father very proudly said, "I am Harry Houdini's brother-in-law and these are all the movies he made." They were old 35 mm film and my father opened one up and showed the inspector. The inspector said, "I am canceling all of your insurance. You could blow up this whole block as these films are very combustible. You must get rid of all of them immediately."

My father was aghast at the whole thing. His beautiful home without insurance—these wonderful movies. Without discussing it with anyone else, other than my mother, who was just as heartbroken, during the night they took every one of the containers of film and put them in cartons in front of the house and stood there as the rubbish men hauled a fortune in Houdini films.

Aunt Bess and Saint then moved to North Winona Boulevard in Hollywood, and were associated with many magic groups, held séances every anniversary of Houdini's death, and made appearances at magic shows, banquets, and conventions. They still came back to New York City and Saint would still work at the filing cabinets. He had added a "Doctor" to his name and was sporting a mustache and short beard. They gave him a very distinguished appearance. In 1936 Saint and Aunt Bess planned for the last séance to try and contact Houdini. It was ten years since Houdini died. The séance was held at the Knickerbocker Hotel in Hollywood. Aunt Bess wrote me that she was "all a jitter about it—and will be so glad when it is all over." Invitations were sent out and the séance was well attended by all the noted magicians and friends and it was recorded on film and a recording was also made. Similar séances were held all over the world, but Houdini was not contacted.

Aunt Bess's trips to New York were getting fewer—I guess the filing cabinets were getting bare. On October 7, 1941, she planned a large family cocktail party. Usually on her trips to New York she would have different members of the family coming to the house. This party was to be as complete and special as possible. All of Aunt Bess's sisters and their husbands, nieces and nephews were invited and they all came. Also there were Houdini's three sisters-in-law and Houdini's sister Gladys. Hardeen was on a tour with his show and was unable to attend. There were fifty guests and relatives. It was the last time the family ever got together.

After the party at Payson Avenue the activities of Aunt Bess and Saint slowed way down. My mother wrote to Aunt Bess in Hollywood daily, and Aunt Bess would answer daily. But the family was worried as we could tell that neither Aunt Bess nor Saint was feeling well. Saint looked like a skeleton and coughed terribly. He died suddenly. Aunt Bess had lots of friends in Hollywood and insisted she could handle everything herself; however, several months later she was hospitalized and then entered a nursing home. She had been told her heart and lungs were in bad shape. She asked my mother to come and bring her back to Payson Avenue. We did not know she was so sick and we prepared joyfully for her coming. Mother was with her several weeks before everything could be settled for the move back to New York.

The picture we saw in the newspaper of Aunt Bess being put on the train told the story. She was wearing an oxygen mask and looked so bad, but her spirits were great. She was so glad to be coming home again; she never lost hope.

While traveling on the train, it was nearing lunch time and Mom and Aunt Bess decided they would like chicken a-la-king to eat. Mom ordered it and was feeding it to Aunt Bess when all of a sudden she realized Aunt Bess had died—no sound—nothing. Mom took her hand mirror and put it up to Aunt Bess's mouth and did not see her breath. Mom pulled the cord for the conductor and asked him to see if there was a doctor on the train. In a few minutes a woman and man came; he was not a doctor, but the woman was a nurse. She verified that Aunt Bess was dead. They waited until the next town was reached, which was Needles, California, before notifying the conductor. The train was stopped and Aunt Bess was taken off. The town was full of soldiers and the hotel was full. An officer kindly gave up his room for my mother. They were so nice to her and took her to the funeral parlor to help make arrangements for a casket for Aunt Bess, and notifying family, friends, and newspapers.

I was making my husband's breakfast and heard on the radio that Mrs. Houdini had died, my lovely Aunt Bess. She was sixty-eight years old. She was shown for three days at a funeral home in Inwood, New York. Magicians came from all over to pay their respects. She was buried in Gate of Heaven Cemetery in Westchester County, New York. Though a plot next to Houdini had been planned for her, she could not be buried there because Machpelah is a Jewish cemetery, Aunt Bess was a Catholic.

Recollection of Hardeen

Sidney H. Radner

AFTER HOUDINI'S DEATH, Hardeen went back into magic. He toured with the "Houdini Show" and performed many of the effects that had made his brother famous. I first got to know him around 1935, when I was sixteen. I was doing shows, billing myself as "America's Foremost Juvenile Escape Artist." I haunted him—going backstage to talk to him, sending letters. Fortunately for me, he took a serious interest in my desire to present an escape act. He had two sons and a nephew, but they did not care about magic or escapes. In later years they seemed to develop an aversion to anything or anybody related to Houdini. In 1937 I bought some handcuffs from Hardeen—the start of my collection. I suspect he was selling off equipment to cover what he lost by gambling and playing the horses.

By 1941 Hardeen decided that I would be the one to carry on the Houdini tradition. I did not sign an oath of secrecy, as Houdini's assistants had done, but I agreed not to reveal the secrets Hardeen gave me. He stayed in close contact with my efforts as I performed a challenge handcuff act at war bond drives for the Treasury Department and at Army Air Force shows. He was then in his sixties, complaining all the time about his ulcers but still a strong, powerful man—gruff, down-to-earth, a great friend and bad enemy. When on furloughs from the Air Force I would visit with him at his unpretentious one-family house in Brooklyn or he would come to my house in Holyoke, Massachusetts.

During this period Hardeen sold or gave me most of my Houdini collection. Among the apparatus I received from him were the Milk Can Escape (two of them); the framework and screens for Walking Through a

Brick Wall; the iron cage from which Houdini escaped in Glasgow; an unusual pillory escape; the Mailbag Escape; the "trapeze artist" automaton attributed by Houdini (wrongly) to Robert-Houdin; the original Houdini bust from which a duplicate was made for the family gravesite; and a unique escape that Houdini probably presented only once, consisting of a perforated wooden box that could be pierced by iron rods whose ends were then welded together. I also acquired about two hundred pairs of handcuffs, two punishment suits, and several straitjackets, including the all-leather escape-proof one that Houdini called the Swansea straitjacket—which Hardeen promised to fix so that I alone could escape from it. A highlight was two scrapbooks, one containing Houdini's clippings and notes from 1894 to 1899, when he was starting out, and another made up of hundreds of playbills announcing his challenges throughout the world.

Hardeen also gave me, gratis, stacks of letters, photos, contracts, posters, and all kinds of miscellaneous material. I refused an offer to take, just for the cost of shipping, hundreds of reels of 35 mm film and the diving suit Houdini invented. I was afraid of storing the highly combustible acetate and had no interest in the suit—a BIG mistake. But in June 1942 Hardeen shipped me the Chinese Water Torture Cell, in my opinion the most famous piece of apparatus in the history of magic. It arrived in Holyoke by Railway Express in five trunks and three crates with a declared weight of 1610 pounds. "You certainly have the greatest collection of Houdini material of anyone in the world," Hardeen wrote me. "I am digging into Trunks and may find a little more. But I am sure not much more." Yet more continued to arrive.

Hardeen planned to assist me in presenting the Water Torture Cell again once the war was over. But he had started to look very drawn and pale, and news of his death in 1945 reached me while I was still stationed in the China-Burma-India theater.

In 1971 I leased key items from my collection to the Houdini Magical Hall of Fame in Niagara Falls, Canada, to enhance its Houdini exhibit. Most of the rest of what I received from Hardeen is now on view at the Houdini Historical Center in Appleton, Wisconsin, opened in 1989. On the evening of April 30, 1995, a spectacular fire of mysterious origin consumed about a third of the Magical Hall of Fame. Among the many items destroyed were the Swansea straitjacket and the Water Torture Cell. The hall will not be rebuilt.

SOURCE GUIDE

To both my satisfaction and regret, the documentation for this biography makes a typescript of one hundred and fifty pages. The great length reflects the fact that my chief sources of information about Houdini's career have been his large correspondence and thirty years' worth of press clippings culled by him and others from hundreds of newspapers and magazines in a half-dozen languages. The thousands of items are scattered among scores of present owners and often pasted into unpaginated scrapbooks or heaped in boxes—each document requiring a lengthy description of its location. What small interest the resulting booklet-about-the-book might have to general readers does not seem to justify the cost of including it here.* The following source guide is offered instead to acknowledge the main repositories, private collections, and secondary literature I have used.

The richest public assemblages of Houdini material are at the Library of Congress, Washington, D.C.; the Houdini Historical Center of the Outagamie County Historical Society, Appleton, Wisconsin; and the Harry Ransom Humanities Research Center, University of Texas, Austin. The library's Rare Book and Special Collections division houses the Harry Houdini Collection, a bequest from Houdini himself. It includes most of his magic library; more than one hundred scrapbooks; forty-plus boxes of clippings, programs, and personal papers; and irreplaceable scrapbooks relating to his flights in Australia and investigation of Margery, compiled after his death by Edward Saint. The division also houses the related

---

*For the magic community, and readers with scholarly interests in the history of magic, the detailed documentation is being issued separately as *Notes to HOUDINI !!!* It will appear under the imprint of the magic publishers Kaufman and Greenberg, in Washington, D.C., to benefit the Houdini fund of the Society of American Magicians. Much thanks to Richard Kaufman for this relief.

McManus-Young Collection of Houdiniana, containing countless primary documents. Many of the most informative are stored in a vertical filing cabinet packed with unclassed folders of correspondence, notes, and transcripts. Photographs, glass slides, and motion pictures of Houdini are separately housed in the Library's Photography division and Film division.

The Houdini Historical Center and the Harry Ransom Humanities Research Center likewise hold hundreds of Houdini's letters, contracts, posters, and the like. The Historical Center owns as well the apparatus and biographically-important scrapbooks mentioned by Sidney H. Radner in his *Recollection*. Also of outstanding biographical interest are two companion scrapbooks, mostly of European and British reviews, gathered by Houdini between roughly 1900 and 1913 and donated by Tad Ware. The Ransom Center owns most of Houdini's surviving notes to Bess Houdini, and a wealth of material on his film activities, including the business papers of his Mystery Pictures Corporation. A dozen or so items in the center's Sir Arthur Conan Doyle papers concern Houdini's involvement with Spiritualism and the assault in Montreal that led to his death.

Among the smaller public collections, the American Museum of Magic in Marshall, Michigan, possesses Houdini's sizable correspondence with F. L. Black, as well as manuscripts and apparatus. (The knowledgeable proprietor of the museum, Robert Lund, died in 1995.) The American Society for Psychical Research, New York City, has stenographic records of the "Margery" sittings, and Houdini's many letters to Walter Franklin Prince, with Prince's replies. The Boston Public Library holds Houdini's unusually revealing correspondence with Quincy Kilby. Other important Houdini letters are at David Price's Egyptian Hall Museum in Brentwood, Tennessee. The Theatre Collection of Harvard University owns Houdini's correspondence with Dr. J. E. Waitte and with Robert Gould Shaw, much of it concerning book collecting. The New York Public Library has the early records of the Society of American Magicians, with secretary's reports and minutes of meetings covering the entire period of Houdini's presidency. Much basic biographical information about Houdini appears in the conveyances, census reports, filings in lawsuits, and similar documents available in the New York City Municipal Archives, the New York City Clerk's Office, and the Cook County Courthouse, Chicago.

Several public repositories hold only one or a few, but very revealing, items. The Huntington Library in San Marino, California, has the manuscript diaries of Charmian London—quoted in the text with the kind permission of Mr. I. Milo Shepard of the Jack London Ranch, Glen Ellen, California. The Minute Book, 1875–92, of Congregation B'ne Jeshurun, Milwaukee, contains entries about the Weiss family, as do the Board Meeting Minutes of the Hebrew Relief Society, 1867–98, at the Meier Library Archives, University of Wisconsin, Milwaukee. Some of Houdini's films, and newsreel footage of him in action, can be seen at the International Museum of Photography and Film, Rochester, New York, and in the SAM film library. The Billy Rose Theatre Collection, New York Public Library for the Performing Arts, owns the Robinson Locke Scrapbooks of Houdini clippings and playbills, covering 1904–16. The Harry Price Collection at the University of London Library includes letters by Houdini about Spiritualism. The Yale University Library, New Haven, has Houdini's correspondence with Walter Lippmann, and a few letters between Houdini and George Pierce Baker. Other public repositories that own miscellaneous papers of Houdini are the American Jewish Historical Society, New York City; the Anderson County Historical Society, Garnett, Kansas; the Chicago Historical Society; the Edison National Historic Site, West Orange, New Jersey; the Museum of the City of New York; the SPR Collection of the Cambridge University Library, Cambridge, England; and the libraries of Brown, Columbia, Duke, Georgetown, and Princeton Universities.

I add my thanks to these institutions for allowing me to use material in their collections, and for the help of their often expert librarians and curators, especially Joan Higbee at the Library of Congress, Jeanne Newlin at the Harvard Theatre Collection, Sara Hodson at the Huntington Library, Jennifer Lee and Don B. Wilmeth at the Brown University Library, Melissa Miller of the Harry Ransom Humanities Research Center, and Moira Thomas and Ben Filene at the Outagamie County Historical Society.

No less of my information about Houdini has come from the holdings of private collectors. Tom Boldt of Appleton, Wisconsin, invited me to read investigative reports prepared for Houdini by Rose Mackenberg and Stewart Griscom, Houdini's account of his visit to Anna Eva Fay, and a hundred-page stenographic record of Houdini's Philadelphia confrontation with J. Malcolm Bird. Mario Carrandi Jr., of Belle Mead, New Jersey, graciously allowed me to take notes on Houdini's quarrelsome correspondence with Martin Beck, and to examine rare cabinet photographs of Houdini. From the large collection of the late Milbourne Christopher (1914–84)—

magician and historian of magic—Mrs. Maurine Christopher permitted me to select for study manuscripts that include some of Houdini's letters to Will Goldston, Harry Kellar, and others, and Houdini's draft of *A Magician Among the Spirits*. David Copperfield gave me entry to his magic museum in Las Vegas, housing many of Houdini's notes on tricks, his wax cylinder recording of patter for the Water Torture Cell, and many unique Houdini posters, lockpicks, and photos. I spent a full day at the home of David Meyer in Glenwood, Illinois, researching his choice scrapbook of clippings and personal memorabilia amassed by Houdini between 1900 and 1905. Stanley Palm of Brooklyn, New York, gave me unlimited consultation of a scrapbook gathered by Houdini in the 1890s and of Houdini's first diary (ca. 1878–79)—key items in my account of Houdini's early career. Most of Houdini's other diaries—indispensable to writing his biography—are owned by a collector who generously allowed me to read them but wishes to remain anonymous.

Other collectors who own and have furnished me with original Houdini material are Roger W. Barrett, Marie Blood, John Bryce, Jr., Mike Caveney, Kevin Connolly, James Crossini, Patrick Culliton, Frank Dailey, John Daniel, Paul Daniels, Edwin A. Dawes, David De-Val, Diego Domingo, Roger E. Dreyer, John Gaughan, Ron Hilgert, Edward Hill, John Hinson, Don Hinz, Volker Huber, Ann M. James, Gene Keeney, Dorothy Young Kiamie, Ken Klosterman, George S. Lowry, William McIlhany, Arthur E. Moses, Henry Muller, Norm Nielsen, Fulton Oursler, Jr., Charles Reynolds, Tom Rozoff, Stephen Sparks, the late Manny Weltman, and Herb Zarrow. They all have my liveliest gratitude, although my exact debt to each is made clear only in the full notes.

Others from whom I received valuable information about Houdini include Barbara Belford, John Booth, Dick Brooks, Mildred L. Buckley, David Charvet, Ormus Davenport (Ira Davenport's great-grandson), Dorothy Dietrich, Carol Durgin, Tom Ewing, Jack Flosso, Ken Force, Stephen James Forrester, Lewis Frumkes, Alfred Holden, Ricky Jay, Walter Johnson, S. T. Joshi, Frank Koval, Kathy Leab, Bill Liles, Norman Mailer, Brooks McNamara, Marion Meade, Joel Miller, Ona Nowina-Sapinsky, Dr. James G. Ravin, Mrs. Alfred W. Roberts, David Roth, Clarice Stasz, Ken Trombly, the late M. Samuel White (Houdini's nephew), Dr. Richard Wresch, and W. Gordon Yadon.

The scrapbooks, diaries, and letters mentioned above are the main sources for following Houdini's career. But I have also mined the leading trade journals of the period—*Billboard*, the *Dramatic Mirror*, *Moving Picture World*, *Variety*—and the leading magic periodicals: *Magic Wand*, *Magical Monthly*, *The Magician Annual*, *Mahatma*, *M-U-M*, *The Sphinx*, and Houdini's own *Conjurers' Monthly Magazine*.

As for secondary sources, some informative books and monographs on Houdini are Lawrence Arcuri, *The Houdini Birth Research Committee's Report* (New York, [ca. 1973]); Patrick Culliton and T. L. Williams, eds, *Houdini's Strange Tales* ([Hollywood], 1992); Bernard M. L. Ernst and Hereward Carrington, *Houdini and Conan Doyle: The Story of a Strange Friendship* (New York, 1932); Stephen James Forrester, *A Bibliography of Classic Authors in Magic and Related Arts* (Calgary, Alta., Can., 1993); Walter B. Gibson, *The Original Houdini Scrapbook* (New York, 1976); Walter B. Gibson and Morris N. Young, *Houdini's Fabulous Magic* (New York, 1961); Milbourne Christopher, *Houdini: The Untold Story*, rev. ed. (New York, n.d.); Doug Henning, *Houdini His Legend and His Magic* (New York, 1977); *Houdini's* History of Magic in Boston 1792–1915 *Researched and Written for Houdini by H. J. Moulton* (Glenwood, Ill., 1983); Jean Hugard, *Houdini's "Unmasking": Fact vs. Fiction* (York, England, 1989); Frank Koval, *The Illustrated Houdini Research Diary* (Oldham, England, 1992–); Bernard C. Meyer, *Houdini: A Mind in Chains* (New York, 1976); The Amazing Randi and Bert Randolph Sugar, *Houdini: His Life and Art* (New York, 1976); Sam H. Sharpe, *Salutations to Robert-Houdin* (Calgary, Alta., Can., 1983); Manny Weltman, *Houdini: A Definitive Bibliography* (Van Nuys, Calif., 1991), and *Houdini: Escape Into Legend* (Van Nuys, Calif., 1993). See also Bernard Drachman, *The Unfailing Light: Memoirs of an American Rabbi* (New York, 1948), and H. P. Lovecraft, *Selected Letters 1925–1929*, ed. August Derleth and Donald Wandrel (Sauk City, Minn., 1968).

For general historical and social background the following books have been helpful: *Baedeker's* travel guides (Leipzig, Germany, 1898–1915); Harvey Green, *Fit For America: Health Fitness Sport and American Society* (New York, 1986); Jeffrey S. Gurock, *When Harlem Was Jewish 1870–1930* (New York, 1979); Larry K. Hartsfield, *The American Response to Professional Crime, 1870–1917* (Westport, Conn., 1985); John D. Klier and Shlomo Lambroza, eds., *Pogroms: Anti-Jewish Violence in Modern Russian History* (Cambridge, England, 1992); Kermit Nathan Miller, *Theodore Roosevelt: A*

Life (New York, 1992); Donald J. Mrozek, *Sport and American Mentality, 1880–1910* (Knoxville, Tenn., 1983); Moses Rischin, *The Promised City: New York's Jews 1870–1914* (1962; reprint, New York, 1964); Charles E. Rosenberg, *The Trial of the Assassin Guiteau: Psychiatry and Law in the Gilded Age* (Chicago, 1968); Thomas J. Schlereth, *Victorian America: Transformations of Everyday Life 1876–1915* (New York, 1991); Clarice Stasz, *American Dreamers: Charmian and Jack London* (New York, 1988); Ronald Steel, *Walter Lippmann and the American Century* (New York, 1981); Mark Sullivan, *Our Times,* 6 vols. (New York, 1926–35); Louis J. Swichkow and Lloyd P. Gartner, *The History of the Jews of Milwaukee* (Philadelphia, 1963); Henri Troyat, *Daily Life in Russia under the Last Tsar,* trans. Malcolm Barnes (Stanford, Calif., 1979); James C. Whorton, *Crusaders for Fitness: The History of American Health Reformers* (Princeton, N.J., 1982).

In recreating various facets of Houdini's career I have drawn on the following:

Aviation: Charles Dollfus and Henri Bouché, *Histoire de l'Aéronautique* (Paris, 1932); Houston Peterson, *See Them Flying: Houston Peterson's Air-Age Scrapbook, 1909–10* (New York, 1969); A. Lawrence Rotch, *The Conquest of the Air* (New York, 1910); Henry Serrano Villard, *Contact! The Story of the Early Birds* (Washington, D.C., 1987); Gabriel Voisin, *Men, Women and 10,000 Kites,* trans. Oliver Stewart (London, 1963).

Sir Arthur Conan Doyle: Arthur Conan Doyle, *Essays on Photography,* comp. John Michael Gibson and Richard Lancelyn Green (London, 1982); *The History of Spiritualism,* 2 vols. (1926; reprint, New York, 1975); *Interviews and Recollections,* ed. Howard Orel (New York, 1991); *Letters to the Press,* ed. John Michael Gibson and Richard Lancelyn Green (Iowa City, 1986); *Memories and Adventures* (Boston, 1921); *The New Revelation* (New York, 1918); *Our American Adventure* (New York, 1923); *Our Second American Adventure* (Boston, 1924); *The Vital Message* (New York, 1919); *The Wanderings of a Spiritualist* (1921; reprint, Berkeley, Calif., 1988). Also John Dickson Carr, *The Life of Sir Arthur Conan Doyle* (1949; reprint, New York, n.d.); Charles Higham, *The Adventures of Conan Doyle: The Life of the Creator of Sherlock Homes* (New York, 1976).

Film: Erik Barnouw, *The Magician and the Cinema* (New York, 1981); William K. Everson, *American Silent Film* (New York, 1978); Will Irwin, *The House That Shadows Built* (New York, 1928); Richard Kozarski, *An Evening's Entertainment: The Age of the Silent Feature Picture 1915–1928*

(New York, 1990); Terry Ramsaye, *A Million and One Nights: A History of the Motion Picture* (New York, 1926); John D. Weaver, *L. A.: El Pueblo Grande* (Los Angeles, 1973); *Hollywood: The First Hundred Years* (New York, 1982); *The Public Is Never Wrong: The Autobiography of Adolph Zukor* (New York, 1953).

   Magic, escapes, and other magicians of the period: David Bamberg, *Illusion Show* (Glenwood, Ill., 1991); Constance Pole Bayer, *The Great Wizard of the North: John Henry Anderson* (Watertown, Mass., 1990); John Booth, *Wonders of Magic* (Los Alamitos, Calif., 1986), *Dramatic Magic* (Los Alamitos, Calif., 1988), and *Conjurians' Discoveries* (Los Alamitos, Calif., 1992); Eugene Burger, *Spirit Theater* (New York, 1986); David Charvet, *Jack Gwynne: The Man, His Mind, and His Royal Family of Magic* (Brush Prairie, Wash., 1986); Gary R. Frank, *Chung Ling Soo: The Man Behind the Legend!* (Calgary, Alta., Can., 1987); Albert A. Hopkins, *Magic: Stage Illusions and Scientific Diversions, Including Trick Photography* (New York, 1899); Ricky Jay, *Learned Pigs & Fireproof Women* (New York, 1986); John Mulholland, *Quicker Than The Eye* (Indianapolis, [1932]); John Novak, *The Art of Escape Vol. 4: Escapes From a Strait Jacket* ([Calgary, Alta., Can.], 1989); Robert E. Olson, *The Complete Life of Howard Franklin Thurston*, 2 vols. (Calgary, Alta., Can., 1993); William V. Rauscher, *Monarch of Magic: The Story of Servais LeRoy* (Woodbury, N.J., 1984); Fred Siegel, "The Vaudeville Conjuring Act," Ph.D. dissertation, New York University, 1993; Samuel Sharpe, *Conjuror's Psychological Secrets* (Calgary, Alta., Can., 1988); Marc Weber Thomas, *Locks, Safes, and Security: A Handbook for Law Enforcement Personnel* (Springfield, Mass., 1971); Grace Thurston as told to William L. Rohde, *My Magic Husband Thurston the Great* [*The Thurston Scrapbook*] (n.pl., 1985); Howard Thurston and Jane Thurston Shepard, *Our Life in Magic* (n.pl., 1989); Peter Warlock, *Buatier de Kolta: Genius of Illusion*, ed. Mike Caveney (Pasadena, Calif., 1993); Bart Whaley, *Who's Who in Magic* (Wallace, Idaho, 1990).

   Spiritualism: J. Malcolm Bird, *"Margery" The Medium* (Boston, 1925); Hereward Carrington, *Eusapia Palladino and her Phenomena* (New York, 1909), *Psychical Phenomena and the War* (New York, 1920), *Laboratory Investigations into Psychic Phenomena* (London, [ca. 1939]), *Psychic Oddities* (London, 1952); John J. Cerullo, *The Secularization of the Soul: Psychical Research in Modern Britain* (Philadelphia, 1982); W. J. Crawford,

The Reality of Psychic Phenomena (New York, 1918); Hamlin Garland, *Forty Years of Psychic Research* (New York, 1937); Emma Hardinge, *Modern American Spiritualism* (1870; reprint, New Hyde Park, N.Y., 1970); William James, *Essays in Psychical Research*, ed. Frederick H. Burkhardt and Fredson Bowers (Cambridge, Mass., 1986); Henry C. McComas, *Ghosts I Have Talked With* (Baltimore, 1935); J. Hewat McKenzie, *Spirit Intercourse: Its Theory and Practice* (New York, 1917); R. Laurence Moore, *In Search of White Crows: Spiritualism, Parapsychology, and American Culture* (New York, 1977); T. L. Nichols, *A Biography of the Brothers Davenport* (London, 1864); Carl Murchison, ed., *The Case For and Against Psychical Belief* (Worcester, 1927); Janet Oppenheim, *The other world: Spiritualism and psychical research in England, 1850–1914* [sic] (Cambridge, England, 1985); Alex Owen, *The Darkened Room: Women, Power and Spiritualism in Late Victorian England* (Philadelphia, 1990); Frank Podmore, *Modern Spiritualism: A History and a Criticism*, 2 vols. (London, 1902); Walter Franklin Prince, *The Enchanted Boundary* (Boston, 1930); *Preliminary Report of the Commission Appointed By The University of Pennsylvania to Investigate Modern Spiritualism* (Philadelphia, 1887); *Proceedings of the American Society for Psychical Research*; Luke P. Rand, *A Sketch of the History of the Davenport Boys* (Oswego, N.Y., 1859); Mark Richardson, L. R. G. Crandon et al., *Margery Harvard Veritas: A Study in Psychics* (Boston, 1925); Charles Richet, *Thirty Years of Psychical Research*, trans. Stanley DeBrath (New York, 1923); Joseph F. Rinn, *Sixty Years of Psychical Research: Houdini and I among the Spiritualists* (New York, 1950); *Scientific American;* Thomas R. Tietze, *Margery* (New York, 1973); John W. Truesdell. *The Bottom Facts Concerning the Science of Spiritualism* (New York, 1883).

Theatrical life: Peter Bailey, ed., *Music Hall: The business of pleasure* [sic] (Philadelphia, 1986); Robert Bogdan, *Freak Show: Presenting Human Oddities for Amusement and Profit* (Chicago, 1988); Benny Brown, ed., *The Last Empires: A Music Hall Companion* (London, 1986); D. F. Cheshire, *Music Hall in Britain* (Newton Abbott, England, 1974); *Circus und artverwandte Künste* (Königstein-Falkenstein, Germany, 1990); Joseph E. DiMeglio, *Vaudeville U. S. A.* (Bowling Green, Ky., 1973); Milton Epstein, "The New York Hippodrome: Spectacle on Sixth Avenue," Ph.D. dissertation, New York University, 1993; Jewgeni Kusnezow, *Der Zirkus der Welt* (Berlin, 1970); Raymond Mander and Joe Mitchenson, *Lost Theatres of*

London (London, 1976); Brooks McNamara, *Step Right Up: An Illustrated History of the American Medicine Show* (New York, 1976); G. J. Mellor, *The Northern Music Hall* (Newcastle-upon-Tyne, England, 1970); A. H. Saxon, *P. T. Barnum: The Legend and the Man* (New York, 1989); Robert Eben Sackett, *Popular Entertainment, Class, and Politics in Munich, 1900–1923* (Cambridge, Mass., 1982); Robert W. Snyder, *The Voice of the City: Vaudeville and Popular Culture in New York* (New York, 1989); Charles W. Stein, ed., *American Vaudeville as seen by its Contemporaries* (New York, 1984); Alexander Whiteley, *Memories of Circus, Variety, etc. As I Knew It* (London, 1981).

Some last thank-yous. I would not have begun this biography without the encouragement of Sidney H. Radner of Holyoke, Massachusetts. Nor could I have completed it without the steady generosity of him and his wife, Helen, of Morris and Chesley Young, and of Stanley Palm. For their varieties of boosting I remain grateful too to John L. Ernst; Buz Wyeth, my editor at HarperCollins; Hugh Rawson, my literary agent; Mrs. Bessie Silverman, my mother; and the members of the festive NYU Biography Seminar.

A final bow, to the secret suppliers of fresh air who have helped me stay under until I could get out. To Steve and Naomi Lemmé, and Pat and Rex Robbins—dear friends. To Willa, Ethan, and the newest members of my family—Benjamin Berkman, Michael Berkman, and Ronit Silverman. And to Jane Mallison—lone audience for my New Year's Eve escape from a padlocked mailbag.

KENNETH SILVERMAN
Washington Square and Highland Lake

INDEX

ABOUT THE AUTHOR

Kenneth Silverman grew up on East Seventy-fifth Street in Manhattan, directly across from the tenement building where Houdini lived as a boy. During his teens, in the early 1950s, he performed as the magician Ken Silvers, working innumerable children's birthday parties and playing lesser hotels on the Catskill Mountain borscht circuit. At the height of his brief career, he magically poured cascades of chocolates from an empty box in a TV commercial for M&M candies.

Today Kenneth Silverman is Professor of English at New York University and codirector of the NYU Biography Seminar. His earlier books have received an Edgar Award from the Mystery Writers of America, the Bancroft Prize for American History, and the Pulitzer Prize in Biography. He is a fellow of the American Antiquarian Society and a card-carrying member of the Society of American Magicians.

NEW HANOVER COUNTY PUBLIC LIB.

3 4200 00421453 8

12/96

DISCARDED
from
New Hanover County Public Library

NEW HANOVER COUNTY PUBLIC LIBRARY
201 Chestnut Street
Wilmington, N.C. 28401

GAYLORD S